CONTENTS

NOTE: ALL PROBLEMS ARE RATED BY ESTIMATED SOLUTION TIME; SEE BEGINNING OF EACH SOLUTION SET AS WELL AS EACH SOLUTION:

{S} LESS THAN 15 MINUTES
{M} 15 TO 40 MINUTES
{L} LONGER THAN 40 MINUTES

ESTIMATED SOLUTION TIME FOR EACH CASE IS PROVIDED AT THE BEGINNING OF EACH CASE SOLUTION.

SOLUTIONS MANUAL TO ACCOMPANY

THE ANALYSIS AND USE OF FINANCIAL STATEMENTS

SECOND EDITION

GERALD I. WHITE, CFA
Grace & White, Inc.

ASHWINPAUL C. SONDHI, Ph.D.
A. C. Sondhi & Associates, LLC

DOV FRIED, Ph.D.
Stern School of Business
New York University

JOHN WILEY & SONS, INC.
New York • Chichester • Weinheim • Brisbane • Singapore • Toronto

Copyright © 1998 by John Wiley & Sons, Inc.

All rights reserved.

Excerpts from this work may be reproduced by instructors
for distribution on a not-for-profit basis for testing or
instructional purposes only to students enrolled in courses
for which the textbook has been adopted. *Any other
reproduction or translation of this work beyond that
permitted by Sections 107 or 108 of the 1976 United States
Copyright Act without the permission of the copyright
owner is unlawful. Requests for permission or further
information should be addressed to the Permissions
Department, John Wiley & Sons, Inc., 605 Third Avenue,
New York, NY 10158-0012.*

ISBN 0-471-17176-X

Printed in the United States of America

10 9 8 7

Printed and bound by Victor Graphics, Inc.

ERRATA FOR FIRST PRINTING

PAGE	DESCRIPTION
164	Exhibit 4-7, note a: "Taxes Payable" should read: "Nonincome Taxes"
211	Question 18A should read: Compute the number of shares used to compute *basic* earnings per share for 1988.
355	Problem 9C, last sentence should read: (Be sure to used both Tables 6 and 7 of Exhibit 7P-2.)
517	Question 4, last line "Explain the decline..." is portion of part (d), not new part (b)
567	Balance sheet years 1994 and 1993 respectively
571	Question 4D reference should be to part C (not B)
575	Problem 9B, reference should be to December 31, 1993
655	Exhibit 12C-5, 1994 data Service cost should be $1,207.0
658	Question 2C should refer to deferred investment loss of $(218) million
684	In 1994 Change in MVA table, first 1993 head should be 1994
740	Exhibit 13P-5, 1993 data, operating profit for Lumex should be 3,881 Corporate and other should be (1,446)
800	Question 4(a), line 2, should read "compute the following financial ratios..."
803	1996 Consolidated Statement of Cash Flows, second line: delete "goodwill" from "Depreciation and goodwill amortization" Replace third bullet at bottom of page with: • 1996 combined depreciation expense equals $580
891	Question 12B(ii), 19X1 should be 1995

979	Case 17-4, question 5.(a) reference should be to Box 3-2, not 3-1.
1026	Second paragraph, after Case 17-1, add: [Share price data given in 3(b)(ii) of that case.]
1102	Last equation on page, first term after summation sign should be $(ROE_j - r)B_{j-1}$
1211	2nd column, line 3 should be Morrison Knudsen
1216	3rd column, line 3, delete "see also" reference
1216	3rd column, first listing under G, should be Hagerman
1221	2nd column, P.H. Glatfelter should be listed under Glatfelter
1223	3rd column, Tobin reference should be to q ratio
1224	3rd column, Westvaco should not be all caps

Chapter 1 - Solutions

Overview:

Problem Length   *Problem #s*
   {S}   *1 to 22*
   [M]   *23*

1.{S}(i) Need to decide whether standards are meant to primarily serve preparers (provide flexibility), auditors (easy to audit) or users (provide information). The standards would also be a function of expected or planned growth in capital markets, the extent of private and government participation in the standard setting process, and the degree of foreign investment sought by the government.

(ii) Relevance indicates that financial statements provide information useful for decision making, even at the cost of precision. Reliability requires that financial data be verifiable even if less relevant. The degree of emphasis placed on relevance versus reliability will depend on decisions made in (i) above.

(iii) Comparability would argue for a single accounting standard for all similar situations. For example, one inventory and one depreciation method for all firms. The standard setters must also decide whether to allow different treatment across industries for similar economic events.

     An additional factor is comparability between the financial statements of Chinese firms and those of firms from other countries. The adoption of IASC or FASB standards by Chinese firms would facilitate such comparisons, especially for non-Chinese investors and creditors.

(iv) Political factors relate to whether financial reporting should serve governmental aims, for example promoting certain economic decisions. Legal factors would include whether financial reporting should conform to tax reporting. Cultural factors would include historic accounting methods in China and whether the country wants to emulate Western accounting standards (such as U.S. or IASC GAAP) or develop another model.

Note: See Davidson, Gelardi, and Li: Analysis of the Conceptual Framework of China's New Accounting System, Accounting Horizons, March 1996.

2.{S}(i)   Short-term lenders are concerned primarily with liquidity. Accounting standards would focus primarily on near-term cash flows and might include cash flow forecasting.

(ii) Long-term equity investors are primarily concerned with the earning power of the firm. Income measurement would be the focus of standards for such users.

(iii) Tax authorities are concerned with the generation of revenue. Accounting standards might limit the ability of firms to shift income from one period to another and place strict controls on the recognition and timing of both revenues and deductible expenditures.

(iv) Corporate managers seek to control their reported earnings, to cast the best possible light on their stewardship. Accounting standards set by managers would be highly flexible, with little supplementary information and footnote disclosure.

3.{S} The matching principle states that revenues should be matched with the expenses that generate them. As the revenues and required expenditures may be incurred in different accounting periods, accrual accounting is required to recognize them in the same period.

4.{S} The going concern assumption states that the enterprise will continue operating in a normal fashion. This assumption permits financial statements to record assets and liabilities based on the cash flows that they will generate as the firm operates. If this assumption were absent, all assets and liabilities would have to be evaluated on a liquidation basis. Accrual accounting could not be used, as the assumption that expenditures would produce future revenues could no longer be made.

5.{S} Public companies must provide current investors with detailed financial statements, mandated by the FASB and the SEC. Because of SEC filing requirements, annual and quarterly financial data are publicly available to potential investors as well. Private companies may not prepare audited financial data. When audited financial statements are prepared, they will lack some disclosures (e.g., earnings per share) and certain SEC-mandated data (such as the management discussion and analysis). In addition, these statements may not be made available to potential investors.

6.{S}All public companies in the United States are required to issue financial statements whose form and content are determined by the FASB after much public debate. The SEC oversees this process and supplements these standards with additional disclosure requirements. As U. S. GAAP have an investor and user orientation, they require detailed disclosures. Financial statements issued by non-U.S. firms follow local (in some cases, IASC) accounting standards, with less disclosure. Local standards reflect legal and political requirements and often do not have the same investor protection objective as in the United States.

7.{S}The FASB sets accounting standards for all audited financial statements prepared under U.S. GAAP. The SEC has jurisdiction over all public companies. Given the overlapping jurisdiction, the SEC generally relies on the FASB to set standards but supplements those standards with additional disclosure requirements deemed necessary to inform and protect investors in public companies.

8.{S}The balance sheet includes only those economic events that qualify as assets and liabilities. As accounting standards define, in effect, assets and liabilities they determine which economic events are accounted for and which are ignored. Events ignored (such as many contracts) are excluded from the process of preparing financial statements. The recognition rules also influence managers' decisions regarding the form of contractual agreements used to acquire assets and incur liabilities, thereby affecting the preparation of financial statements.

9.{S}Liabilities represent the assets of the firm funded by trade and financial creditors. Equity represents the permanent capital of the firm, and is the residual after all liabilities have been satisfied. Thus the distinction between liabilities and equity is the difference between prior claims and permanent capital. Misclassification will over- or understate the firm's reported debt and the degree of leverage or financial risk.

10.{S}Historical cost is more reliable as it reflects actual past transactions. Market values are less reliable as they may require assumptions and estimates. However, general inflation and specific price changes make historical costs less useful (relevant) as time passes. Market values always have relevance as they represent the current value of the firm's resources. The nature of the markets (liquidity, volatility, and transparency) affects the reliability of the values reported.

11.{S}Contra accounts are deductions from asset or liability accounts that accumulate valuation or other adjustments (such as accumulated depreciation) and reduce the asset or liability account to its "net" amount. Adjunct accounts (such as valuation adjustments for marketable securities under SFAS 115) are reported separately.

12.{S}A. Revenues and expenses result from the firm's operating activities; gains and losses result from valuation and other non-operating events. The latter are peripheral to the normal activities of the firm and, therefore, should be separated for analytic purposes.

B. Comprehensive income includes all changes in equity other than transactions with stockholders. It encompasses operating earnings, "non-recurring" items, valuation adjustments, and the cumulative effect of accounting changes. Comprehensive income could serve as a bridge between "income from continuing operations" (most useful for earnings forecasting) and the net change in stockholders' equity (excluding transactions with owners).

13.{S}Recurring income refers to income from continuing operations, the best measure of the operating profits of the firm for that time period, and therefore the best base for forecasting and valuation. Non-recurring items are unusual or infrequent in nature, and usually result from non-operating factors.

14.{S}The classification of cash flows into three categories highlights their differing natures. Cash from operations reports the cash generated or used by the firm's operating activities. Cash for investment measures the outflow for investments in capacity, for acquisitions, or for long-term investments. Cash from financing indicates the source (debt or equity) of any financing required by the firm as well as distributions to preferred and common stockholders.

These classifications should be viewed over time as indicators of the firm's liquidity and solvency. The relationship among these classifications is especially important.

15.{S}Footnotes are an integral part of the financial statements and are included in the audit. They supply detail that supplements financial statements (e.g. employee benefit plan data). Supplementary schedules may be included within the financial statements (e.g. oil and gas disclosures) but may not be audited.

16.{S}The Management Discussion and Analysis is intended to explain changes in reported income statement, balance sheet, and cash flow items and therefore help financial statement users to interpret these financial statements. The MD&A should discuss trends, including those expected to continue in the future. This discussion should aid the prediction of future cash flows and earnings.

17.{S}(i) The opinion should report any changes in accounting principles used and may refer to the footnote providing additional information on the change.

(ii) Changes in accounting estimates are <u>not</u> referred to in the auditor's opinion.

(iii) The auditor's report must describe uncertainties when they are material to the firm's financial position.

(iv) While the auditor's opinion provides reasonable assurance that there are no material errors in the financial statements, it is not a guarantee against error or even fraud.

In 1997, after the text went to press, the AICPA adopted Statement on Auditing Standards 82, effective for period ending after December 15, 1997. SAS 82 requires auditors to assess the risk of financial statement fraud.

18.{S}A. Deere changed its accounting method for income taxes, adopting SFAS 109 in fiscal 1992. The argument for including a reference to the change in the auditor's report is that accounting changes reduce the comparability of financial statements as different methods are used in different years. The argument against reporting the change is that there was no material effect in the year of the change.

   B. While the effect of SFAS 109 may not have been material in fiscal 1992, the new standard may affect reported net income in future years. Some events may be reported differently under the new accounting method than under the old one.

19.{S}The preparer gathers financial data, chooses accounting principles and estimates, and assembles the data into financial statements using those methods and estimates. The auditor examines the financial statements for errors, and checks that the accounting methods and assumptions are permissible under GAAP and whether they have been applied consistently over time.

20.{S}Companies generally prepare financial statements using the accounting principles of their home country. When selling securities in a foreign jurisdiction, they may be required to prepare supplementary financial statements using the accounting standards of that country. The cost and inconvenience of this extra work may dissuade the firm from selling securities in that country, thus depriving that country's investors of the opportunity to invest.

   On the other hand, investors must choose between that firm's securities and those of home country firms using local accounting principles. If the foreign firm uses different accounting principles, investors may make poor investment decisions because of their inability to separate real differences between firms from differences caused by alternative accounting principles.

21.{S}A. Because the probability of loss is so low (less than one in ten thousand), Bonnywill will report no loss. If a fire occurs, the firm will then accrue the estimated loss.

  B. An alternative method would accrue the expected value of the loss, computed by multiplying the number of units sold by the expected loss per unit. The result would be 10,000 x .00009 x $100,000 = $90,000.

22.{S}A. For firm A the probability of loss is remote (.3%) so that no liability should be recognized. If an accident occurs, the firm would recognize a liability equal to the expected loss.

  B. Firm B expects to have 10 workers' compensation claims each year (10,000/1,000) with a loss of $10,000 per claim. Thus firm B should accrue $100,000 per year. The difference from firm A is that the employee population is large enough to make the loss predictable.

23.{M}A. While Bristol-Myers (BMY) did not report any accrual for breast implant litigation in 1992, the footnote did warn investors that a large potential liability might exist. When such disclosures are made, financial statement users must make their own evaluation of the possible outcome.

  B. If BMY had not accrued the expected insurance recovery, the 1993 special charge would have been $1 billion greater, reducing earnings further. The insurance claim is an additional risk factor that makes the ultimate financial outcome for BMY uncertain. Note that the insurance recovery has not been offset (netted) against the liability; BMY has the primary liability to pay claims.

  C. The actual cash outflow can be estimated as follows:

	1994	1995
Net liability* 1/1	$ 470 million	$ 868 million
Net liability* 12/31	868	1,386
Increase	$ 398	$ 518
Special charge	(750)	(950)
Cash outflow	$(352) million	$ (432) million

  * The liability amounts are shown net of the expected insurance recovery.

Chapter 2 - Solutions

Overview:

Problem Length	*Problem #'s*
{S}	*1,2,3,4,5,6,9,10*
{M}	*7,8,11,12,13,14*

1.{S}(i) When the product is a commodity with a known price and liquid market.

(ii) When collection is assured because the risk of non-payment can be estimated.

(iii)When collection is uncertain because the risk of non-payment cannot be estimated.

2.{S}A. (i) Terry can recognize revenue as long as collection is assured (it can estimate bad debts).

(ii) Terry cannot recognize revenue until the return period has passed and it is possible to determine actual sales.

B. Early recognition of sale results in the overstatement of accounts receivable, the understatement of inventory (that should not have been considered sold), and the overstatement of retained earnings (as income has been recognized too soon).

3.{S}A. Under the completed contract method, reported earnings are more volatile because all recognition is delayed until completion. As a result, net income is reported only in periods when projects are completed, and depends on the number and profitability of projects completed in each period.

B. With many contracts, some averaging occurs so that the volatility of firm results is not as great (although it is still greater than under the percentage of completion method).

C. When a firm has relatively few projects and uses the completed contract method, reported revenues and net income are highly variable. The volatility makes forecasting extremely difficult. With a greater number of contracts, volatility is reduced, and forecasting is easier. The percentage of completion method, by reporting revenues and net income as earned over the life of the project, provides better data regarding the operations of the firm. However, reported cash flows are not affected by the choice of accounting method.

4.{S}(i) Under the completed contract method, no revenues or cost-of-goods-sold are recognized until completion; both are lower during the project but higher in the period when completion takes place. Their trend is highly volatile. Under the percentage of completion method, revenues and COGS are recognized as projects progress; they are higher during the project but lower at completion. The trend will reflect the overall level of activity and will be less volatile.

(ii) Earnings recognition follows the same pattern as revenue recognition, as explained in (i), assuming that estimates of project profitability prove to be accurate. Under the percentage of completion method, revised estimates of profitability increase the volatility of income as the past over- or underaccrual of income must be offset in the period of revision.

(iii) No difference between methods; operating cash flows are not affected by the choice of accounting method.

(iv) Accounts receivable will always be higher under the percentage of completion method, as that method recognizes revenue sooner, creating accounts receivable. Total current assets will also be higher as the higher level of accounts receivable under the percentage of completion method more than offsets the higher level of inventory under the completed contract method. Long-term assets are not affected by the choice of method.

5.{S}

ACCOUNT	Part A	Part B
Costs and earnings in excess of billings on uncompleted contracts	This account reflects the costs actually incurred and the proportionate share of profits on those contracts for which the amount of revenue recognized exceeds payments received from customers	The account is similar to Accounts Receivable which also reflects the excess of revenue recognized over cash payments received.
Billings in excess of costs and earnings on uncompleted contracts	This account reflects the contracts where payments received exceed revenue recognized.	The account is similar to Advances from Customers.

C. The company uses the percentage-of completion method. This is evident from the fact that the accounts

   Costs and earnings in excess of billings on uncompleted contracts Billings in excess of costs and earnings on uncompleted contracts

both reflect "earnings on uncompleted contracts". Under the percentage of completion method the company recognizes revenue on the contract prior to completion of the contract; payments received from customers are not related (directly) to the level of revenue recognized.

6.{S}A. (i) and (ii)

    19X6:   Revenue = 20% x $6 million = $1.2 million

         Costs incurred = 20% x $4.5 million = $.9 million.

           (Income recognized is $.3 million difference.)

    19X7:   Revenue = 60% x $6 million = $3.6 - $1.2 = $2.4 million

           Costs incurred (cumulative) = 60% x $4.8 million = $2.88 million. As 19X6 recognition was $.9 million, 19X7 recognition must be $ 1.98 million ($2.88 - $0.9).

           (Income recognized is $.42 million difference, making cumulative recognition $.72 million for two years.)

B.   There should be no effect; expenditures that do not contribute to the completion of the project do not affect revenue or income under the percentage of completion method.

7.{M} (All data in $ millions)

A. Under the percentage-of-completion method, revenues,
   expenses and income are based on the percentage of the work
   completed based upon costs incurred. Therefore:

Year	Cumulative %	Cumulative Revenue	Current Revenue	Expense	Profit
1994	4.7/24 = 19.58%	$ 5.2875	$ 5.2875	$ 4.7000	$0.5875
1995	14.1/24 = 58.75%	$15.8625	$10.5750	$ 9.4000	$1.1750
1996	24.0/24 =100.00%	$27.0000	$11.1375	$ 9.9000	$1.2375
			$27.0000	$ 24.0000	$3.0000

B. The total (expected) cost will now be ($4.7 + $10.0 + 10.3)
   $25 million of which $14.7 million has been incurred by the
   end of 1995. Thus, cumulative revenue to the end of 1995
   equals $14.7/$25 = 58.8% of $27 million or $15.876 million.
   As $5.2875 million had been recognized in 1994, ($15.8760 -
   $5.2875)$10.5885 must be recognized in 1995. The approach
   for 1996 is similar:

Year	Cumulative %	Cumulative Revenue	Current Revenue	Expense	Profit
1994	4.7/24 = 19.58%	$ 5.2875	$ 5.2875	$ 4.7000	$0.5875
(1994 based on original estimates unchanged from part A)					
1995	14.7/25 = 58.80%	$15.8760	$10.5885	$10.0000	$0.5885
1996	25.0/25 =100.00%	$27.0000	$11.1240	$10.3000	$0.8240
			$27.0000	$25.0000	$2.0000

8. {M}   (All data in $ millions)
    A.

	19X5	19X6	19X7	Total
Revenue*	$2.75	$4.40	$3.85	$11.00
Profit*	.25	.40	.35	1.00
CFO	(.50)	(.50)	2.00	1.00

*For each year James recognizes both revenue and profit based on the percentage of the tunnel completed as measured by costs incurred.

   B.

	19X5	19X6	19X7	Total
Revenue*	---	---	$11.00	$11.00
Profit*	---	---	1.00	1.00
CFO	(.50)	(.50)	2.00	1.00

*Under the completed contract method, all revenue and income recognition takes place at completion of the tunnel in 19X7. CFO is identical, however.

   C.   Estimated total profit is now zero. As James recognized $.25 of profit in 19X5, it must recognize a *loss* of $.25 in 19X6 in order to bring the cumulative profit to zero.

If completion is measured by cost incurred, then cumulative revenue (through 19X6) will now be $6.50 million (equal to cost incurred). As $2.75 million of revenue was recognized in 19X5, only $3.75 million ($6.50 - $2.75) can be recognized in 19X6. Note that, while *cumulative* results are correct, revenues and profit may not reflect the operating results for either 19X5 or 19X6.

   D.   The completed contract method has the advantage of delaying recognition of revenue and profit until all risk has been eliminated. The disadvantage is that, under normal circumstances, the performance of the firm is understated.

The percentage of completion method has the advantage of reporting revenues and profits as earned. The disadvantage is the risk of surprise if estimates must be revised during the project.

9.{S}A.

	Able	Baker	Charlie	David
Sales	$ 170,000[1]	$ 160,000[2]	$ 100,000	$ 50,000[3]
COGS	85,000	80,000	50,000	25,000
Net Income	$ 85,000	$ 80,000	$ 50,000	$ 25,000

[1]Sales = goods shipped + inventory + backorders, all measured at selling price.
[2]Sales = goods shipped + inventory
[3]Cash collected = sales - accounts receivable

B. & C.   CFO and cash balances will be identical; revenue and net income differences reflect only the choice of accounting method, not any economic differences among the companies.

10.{S}A. (i) & (ii) The pattern of income and revenue recognition are identical. Therefore, the answers to A(i) and A(ii) are identical.

To maximize the present value of the bonus, you should prefer the method that recognizes revenue (and income) earlier. Thus, you should prefer the percentage of completion method to the completed contract method.

The pattern of recognition is (1/2, 1/4, 1/4) for the percentage of completion method and (1/3, 1/3, 1/3) for the installment method. Since on a cumulative basis, the percentage of completion method (1/2, 3/4, 1) dominates the installment method (1/3, 2/3, 1) it is preferred.

(iii) All three methods show identical CFO patterns and you would be indifferent under the third bonus criterion.

B.   Over the project's life all three methods generate identical total revenue, income, and CFO. Since payment is made at completion, you are indifferent.

11.{M} This problem provides a good opportunity to discuss the subtleties and implications of revenue and expense recognition criteria.[1]

  A. Revenue recognition is predicated on the following two criteria:
     (1) Collectibility of cash
     (2) Provision of service.

     Criterion (1) is satisfied as the license fee is paid in advance.

     The focus of the question becomes criterion (2) - provision of service. Some students will argue that the service is only provided when the games are actually played. This argument holds only for the revenues from the *season tickets* themselves *not the license fee* - as the former is refundable if games aren't played (player's strike) or if the team "folds". The license fee is presumably nonrefundable no matter what happens. Thus, it is reasonable to recognize the full amount of the license fee as revenue immediately.

     [The discussion can be enhanced by considering what would happen if the Raptors did not sell the ticket and license fee separately but rather sold lifetime season tickets --- i.e. one payment up front entitled the buyer to attend all games forever without additional payment.
         The first issue that would have to be addressed is similar to the above; i.e. what is refundable if games are canceled? If it was assumed that nothing is refundable then would one recognize the full amount as revenue immediately even though no games were played? This would lead to the team recognizing revenues without as yet incurring expenditures in performing the service.
         If one argued that the revenues should be recognized pro-rata -- over how many years should the revenues be recognized? Remember the tickets are sold as a "lifetime" right. Finally, if one made the pro-rata argument for this latter case, one would have to argue as to why it is different than the license portion in the

---

[1] Conceptually, the issues in this problem are similar to those in the Thousand Trails case. The license fee is similar to the initial membership sales and the **season** tickets are similar to the annual membership dues.

case where there is a separate license and season ticket fee.]

B.   A corporation that purchased the license fee would have a "lifetime" asset. For accounting purposes, therefore, it should probably not recognize any expense for the license fee. Practically speaking, however, one would expect the firm to amortize the fee over some arbitrary number of years (probably 40).

C.   In analyzing expected earnings, license fees for a given seat sold are a one-time event. Although licenses for other seats may be sold in future years, as capacity is fixed, in the long run revenues from license fees are nonrecurring. *The long-run earnings potential depends on season ticket sales.*

The license fees, however, provide a valuable input in forecasting future season ticket sales. It is reasonable to assume that (relative to a season ticket holder without a license) there is a greater probability that a licensee will either buy season-tickets themselves or (if they are not interested) they will try to find someone to sell their license to who would be willing to buy season tickets.

Thus, the number of licensees acts as a base or threshold level for anticipated season tickets sold each year. The more licenses sold the higher the expected recurring revenues from season ticket sales.

12.{M}A. Projects for which work was done in previous years were completed in 1991 and revenue was recognized. Under the percentage of completion method, revenue for those projects was recognized in 1990 and prior years. Apparently completions were larger in 1991 than in 1990. However, revenue recognized in 1991 under the percentage of completion method was less than revenue under that method for 1990.

B. Similar to A, projects begun pre-1989 were completed in 1989-1991. The fact that the completed contract shows more revenue may be a signal that current business was declining.

C. **Completed Contract Method**

	1989	1990	1991
Sales	$ 100,436	$ 79,865	$ 98,747
COGS	83,884	64,211	76,872
Gross Margin	$ 16,552	$ 15,654	$ 21,875
Percent	16.48%	19.60%	22.15%

Percentage of Completion Method

	1989	1990	1991
Sales	$ 95,974	$ 92,160	$ 89,309
COGS	79,473	74,203	69,225
Gross Margin	$ 16,501	$ 17,957	$ 20,084
Percent	17.19%	19.48%	22.49%

Gross Margin is improving over time indicating that the "markup" on recent projects is higher. The percentage of completion method picks this up earlier as it recognizes profits from more recent projects sooner. Thus, the profit margin under this method is higher (except for 1990 when the difference is marginal.)

D. Changing to the percentage of completion method should increase Newcor's accounts receivable (faster revenue recognition) but decrease inventory and customer advances. The result will increase the current ratio and change turnover ratios for these accounts.

13.{M}A. The settlement with the IRS and the reversal of previous year's writeoffs are not related to the company's 1994 performance. The IRS settlement dates back to an event occurring in 1985 and the interest earned thereon is related to the 1985-1994 period - not only 1994. Similarly, the $49 million reversal of pretax income is a correction of an incorrect estimate made in 1992 and 1993 and certainly does not relate to 1994 performance. If we eliminate these amounts, after tax income would be reduced by $51 million.

Elimination of IRS settlement	$ 21 million
Elimination of restructuring reversal*	30 million
	$ 51 million

*From IRS settlement we estimate tax rate of (1 - 21/33 =) 38%
Therefore, aftertax $49 million equals $30 million)

Adjusted Net Income = $622 - $51 = $571

Note : No adjustment is required for equity as since these amounts "belong" to previous years, they should be incorporated in equity in those previous years.

Adjusted ROE $\frac{\$571}{\$2902}$ = 19.7%

If these adjustments are included then the "annual incentive award of achieving or exceeding a net income goal" would likely be reduced as net income is reduced by 8% or $51 million. Similarly, the stock options should not be issued as the ROE of 19.7% is less than 20%.
On the other hand, one might argue that the one time (after-tax) charge of $55 million should also not be charged against 1994 income. Even though the charge was taken in 1994, these charges are for staff reductions and closures to be taken in *future* years and do not reflect current operations. Were these charges not included

Adjusted net income   = $571 + $55 = $626
Adjusted 1994 equity   = $2,948 + $55 = $3,003
Adjusted average equity =.5 x ($2,855 + $3,003) = $2,929

Adjusted ROE $\frac{\$626}{\$2,929}$ = 21.4%

After this adjustment, net income would be higher and ROE would be above the threshold level of 20% entitling the CEO to the various incentives.

B. These non-recurring charges should be excluded when assessing current performance. The charges (often) reflect expenses of past (or future) years. Moreover, as they are subject to management discretion, they can be used to manipulate both performance goals and performance trends.

However, ignoring them totally raises another problem. These are real costs and someone must be held accountable for them. Otherwise, management can "warehouse" and bury such recurring costs on a year to year basis and then clean the slate in a series of lump sum "nonrecurring" charges.

This suggests that incentives should perhaps be based on both current performance ignoring noncurrent charges as well as nonrecurring charges using a measure of "average" performance taken over a few years.

C. The best estimate of the level of reported "recurring" profits and ROE would start with this year's "recurring" level of $571 and 19.7%. Given the restructuring, one might expect future profits to increase as future employee costs will be lowered.

However, the *reported* "recurring" levels may not paint an accurate picture of Monsanto's profitability. One must not ignore the fact that Monsanto may be "warehousing" costs and periodically charging them off as "nonrecurring". The firm's profit levels should be adjusted downwards to reflect these periodic non-recurring charges perhaps by averaging the nonrecurring costs over a number of years. These adjusted levels should then be used to forecast future "real" profitability rather than future "reported" profitability.

14.{M}A.& B. ATT's adjusted income before nonrecurring charges is computed by adding back the non-recurring charges to reported income.

All Data in Billions of $

	1985	1986	1987	1988	1989	1990	1991	1992	1993	1994	1995
Revenues	63.2	62.0	60.7	62.1	61.6	63.2	64.5	66.6	69.4	75.1	79.6
Income											
Reported	3.6	1.0	4.1	-2.5	4.8	5.4	1.4	6.5	6.5	7.9	1.2
Restructuring	0.0	3.2	0.0	6.7	0.0	0.0	4.5	0.0	0.5	0.0	7.8
Adjusted	3.6	4.2	4.1	4.2	4.8	5.4	5.9	6.5	7.0	7.9	9.0

Comparing the adjusted and reported amounts, we find that the adjusted amounts follow a smooth pattern mirroring that of the revenue stream. The reported amounts however are erratic and although, overall, the trend is upwards, the path is volatile and follows no discernible pattern.

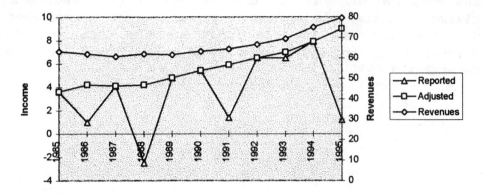

C. At first glance it would seem that if the objective is to forecast future *reported recurring* operating data then the adjusted data are more relevant. They follow a smooth trend consistent with that of revenues, are recurring in nature and are not subject to random fluctuation. However, the repetitive nature of AT&T's "non-recurring" restructuring charges indicates that the firm is engaging in smoothing/big bath behavior. The firm is storing costs and periodically charging them out in order to make "recurring" operating income look better. Thus, to analyze AT&T's actual economic performance or future earnings power the non-recurring items must be considered and the reported operating income used. Over the 11 year period, nonrecurring items totaled $22.7 billion. Charging an average of approximately $2 billion to each year results in the "smoothed" line on the graph (below). It still follows the pattern implied by revenues, albeit at a much lower level.

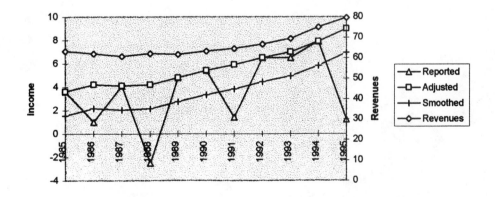

D. AT&T adopted SFAS 121 in 1995 and took a $7.8 billion pretax restructuring charge that year. Included in that restructuring charge is a charge for asset impairments as provided by SFAS 121. That *charge did affect* ATT's reported results. However, the *adoption of SFAS 121 did not affect* the results as AT&T claims that it would have made the identical charge whether or not SFAS 121 was in effect. (Given the empirical findings discussed in pp. 403-406 of the text, that statement is debatable.]

Case 2-1 - Solution

Estimated time to complete this case is 1 to 1½ hrs

1. Thousand Trails' revenues from membership sales increased by $40 million or almost 100% in the 1981 - 1983 period. Two issues need to be addressed with respect to these revenues. First, revenues were recognized in the year of the sale even though customers who bought them were granted "lifetime" privileges from the company. Secondly, (for a portion of the sales) revenue was recognized prior to cash collection as sales were made on an installment basis with an average term of 5 years (61 months).

    These two issues speak directly to the two major criteria underlying revenue recognition;

    1. Has the company provided all or substantially all the service to its customers?
    2. Was cash collectibility reasonably assured?

    With respect to criterion 1, it can be argued that part of the lure of membership was the accessibility of both current and future campgrounds promised by Thousand Trails. Thus Thousand Trails' service was complete only when future campgrounds materialized. This point is, however, not relevant. Under the terms of the membership sales agreement, however, no refunds were available once memberships were sold, even if future campsites were not completed. Thus this criterion suggests that revenue recognition was appropriate.

    The second criterion is more problematic. The potential for a lag between cash collections and revenue recognition is highlighted by the following (interrelated) issues:

    - What percentage of sales was made for cash?
    - For installment sales, what was the creditworthiness of the customers and what were the terms of payment? Note that the customer base was individuals rather than companies.

    These questions, in addition to having relevance for criterion 2, also reopen consideration of criterion 1. While it is true that the company did not have to *refund* any moneys collected if customers canceled, at the same time, it had no recourse in terms of collecting any unpaid balances upon cancellation. *Thus, if customers stopped paying (effectively canceling their memberships), previously recognized revenues might have to be reversed.* As customers purchased memberships with the expectation that future campsites would be opened and/or current ones would be upgraded, if these expectations were not met they might well stop paying the remaining balances owed on their memberships. Thus the appropriateness of the revenue recognition may well hinge on whether the company has "provided all or substantially all the service to its customers"

2. For expense recognition, Thousand Trails' took the opposite tack. Expense recognition of preserve improvements was deferred to years after the actual cash outlay for those improvements.

Note that Thousand Trails' "percentage of completion" method of recognizing expenses differs from the one discussed in the chapter. In the chapter, the customer for the project had already contracted for it. For Thousand Trails, the customer had still to be found.

The appropriateness of their expense recognition method was clearly a function of whether the planned sales would occur. Note that management forecast that total memberships (based on existing preserves) would be three times the current level. Management forecasts used as accounting inputs must be examined carefully as misestimation, whether purposeful or not, may have significant effects on reported earnings and asset values.

Taken together with Thousand Trails' revenue recognition methods, the following picture emerges. Thousand Trails attempted to have the best of both worlds. It made large outlays for preserve improvements based on optimistic estimates of future cash flows. Current cash outflows were capitalized (deferred to future periods), while all estimated future cash inflows were recognized as revenue immediately.

3. Thousand Trails took an "aggressive" position in recognizing revenues (and expenses). Sales were recognized in full, although only a portion of the cash was collected. Expenses, on the other hand, were deferred to periods following the cash outlay. Given the long collection period, there was a built-in lag between present cash

outflows and future cash inflows. Thus reported income was not a good indicator of near-term cash flows.

Moving beyond the issue of whether this accounting complied with GAAP, the implications of the gap between revenue and expense recognition and cash flows should be clear. Assuming for the moment that the growth rate could be maintained, the gap would still indicate potential liquidity and solvency problems.

However, analysis suggests that maintaining Thousand Trails' past growth rates was unlikely. The only way to maintain the growth rate was for membership sales to grow at the same rate as in the past. These sales would require new campgrounds, which would result in further cash outlays and deferral of costs. This cycle assumed, to some extent, the existence of a large untapped market. Even if this market existed, the cash flow (liquidity) constraint could eventually overwhelm the company.

All markets reach saturation eventually. For every company that maintains a very high growth rate year after year (Wal-Mart, for example), there are others that fail to sustain earlier high rates of growth. In most cases, the current growth rate of sales and income must be expected to decline in the future.

Given the "lifetime" nature of membership sales, customers do not return for second purchases, and future membership sales are purely a function of demographics and population trends. Note it took at least three years to reach a membership level of 50,000. How long might it take to reach its forecast of 100,000 more members on its current campgrounds? The increase in memberships was dependent to some extent on new campgrounds being opened, which, again would require expansion of the market. The answer to this question exists outside the financial reports. Demographic and population trends, competition, and other factors would need to be examined; parameters which require data from outside of the financial statements.

4. Once saturation is reached, the company's main source of income would be annual dues and interest on installment sales rather than membership sales. Thus, for "long-run" analytic purposes, we must recognize that these recurring components of income are more important than income from membership sales, which had historically been the most prominent factor.

This does not mean that historical membership sales are irrelevant. On the contrary, they are the primary inputs in estimating the level of future annual membership dues. This underscores the use of financial statements in general, and the income statement in particular, as (part of) a database used to predict the company's future.

5. Assets represent economic resources that provide future benefits. Consistent with a long-run "going concern" perspective of the firm, these future benefits can be

   - *their earnings generating ability;* or
   - *their cash collectibility.*

Fixed assets and inventory, for example, are assets primarily because they help generate future sales and earnings. In the Thousand Trails case, operating preserves represent such assets. Receivables, which arise after the earnings generating process has been completed, are forecasts of cash collections. They are an asset to the extent that they will result in the collection of cash. The service has already been provided; conversion to cash is now awaited.

Our previous discussion indicated some question as to the eventual collectibility of Thousand Trails' receivables due to both the creditworthiness of the customers and the limits to growth.

Furthermore the cash outflows for operating preserves and improvements therein are assets if they are expected to provide future services. Our analysis questions this assumption. For the operating preserves to be an asset, nearly three times the current membership levels would have to be reached. If anticipated future sales do not materialize and a ready market[1] for the assets does not exist, then the carrying value of the assets should be viewed as nothing more than unexpired costs; "expenses waiting to happen." When there is no expectation of future revenues, there is nothing to "match" those expenses

---

[1] For the operating preserves, although the land may have had some market value (for alternative uses), most of the carrying cost was for improvements. These have value only if used as campgrounds, which, we have already pointed out, depended on the achievement of optimistic assumptions.

against, and the carrying amount of the assets will be overstated.

   To a great extent therefore, these assets (receivables and operating preserves) exist only as a function of Thousand Trails' revenue and expense recognition methods.

   The seriousness of this issue can be brought home if we take a peek at Exhibit 3C-2 (text p.121). Thousand Trails' December 31, 1983, balance sheet shows that approximately 85% of Thousand Trails' assets of $151.8 million consisted of receivables (56%) and operating preserves (29%):

		% of Total Assets
Receivables (net of allowance)		
Current	$20.8 million	13.7%
Noncurrent	64.1	42.2%
Total	$84.9 million	55.9%
Operating preserves	$43.8 million	28.8%

   Take these "assets" away and there are few assets left.

Chapter 3 - Solutions

Overview:

Problem Length	*Problem #'s*
{S}	1,2,3,5
{M}	4,7,8,10
{L}	6,9,11,12,13

1.{S}A.   **Palomba Pizza Stores**
         Statement of Cash Flows
         Year Ended December 31, 1991

Cash Flows from Operating Activities:		
Cash Collections from Customers	$250,000	
Cash Payments to Suppliers	(85,000)	
Cash Payments for Salaries	(45,000)	
Cash Payments for Interest	(10,000)	
Net Cash from Operating Activities		$ 110,000
Cash Flows from Investing Activities:		
Sales of Equipment	38,000	
Purchase of Equipment	(30,000)	
Purchase of Land	(14,000)	
Net Cash for Investing Activities		$ (6,000)
Cash Flows from Financing Activities:		
Retirement of Common Stock	(25,000)	
Payment of Dividends	(35,000)	
Net Cash for Financing Activities		$ (60,000)
Net Increase in Cash		$ 44,000
Cash at Beginning of Year		50,000
Cash at End of Year		$ 94,000

B.   Cash Flow from Operations (CFO) measures the cash
     generating ability of operations, in addition to
     profitability. If used as a measure of performance, CFO
     is less subject to distortion than net income. Analysts
     use the CFO as a check on the quality of reported
     earnings, although it is not a substitute for net
     income. Companies with high net income and low CFO may

be using overly aggressive income recognition techniques. The ability of a firm to generate cash from operations on a consistent basis is one indication of the financial health of the firm. Analysts search for trends in CFO to indicate future cash conditions and potential liquidity or solvency problems.

Cash Flow from Investing Activities (CFI) reports how the firm is investing its excess cash. The analyst must consider the ability of the firm to continue to grow and CFI is a good indication of the attitude of management in this area. This component of total cash flow includes the capital expenditures made by management to maintain and expand productive capacity. Decreasing CFI may be a forecast of slower future growth.

Cash Flow from Financing (CFF) indicates the sources of financing for the firm. For firms that require external sources of financing (either borrowing or equity financing) it communicates management's preferences regarding financial leverage. Debt financing indicates future cash requirements for principal and interest payments. Equity financing will cause future earnings per share dilution.

For firms whose operating cash flow exceeds investment needs, CFF indicates whether that excess is used to repay debt, pay (or increase) cash dividends, or repurchase outstanding shares.

C.   Cash payments for interest should be classified as CFF for purposes of analysis. This classification separates the effect of financial leverage decisions from operating results. It also facilitates the comparison of Palomba with other firms whose financial leverage differs.

D.   The change in cash has no analytic significance. The change in cash (and hence, the cash balance at the end of the year) is a product of management decisions regarding financing. For example, the firm can show a large cash balance by drawing on bank lines just prior to year end.

2.{S} A.(i) *Cash Flows from operating activities*

Cash Collections from Customers	$260
Cash payments to Merchandise suppliers	(85)
Cash payments for salaries	(35)
Cash payments for interest	(12)
	$128

(ii) *Cash Flows from investing activities*

Purchase of land	(8)
Purchase of equipment	(40)
Sale of equipment	30
	$(18)

(iii) *Cash Flows from financing activities*

Retirement of common stock	(32)
Payments of dividends	(37)
	$(69)

B. It may be more appropriate to reclassify cash paid for interest from CFO to cash flows for investing activities. This would result in

Cash flows from operating activities	$140
Cash flows for investing activities	(18)
Cash flows from financing activities	(81)

C. Depending on the purpose of analysis, free cash flows may or may not include cash flows for interest payments:

	Interest Included IN CFO	Interest Not Included In CFO
Cash flows from operating activities	$ 128	$ 140
Cash flows for investing activities	(18)	(18)
Free cash flows	**$ 110**	**$ 122**

3.{S} A.

Cash from customers	$ 150,000
Cash Paid for:	
salaries	(60,000)
suppliers	(40,000)
Cash from operations	$ 50,000

B. Based on SFAS 95 the $20,000 would reduce the CFO to $30,000. However, as noted in the chapter, interest costs may be more properly considered as a financing cost and as such would be ignored in calculating CFO.

4.{M}A.

	19X0	19X1	19X2	19X3	19X4	19X5
Sales	$ ---	$ 140	$ 150	$ 165	$ 175	$ 195
Bad debt expense	---	7	7	8	10	10
Net receivables	30	40	50	60	75	95
Cash collections[1]	$ ---	$ 123	$ 133	$ 147	$ 150	$ 165

[1]Sales - bad debt expense - increase in net receivables

B. The bad debt provision does not seem to be adequate. From 19x1 - 19X5 sales increased by approximately 40%, while net receivables more than doubled, indicating that collections have been lagging. The ratios calculated below also indicate the problem. While bad debt expense has remained fairly constant at 5% of sales over the 5 year period, net receivables as a percentage of sales have increased from 29% to 49%; cash collections relative to sales have declined. Other possible explanations for these data are that stated payment terms have lengthened or that Stengel has allowed customers to delay payment.

	19X1	19X2	19X3	19X4	19X5
Bad debt expense/sales	5.0%	4.7%	4.9%	5.7%	5.1%
Net receivables/sales	28.6	33.3	36.4	42.8	48.7
Cash collections/sales	87.9	88.7	89.1	85.7	84.6

5. {S}Niagara Company
Statement of Cash Flows 19X2

Cash Collections	$ 980		[Sales - Δ A/C Receivable]
Cash Inputs	(670)		[COGS + Δ Inventory
Cash Expenses	(75)		[S & G Exp - Δ A/C Payable[1]]
Cash Interest Paid	(40)		[Int. Expense - Δ Int. Pay.]
Income Taxes Paid	(30)		[Income Tax Exp. - Δ Deferred Tax]
Cash from Operations		$ 165	
Purchase of Fixed Assets	(150)		[Depreciation Expense + Δ Fixed
Cash Used for Investing		(150)	Assets (net)]
Increase in LT Debt	50		
Decrease in Notes Pay.	(25)		
Dividends Paid	(30)		
Cash Used for Financing		(5)	[Net Income - Δ Retained earnings]
Net Change in Cash		$ 10	
Cash Balance 12/31/X1		50	
Cash Balance 12/31/X2		$ 60	

[1]Can also be used to calculate cash inputs, decreasing that outflow to $645 while increasing cash expenses to $100.

6.{L}A.   **G Company**
         Income Statement, 19X4 ($ thousands)

Sales	$ 3,841	[receipts from customers + increase in accounts receivable]
COGS + Operating Expenses[1]	3,651	[payments - increase in inventory + increase in accounts payable]
Depreciation	15	[increase in accumulated depreciation]
Interest	41	[payments]
Taxes	42	[payment + increase in tax payable]
Net Income	$ 92	[check = change in retained earnings as there are no dividends]

[1]Note that these two cannot be calculated separately from the information available.

B.   **M Company**
     Cash Receipts and Disbursements, 19X4 ($ thousands)

Cash receipts from:		
Customers	$ 1,807	[Sales - increase in receivables]
Issue of stock	3	[Increase in account]
Short-term debt	62	[Increase in liability]
Long-term debt	96	[Increase in liability]
Total	$ 1,968	
Cash disbursements for:		
COGS/operating exp.	$ 1,843	[COGS + operating expense + increase in inventory + decrease in accounts payable]
Taxes		
Interest	3	[Expense - increase in tax payable]
Total	51	
	$ 1,952	[Expense]
Change in cash		
	$ 16	

NOTE: This is not a true receipts and disbursements schedule as it shows certain amounts (e.g., debt) on a net basis rather than gross. Such schedules (and cash flow statements) prepared from published data can only show some amounts net, unless supplementary data is available.

C. The cash flow statements are presented with the income statement for comparison purposes in answering Part D.

M Company--Statement of Cash Flows   ($ thousands)

	19X0	19X1	19X2	19X3	19X4
CFO:					
From customers	$1,165	$1,210	$1,327	$1,587	$1,807
Less outlays for:					
COGS/Op. Exp.	1,130	1,187	1,326	1,672	1,843
Interest	15	19	16	21	51
Taxes	23	19	9	9	3
	$ (3)	$ (15)	$ (24)	$ (115)	$ (90)
CFI:					
PP&E purchase	(14)	(17)	(37)	(30)	(33)
CFF:					
Issue of stock	5	5	8	3	3
Short-term debt	64	65	--	153	62
Long-term debt	--	--	100	--	96
Dividends	(20)	(21)	(21)	(21)	(22)
Repurchase of stock	(22)	(14)	--	(10)	--
Repayment of LT debt	(2)	(2)	(3)	--	--
Repayment of ST debt	--	--	(8)	--	--
	$ 25	$ 33	$ 76	$ 125	$ 139
Change in Cash	$ 8	$ 1	$ 15	$ (20)	$ 16

M Company--Income Statement ($ thousands)

	19X0	19X1	19X2	19X3	19X4
Sales	$ 1,220	$ 1,265	$ 1,384	$ 1,655	$ 1,861
COGS	818	843	931	1,125	1,277
Operating exp.	298	320	363	434	504
Depreciation	9	10	11	12	14
Interest	15	19	16	21	51
Taxes	38	33	27	26	6
Total	$ 1,178	$ 1,225	$ 1,348	$ 1,852	$ 1,852
Net Income	$ 42	$ 40	$ 36	$ 37	$ 9

3-7

G Company--Statement of Cash Flows   ($ thousands)

	19X0	19X1	19X2	19X3	19X4
CFO:					
From customers	$1,110	$1,659	$2,163	$2,809	$3,679
Disbursements:					
COGS/Op. Exp.	1,214	1,702	1,702	2,895	3,778
Interest	11	13	23	29	41
Taxes	13	15	16	29	35
CFO	$ (128)	$ (71)	$ (93)	$ (144)	$ (175)
CFI:					
PP&E purchase	---	---	(20)	(10)	---
CFF:					
Issue of stock	10	---	5	45	30
Short-term debt	80	52	91	3	60
Long-term debt	40	23	20	125	50
CFF	$ 130	$ 75	$ 116	$ 173	$ 140
Change in Cash	$ 2	$ 4	$ 3	$ 19	$ 35

G Company--Income Statement   ($ thousands)

	19X0	19X1	19X2	19X3	19X4
Sales	$ 1,339	$ 1,731	$ 2,261	$ 2,939	$ 3,841
COGS	1,039	1,334	1,743	2,267	---
Operating exp.	243	312	398	524	3,651
Depreciation	10	10	12	14	15
Interest	11	13	23	29	41
Taxes	13	20	27	31	42
Total	$ 1,316	$ 1,689	$ 2,203	$ 2,865	$ 3,749
Net Income	$ 23	$ 42	$ 58	$ 74	$ 92

D. Both companies are credit risks. Although both are profitable, their CFO is increasingly negative. If current trends continue they face possible insolvency. However, before rejecting both loans outright, it is important to know whether CFO and income differ because the companies are doing poorly or because they are growing too fast.

Both companies increased sales over the 5 year period; Company M by 50%, Company G by more than 300%. Are these sales real (will cash collections materialize)? If they are "growing too fast", it may be advisable to make the loan but also to force the company to curtail its growth until CFO catches up. One way to verify whether the gap is the result of sales to poor credit risks is to check if the growth in receivables is "proportional" to the sales growth. Similar checks can be made for the growth in inventories and payables. In this case, the inventory of M company has doubled from 19X0 to 19X4 while COGS increased by only 56%. The inventory increase would be one area to investigate further.

There is a significant difference in the investment pattern of the two companies. Company M has made purchases of PPE each year, while Company G has made little net investment in PPE over the period. Yet Company G has grown much faster. Does this reflect the nature of the business (Company G is much less capital intensive) or has Company G used off balance sheet financing techniques?

The cash from financing patterns of the two companies also differ. Both tripled their total debt over the period and increased the ratio of total debt to equity. Given Company M's slower growth (in sales and equity), its debt burden has grown much more rapidly. Despite this, Company M has continued to pay dividends and repurchase stock. Company G has not paid dividends and has issued new equity. These two factors account for its larger increase in equity from 19X0 to 19X4.

Based only on the financial data provided, G looks like the better credit risk. Its sales and income are growing rapidly, while M's income is stable to declining on modestly growing sales. Unless further investigation changes the insights discussed here, you should prefer to lend to Company G.

7. {M}   **Statement of Cash Flows - Indirect Method**

Cash from operations

Net Income		$1,080
Add Non cash expense - depreciation		600

Add/Subtract Changes in working capital

A/R	(150)	
Inventory	(200)	
Accruals	80	
A/P	120	(150)
		1,530

Cash from investing

Capital Expenditures	**1,150**

Cash from financing

Short term borrowing	550
Long-term repayment	(398)
Dividends	(432)
	(280)

Net Change in Cash	**$ 100**

Worksheet for (Direct Method) Cash Flow Statement

	Income Statement	Balance Sheet 12/31/95	12/31/96	Change	Cash Effect
Net Income	1080				1080
Depreciation	600				600
A/R		1500	1650	150	(150)
Inventory		2000	2200	200	(200)
Accruals		800	880	80	80
A/P		1200	1320	120	120
Depreciation	(600)				(600)
Net fixed assets		6500	7050	550	(550)
Capital Expenditures					*(1150)*
Note payable		5500	6050	550	550
Short-term borrowing					*550*
Long-term debt		2000	1602	(398)	(398)
Long-term debt repayment					*(398)*
Net Income	(1080)				(1080)
Retained Earnings		500	1148	648	648
Dividends					*(432)*
	0				100

3-10

The worksheet to create the cash flow statement is presented above. Each balance sheet change (other than cash) is accounted for and matched with its corresponding activity. Furthermore the operating account changes are grouped together and matched to their corresponding income statement item. As a last check, the net income and the add-backs of non-cash items are balanced and "closed" to their respective accounts (PP&E and retained earnings) providing the amounts of capital expenditures and dividends.

8. {M}   **Statement of Cash Flows - Direct Method**
   Cash from Operations

Cash Collections	$9,850
Cash payments for merchandise	(6,080)
Cash paid for SG&A	(920)
Cash paid for interest	(600)
Cash paid for taxes	(720)
	1,530

   Cash for investing activities

Capital Expenditures	**(1,150)**

   Cash for financing activities

Short-term borrowing	550
Long-term debt repayment	(398)
Dividends	(432)
	(280)

   Net Change in cash   **$ 100**

The worksheet to create the cash flow statement is presented below. Each balance sheet change (other than cash) is accounted for and matched with its corresponding activity. Furthermore the operating account changes are matched to their corresponding income statement item. As a last check, the net income is balanced and "closed" to retained earnings providing the amount of dividends.
Note that there is no difference between the indirect and direct methods in the cash flow statement and in the worksheet for cash for investing and financing activities,

Worksheet for (Indirect Method) Cash Flow Statement

	Income Statement	Balance Sheet 12/31/95	12/31/96	Change	Cash Effect
Sales	10000				10,000
A/R		1500	1650	150	(150)
Cash Collections					**9,850**
COGS	(6000)				(6,000)
Inventory		2000	2200	200	(200)
A/P		1200	1320	120	120
Cash payments for merchandise					**(6,080)**
SG&A	(1000)				(1,000)
Accruals		800	880	80	80
Cash paid for SG&A					**(920)**
Interest Exp	(600)				(600)
Cash paid for interest					**(600)**
Taxes	(720)				(720)
Cash paid for taxes					**(720)**
Depreciation	(600)				(600)
Net fixed assets		6500	7050	550	(550)
Capital Expenditures					**(1,150)**
Note payable		5500	6050	550	550
Short-term borrowing					**550**
Long-term debt		2000	1602	(398)	(398)
Long-term debt repayment					**(398)**
Net Income	(1080)				(1,080)
Retained Earnings		500	1148	648	648
Dividends					**(432)**
	0				100

9.{L}A. **Mercantile Stores**
Cash Flow from Operations, Direct Method
Year Ended January 31, 1992
($ thousands)

Net sales	$ 2,442,425	
Δ in accounts receivable	20,467	
Cash collections		$ 2,462,892
Cost of goods sold	(1,720,947)	
Depreciation expense[1]	70,607	
Δ in inventories	11,898	
Δ in accounts payable	(1,698)	
Merchandise purchases		(1,640,140)
Selling & admin. expense	(546,682)	
Δ in other current assets	669	
Δ in other current liabilities	(1,751)	
Δ in accrued payroll	(2,147)	
Unidentified changes[2]	(3,601)	
Cash operating expense		(553,512)
Interest expense	(23,390)	
Δ in accrued interest[3]	(7)	
Interest paid		(23,397)
Interest income	4,511	
Other income	30,485	
Δ in other receivables	(9,295)	
Undistributed equity income[4]	(931)	
Cash other income		24,770
Income tax expense	(72,363)	
Δ in deferred income tax (c/a)	$ 198	
Δ in deferred income tax (lt/l)	697	
Subtotal deferred taxes	$ 895	
Δ in accrued income tax (c/1)	(273)	
Income tax paid[5]		(71,741)
Cash Flow from Operations		$ 198,872

[1] As depreciation is not separately identified in the income statement, it must be removed. We assume that it is entirely included in cost of goods sold.

3-13

[2] Some of the "adjustments to reconcile" in the indirect method cash flow statement cannot be derived from the financial data provided. Some of the adjustments in the direct method statement (note 3, for example) are not shown in the indirect method statement. Yet both must produce the same cash flow from operations. These problems require a "plug" figure that is the "net" of all of these items:

Shown in indirect method statement:		
Pensions		$ (4,256)
Other working capital changes		(2,854)
Subtotal		$ (7,110)
Shown in direct method statement:		
Other current assets	669	
Other current liabilities	(1,751)	
Accrued payroll	(2,147)	
Interest Payable	(7)	
Income tax accruals (net)	(273)	
Subtotal		(3,509)
Difference: unidentified changes (plug)		$ (3,601)

[3] The supplemental cash flow information discloses interest paid; the difference from interest expense must reflect a decrease in accrued interest payable.

[4] This represents Mercantile's share of earnings not received as dividends; equity earnings (see Chapter 3) are assumed to be part of other income.

[5] Computed income taxes paid equal the amounts disclosed in the supplemental cash flow information; no adjustment is required.

B. While the direct method statement for one year can
    provide only limited insight into cash flow
    relationships, there is some benefit. For example,
    compare the ratios of COGS and operating expenses to
    sales as shown in the income statement with their cash
    analogues:

	% Sales		% Collections
Cost of goods sold	70.5%	Merchandise purchases	66.8%
Selling and admin.	22.4	Cash operating expense	22.6

While depreciation expense accounts for most of the
difference between the ratios, purchases are a lower
percent (although collections exceed sales) as Mercantile
controlled inventories to cope with recessionary
conditions.

The direct method cash flow statement also permits
the comparison of income statement accruals and their
cash analogues (e.g., cost-of-goods sold and merchandise
purchases). Both short- and long-term divergences may
convey information about the impact of accounting choices
and economic events. For example, an excess of
merchandise purchases over COGS may indicate (if short-
term) disappointing sales or purchases in anticipation of
future orders. If long-term, the excess may indicate
obsolete or excessive inventory.

Given more than one year of data, the direct method
statement should facilitate analysis by providing
comparisons (such as those above) not available from the
indirect cash flow statement.

10.{M}A.   **Hertz Corp. ($ millions)**

	1989	1990	1991
Reported cash flow from operations	$ (117)	$ 92	$ 286
Add back: purchases of equipment	3,003	4,024	4,016
Subtract: sales of equipment	(2,354)	(3,434)	(3,784)
Adjusted cash flow from operations	$ 532	$ 682	$ 518

B.   As reported, cash flow from operations shows steady improvement over the period 1989-1991, changing from a negative to a positive amount. After adjustment, the trend is eliminated; cash flow from operations is lower in 1991 than in either 1989 and 1990. The improvement in reported cash flow from operations was the result of reducing Hertz's net investment in rental equipment.

C.

	1989	1990	1991
Reported cash flow for investing	$ (133)	$ (79)	$ (72)
Subtract: purchases of equipment	(3,003)	(4,024)	(4,016)
Add back: sales of equipment	2,354	3,434	3,784
Adjusted cash flow for investing	$ (782)	$ (669)	$ (304)

D.   Reported cash flow for investing shows little change over the three year period. After reclassification of equipment purchases and sales, cash flow for investing drops by more than half in 1991. After reclassification it reflects the sharp drop in net car and truck purchases in that year.

E.   Free cash flow can be defined as cash flow from operations less investment required to maintain productive capacity. If we assume that Hertz's investments are solely to maintain existing capacity, then free cash flow equals cash flow from operations less cash flow for investing:

	1989	1990	1991
Reported cash flow from operations	$ (117)	$ 92	$ 286
Less: reported cash flow for investing	(133)	(79)	(72)
Equals: free cash flow	$ (250)	$ 13	$ 214

Note that reclassification of purchases and sales of revenue equipment has no effect on free cash flow:

	1989	1990	1991
Adjusted cash flow from operations	$ 532	$ 682	$ 518
Less: adjusted cash flow for investing	(782)	(669)	(304)
Equals: free cash flow	$ (250)	$ 13	$ 214

Thus by defining free cash flow in a manner which subtracts out all expenditures required to maintain the operating capacity of the firm, whether capitalized or not and regardless of classification, the effects of accounting and reporting differences can be overcome. This solution requires, of course, the identification of the amounts of such items.

F.   When equipment is purchased, the full amount is reported as an operating cash outflow. For leased equipment, only the periodic lease payments are reported as operating cash outflows. Thus, for Hertz, leasing increases reported cash flow from operations.

G.   When equipment purchases are classified as investing cash flows, then leasing reduces operating cash flows relative to purchases. That is because the outflow connected with purchases (or any other capitalized expenditure) is never classified as an operating outflow. [See Chapter 11 for a detailed analysis of this issue.]

11.{L} The cash flow statement shows a steady deterioration in CFO; albeit CFO remains positive. Income (before extraordinary items) on the other hand increases steadily at approximately 8%-10% per year.

To explain the cause for the discrepancy between the pattern of income and CFO, we first compute the direct method cash flow statement and then compare the cash flow components with their income statement counterparts.

The (abbreviated) cash flow statement under the direct method is presented below:

	1992	1993	1994
Cash from operating activities			
Collections from customers	$2,135,805	$2,420,961	$2,744,159
Payments for merchandise	(1,502,414)	(1,742,149)	(2,064,815)
Payments for SG&A	(453,449)	(523,474)	(601,575)
Interest Paid	(37,883)	(33,367)	(33,048)
Taxes paid	(12,414)	(22,989)	(8,408)
Other (Plug)	(29,505)	(247)	(5,519)
	100,140	98,735	30,794
Cash for investing activities			
Capital expenditures	(48,878)	(110,534)	(90,009)
Acquisition of leaseholds	(30,602)	(21,894)	(8,025)
	(85,480)	(132,428)	(98,034)
Cash for financing activities			
Borrowings - Long-term	(3,276)	(23,831)	(19,432)
Borrowings - revolving credit			70,243
Common stck, options & warrant	1,995	54,460	1,050
	(1,281)	30,629	51,861
Net Change in Cash	$ 13,379	$ (3,064)	$ (15,379)

The required calculations for the operating items are presented in Exhibit 3S-1. The last item "other" is the plug figure used to arrive at the CFO presented in the indirect cash flow statement (Exhibit 3P-4).

Exhibit 3S-1: Worksheet for Operating Items for Direct Method SoCF

	1992	1993	1994
Sales	2,127,684	2,414,124	2,748,634
Change in Receivables	8,121	6,837	(4,475)
Collections from Customers	**2,135,805**	**2,420,961**	**2,744,159**
COGS	(1,527,731)	(1,742,276)	(1,975,332)
Change in inventory	(28,401)	(60,893)	(82,863)
Change in A/P	53,718	61,020	(6,620)
Payments for merchandise	**(1,502,414)**	**(1,742,149)**	**(2,064,815)**
SG&A	(458,804)	(520,685)	(605,538)
Change in prepaid expenses	1,317	(2,137)	(3,358)
Change in accrued wages	4,038	(652)	7,321
Payments for SG&A	**(453,449)**	**(523,474)**	**(601,575)**
Interest Expense	(39,934)	(34,904)	(34,048)
Amortization of debt issuance costs	2,051	1,537	1,000
Interest Paid	**(37,883)**	**(33,367)**	**(33,048)**
Tax expense	(25,507)	(26,152)	(27,569)
Change in Taxes payable	9,003	2,662	17,567
Deferred taxes	4,090	501	1,594
Taxes paid	**(12,414)**	**(22,989)**	**(8,408)**

The comparison of the cash flow and income statement components is presented below:

	1992	1993	1994	%change 1992-1993	%change 1993-1994	%change 1992-1994
Sales	2,127,684	2,414,124	2,748,634	13.5%	13.9%	29.2%
Collections from Customers	2,135,805	2,420,961	2,744,159	13.4%	13.3%	28.5%
Collections/Sales	100.38%	100.28%	99.84%			
COGS	(1,527,731)	(1,742,276)	(1,975,332)	14.0%	13.4%	29.3%
Payments for merchandise	(1,502,414)	(1,742,149)	(2,064,815)	16.0%	18.5%	37.4%
Payments/COGS	98.34%	99.99%	104.53%			
SG&A	(458,804)	(520,685)	(605,538)	13.5%	16.3%	32.0%
Payments for SG&A	(453,449)	(523,474)	(601,575)	15.4%	14.9%	32.7%
Payments/SG&A	98.83%	100.54%	99.35%			

A comparison of cash collections with sales indicates that sales have been increasing at a slightly faster pace than collections. The collections/sales ratio has decreased from 100.38% in 1992 to 99.84% in 1994. The difference however is very small (just over .5%) and it does not seem that credit and collections is responsible for the deterioration in CFO.

The inventory story however is another matter. Payments for inventory increased by 37% whereas COGS only increased by 29%. This is indicative of inventory being bought, paid for and piling up as the merchandise is not being sold. The proportion of payments to COGS increased accordingly from 98.3% to 104.5% in two years. This increase of 6% translates (based on COGS of close to $2,000,000) to an increased annual cash requirement of $120,000.

Thus, the first cause of Radloc's problems may be facing would seem to be inventories. Its income may be overstated as inventory may have to be written down if it cannot be sold. Even if inventory is eventually sold and the purchases now being made now are to satisfy future growth, the firm may still face liquidity problems as they require cash to purchase (and carry) the new inventory.

However, as CFO is still positive *ceterus parabus* the firm may still be a good candidate for credit.

Further insights as to the impact of growth can be seen if we compare free cash flows (CFO - CFI) with income and CFO.

	1992	1993	1994
Earnings bef. extraordinary items	$37,262	$41,378	$44,359
CFO	100,140	98,735	30,794
Free Cash Flows	14,660	(33,693)	(67,240)

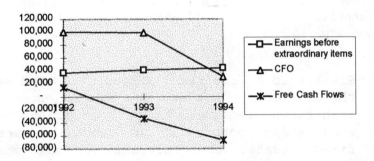

Although income rises, CFO and free cash flows fall. CFO exceeds income in 1992 and 1993 as the noncash depreciation addback increases CFO relative to income. By 1994, however, CFO, (although positive) falls below income. This indicates that the firm *may* have problems in covering the replacement of *current* productive capacity.

Free cash flows is negative in 1993 and 1994 and "barely" positive in 1992. This indicates that the firm's growth (in addition to inventory) requires cash that Radloc cannot supply internally.

Where is the cash coming from?

In 1993, it met its requirements by issuing stock; in 1994 the firm's short term debt increased considerably as it drew down its revolving credit lines.

Thus, the firm seems to be facing a credit crunch and one might hesitate to give it a loan.

PS Radloc is an anagram for Caldor and the financial statements in Exhibit 3P-4 are taken from Caldor's. Caldor, a wholesaler, entered Chapter 11 bankruptcy soon after the 1994 statements were published.

12.{L}A. As Castle had no non-U.S. operations prior to the acquisition of Norton, balance sheet changes that differ from the corresponding cash flows must be the result of the acquisition of Norton. This relationship allows us to deduce the assets and liabilities of Norton that Castle acquired ($ thousands):

	Balance Sheet Change	-	Cash Flow Change	=	Difference
Accounts receivable	$ (2,025)	-	$ (3,818)	=	$ 1,793
Inventories	17,594	-	13,592	=	4,002
Accounts payable	(8,605)	-	(11,709)	=	3,104

B. Similar to A, the fixed assets of Norton acquired must be the discrepancy between the balance sheet change and the cash flows. Because we must account for depreciation and asset sales, both of which reduce the carrying amount of fixed assets, the calculations are more complex ($ thousands):

Balance sheet change	$ 9,490
Depreciation expense	5,215
Basis of assets sold[1]	17
Assets acquired	$14,722
Less: capital expenditures[2]	(13,390)
Equals: Norton assets	$ 1,332

[1]The cash flow statement reports that the proceeds from assets sold were $34 and the gain was $17, indicating that the cost basis of assets sold was $17 ($34-$17).
[2]From the cash flow statement.

C. (i) While net income almost vanished in 1991, Castle reduced both accounts receivable and inventories during the year (lower receivables reflect lower sales). While lower payables offset part of these declines, nondebt current accounts fell by more than $20 million in 1991, in contrast to a rise of nearly $25 million in 1990. As a result, cash from operations swung from an outflow of nearly $15 million in 1990 to an inflow of $25 million for 1991.

(ii) The acquisition of Norton in 1990 increased Castle's inventories and accounts receivable, as shown in part A. The purchase of these assets was reflected in cash from investing activities. If the 1991 reduction included Norton operating assets acquired in 1990, then 1991 cash from operations is inflated. These assets were not acquired through operations and their sale distorts the trend of cash from operations.

13.{L}A. This part of the question requires an understanding of SFAS 95, which governs the preparation of the Statement of Cash Flows. SFAS 95 permits use of either the direct or indirect method. As an initial step under either method, the effect of the Kraft acquisition must be removed as follows:

Balance Sheet Changes ($ in millions}

	As Reported 1987	As Reported 1988	Total Change 1987-1988	Less Kraft	Adjusted Change
Receivables	$ 2,065	$ 2,222	$ 157	$ 758	$ (601)
Inventory	4,154	5,384	1,230	1,232	(2)
PPE	6,582	8,648	2,066	1,740	326
Goodwill	4,052	15,071	11,019	10,361	658
ST debt	1,440	1,259	(181)	700	(881)
A/C Payable	791	1,777	986	578	408
Accrued li-abilities	2,277	3,848	1,571	530	1,041
LT debt	6,293	17,122	10,829	900	9,929

Transactional Analysis Worksheet ($ Millions)

Revenues	$31,742		
Decrease in receivables	601		
Cash collections		$ 32,343	
Cost of goods sold	(12,156)		
Decrease in inventory	2		
Increase in accounts payable	408		
Cash inputs		(11,746)	
Selling & admin. expense	(14,410)		
Increase in accrued liabilities	1,041		
Cash expenses		(13,369)	
Income tax expense	(1,390)		
Increase in income taxes payable	362		
Decrease in deferred income taxes	(325)		
Income taxes paid		(1,353)	
Interest expense		(670)	
Cash flow--operating activities		$ 5,205	
Depreciation expense	$ (654)		
Increase in net PPE	(326)		
Cash invested in PPE		$ (980)	
Goodwill amortization	(125)		
Increase in goodwill	(658)		
Goodwill purchased		(783)	
Decrease in investments		405	
Acquisition of Kraft		(11,383)	
Cash flow--investing activities		$(12,741)	
Dividends declared	$ (941)		
Increase in dividends payable	47		
Dividends paid		$ (894)	
Decrease in stockholders' equity			
(repurchase)*		(540)	
Net change in short-term debt		(881)	
Net change in long-term debt		9,929	
Cash flow--financing activities		$ 7,614	
Increase in cash and equivalents			$ 78

*The net issuance or repurchase of equity is computed by reconciling the stockholders' equity account:

Reconciliation of Stockholders' Equity

12/31/87 Balance	$ 6,823
1988 Net income	2,337
Dividend declared	(941)
Total	$ 8,219
12/31/88 Balance	(7,679)
Decrease in stockholders' equity (repurchase)	$ 540

If the "indirect method" is used, the following presentation is appropriate:

Philip Morris Companies, Inc.
Worksheet for Statement of Cash Flows
Year Ended December 31, 1988   ($ Millions)

Cash flows from operating activities:			
Net income	$ 2,337		
Adjustments to cash basis:			
Depreciation expense	654		
Amortization of goodwill	125		
Decrease in accounts receivable	601		
Decrease in inventory	2		
Decrease in deferred taxes	(325)		
Increase in accounts payable	408		
Increase in accrued liabilities	1,041		
Increase in income taxes payable	362		
Net cash flow--operating activities		$ 5,205	
Cash flows from investing activities:			
Increase in PPE (before depreciation)	$ (980)		
Increase in goodwill (before amort)	(783)		
Decrease in investments	405		
Acquisition of Kraft	(11,383)		
Net cash used by investing activities		(12,741)	
Cash flows from financing activities:			
Decrease in short-term debt	$ (881)		
Increase in long-term debt	9,929		
Decrease in stockholders' equity (repurchase)	(540)		
Dividends declared	(941)		
Increase in dividends payable	47		
Net cash provided by financing activities		7,614	
Net increase in cash		$ 78	
Supplementary disclosure of cash flow information:			
Interest paid during year			
Income taxes paid during year		$ 670	
		$ 1,353	
Schedule of noncash investing & financing activities:			
		$---	

B. The simplest calculation would be operating cash flow less capital expenditures: $5,205 - $980 = $4,225 million. But many variations are possible.

The more important part of the question is the connection between free cash flow and future earnings and financial condition. Possible uses of free cash flow include:

1) Repayment of debt resulting in lower interest cost and higher earnings. This also reduces debt ratios and improves interest coverage, possibly leading to higher debt ratings.

2) Repurchase of equity may raise earnings per share and (if repurchased below stated book value or real value per share) increase these.

3) Acquisitions (such as Kraft) that may provide future growth, better diversification, lower risk, etc.

4) Expenditures to fund internal growth through capital spending, research and development, new product costs, etc.

C. If the acquired inventories and receivables are sold the proceeds will be reported as cash flow from operations (CFO). As their acquisition was reported as cash used for investment, CFO will be inflated. This will occur if Kraft reduces its required level of inventories and receivables because of operating changes (such as changes in product lines or credit terms) or the use of financing techniques that remove these assets from the balance sheet.

Case 3-1 - Solution

Estimated time to complete this case is 2 hrs

In Thousand Trails Part I, we questioned whether the growth assumptions made by the company resulted in an overstatement of revenues and understatement of expenses. In Part II we continue the analysis of the company's profitability and liquidity by examining the company's cash flow statement.

Thousand Trails: Defining CFO

The statement of changes shown in Exhibit 3C-1 was prepared prior to the issuance of SFAS 95. A large portion of the cash outflows reported by Thousand Trails related to expenditures for "preserve improvements," the transformation of undeveloped land into land suitable for campgrounds. Do these costs represent investing or operating outflows? Thousand Trails classified them as operating cash flows. A strong argument can be made that preserve improvement costs are investments, given their long-term nature; under a strict reading of SFAS 95, they are not part of operations. They are conceptually similar to the costs incurred in building a hotel or apartment building.

On the other hand, unlike property, plant, and equipment, which produce the product to be sold, the preserves are similar to operating items such as inventory, as it is the preserves themselves (or access to them) that are being sold and thus classification as operations would be appropriate.

Upon further reflection, however, it should be clear that the classification of a given cash flow is irrelevant; what is important is the implication. Analysts can (and should) reclassify cash flows if the resulting data provide better analytic insights. In the case of Thousand Trails, the need to expand and improve campgrounds was a constant cash drain. The relationship between CFO and cash required for preserve improvements (free cash flows) will therefore be our main focus for analysis.

Comparing Income and Cash Flows

We begin by comparing net income and CFO overall.

Net Income and CFO
(millions of $)

	1981	1982	1983
Net Income	$3.33	$7.76	$12.00
Cash used in Operations			
Before Preserve Improvements	(0.60)	4.31	3.78
After Preserve Improvements	(7.44)	(6.97)	(14.68)

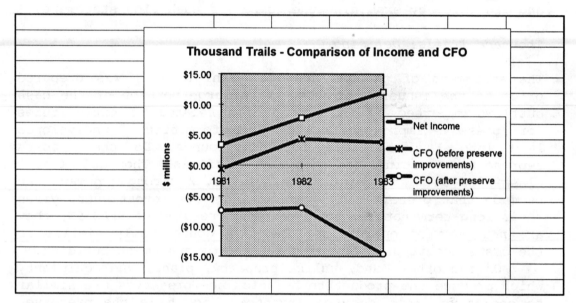

CFO (however measured) lagged reported income. In Thousand Trails Part I, we noted that the lag between CFO and income may be due to the company's revenue and expense recognition methods. The company
1. recognized revenues early, prior to collection of cash or establishing its collectibility; and
2. deferred expense recognition to many years after the outlay of cash, based on forecasts of future sales.

However, CFO did not just lag reported income; it headed in the opposite direction! Income increased fourfold from 1981 to 1983. Cash used in operations before preserve improvements, on the other hand, declined in 1983 even as income increased by 50%. Cash flow after preserve improvements was negative each year 1981-1983 and the deficiency increased by over 100% in 1983. Although one can argue that the deficiency is a result of the nature of the company's business (investing in preserves and preserve improvements up front to grow as it sold memberships); the divergent pattern of income and CFO raises serious questions as to the company's profitability and liquidity.

and preserve improvements up front to grow as it sold memberships); the divergent pattern of income and CFO raises serious questions as to the company's profitability and liquidity.

Analyzing Cash Flow and Income Components

When we examine components of the cash flow statement we see that the cash deficiency increased each year.

Membership Sales: Comparison of Revenue Recognized and Cash Inflows (in $ millions)

	1981	1982	1983
Revenue	$ 40.0	$ 56.5	$ 80.0
Cash inflow*	(27.1)	(35.3)	(46.2)
Difference	$ 12.9	$ 21.2	$ 33.8

*Defined as the sum of cash received from membership sales plus collections on contracts receivable, less interest income. Thus, for 1983, cash inflow = $27.7 + $28.6 - $10.1 = $46.2 million. (We have made the simplifying assumptions that interest income all relates to membership contracts and is received in cash.)

The annual difference between revenues and cash inflows grew from year to year. *Furthermore, even on a lagged basis, the difference grew.* Collections in 1982 ($35.3 million) were less than revenue recognized in 1981 ($40.0 million); similarly, in 1983 ($46.2 million versus $56.5 million). The lag grew on both an absolute ($4.7 million rising to $10.3 million) and percentage (12% rising to 18%) basis.

A similar pattern emerges when we compare preserve improvement expenditures with those recognized as an expense. *In all years, cash outflows exceed expense recognition and the annual gap increased.*

Preserve Improvement Costs: Comparison of Expense Recognized and Cash Outflows (in $ millions)

	1981	1982	1983
Expense	$ 5.8	$ 8.4	$13.0
Cash outflow*	(6.8)	(11.3)	(18.4)
Difference	$(1.0)	$(2.9)	$(5.4)

*Defined as cash expended for preserve improvements

Going Beyond the Cash Flow Statement

Focusing on the cash requirements of Thousand Trails allows us
to expand our analysis. In addition to preserve improvements,
Thousand Trails made additional outlays for the preserves
themselves as it continued to expand. From the balance sheet
(Exhibit 2C-2), we can compute the following increase in the
investment in preserves during 1983:

Operating preserves (land and improvements)* $26.1 million
Preserves under development   4.3
  Total increase $30.4 million

*Before deductions for "costs applicable to membership sales."

Of this $30 million increase, *Thousand Trails only reported
$18.4 million as cash expended for preserve improvements.* The
remaining expenditure did not appear in the cash flow statement
at all. We can infer that the remaining increase represents
preserves acquired for debt (noncash transactions). In
addition, (as noted below) the statement of changes data
suggest a significant decline in debt during 1983, yet the
balance sheet shows a significant increase.[1]

Under SFAS 95, such transactions would not appear in the
cash flow statement either. Rather, they would be given
separate disclosure as "Significant Noncash Financing and
Investment Activities." For analytic purposes, however, these
amounts need to be considered when analyzing the free cash
flows and solvency of a company. It is interesting to note that
Thousand Trails classifies the payments on such debt (see $4.3
million---Principal payments on debt related to preserve
properties) as part of cash from operations.

Our analysis goes a step farther. As we have argued that
the cost of acquiring preserves should be considered an
operating outflow, the debt incurred to acquire preserves
should be included in that outflow. *Thus we would argue that
Thousand Trails' cash flow requirement was significantly
greater than the $14 million outflow actually reported for
1983, perhaps as much as $26 million.*[2]

---

[1] Footnote data (not reproduced in the case) confirm that Thousand Trails
acquired preserves by incurring debt.

[2] As the balance sheet only shows two years of data , we cannot make this
analysis for 1981-1982.

Financing Cash Flows

How did Thousand Trails finance itself? From the Cash Flow statement we find the following borrowings (repayments)

Net Borrowings
($ millions)

	1981	1982	1983
From CFO section:			
Payments on debt related to preserve improvements	$(2.0)	$(3.7)	$(4.3)
From Other Sources section:			
Proceeds of borrowings	9.1	8.6	0.9
Payments	(0.7)	(0.7)	(1.1)
	$ 6.4	$4.2	$(4.5)

In 1981 and 1982, based on the "cash flow" statement, the company borrowed a total of $10.6 million. In 1983, however the statement shows repayments of $4.5 million. Funding, that year, came from a common stock issuance of $17.8 million.

Going beyond the cash flow statement, however, a different picture emerges. For 1983, for example:

Change in
Current portion of long-term debt ($5.9 - $4.4) $1.5
Long term debt   ($47.3 - $43.1)   4.2
                                                     $5.7

From the balance sheet we note that Thousand Trails' debt increased $5.7 million - despite repayments of $4.5 million! The difference bypassed the cash flow statement because, as noted, the company only reported actual cash flows and not debt resulting from acquisition of property[3].

---

[3] One can infer that new debt of ($5.7 + $4.5) $10.2 was incurred for the acquisition of preserves. This approximates the $12 million of preserve improvements ($30.4 - $18.4) not shown in the "cash flow " statement.

Implications of the Analysis

The above analysis as well as Thousand Trails: Part I indicates

1. The *negative CFO indicated potential liquidity and solvency problems* even if one assumed that the growth rate could be maintained, Thousand Trails continually accessed the capital markets. Given its increasing cash needs, there was increased risk that the company would approach its borrowing capacity.

2. *The difference between reported CFO and reported income was a function of Thousand Trails' choice of accounting policies.* Thousand Trails took an "aggressive" position in recognizing revenues (and expenses). Sales were recognized in full, although only a portion was collected. Given the long collection period, there was a built-in lag between present cash outflows and future cash inflows. Expenses, on the other hand, were deferred to periods following the cash outlay. Thus reported income was not a good indicator of near-term cash flows. Income (again assuming that forecast growth could be achieved) might have been a good indicator of long-term cash flows.

3. *The disparity between CFO and income questions the validity of the going concern assumption.* Given the lags and the discussion in Thousand Trails Part I, we can ask whether the assumption of eventual cash collectibility was tenable? There was some doubt as to whether the cash would eventually be collected; thus the CFO acts as a "check" on reported income. Additionally, Thousand Trails' expense recognition methods hinged on these eventual sales. If these sales did not materialize, then the expenditures already made would have to be written off against membership sales made to date. The unallocated expenditures of $43.8 million by themselves would wipe out the firm 's retained earnings of $30.9 million (both at December 31, 1983).

As the analysis indicates, it is important to use all financial data; no single statement provides all the needed information. The relationship between cash flow from operations and net income is one of timing. The income statement reflects the firm's operations but does not provide information about the extent to which the firm's cash and liquidity needs are generated internally. Free cash flow does provide that information.

Chapter 4 Solutions

Overview:

Problem Length	*Problem #s*
{S}	*9*
{M}	*2, 4, 5, 6, 10,*
{L}	*1, 3, 7, 8, 11, 12,*

1.{L} The Walt Disney Company

   (i) Accounts receivable turnover = Revenue/receivables
       = $ 8,529 / $1,390 = 6.14
       This ratio measures the effectiveness of the firm's
       credit policies and the capital required to maintain
       the firm's sales level.

   (ii) Total asset turnover = Sales / total assets
       = $ 8,529 / $ 11,751 = 0.73
       This ratio is designed to evaluate the efficiency of
       long-term capital investment in productive capacity by
       measuring sales generated by investments in total
       assets.

   (iii)Current ratio = Current assets /current liabilities
       = $ 4,251 / $ 2,821 = 1.51
       The current ratio is the broadest measure of current
       and potential resources available to meet obligations.

   (iv) CFO to current liabilities = $ 2,145 / $ 2,821 = 0.76
       Unlike the current ratio, this measure compares actual
       cash flows to current obligations.

   (v) Debt to equity = $ 2,386 / $ 5,030 = 0.47
       A measure of risk compared to the owners' investment in
       the firm. Note that this ratio should include the
       current portion of financial obligations in the
       numerator. An alternative computation is based on the
       sum of operating and financial obligations:
       ($ 2,821 + $2,386) / $ 5,030 = 1.04.

   (vi) The times interest earned ratio = EBIT/interest
       expense = ($ 1,074 + $ 158) / $ 158 = 7.80
       is an indicator of safety for creditors as it measures
       the extent to which earnings are available to meet
       interest charges.

   (vii)Operating income to sales = $ 1,724 / $ 8,529 = 0.20
       This is a measure of the profitability of a firm's
       "core" business.

(viii) Return on sales = Net income / sales
= $ 671 /$ 8,529 = 7.87%
An indicator of overall profitability.

(ix) Return on assets = (Net income + after-tax interest)/
total assets = ($671 + $98.71)/$ 11,751 = 6.55%
This ratio measures the efficiency of the use of assets
in generating operating profits and of the return
accruing to capital used in the operations. It may also
be measured on a pretax basis to exclude the impact of
differences in tax position and financial policy:
EBIT / total assets = $ 1,232 / $ 11,751 = 10.48%

2.{M}A. **Five component disaggregation of ROE:**

				1989	1993
	1. Operating margin	EBIT/Sales	=	25.62%	14.44%
x	2. Interest burden	Pretax income/EBIT	=	0.98X	0.87X
x	3. Tax burden	Net income/Pretax income	=	0.61X	0.62X
x	4. Asset turnover	Sales/Average assets	=	0.69	0.73
x	5. Leverage	Average assets/Average equity	=	2.19X	2.34X
=	Return on equity	Net income/Average equity	=	23.15%	13.30%

B. The primary cause of the decline in ROE is the lower
operating margin. This component has fallen because
operating expenses have risen sharply and the firm has
reported significant losses from Euro Disney. ROE is
also adversely affected by the sharply higher interest
burden due to the increase in borrowings.

*Problems 3 to 6 will take 2 hours and 30 minutes to solve if
assigned together.*

3.{L}   A.   **Activity Ratios:**
(i)   Inventory turnover = COGS/Average inventory
= $8,048 / $1,919 = **4.19X**

(ii) Accounts receivable turnover = Sales/ Average
receivables
= $12,065 / $2,545 = **4.74X**

(iii) Fixed asset turnover = Sales/Average property
= $12,065 / $1,304 = **9.26X**

(iv) Total asset turnover = Sales/Average assets
= $12,065 / $6,425 = **1.88X**

B. **Liquidity Ratios:**

   (i)   Operating cycle = 365 [1/inventory turnover +
         1/receivable turnover]
         = 365 [1/4.19 + 1/4.74] = **164.1 days**

   (ii) Cash cycle:
         Purchases = COGS + Increase in accounts
         payable
         = $8,048 + $448 = $8,496

         Number of days payable = 365 x Average
         payables/purchases
         = 365 x $709/$8,496 = 30.5 days

         Therefore cash cycle = 164.1 − 30.5 =
         133.6 days

   (iii) Current ratio = Current assets/Current
         liabilities
         = $6,360/$3,945 = **1.61X**

   (iv) Quick ratio = (Cash + Receivables)/Current
         liabilities
         = $3,924/$3,945 = **0.99X**

   (v)   Cash ratio = Cash/Current liabilities
         = $325/$3,945 = **0.08X**

   (vi) Cash from operations to current liabilities
         = Cash from operations/Current liabilities
         = $(256)/$3,945 = **(0.06)X**

   (vii) Defensive interval
         = 365 x [Cash + Receivables]/Projected
         expenditures
         = 365 x $3,924/$9,828 = **146 days**

         Where projected expenditures estimated as
         total costs and expenses less depreciation
         = $10,151 − $323 = $9,828

C.   **Solvency Ratios**

(i)   Debt to equity = Debt (nontrade)/Equity
      = $1,170/$3,803 = **0.31**

(ii) Debt to capital = Debt/(debt + equity)
      = $1,170/$4,973 = **0.24**

(iii) Times interest earned = Earnings before
      interest and tax/interest expense
      = $2,337/$78 = **29.96X**

(iv) Capital expenditures ratio = Cash from
      operations/Capital expenditures
      = $(256)/$798 = **(0.32)X**

D.   **Profitability Ratios**

(i)   Gross Margin: = (Sales - COGS)/Sales
      = ($12,065 - $8,048)/$12,065 = **33.3%**

(ii) Operating income to sales = Operating
      income/Sales
      = $2,337/$12,065 = **19.4%**

(iii) Return on sales = Net income / Sales
      = $1,265/$12,065 = **10.5%**

(iv) Return on assets = (Net income + [Interest
      expense (1-tax rate)]) / Average Assets
      = ($1,265 + [$78 (1-.44)])/$6,425 = **20.4%**

      Return on assets (pretax) = Earnings before
      interest and taxes/Average assets
      = $2,337/$6,425 = **36.4%**

(v)   Return on equity = Net income/Average equity
      = $1,265/$3,336 = **37.9%**

4.{M}**Three component disaggregation of ROE:**

	1. Profitability	Net income / Sales	=	10.5%
x	2. Asset turnover	Sales / Average assets	=	1.88X
x	3. Leverage	Average assets/Average equity	=	<u>1.93X</u>
=	Return on equity	Net income / Average equity	=	37.9%

Five component model:

	1. Operating margin	EBIT / Sales	=	19.4%
x	2. Interest burden	Pretax income / EBIT	=	0.97X
x	3. Tax burden	Net income / Pretax income	=	0.56X
x	4. Asset turnover	Sales / Average assets	=	1.88X
x	5. Leverage	Average assets/Average equity	=	<u>1.93X</u>
=	Return on equity =	Net income / Average equity	=	37.9%

5.{M}A.   Although ratio analysis has an implicit proportionality assumption, these relationships are not always proportional. When the scale of operations changes dramatically, relationships between variables that hold at one level of operations may not hold at another level. (The asset turnover ratio described in Figure 4-1 is one example.)

   B.   (i)   Use the average of end of year and end of first quarter assets in denominator, or alternatively, use end of year assets.
   (ii) Use weighted average: .25 x opening assets + .75 closing assets; this matches the numerator that reflects a return on the additional assets for 3/4 of the year.
   (iii) Average of opening and closing assets is weighted average.
   (iv) Use weighted average: .75 x opening assets + .25 closing assets.

6.{M}A. Estimate of 19X5 fixed and variable costs:
 S = Sales
 F = Fixed costs
 V = Variable costs
 v = Variable costs as a percentage of sales
TC = Total costs = F + V = F + vS

$$v = \frac{TC(\text{year } 2) - TC(\text{year } 1)}{S(\text{year } 2) - S(\text{year } 1)}$$

$$= \frac{\$10,151 - \$6,403}{\$12,065 - \$7,570}$$

$$= .8338$$

F = TC - vS
 = $10,151 - (.8338 x $12,065)
 = $91

B. Financial Leverage Effect (FLE) = Operating income/net income
19X4: FLE = $1,450/$800   19X5: FLE = $2,337/$1,265
        = **1.81**   = **1.85**

Operating Leverage Effect (OLE) = Contribution margin/operating income
19X4: OLE = $1,520/$1,450 19X5: OLE = $2,351/$2,337
        = **1.05**   = **1.01**
where contribution margin is pretax income plus fixed costs ($92 for both years).

Total Leverage Effect (TLE) = OLE x FLE = Contribution margin/net income
19X4: TLE = $1,520/$800   19X5: TLE = $2,351/$1,265
        = **1.90**   = **1.86**
        = 1.05 x 1.81   = 1.01 x 1.85

C. The basic formula used to estimate fixed and variable costs assumes that the underlying relationships are constant. Chicago's rapid growth may require a fixed-to-variable cost ratio for 19X5 that may be quite different from that based on 19X4 data.

     As a result, the part A estimate of fixed costs is certainly too low. The primary reason is the high growth rate of Chicago during 19X5. A partial solution would be to deduct known fixed costs like depreciation and interest expense from total costs before applying the formula. However, the lack of information about depreciation eliminates this method. All of the problems discussed in Appendix 4-A, including relevant range and the non-linear relationship between costs and output, apply in this case as well.

The calculation of OLE in part B is not meaningful given the inability to estimate variable and fixed cost components. Chicago's operating leverage is surely greater than the OLE calculated. The total leverage effect (TLE) is also understated in the part B computation.

7.{L}

Description	Ratio	Method of Calculation
1. Inventory turnover	3.71X	Asset turnover x (COGS/sales) x (assets/inventory)
2. Receivable turnover	5.65X	Asset turnover x (assets/ receivables)
3. Days of inventory Days of receivables Operating cycle	98 days 65 163 days	365/inventory turnover 365/receivable turnover Total
4. Days of payables Cash cycle	(72) days 91 days	365/payables turnover (calculated as 5.06X using COGS instead of purchases) Operating cycle less days of payables
5. Fixed asset turnover	2.67X	Asset turnover divided by (PPE/ assets)
6. Cash ratio	0.08X	Cash/current liabilities
7. Quick ratio	0.79X	(Cash + receivables)/Current liabilities
8. Current ratio	1.67X	Current assets/Current liabilities
9. Debt-to-equity	0.60	(Debt payable + long-term debt)/ equity
10. Interest coverage	11.0X	Operating income/interest expense
11. EBIT/sales	11.0%	Given directly
12. Sales/assets	0.96	(Asset turnover) Given directly
13. EBIT/assets	10.6%	(EBIT/sales) x (sales/assets)
14. EBT/assets	9.6%	(EBT/sales) x asset turnover
15. Assets/equity	2.50X	Inverse of equity/assets (given)
16. EBT/equity	24.0%	(EBT/assets) x (assets/equity)

8.{L}A.

Company	Industry
1	Chemicals and drugs (Monsanto)
2	Aerospace (Boeing)
3	Computer software (Altos Computer)
4	Department stores (J.C. Penney)
5	Consumer foods (Quaker Oats)
6	Electric utility (SCEcorp)
7	Newspaper publishing (Knight Ridder)
8	Consumer finance (Household Finance)
9	Airline (AMR Corp.)

B. The airline, consumer finance, and electric utility industries are service industries. They are characterized by the absence of cost of goods sold and inventories. Companies 6, 8, and 9 have the lowest ratios (COGS/sales and inventories/total assets). Newspaper publishing may also be considered a service industry; we will return to this later.

Company 8 is the consumer finance company. It has a high level of debt balanced by a high level of receivables and investments (loans and securities). Much of its debt is short-term, reflecting the short maturities of its loans. It has almost no fixed assets. The ratio of interest expense to revenues is the highest for this company.

Both the electric utility and airline firms would have high fixed assets; utilities generally have higher assets (lower asset turnover), are more profitable, and have higher debt and interest expense. Airlines, on the other hand, have high current liabilities for trade payables (payments to suppliers) and for advance ticket sales (other current liabilities). We conclude that company 6 is the electric utility and company 9 is the airline.

Companies 1, 2, and 3 have high R&D expense, consistent with the aerospace, chemicals and drugs, and computer software industries. Aerospace would have the highest inventory (low inventory turnover). Customer prepayments under long term contracts result in lower receivables and large customer advances (other current liabilities). Therefore, company 2 is the aerospace firm.

Distinguishing company 1 from company 3 is difficult. Computer software and drugs are both characterized by high R & D. The inclusion of chemicals, however, should lower the intensiveness of R&D, suggesting that company 3 is the computer software firm. Computer software, lacking manufacturing, is less capital intensive than chemicals and drugs and the latter is generally more profitable. Further, the chemical industry (being older) should have "older" plant (greater proportion depreciated). Company 1 is, therefore, the chemical and drugs firm and company 3 is in the computer software industry.

Companies 4, 5, and 7 remain. Company 4 has high inventories and COGS, the highest receivables relative to assets, and high asset turnover, all of which suggest a retailer. It has no R&D, high advertising expense, and low pretax profit margins. Company 4 is the department store firm.

Company 5 has high net property relative to assets, and the highest ratio of advertising to revenues. Company 5 must be the consumer foods company.

Company 7 is the newspaper publisher. It has very low inventory but high cost of goods sold; inventory is primarily newsprint while cost of goods sold includes the high cost of reporting and production. Company 7 has the highest intangibles (newspapers purchased) and very high pretax profit margins (most newspapers have only indirect competition).

This exercise was intended to show that industries have balance sheet and income statement characteristics that set them apart from others. These characteristics are often used to compare firms within an industry (e.g. advertising as a percentage of sales for consumer goods firms). Summarized data should be used with caution, however. Different firms (even in the same industry) classify identical items differently. Thus the analyst should examine original financial statements to achieve better comparability. Differences among firms may be due to operational or classification differences. When management is available to answer questions, these differences are often useful starting points for obtaining a better understanding of the firm.

9.{S)Common size statements are the first step in developing insights into the economic characteristics of different industries and of different firms in the same industry. They are also used to standardize components of financial statements by expressing them as a percentage of a relevant base, e.g. total assets for the balance sheet or cash flow from operations for the cash flow statement.

10.(M)A.

	19X1	19X2	19X3
Current ratio	2.00X	2.00X	2.00X
Quick ratio	1.20	1.10	1.00
Cash ratio	.40	.30	.25

B.   Common size statements would show that cash as a percentage of (current) assets is declining; accounts receivable and inventory are growing. Similarly, current liabilities would show the proportion of (bank) borrowing growing relative to credit granted by suppliers.

C.   Although the current ratio has remained constant over the 19X1-19X2 period, its components have not. The quick and cash ratios have deteriorated. The firm's liquidity position has weakened over the period as its current assets are less liquid (more inventory and receivables, less cash). At the same time its debt financing relative to trade credit has grown.

D.   The CFO to current liabilities and turnover ratios would be used to measure the length of the operating and cash cycle. We would expect slower turnover and therefore longer operating and cash cycles. Similarly, CFO and the CFO to current liabilities ratio would be expected to decline.

11.(L)A. **Identification of common-size statements**: Company C is highly automated with higher gross plant assets ($175,000 versus $65,000). Therefore it would tend to have higher fixed operating costs. As sales drop, COGS as a percentage of sales should increase more than for a firm with lower fixed costs. As Company C is more capital intensive it would be expected to have higher debt and (as a percentage of sales) interest costs. *Thus, the second set of common size statements is for Company C. The first set belongs to Company L.*
Identification of ratios:

As Company C operates in a JIT inventory environment and has prompt payments and collections, it should have the higher turnover ratios:

Turnover	Company L	Company C
Inventory	6.667	16.667
Receivables	7.409	11.111
Payables	4.444	25.000

Similarly Company C would be expected to have more long-term debt as it is more capital intensive. Therefore the debt to capital ratio of .429 (.195) applies to Company C (Company L).

B. **Creation of income statement, Company C, 19X2:**

Since CFO/current liabilities = 5.275 and CFO = $52,750, then current liabilities = $10,000
Since the current ratio (current assets/current liabilities) = 9.475 and current liabilities = $10,000, then current assets = $94,750
Similarly the quick ratio [(cash + receivables)/current liabilities] = 8.875 yields cash + receivables = $88,750 and therefore:
Inventory (19X2) = (current assets less quick assets)

= ($94,750 - $88,750) = $6,000
As there was no inventory change in 19X2, inventory(19X1) = $6,000

As average inventory = $6,000 and 19X2 inventory turnover was 16.667, then
COGS(19X2) = 16.667 x $6,000 = $100,000
Using COGS and the common size statement for Company C, we can now reconstruct the income statement for 19X2:

Sales	100.00%	$150,000
COGS	66.67%	$ 100,000
SG&A	20.00%	30,000
Interest	4.67%	7,000
Taxes	2.17%	3,250
Total Expense	93.50%	$ 140,250
Net Income	6.50%	$ 9,750

Creation of income statement, Company C, 19X1:

Since sales dropped by 1/6 from 19X1 to 19X2, and sales in 19X2 were $150,000; sales in 19X1 were $180,000. This amount and the common size income statement for 19X1 can be used to prepare the income statement for 19X1:

Sales	100.00%	$180,000
COGS	58.33%	$ 105,000
SG&A	17.78%	32,000
Interest	3.89%	7,000
Taxes	5.00%	9,000
Total Expense	85.00%	$ 153,000
Net Income	15.00%	$ 27,000

Creation of income statement, Company L, 19X2:

This follows the methodology used for Company C.

Since CFO/current liabilities = .807 and CFO = $28,250, then current liabilities = $30,000
Since current ratio = 3.592, and current liabilities = $30,000, then current assets = $107,750
Similarly the quick ratio of 3.192 yields quick assets of $95,750 (3.192 x $30,000) and therefore inventory(19X2) of $12,000 ($107,750 - $95,750).

As the 19X2 change in inventory was (6,000), inventory(19X1) was $18,000.

As average inventory = $15,000 and inventory turnover = 6.667, then
COGS (19X2) = 6.667 x $15,000 = $100,000

We can now reconstruct the income statement for 19X2:

Sales	100.00%	$ 150,000
COGS	66.67%	$ 100,000
SG&A	20.00%	30,000
Interest	2.00%	3,000
Taxes	2.83%	4,250
Total Expense	91.50%	$ 137,250
Net Income	8.50%	$ 12,750

Creation of income statement, Company L, 19X1:

Since sales dropped by 1/6, sales in 19X1 were $180,000. The income statement for 19X1 is:

Sales	100.00%	$ 180,000
COGS	63.89%	$ 115,000
SG&A	19.44%	35,000
Interest	1.67%	3,000
Taxes	3.75%	6,750
Total Expense	88.75%	$ 159,750
Net Income	11.25%	$ 20,250

C. Interest costs (Company C = $7,000; Company L = $3,000) are fixed for both companies. The breakdowns for COGS and SG&A follow:

Company C: 19X2 sales decreased by $30,000, COGS decreased by $5,000, and SG&A decreased by $2,000. Therefore, variable costs as a percentage of sales are:
COGS = $5,000/$30,000   =   16.67%
SG&A = $2,000/$30,000   =   6.67
    Total   23.34%

Therefore,(using 19X1 income statement), fixed costs equal
COGS = $105,000 - (.1667 x $180,000)   = $75,000
SG&A = $ 32,000 - (.0667 x $180,000)   =   20,000
    Total $95,000

Company L: 19X2 sales decreased by $30,000, COGS decreased by $15,000, and SG&A decreased by $5,000. Therefore, variable costs as a percentage of sales are:

$$COGS = \$15,000/\$30,000 = 50.00\%$$
$$SG\&A = \$\ 5,000/\$30,000 = \underline{16.67}$$
$$Total \qquad\qquad\qquad\qquad \overline{66.67\%}$$

Therefore, (using 19X1 income statement), fixed costs equal

$$COGS = \$115,000 - (.5000 \times \$180,000) = \$25,000$$
$$SG\&A = \$\ 35,000 - (.1667 \times \$180,000) = \underline{\ \ 5,000}$$
$$Total \qquad\qquad\qquad\qquad\qquad\qquad\qquad \overline{\$30,000}$$

Taxes are a constant 25% of pretax income.

D. The 19X3 sales forecast is .8 x 19X2 sales = .8 x $150,000 = $120,000 for both companies. Projected income statements for 19X3 follow:

E.

	Company C	Company L
Sales	$ 120,000	$ 120,000
COGS[1]	95,000	85,000
SG&A[2]	28,000	25,000
Interest	7,000	3,000
Total expenses	$ 130,000	$ 113,000
Pretax income	(10,000)	7,000
Taxes (25%)	2,500	(1,750)
Net income	$ (7,500)	$ 5,250

[1] Company C: $75,000 + (.1667 x $120,000) = $95,000
  Company L: $25,000 + (.5000 x $120,000) = $85,000
[2] Company C: $20,000 + (.0667 x $120,000) = $28,000
  Company L: $ 5,000 + (.1667 x $120,000) = $25,000

E. With higher fixed operating costs and interest costs, Company C has higher operating as well as financial leverage. The effects can be demonstrated by reference to the following schedule that uses 19X2 as its reference point:

	19X1	19X2	19X3
Sales (both) % change from 19X2	$180,000 20%	$150,000 ---	$120,000 (20%)
Net income: Company C % change from 19X2	$ 27,000 177%	$ 9,750 ---	$ (7,500) (177%)
Net income: Company L % change from 19X2	$ 20,250 59%	$ 12,750 ---	$ 5,250 (59%)

With higher sales in 19X1, the leverage effect works in Company C's favor and its income is higher. However, when sales decline in 19X2 and 19X3, Company L's income is higher as it does not bear the burden of high fixed costs.

Using 19X2 as the base period, (since percentage changes in sales are symmetric to that year) we find that Company C's total leverage effect is 8.85 as a 20% change (higher or lower) in sales results in a 177% change in net income.

% Change in income = TLE x % change in sales
177% = 8.85 x 20%

Company C's TLE is three times as large as Company L's whose TLE (with a 19X2 base) is only 2.95:

% Change in income = TLE x % change in sales
59% = 2.95 x 20%

NOTE: The components of the TLE, the Operating Leverage Effect (OLE) and Financial Leverage Effect (FLE), can be calculated by converting the 19X2 income statements into the following format (on a pretax basis):

	Company C	Company L
Sales	$150,000	$150,000
Variable COGS & SG&A	(23.33%) (35,000)	(66.67%) (100,000)
Contribution	$115,000	$ 50,000
Fixed costs	(95,000)	(30,000)
Operating income	$ 20,000	$ 20,000
Interest	(3,000)	(3,000)
Pretax income	$ 13,000	$ 17,000

As the following breakdown indicates, the OLE is the major contributor to the TLE for both companies and is the primary difference between the two companies as well. The difference in OLE is then further magnified by the difference in FLE:

	Co. C	Co. L
OLE = Contribution/operating income	5.75	2.50
FLE = Operating income/pretax income	1.54	1.18
TLE = OLE x FLE = Contribution/pretax income	8.85	2.95

The calculations can also be done on a posttax basis but that would require "tax effecting" the contribution margin and operating income as well as net income. For example, for Company C, the contribution margin is $86,250 (.75 x $115,000), operating income is $15,000 (.75 x $20,000) and net income is $9,750 (.75 x $13,000).

12. (L) A. **Balance Sheet - Company C:**

	19X1	19X2
Cash	$ 25,000	$ 76,750
Receivables	15,000	12,000
Inventory	6,000	6,000
Property	175,000	175,000
(Depreciation)	(80,000)	(120,000)
Totals	$141,000	$149,750
Payables	$ 4,000	$ 4,000
S.T.Debt	7,000	6,000
L.T.Debt	60,000	60,000
Equity	70,000	79,750
Totals	$141,000	$149,750

These amounts can be calculated from the data provided as follows:

Property, Plant and Equipment:
Given at $175,000 for 19X2. Since cash for investing is zero, the same level applies to 19X1.

Accounts Receivable:
For 19X2, A/R turnover of 11.1111 and sales of $150,000 imply average receivables of $13,500. Since receivables decreased by $3,000 in 19X2, they must have been $15,000 in 19X1 and $12,000 in 19X2.

Inventory:
From the answer to problem 11-B, Inventory (19X2) = Inventory (19X1) = $6,000

Cash:
Since current assets = $94,750, and cash = current assets less receivables and inventory, then cash (19X2) = $94,750 - $12,000 - $6,000 = $76,750.
        Since the 19X2 change in cash = CFO + cash from financing + cash from investment = $52,750 - $1,000 + $0 = $51,750, then cash (19X1) = $76,750 - $51,750 = $25,000

Accounts Payable:
With no change in inventory and COGS = $100,000, 19X2 purchases must be $100,000.
        19X2 accounts payable turnover of 25 and purchases of $100,000 imply an average accounts payable of $4,000. Since there was no 19X2 change in payables,

then A/P (19X1) = A/P (19X2) = $4,000

Short-term debt (S.T.Debt):

Short term debt = Current liabilities - accounts payable

For 19X2, current liabilities of $10,000 imply short term debt of $10,000 - $4,000 = $6,000. Given a decrease of $1000 in 19X2, S.T.Debt (19X1) = $7,000.

Equity:

ROE = 0.13 and net income of $9750 imply average equity = $75,000

Since only change in equity is net income of $9,750, equity (19X1) = $70,000, and equity (19X2) = $79,750.

Long-term Debt (L.T.Debt):

With L.T.Debt/capital of 0.429 and equity of $79,750, L.T.Debt = $60,000.

Accumulated Depreciation:

Total liabilities + equity = $141,000 and $149,750 for 19X1 and 19X2 respectively.

Total assets must be same, yielding accumulated depreciation of $80,000 and $120,000 for those years. The 19X2 increase must be depreciation expense for that year (as no property was sold or retired) of $40,000.

Alternate Method of Calculation:

CFO = income + noncash items + changes in operating assets

$52,750 = $9,750 + noncash items + $3,000

Therefore, noncash items (depreciation expense in this case) = $40,000

Balance Sheet - Company L:

	19X1	19X2
Cash	$ 54,500	$ 77,750
Receivables	22,500	18,000
Inventory	18,000	12,000
Property	65,000	65,000
(Depreciation)	(30,000)	(40,000)
Totals	$130,000	$132,750
Payables	$ 23,650	$ 18,650
S.T.Debt	16,350	11,350
L.T.Debt	20,000	20,000
Equity	70,000	82,750
Totals	$130,000	$132,750

The methodology is the same as for Company C:

Property, Plant and Equipment:
Given at $65,000 for 19X2. Since cash for investing is zero, the same level applies to 19X1.

Accounts Receivable:
For 19X2, A/R turnover of 7.409 and sales of $150,000 imply average A/R = $20,250.
Since A/R decreased by $4,500, A/R (19X1) = $22,500 and A/R (19X2) = $18,000

Inventory:
From 11-B, inventory (19X2) = $12,000 and inventory (19X1) = $18,000

Cash:
Since current assets = $107,750, cash (19X2) = $107,750 - $12,000 - $18,000 = $77,750

19X2 change in cash
= CFO + cash from financing + cash from investment
= $28,250 - $3,000 + $0
= $23,250

and cash (19X1) = $77,750 - $23,250 = $54,500

Accounts Payable:
With inventory change of $(6,000) and COGS of $100,000; purchases = $94,000

For 19X2, accounts payable turnover of 4.444 and purchases of $94,000 imply an average A/P of $21,150. Since the change in A/P was (5,000), A/P (19X1) = $23,650 and A/P (19X2) = $18,650

Short-term Debt:
Short-term debt = Current liabilities - accounts payable = $30,000 - $18,650 = $11,350

Since S.T.Debt decreased by $5,000 in 19X2, S.T.Debt (19X1) = $16,350

Equity:
ROE = 0.167 and net income = $12,750, therefore average equity = $76,350.

Since only change in equity is net income of $12,750, equity (19X1) = $70,000, and equity (19X2) = $82,750.

Long-term Debt (L.T.Debt):
L.T.Debt/capital = 0.195 and equity = $82,750; L.T.Debt = $20,000.

Accumulated Depreciation:
Total liabilities + equity = $130,000 and $132,750 for 19X1 and 19X2 respectively.

Total assets must be same, yielding accumulated depreciation of $30,000 and $40,000. Change is depreciation expense of $10,000:

Alternate Method of Calculation:
CFO = income + noncash items + changes in operating assets
28,250 = $12,750 + noncash items + $5,500
Therefore noncash depreciation expense = $10,000

B. **19X3 Forecast Balance Sheet - Company C:**

Cash	$111,650	Accounts payable	$ 4,000
Acct. receivable	9,600	Short-term debt	6,000
Inventory	6,000	Long-term debt	60,000
Property, plant	175,000		
(Depreciation)	(160,000)	Equity	72,250
Total assets	$142,250	Total equities	$142,250

Explanation: Given the JIT environment, and the patterns for 19X1 and 19X2, we assume that inventory and payables stay at the same level even with the decline in sales. These levels are presumably "minimum" working levels. To maintain the receivable turnover ratio of 11.111, accounts receivable (19X3) = $9,600. Assuming no new investments or debt repayment implies a change in cash solely due to cash flow from operations. In 11-D, 19X3 net income was projected at $(7,500).

19X3 CFO = Net income + depreciation + Δ in operating accounts = $(7,500) + $40,000 + $2,400 = $34,900
Therefore, cash (19X3) = $76,750 + $34,900 = $111,650.

19X3 Forecast Balance Sheet - Company L:

Cash	$ 96,700	Accounts payable	$ 20,250
Accounts receivable	14,400	Short-term debt	11,350
Inventory	13,500	Long-term debt	20,000
Property, plant	65,000		
(Depreciation)	50,000	Equity	88,000
Total assets	$139,600	Total equities	$139,600

Explanation: For Company L, we assume that all turnover ratios are maintained.

A/R turnover of 7.409 with sales of $120,000 implies average inventory of $16,200. From part A, we have A/R (19X2) = $18,000. Thus A/R (19X3) equals $14,400.

Inventory turnover of 6.667 with COGS of $85,000 (see 11-D) implies average inventory of $12,750. Given inventory (19X2) of $12,000, inventory (19X3) = $13,500.

Purchases = COGS + increase in inventory = $85,000 + $1,500 = $86,500.

With accounts payable turnover of 4.444, average payables = $19,450. Since 19X2 payables are $18,650, A/P for 19X3 = $20,250.

Assuming no new investment or debt repayment implies a change in cash solely due to cash from operations. In 11-D, 19X3 net income was projected at $5,250.

CFO = Net income + depreciation + change in operating accounts = $5,250 + $10,000 + [$3,600 + $(1,500) + $1,600] = $18,950

Cash (19X3) = $77,750 + $18,950 = $96,700

C. Although both companies have positive CFO and "seem" to be cash rich, the picture is not as rosy as it appears. CFO does not make allowance for the replacement of productive capacity. The fixed assets of both companies are almost fully depreciated and may have to be replaced soon. Also any improvement in sales will require additional working capital, especially for Company L. Thus, cash is not really "excess" as it may be needed for working capital and future capital expenditures to maintain present productive capacity.

13.{M}A. Since there is no debt, ROA and ROE are identical at 10%.

B. ROE = ROA + D/E [ROA - cost of debt] where cost of debt is measured on an after-tax basis. This formula is used to prepare the following table showing the expected ROE at each level of debt:

	{A} Debt/ Equity	{B} Pretax Interest	{C}= .80 x {B} Aftertax Interest	{D} = 10% + [{A}(10%-{C})] ROE
(1)	0.25X	6.0%	4.8%	11.3%
(2)	0.50	8.0	6.4	11.8
(3)	1.00	10.0	8.0	12.0
(4)	1.50	12.0	9.6	10.6
(5)	2.00	15.0	12.0	6.0

C. Detailed calculations for cases (1) and (5):

Case Number	(1)	(5)
Debt Equity	$200,000 800,000	$666,667 333,333
Income before interest and taxes Interest expense Income before tax Tax expense Net income	$125,000 (12,000) $113,000 (22,600) $ 90,400	$125,000 (100,000) $ 25,000 (5,000) $ 20,000
ROE	$ 90,400 = 11.3% $800,000	$ 20,000 = 6.0% $333,333

D. Leverage works up to a point. As a firm takes on more debt the interest rate tends to rise (riskiness of debt increases). When the interest rate exceeds the firm's ROA then the benefits of leverage are lost. This trend is accelerated when ROA declines with increasing amounts of investment as more attractive (higher ROA) investments are made first.

In theory, the firm should borrow as long as the expected ROA exceeds the cost of debt. In practice, firms place their "hurdle rate" for new investments above the cost of capital to allow for risk. Many investments fail to achieve their expected ROA. When the realized ROA falls short of the cost of debt, the investment reduces ROE.

14.{L} In this problem the debt/equity ratios and cost of debt have to be adjusted to include all the debt (even that which is non-interest bearing).

A. The D/E ratio without any *bank* borrowing is
$200,000/$800,000 = .25
Therefore ROE = 10% + .25[10% - 0] = 12.5%

B. Calculations for the table that follows can be illustrated using case (1) with a D/E ratio of 25% and interest rate of 6%.

Total assets are $1,000,000 and trade payables equal $200,000. That leaves $800,000 to be divided between bank debt and equity. A D/E ratio of 25% implies bank debt of $160,000 and equity of $640,000.
    The actual D/E ratio (including trade payables) is therefore: $360,000/$640,000 = 0.56.
    Interest (on bank debt only) at 6% = $9,600. The interest rate on total debt of $360,000 (bank debt + trade payables) can be computed as:
    $9,600/$360,000 = 2.67%

Therefore, ROE = ROA + D/E [ROA - (1-tax rate)cost of debt] = 10% + .56 [10% - .8 x 2.67%] = 14.4%

Data for all five cases follows:

	Stated D/E Ratio	Stated Interest Rate	Bank Loan Amount	Actual D/E Ratio	Actual Interest Rate	ROE
(1)	0.25	6.0%	160,000	0.56	2.67%	14.4%
(2)	0.50	8.0	266,667	0.88	4.57	15.6
(3)	1.00	10.0	400,000	1.50	6.67	17.0
(4)	1.50	12.0	480,000	2.13	8.47	16.9
(5)	2.00	15.0	533,333	2.75	10.91	13.5

C.

Case Number	(1)	(5)
Debt	$160,000	$533,333
Equity	640,000	266,667
Income before interest and taxes	$125,000	$125,000
Interest expense	(9,600)	(80,000)
Income before tax	$115,400	$ 45,000
Tax expense	(23,080)	(9,000)
Net income	$ 92,320	$ 36,000
ROE	$ 92,320 / $640,000 = 14.4%	$ 36,000 / $266,667 = 13.5%

D. Trade debt appears to be interest free credit (in fact the cost of credit is often included in the price of the goods sold). The result of such debt is a higher return on equity as the same return is earned on a smaller investment. While the numbers change from problem 13, the conclusion is the same. Leverage enhances returns only when the cost of credit is less than the return on assets. As in problem 13, the highest ROE is earned at a debt/equity ratio of 1.

15.{M} A.and B: The following liquidity, solvency, and
                 profitability ratios can be used to support the
                 conclusions reached in Problem 6 of Chapter 3:

	19X1	19X2	19X3	19X4	19X5
M COMPANY					
Turnover Ratios:					
Inventory	3.60	3.43	3.27	3.17	2.96
Receivables	3.34	3.22	3.09	3.24	3.25
Payables	7.87	7.47	7.76	10.85	12.79
Number of days:					
Inventory	101.29	106.51	111.54	115.02	123.33
Receivables	109.20	113.25	118.00	112.70	112.00
Payables	(46.40)	(48.90)	(47.00)	(33.60)	(28.50)
Cash cycle	164.09	170.86	182.54	194.12	206.83
Current ratio	1.71	1.57	1.75	1.55	1.60
Quick ratio	1.09	0.99	1.11	0.91	0.93
Debt-to-equity	0.78	0.97	1.17	1.60	2.14
Interest coverage	6.33	4.84	4.94	4.00	1.35
Return on equity	0.14	0.13	0.11	0.11	0.03
G COMPANY					
Turnover ratios:					
Inventory	3.43	3.84	3.87	3.84	4.73
Receivables	5.38	6.07	6.11	6.07	6.10
Payables	10.19	10.61	10.52	10.34	12.47
Number of days:					
Inventory	106	95	94	95	77
Receivables	68	60	60	60	60
Payables	(36)	(34)	(35)	(35)	(29)
Cash cycle	138	121	119	120	108
Current ratio	2.23	2.13	1.95	2.29	2.30
Quick ratio	1.07	1.01	0.92	1.08	1.05
Debt-to-equity	0.38	0.49	0.63	0.71	0.74
Interest coverage	4.27	5.77	4.70	4.62	4.27
Return on equity	0.05	0.09	0.11	0.12	0.12

C. The deterioration in M company's liquidity and financial position can be seen from the cash cycle, which increased to 207 days in 19X5 from 164 days in 19X1. Also see the decline in the current and the quick ratios. M company's debt-to-equity ratio has more than doubled from 0.78 to 2.14, accompanied by a decline in interest coverage from 6.33x to 1.35x. That decline resulted from both the increasing leverage and the decreasing ROE (from .14 in 19X1 to .03 in 19X5).

G company's cash cycle has declined (improved) and its liquidity ratios remained steady. The problem here is the higher leverage and low interest coverage (albeit, a steady 4.27 with modest change during the five years shown). Profitability (ROE) increased from .05 to .12. The substantial growth has been managed well so far but it remains to be seen whether the firm can manage future growth as well.

16.{L}Sales growth: revenues grew at a 25% compound annual rate from $287 million in 1985 to $865 million in 1990. However, a substantial portion of this increase came in 1987 (from $295 million to $685 million). Sales grew at a less than 9% compound annual rate from 1987 to 1990. Gross margin was stable and averaged 26% over the 1985-1990 period. The explosive growth in net income came in part from cost controls (e.g. S,G&A as a percentage of sales was 20% in 1985 and 17% in 1990). Interest expense declined considerably (1988-1990) after three years of high debt levels. These trends can be seen from the disaggregation of ROE that follows.

The ratios used in the following analysis are based on income before extraordinary items and discontinued operations. 1985 ratios use year-end balances; average balances are used for all other years. *Note: ATA = average total assets.*

Year	Net income / Sales	x	Sales / ATA	=	Net income / ATA	x	ATA / Ave. equity	=	ROE
1985	0.92%	x	2.52X	=	2.31%	x	24.69X	=	57.14%
1986	1.46	x	1.34	=	1.95	x	14.34	=	28.01
1987	2.58	x	1.94	=	4.99	x	7.95	=	39.68
1988	3.59	x	1.94	=	6.95	x	4.24	=	29.43
1989	4.12	x	2.03	=	8.36	x	2.81	=	23.47
1990	4.43	x	2.20	=	9.74	x	2.22	=	21.58

The interesting result shown by the disaggregation is that ROE declined sharply at the same time that profit margins (net income/sales) were rising. The steady decline in equity turnover explains this apparent contradiction. Equity grew from a nominal amount in 1985 (4% of assets) to nearly half of total assets by the end of 1990. Not only did Harley pay nominal if any dividends to stockholders but the firm sold equity as well. (Net income was about $120 million over the 1986-1990 period while equity increased by $194 million.)

Harley is a classic case of deleveraging. Total debt (current + long-term) declined by $138 million, from about $210 million at the end of 1986 to barely $72 million four years later. Thus more than 70% ($138/$194) of the equity increase over the 1986-1990 period was used for debt reduction rather than for investment purposes.

Harley's return on assets did multiply fourfold over the 1985-1990. The firm's 21.58% return on equity in 1990, while very respectable, is far below what it would have been if Harley had remained highly leveraged.

17.{L}A.   Basic Earnings per share for 1992
= Earnings available to common shareholders/ Weighted average number of common shares outstanding
= Net income - preferred dividends
= $ 6,500,000 - $ 140,000 = $ 6,360,000 / 2,500,000
= $ 2.54 per share

B.   The convertible bonds are common equivalents because their effective yield, 5%, was less than two-thirds of the Aa bond rate, 8.5%, at the time of issuance.

The convertible preferred shares are not common equivalents as their effective yield was greater than two-thirds of the Aa bond yield (5.5% versus 2/3 of 7.5%) at the issue date.

The options must be included in the computation of primary earnings per share because they are dilutive (the average market price exceeds the exercise price). The number of shares outstanding (primary) equal:

Average # of shares actually outstanding	2,500,000
Shares issuable upon bond conversion[*]	400,000
Effect of options	50,000
Total common and common equivalent shares	2,950,000

[*] $12,000,000/$30

Treasury stock method: Proceeds on exercise of 200,000 options @ $15 = $3,000,000. At the average price of $20, can repurchase 150,000 shares ($3,000,000/$20). Thus the incremental number of shares is the difference (200,000 less 150,000).

C. Net income $ 6,500,000
   Less: preferred dividends
     (70,000 x $4.00 x 1/2)   (140,000)
   Plus: interest on bonds assumed converted*   360,000
   Net income after adjustment $ 6,720,000
   * $12 million x 5% x .6 (tax adjustment)

Earnings per common and common equivalent share are:
$6,720,000/2,950,000 = $2.28

D. For the fully diluted calculation, the convertible preferred shares are assumed to be converted (for the one-half year outstanding). In addition, the treasury stock calculation is based on the year-end price when it exceeds the average price. The number of shares outstanding (fully diluted) is therefore:

Average # of shares actually outstanding 2,500,000
Shares issuable upon bond conversion*   400,000
Shares issuable upon preferred conversion# 175,000
Effect of options   80,000
Total common and common equivalent shares 3,155,000
* $12,000,000/$30
# 70,000 x 5 x 1/2

Treasury stock method:
Proceeds on exercise of 200,000 options @ $15 = $3,000,000. At year-end price of $25, can repurchase 120,000 shares ($3,000,000/$25). Thus the net number of shares is the difference (200,000 less 120,000).

Basic EPS is based on the weighted average number of shares outstanding at year-end with no adjustments for dilution. *Primary* EPS incorporates some dilution stemming from convertible bonds and options; *Fully diluted EPS* reflects maximum possible dilution. It includes the expected dilutive effect of convertible preferred.

Differences among number of shares used for Basic, Primary, and Fully diluted EPS

For Basic EPS: Weighted average number of shares
actually outstanding   **2,500,000**
Add:Shares issuable upon bond conversion[*]   400,000
Effect of options   50,000
Equals:Shares used to compute *Primary EPS* 2,950,000
Add: Shares issuable upon
     preferred stock conversion[#]   175,000
Incremental effect of options   30,000
Equals: Shares used for fully diluted EPS **3,155,000**
[*] $12,000,000/$30
[#] 70,000 x 5 x 1/2

E.   Net income $ 6,500,000
Plus: interest on bonds assumed converted[*]   360,000
Net income after adjustment $ 6,860,000
[*] $12 million x 5% x .6 (tax adjustment)

Fully diluted earnings per share equal:
    $6,860,000/3,155,000 = $2.17

Differences between earnings used for Basic, Primary, and Fully diluted EPS

Net income $ 6,500,000
Less: preferred dividends
    (70,000 x $4.00 x 1/2)   140,000)
Equals: Earnings for Basic EPS $ 6,360,000
Plus: interest on bonds assumed converted[*]   360,000
Equals: Earnings for Primary EPS $ 6,720,000
Less: preferred dividends   140,000
Equals: Earnings for Fully Diluted EPS $ 6,860,000
[*]$12 million x 5% x .6 (tax adjustment)

F.   (i)   Only the fully diluted calculation would change. At a closing price of $30, only 100,000 shares could be repurchased, resulting in 100,000 net shares outstanding, an increase of 20,000.

    (ii)   There would be no effect. The two-thirds rule is applied only at issuance and the classification is not affected by later events.

G.   (i)   Pooling transactions result in the addition of
          (a) earnings of acquired or merged firm to that
          of the buyer or surviving firm and (b) all
          shares issued are assumed to be outstanding for
          the entire period. If the acquisition had not
          been made, the basic and primary earnings per
          share would be:

Basic EPS = net income	$ 6,500,000
Less: addition due to pooling	(600,000)
Adjusted basic EPS net income	$ 5,900,000

Basic EPS: common shares	2,500,000
Less: addition due to pooling	(240,000)
Adjusted basic shares	2,260,000

Adjusted basic EPS is $5,900,000/2,260,000 = $2.61

Primary EPS:

net income after adjustment	$ 6,720,000
Less: addition due to pooling	(600,000)
Adjusted primary EPS net income	$ 6,120,000

Primary EPS: total common and common equivalent shares	2,950,000
Less: addition due to pooling	(240,000)
Adjusted primary EPS shares	2,710,000

Adjusted primary EPS = $6,120,000/2,710,000 = $2.26

(ii) Assuming a purchase method acquisition, the
      issued shares are considered outstanding for,
      and the earnings of the acquired firm are
      included only for the period following the
      acquisition. Since the acquisition was made on
      March 31, 1992, only 3/4ths of the income or
      $450,000 can be included and the additional
      equivalent shares are 180,000 (.75 x 240,000).

Basic EPS net income (part i)	$ 5,900,000
Plus: purchase method adjustment	450,000
Readjusted basic EPS net income	$ 6,350,000

Adjusted basic EPS shares (part i)	2,260,000
Plus: purchase method adjustment	180,000
Readjusted basic EPS shares	2,440,000

Readjusted basic EPS = $6,350,000/2,440,000 = $2.61

Adjusted primary EPS net income	$ 6,120,000
Plus: purchase method adjustment	450,000
Readjusted primary EPS net income	$ 6,570,000
Adjusted primary EPS shares	2,710,000
Plus: purchase method adjustment	180,000
Readjusted primary EPS shares	2,890,000

Readjusted primary EPS = $6,570,000/2,890,000 = $2.27

18.{M}A. Basic EPS cannot be calculated since no income data is provided in the example. However, the number of shares outstanding for Basic EPS would be:

Number outstanding at December 31, 1987	2,000,000
Effect of stock dividend (10%)	200,000
Number of shares	2,200,000

B. The stock dividend shares are considered outstanding for the entire year. The additional shares resulting from other securities are considered outstanding only for the portion of the year following their issue.

The number of common and common equivalent shares is:

Number outstanding at December 31, 1987	2,000,000
Effect of stock dividend (10%)	200,000
Shares issuable on bond conversion*	1,000,000
Total	3,200,000

* As effective yield (5%) is less than two-thirds of the Aa bond yield (8%) at issue date, the convertible bonds are considered common equivalents. The number of shares is $10,000,000 / $5 or 2,000,000; as the bonds were sold on July 1, only half the number of shares is included.

The warrants are *not* reflected because they are anti-dilutive; the exercise price exceeds the average stock price for the period outstanding.

C. For the fully diluted calculation, the treasury stock method is based on the (higher) closing price of Champion shares ($8). At that price, the proceeds of exercise (800,000 x $5 = $4,000,000) could be used to repurchase 500,000 shares ($4,000,000/$8) resulting in a net issuance of 300,000 shares. For one-quarter year, 75,000 shares are deemed outstanding. Thus the fully diluted number of shares outstanding is:

Number outstanding at December 31, 1987	2,000,000
Effect of stock dividend (10%)	200,000
Shares issuable on bond conversion*	1,000,000
Effect of stock options	75,000
Total	3,275,000

D. (i)   At a closing price of $10, the treasury stock method would result in repurchase of 400,000 shares ($4,000,000/$10) and net issuance of 400,000 shares (800,000 less 400,000). For one quarter year, the net effect would be 100,000, an increase of 25,000 from the total in part B. The closing price only affects fully diluted EPS.

(ii) At an average price of $8, the warrants are dilutive in the primary calculation. The proceeds of exercise ($4,000,000) could repurchase 500,000 shares, resulting in a net issuance of 300,000 shares. The effect for one quarter year is 75,000 shares, making the number of common and common equivalent shares equal to 3,275,000.

(iii) No effect. The determination of common equivalent classification is made at the time of issue and is not changed by subsequent events.

Note: There is no effect on the number of shares used for basic EPS of any of these events.

CASE 4-1 Solution

Estimated solution time is four to five hours.

Case overview: The objective of this case is to prepare a comprehensive ratio analysis of one U.S. and one U.K. company. The ratios are compared with those for duPont, a major competitor.

1. Exhibits 4CS-1A and D contain the required ratios.

2. *Activity Analysis:* DuPont reports higher inventory, receivables, and total assets turnover ratios. These ratios reflect better operating performance than both Dow and ICI. DuPont's fixed asset turnover is poorer than that reported by the other firms.

    These comparisons are affected by different inventory methods. (Unlike the others, ICI uses FIFO) and differences in business mix, lease versus purchase, timing of the purchases of fixed assets, write-offs, and depreciation methods used.

    Liquidity Analysis: Both ICI and Dow report longer operating cycles than DuPont. However, ICI and Dow take significantly longer to pay their suppliers. This allows ICI to report the shortest and most efficient cash cycle. Dow's operating cycle is the longest and the longer time taken to pay suppliers does not overcome the problems suggested by the operating cycle.

    Dow reports generally poorer conventional liquidity ratios. DuPont's cash from operations ratio and the defensive interval show its relative strength and operating efficiency. Again, some ratios may differ because DuPont and Dow use LIFO. FIFO enables ICI to report a higher current ratio compared to DuPont and Dow.

    Solvency Analysis: ICI reports the lowest debt to equity and capital ratios. This advantage disappears when debt includes trade payables. Dow remains the most highly leveraged regardless of measure used. DuPont reports higher interest coverage and CFO to debt ratios. ICI's reported coverage suffers because it is not allowed to capitalize interest. Overall, DuPont has lower leverage and a better cash generating ability.

Exhibit 4CS-1A
ACTIVITY ANALYSIS
($ in millions for DuPont and Dow; £ in millions for ICI)

	DUPONT	ICI	DOW
Inventory Turnover[1]	5.64	5.35	5.05
Average number of days inventory[2]	65	68	72
Accounts Receivable turnover[3]	9.52	7.14	6.73
Average number of days receivables[4]	38	51	54
Fixed Assets Turnover[5]	1.85	2.33	2.31
Total Assets Turnover[6]	1.06	1.01	0.77

[1]Inventory Turnover = COGS/Avg. Inventory.
ICI=(6,502/((1,233+1,199)/2)=5.35;
Dow=13,219/((2,712+2,526)/2))= 5.05

[2]Average number of days inventory in stock=365/Inventory Turnover
ICI=365/5.35=68;Dow=365/5.05=72.

[3]Accounts Receivable Turnover =Net Sales/Average Trade Receivables
ICI=(9,189/((1,360+1,214)/2))=7.14;
Dow=20,015/((3,359+2,587)/2)=6.73

[4]Average number of days receivables on hand =365/Accounts
Receivable Turnover ICI=365/7.14 = 51;Dow = 365/6.73 = 54.

[5]Fixed Assets Turnover = Sales/Average Fixed Assets
ICI=(9,189/((3,861+4,024)/2))=2.33;
Dow=20,015/((8,726+8,580)/2))= 2.31.

[6]Total Assets Turnover = Sales/Average Total Assets =
ICI=(9,189/((9,004+9,229)/2))=1.01;
Dow=(20,015/((26,545+25,505)/2))=0.77.

Exhibit 4CS-1B

Liquidity Analysis Year ended December 31, 1994
($ in millions for DuPont and Dow; £ in millions for ICI)

	DUPONT	ICI	DOW
Average no. of days inventory in stock[1]	65	68	72
+ Days receivables outstanding[2]	38	51	54
Length of Operating Cycle	103	119	126
– Days Payables outstanding[3]	29	53	46
Length of Cash Cycle	74	66	80
Current ratio[4]	1.47	1.81	1.31
Quick ratio[5]	0.84	1.18	0.68
Cash ratio[6]	0.15	0.66	0.17
Cash from operations ratio[7]	0.75	0.23	0.40
Defensive interval no. of days[8]	71	135	101

[1]Average no. of days inventory in stock computed in Exhibit 4C-1A.

[2]Days receivables outstanding computed in Exhibit 4C-1A.

[3]Purchases = COGS + Change in Inventory. ICI= 6,502+(1,233-1,199)= 6,536.
Dow=13,219+(2,712-2,526)= 13,405.
Average no. of days payables outstanding = 365*[Average AP(Trade)/Purchases];
ICI=365*[((993+888)/2)/6,536]=53.
Dow=365*[((1,928+1,479)/2)/13,405=46.

[4]Current ratio = Current Assets / Current Liabilities. ICI=4,733/2,608=1.81 (Reported current assets minus long-term prepayments of 239; see Footnote 16, p. 1181).
Dow=8,693/6,618=1.31.

[5]Quick ratio = (Cash + Marketable Securities + AR)/Current Liabilities. ICI=(235+1475+1360)/2,608=1.18. (Reported Marketable securities 1524 minus restricted 49, Footnote 17, p. 1182).
Dow=(569+565+3,359)/6,618=0.68.

[6]Cash ratio = (Cash + Marketable Securities/Current Liabilities)
ICI=(235+1475)/ 2,608=0.66. Dow =(569+565)/6,618=0.17.

[7]Cash from operations ratio = CFO/Current Liabilities =
ICI = 612/2,608 = 0.23. (ICI CFO is after interest paid, and dividends paid and received, see cash flow statement on p.1171).Dow = 2,635/6,618 = 0.40.

[8]Projected Expenditures = COGS + Other operating expenses except depreciation expense. ICI = 6,502+ 1,778 = 8,280 (see Footnote 12 for depreciation expense).
Dow = 13,219 + 4,491 - 1525 = 16,185.
Defensive interval no. of days = 365*[(Cash + Marketable Securities +AR)/Projected Expenditures]. ICI= 365*[3,070/8,280] = 135.
Dow = 365* [4,493/16,185] = 101.

Exhibit 4CS-1C
LONG TERM DEBT AND SOLVENCY ANALYSIS
($ in millions for DuPont and Dow; £ in millions for ICI)

Capitalization Table	DUPONT	ICI	DOW
Short-term debt	714	142	741
Current long-term debt	578	181	534
Long-term debt	6,376	1,575	5,303
Total Debt	7,668	1,898	6,578
Trade payables[1]	3,565	1,302	2,738
Total Debt (including trade)	11,233	3,200	9,316
Total equity	12,822	3,736	8,212
Total Capital	20,490	5,634	14,790
Total Capital (including trade)	24,055	6,936	17,528
Debt			
To equity[2]	0.60	0.51	0.80
To capital[3]	0.37	0.34	0.44
Debt (including trade)			
To equity[4]	0.88	0.86	1.13
To capital[5]	0.47	0.46	0.53
Times interest earned[6]	8.84	3.19	4.82
Capital expenditures ratio[7]	2.16	2.96	2.45
CFO to debt[8]	0.74	0.32	0.40

[1]Trade Payables = Trade accounts payable + Income taxes payable + other accrued taxes
ICI=993+233+76=1,302; Dow = 1,928+664+146=2,738.
[2]Debt to Equity = Total debt to total equity ICI=1,898/3,736=0.51
Dow = 6,578/8,212=0.80.
[3]Debt to Capital = Total debt/Total capital ICI = 1,898/5,634 = .34
Dow = 6,578/14,790=0.44
[4]Debt (including trade) to Equity = Total debt (including trade) to total equity ICI=3,200/3,736=0.86; Dow = 9,316/8,212=1.13.
[5] Debt (including trade) to Capital (including trade) = Total debt (including trade /Total capital (including trade
ICI = 3,200/6,936=0.46; Dow = 9,316/17,528=0.53
[6]Times interest earned = EBIT/Interest expense =
ICI = 594/186 = 3.19; Dow = 2,589/537 = 4.82
[7]CFO/Capital expenditures ICI=612/207 = 2.96; Dow=2,635/1,072=2.45.
[8]CFO to debt = CFO to total debt.
ICI = 612/1,898= 0.32 Dow = 2,635/6,578 = 0.40

Exhibit 4CS-1D

PROFITABILITY ANALYSIS

($ in millions for DuPont and Dow; £ in millions for ICI)

	DUPONT	ICI	DOW
Gross margin[1] (%)	44.13	29.24	33.95
Operating margin[2] (%)	9.85	6.40	11.72
Pre-interest and tax margin[3] (%)	12.56	6.46	12.94
Pretax margin[4] (%)	11.14	4.44	10.25
Profit margin[5] (%)	6.93	2.66	4.69
ROA (pre-interest)			
After-tax[6] (%)	8.32	4.04	5.11
Pretax[7] (%)	13.36	6.52	9.95
ROE			
After-tax[8] (%)	22.68	6.40	11.55
Pretax[9] (%)	36.44	10.70	25.26
ROTC (preinterest)			
After-tax[10] (%)	14.98	6.31	8.94
Pretax (%)[11]	24.07	10.17	17.39

[1]Gross margin = Gross Profit/Sales. ICI = 2,687/9,189 = 29.24
Dow = 6,796/20,015= 33.95
[2]Operating margin = Operating Profit/Sales. ICI = 588/9,189=6.40
Dow = $2,345/$20,015 = 11.72
[3]Pre-interest and tax margin = EBIT/Sales. ICI = 594/9,189=6.46
Dow = 2,589/20,015=12.94.
[4] Pretax margin = EBT/Sales. ICI = 408/9189 = 4.44
Dow 2,052/20,015 = 10.25
[5]Profit margin = Net income/Sales. ICI= 244/9,189 = 2.66,
Dow = 938/20,015= 4.69
[6]Aftertax ROA = {[Net income + (Interest expense*(1-effective tax rate)]/Average Assets}
ICI = {[244 + (186*0.67)]/{[9,004+9,229]/2} = 4.04
Dow = {[938 + (603*0.65)]/{[26,545+25,505]/2} = 5.11
[7]Pretax Return on Assets = EBIT/Average Assets.
ICI = 594/9,116 = 6.52; Dow = 9.95
[8]After tax (%) = (Net Income/Average Equity)*100.
ICI = (244/((3,736 + 3,888)/2)) = 6.40;
Dow = (938/((8,212 + 8,034)/2)) = 11.55
[9]Pretax (%) = (EBT/Average Equity)*100
ICI = (408/3,812)*100 = 10.70; Dow = (2,052/8,123)*100 = 25.26
[10]After tax (%) = {[Net income + (Interest expense*1-effective tax rate)]/Average Total Capital}
ICI = {[244 + (186*0.67)]/{[5,634+6,045/2} = 6.31
Dow = {[938 + (603*0.65)]/ {[14,790+14,978]/2} = 8.94
[11]Pretax (%) = {EBIT/Average Total Capital}
ICI = {594/((5,634+6,045)/2))=10.17.
Dow = {2,589/{[14,790+14,978]/2} = 17.39

Profitability Analysis: Exhibit 4CS-1D shows that DuPont reports higher profitability and returns across nearly all measures. Its EBIT and operating margin are lower than those reported by Dow. ICI is the poorest performer of the three firms analyzed.

Limitations and Additional Data needs: All the ratios computed and analyzed in the preceding exhibits are affected by different accounting methods used by the three firms. We need data (for example, trends in capital expenditures, writeoffs, debt and equity financing over the last three to five years) from previous years to evaluate trends. The analysis of ratios at a single point in time is incomplete and potentially misleading.

3. Exhibits 4CS-2A and 4CS2-B provide an integrated ratio analysis of Dow and ICI.

4. *Changes in ROE from 1993 to 1994*: DuPont reported a significant improvement in ROE (from 4.83% to 22.68%) due to a substantial increase in operating profitability. Changes in turnover and leverage did not significantly affect ROE.

    ICI reported higher ROE in 1994 because of significant improvement in profitability and more efficient use of assets.

    Dow shows less improvement than either DuPont or ICI. Leverage has decreased slightly, offsetting improvements in profitability and turnover.

Exhibit 4CS-2A DISAGGREGATION OF PRETAX ROA AND ROE
DUPONT, ICI AND DOW
Year ended December 31, 1994

	Return on Assets					Interest		Return on Equity			
	Preinterest & Tax Margin[1]	*	Asset Turnover[2]	=	Preinterest ROA[3]	-	Interest on assets[4]	=	Postinterest ROA[5]	*	Leverage[6]	=	Pretax ROE[7]
	EBIT/Sales (%)		Sales/Avg total assets		EBIT/Avg total assets (%)		Interest expense/Avg total assets (%)		EBT/Avg total assets (%)		Avg total assets/Avg common equity		EBT/Avg common equity (%)
DUPONT												
1993	4.18	*	0.98	=	4.09	-	1.56	=	2.51	*	3.30	=	8.33
1994	12.56	*	1.06	=	13.36	-	1.51	=	11.85	*	3.07	=	36.44
ICI												
1993	5.20	*	0.91	=	4.75	-	2.73	=	2.02	*	2.37	=	4.79
1994	6.46	*	1.01	=	6.52	-	2.04	=	4.48	*	2.39	=	10.70
DOW												
1993	11.77	*	0.71	=	8.33	-	2.35	=	5.98	*	3.17	=	18.96
1994	12.94	*	0.77	=	9.96	-	2.06	=	7.88	*	3.20	=	25.25

1994 Calculation Numbers have been rounded

Note: DuPont calculations are provided in Exhibit 4-12.
ICI and Dow 1993 calculations use year-end data as averages cannot be computed from 1994 financial statements..

		ICI	DOW
1. Preinterest and tax margin (%) = (EBIT/Sales)*100		594/9,189=6.46	2,589/20,015=12.94
2. Asset Turnover = Sales/Avg total assets		9,189/9116.5=1.01	20,015/26,025=0.77
3. Preinterest ROA = Preinterest and tax margin * Asset Turnover	6.46*1.01=6.52	12.94*0.77=9.96
4. Interest on assets = (Interest expense/Avg total assets)	186/9116.5=2.04	537/26,025=2.06
5. Postinterest ROA = Preinterest ROA - Interest on assets	6.52-2.04=4.48	9.96-2.06=7.88
6. Leverage = Avg total assets/Avg common equity	9,116.5/3,812=2.39	26,025/8,123=3.20
7. Pretax ROE = Postinterest ROA * Leverage	4.48*2.39=10.70	7.88*3.20=25.25

EXHIBIT 4CS-2B: DISAGGREGATION OF RETURN ON EQUITY (AFTER TAX)
DUPONT, ICI, AND DOW

A. Three-Component Disaggregation of ROE

	(Profitability	x	Turnover)	x	Solvency	=	ROE
	Net Income / Sales	x	Sales / Average Total Assets	=	Net Income / Average Total Assets	x	Average Total Assets / Average Common Equity	=	Net Income / Average Common Equity

DuPont	Net Income / Sales	x	Sales / Average Total Assets	=	Net Income / Average Total Assets	x	Average Total Assets / Average Common Equity	=	Net Income / Average Common Equity
1993	1.50%	x	0.98	=	1.47%	x	3.30	=	4.83%
1994	6.93%	x	1.06	=	7.37%	x	3.07	=	22.68%
ICI									
1993	0.79%	x	0.91	=	0.72%	x	2.37	=	1.71%
1994	2.66%	x	1.01	=	2.69%	x	2.39	=	6.43%
Dow									
1993	3.57%	x	0.71	=	2.53%	x	3.17	=	8.02%
1994	4.69%	x	0.77	=	3.61%	x	3.20	=	11.55%

B. Five-Component Disaggregation of ROE

(Profitability x Turnover) x Solvency = ROE

Effects of: Taxes Financing Operations

	Net Income / EBT	x	EBT / EBIT	x	EBIT / Sales	=	Net Income / Sales	x	Sales / Average Total Assets	=	Net Income / Average Total Assets	x	Average Total Assets / Average Common Equity	=	Net Income / Average Common Equity
DuPont															
1993	0.58	x	0.62	x	4.18%	=	1.50%	x	0.98	=	1.47%	x	3.30	=	4.83%
1994	0.62	x	0.89	x	12.56%	=	6.93%	x	1.06	=	7.37%	x	3.07	=	22.68%
ICI															
1993	0.36	x	0.42	x	5.20%	=	0.79%	x	0.91	=	0.73%	x	2.37	=	1.73%
1994	0.60	x	0.69	x	6.46%	=	2.67%	x	1.01	=	2.70%	x	2.39	=	6.43%
Dow															
1993	0.42	x	0.72	x	11.77%	=	3.56%	x	0.71	=	2.53%	x	3.17	=	8.02%
1994	0.46	x	0.79	x	12.94%	=	4.72%	x	0.77	=	3.63%	x	3.20	=	11.55%

5. DuPont reports the highest ROE (22.68%) due to its high profitability, efficient use of assets (highest asset turnover), and (relative to ICI) high leverage.

    Differences in ROE of the three firms over time are due to:

    - Relative profitability and capital intensity of different business segments
    - trends in operating and financial leverage
    - financial reporting methods

    We would need additional financial statement and operating data to evaluate the impact of those differences on ROE.

6. *Balance Sheet Comparisons*: DuPont and ICI are stronger financially than either DOW or the chemical industry composite (21% debt compared to 25% for Dow and 26% for the industry). ICI reports the highest proportion of cash and securities implying the lowest net debt burden. ICI also reports the highest ratio of equity to total assets; both DuPont and Dow have less equity than the industry composite.

    At 30% and 33% respectively, both DuPont and Dow have significantly lower current assets as a proportion of total assets; The ICI and industry composite ratios are higher at 53 and 58% respectively. DuPont and Dow have significantly lower investments in inventories and receivables.

    Both DuPont and ICI have high property investments (at 57% and 43%, respectively) compared to Dow and the industry (at 33% and 32%, respectively).

    Income Statement: DuPont is the most profitable and has the highest gross margin and net income as a percentage of sales. ICI is less profitable than the industry as its gross margin is 29% compared to 32% and net income as a percentage of sales is 2% compared to the industry average of 5%.

    Limitations: The analysis is based on data for a single year and the chemical industry composite includes firms in different sectors whose contribution to the common size statements may differ from that reported by DuPont, Dow, and ICI. Financial reporting differences also affect the comparisons.

Chapter 5 - Solutions

Overview:

Problem Length	*Problem #'s*
{S}	*1,4,5,6,11,12*
{M}	*2,3,7,8,10*
{L}	*9*

NOTE: The problems in this chapter are designed primarily as a basis for discussion of the issues covered in this chapter. There are no absolutely right/wrong answers. The solutions below should be viewed in that spirit.

1.{S}The FASB view of neutrality is consistent with the classical approach, that takes the position that an "ideal" accounting paradigm can and should be designed disregarding potentially adverse impacts.

Market-based researchers, however, argue that the costs and benefits of accounting policy setting should be subject to economic analysis. Neutrality as defined in the quotation is therefore *not a desirable objective*. The fact that certain firms would be adversely affected by accounting standards renders the standard non (pareto[1]) optimal. Thus, although the efficacy of an accounting system is measurable by its market impact (information content), that same impact means that it is not possible to use information content to determine accounting policy.

The "positive" approach argues that *de facto* neutrality is *not a feasible objective*. The accounting standard setting process is influenced by the impact, favorable or unfavorable, that standards have on firms. Firms lobby (in many cases successfully) for or against certain standards precisely for that reason. This is not necessarily bad. Rather it is a "fact of life" and in this view, accounting standards and the standard setting process cannot be determined exogenously of firms' production-investment decisions.

---

[1] Pareto optimality is defined as the condition where a change to a new equilibrium leaves nobody worse off and at least one participant is better off.

2.{M}A.   This question is difficult to answer without knowing the total information set provided by each system in its first report. However, assuming that in other respects they are identical, information system Alpha is a superior system insofar as it provides a better prediction of the second report.

B.   Since, under the Alpha system, the second report could be forecasted better, at the time of its issuance it would contain fewer "surprises" and show less information content. The Gamma system, however, would contain a greater degree of "surprise" and, therefore, show greater information content.

C.   The answers to parts A and B point out the problems of focusing only on the market reaction to one report at a specific point in time. Although market reaction may tell us something about the information content of that given report, it does not tell the whole story.

Accounting reports may contain information that will only be known at a later point in time (outside the "window" examined). Similarly, nonreaction may be due to knowledge generated by previous information provided by the system (alone or in conjunction with external information sources); the better a system predicts, the less "information" content in subsequent reports.

D.   Ingberman and Sorter viewed accounting systems as part of an overall data base whose purpose is to aid in forecasting the impact on the firm of changes in the firm and the environment. Thus, their view suggests the following "scenario":

1.   Financial statements provide information as to how previous changes in the environment impacted the firm.

2.   A change occurs in the environment. Market participants use their previous knowledge (see #1) to assess the potential impact of that change on the firm. Market reaction occurs at this time.

3. Subsequent reports update and confirm the extent to which the environmental change affected the firm. A small (or nonexistent) market reaction at the time of issuance of these reports means that most (or all) of the reaction occurred earlier.

4. The measures of the effects on the firm provided by the subsequent reports are then used to update the database and make projections.

Similar to the situation described by the Alpha and Gamma information systems, Ingberman and Sorter argued that focusing on the specific point in time when a given accounting report is issued may be the wrong way to assess the value of the information provided by accounting reports.

3.{M}A. (i) The efficient market hypothesis (EMH) states that a market is efficient if security prices immediately and fully reflect all available relevant information. If the market fully reflects information, the knowledge of that information would not allow anyone to profit from it because stock prices already incorporate the information.

The weak form asserts that stock prices already reflect all information that can be derived by examining market trading data such as the history of past prices and trading volume.

Technical analysis in the form of charting involves the search for recurrent and predictable patterns in stock prices to enhance returns. The EMH implies that this type of analysis is without value. If past prices contain no useful information for predicting future returns, there is no point in following any technical trading rule for timing the purchases and sales of securities. According to weak-form efficiency, no investor can earn excess returns by developing trading rules based on historical price and return information. A simple policy of buying and holding will be at least as good as any technical procedure. Tests generally show that technical trading rules do not produce superior returns after making adjustments for transactions costs and taxes.

(ii) The semistrong form says that a firm's stock price already reflects all publicly available information about a firm's prospects. Examples of publicly available information are annual reports of companies and investment advisory data. Empirical evidence mostly supports the semistrong form, but occasional studies are inconsistent with this form of market efficiency.

Fundamental analysis uses earnings and dividend prospects of the firm, expectations of future interest rates, and risk evaluation of the firm to determine proper stock prices. The EMH predicts that most fundamental analysis is doomed to failure. According to semistrong-form efficiency, no investor can earn excess returns from trading rules based on any publicly available information. Fundamental analysis is no better than technical analysis in enabling investors to capture above-average returns. Only analysts with unique insight earn superior returns.

The strong form of the EMH holds that market prices incorporate both publicly available and privately held (insider) information. [However, empirical evidence suggests insiders may earn abnormal returns using inside information.] Both technical and fundamental analysis would not be able to earn abnormal returns under the strong form.

In summary, the EMH holds that the market appears to adjust so quickly to information about individual stocks and the economy as a whole that no technique of selecting a portfolio -- using either technical or fundamental analysis-- can consistently outperform a strategy of simply buying and holding a diversified group of securities, such as those making up the popular market averages,

B. Even in perfectly efficient markets, portfolio managers have several roles. Two of these deal with the crux of any investment decision risk and return.

  1. *Identify the risk/return objectives for the portfolio given the investor's constraints and develop a well-diversified portfolio with the selected risk level.*

     In an efficient market, portfolio managers are responsible for tailoring the portfolio to meet the investor's needs rather than to beat the market, which requires identifying the clients requirements and risk tolerance. Although an efficient market prices securities fairly, each security still has firm-specific risk that portfolio managers can eliminate through diversification, Therefore, rational security selection requires selecting a well-diversified portfolio that provides the level of systematic risk that matches the investor's risk tolerance.

  2. *Develop capital market expectations for appropriate asset-allocation decisions.*

     As part of the asset-allocation decision portfolio managers need to consider their expectations for the relative returns of the various capital markets to choose an appropriate asset allocation.

C. The empirical evidence generally supports the weak form and to a great degree the semistrong firm. However, the existing anomalies suggest that *superior* analysis of available information may result in excess or abnormal returns. Furthermore, as market efficiency is often explained as being the product of the plethora of analysts analyzing information, neglected areas such as smaller firms, firms which have fallen "out of favor" or sources of information not readily available to (or used by) all analysts are areas which analysts can most readily exploit. A word of caution - however - if many analysts simultaneously try to exploit these sources, then once again efficiency will prevail.

4. {S}Standard research procedures abstract from (i.e. eliminate) general market conditions to test for (market) reaction specific to a firm or sample of firms. If an accounting

standard affects all firms equally, then a test looking for firm-specific reaction will not find anything as the informational impact is (inadvertently) included in "general" market conditions. Even if the standard does not affect all firms, but only a sizable proportion of them, then standard research designs would be unlikely to find (significant) market reaction. Thus, somewhat paradoxically, the more pervasive the impact of an accounting change the less likely that market reaction will be found. Only if studies are designed to measure the differential effect of such changes on particular firms can a market reaction be found.

Examples of pervasive accounting standards are:
1. Changing prices (SFAS 33[*])
2. Pension plans (SFAS 87)
3. Income taxes (SFAS 109)
4. Postretirement benefits (SFAS 106)

[*]This argument may explain the insignificant results (see Appendix 8-A) found by studies that examined the impact of SFAS 33.

5. {S}This statement is most consistent with the positive approach to accounting theory. Proponents of the classical and market-based approaches might agree with the descriptive validity of the statement. However, the political process is viewed by classicists as an undesirable 'fact of life' to be overcome and as irrelevant by the market-based proponents. The positive approach, on the other hand, holds that the ramifications and implications of this political process are an essential element in understanding how accounting standards are developed and the motivation of firms in opting for alternative choices.

6. {S}Pharmaceutical companies are often the subject of attack by politicians and consumer groups that drug prices are too high.

The political cost hypothesis argues that firms may choose to "artificially" depress earnings if they fear legislative or regulatory actions would be taken against them if it was perceived that their earnings were excessive.

1993, at the beginning of President Clinton's term was the year that his wife Hillary Rodham Clinton headed a committee whose objective was to create a nation-wide health care system. As part of that process, drug prices (and profits) were under extreme scrutiny. This environment may explain why the Pfizer company "managed down earnings".

7. {M} *NOTE: Most, if not all, of the items listed have analytical implications that are independent of financial statements, i.e., they would have to be considered whether or not the firm issued financial statements. We focus here only on the implications of these items in the context of financial statements.*

   (i) To the extent that a firm's labor costs are related to profitability, (e.g. profit sharing plans), management may have an incentive to select accounting policies that dampen reported profits. Lower reported profits may also keep down demands for higher wages and benefits. Thus, the analyst should be prepared to "adjust" the firm's reported performance upwards as the firm may have been too conservative.

        Similarly, if a labor contract is coming up for renewal, and the firm's financial statements show strong performance, then one can expect higher demands from labor, increased probability of a strike, and increased labor costs in the future. (Also see iii below)

   (ii) Market efficiency is increased by analysts competing to "beat the market." This motivation and the resultant behavior (somewhat paradoxically) leads to information being immediately impounded in prices. If this is true then the degree of efficiency should be (positively) related to the number of analysts covering the firm. Thus, an analyst who wants to uncover and exploit information not recognized by the market should look for firms that are covered by few other analysts. (Also see iv below)

   (iii) The bonus plan hypothesis is that managers will act to enhance their well being even if it may not be in the firm's best interest. For example, managers may opt for financial reporting methods that increase income if their compensation is directly (or indirectly) tied to the firm's income. Analysts need to be aware of this phenomenon to better understand the effect of this behavior on the firm's reported performance. (Also see v below)

More sophisticated manifestations of this behavior include:

(1) taking a "big bath" in a year when performance is below some threshold anyway, thereby increasing the probability that the threshold level will be achieved in the future.

(2) alternatively, if a threshold has been achieved and no further benefit (to managers) accrues from exceeding that threshold, they may engage in income smoothing to "store" income for future years when adverse business conditions make the threshold harder to achieve.

(iv) (1) One of the documented anomalies of the efficient market hypothesis is the small firm effect. Small firms tend to earn abnormal positive returns (even after compensating for risk). This phenomenon may be related to item ii, the number of analysts covering the firm, as larger firms tend to have more of an analyst following. This argues for more emphasis on the analysis of smaller firms.

However, there is a cost-benefit tradeoff. An investor with $100 million to invest may have to choose between investing in ten larger firms or 100 smaller firms. The additional return earned on the latter may not compensate for the higher research costs (especially time) and lower liquidity. For a given research effort that results in an additional 1% return, the benefits will differ considerably depending on the size of the firm. The 1% additional return for a firm whose capitalization is $100 million is considerably greater than a 1% return on a firm whose capitalization is only one million dollars. The $10,000 return earned on the latter may not compensate for the research time and money expended.

(2) On the other hand, the political cost hypothesis argues that larger firms are more sensitive to certain accounting changes and patterns of income. Analysts should be on the lookout to see if large firms have chosen accounting methods that shield them from political costs.

(v) As noted earlier (item iii) managers may have incentives to take actions that enhance their position at the expense of the firm. The incentives for this behavior are reduced when managers are also owners of the firm. Thus, the more a firm is controlled by its owners, the lower the potential effects of agency costs.

(vi) Companies in the same industry tend to choose similar accounting methods. When a company deviates from these policies, in addition to adjusting for the alternative methods the analyst should ask what motivates these divergences and what can be learned about the company's "corporate profile." Do the changes signal a shift in emphasis from one segment (industry) to another?

Additionally, for firms in certain industries (oil and gas, banking) the political cost hypothesis discussed earlier is a relevant consideration.

8.{M}A&B. Assuming external validity and generalizability of the survey, there are three possible explanations for the results:

(1) Firms were not aware of the magnitude of their postretirement health benefits until they were forced to calculate them by the new accounting rule.

(2) The mandated balance sheet recognition and disclosure of health care liabilities was directly responsible for their curtailment by firms.

(3) There is no direct cause and effect between balance sheet recognition and the curtailment of benefits. The events are only correlated with another.

The first explanation assumes that managers (as well as investors) are "fixated" on annual reports and that managers have no appreciation of actual costs unless and until they are contained in the financial reporting system. Previous research on leases and foreign currency translation suggest that managers do pay more attention to events that they must account for. Similarly, field tests carried out when the health cost disclosure was first introduced indicated that (some) managers had difficulty in complying with the requirements because of a lack of data availability.

Because of this lack of data and the complexity of calculating the present value of these benefits (see Chapter 12) it is possible that some firms had only the haziest idea of the cost of these benefits. Postemployment benefits were often granted to unionized employees as trade offs for current wages, that had to be recognized as expense immediately. Managers had a clear incentive to trade future costs for present costs. [A senior manager of one Fortune 100 company told one of the authors that he thought the benefits would not have been granted if management had known their cost.]

The second explanation is consistent with the "economic consequences" branch of the positive accounting approach. By adversely affecting the company's reported performance, the new accounting standard may impact one or more of the following:
    (1) management compensation,
    (2) bond covenants on existing debt,
    (3) the terms of any new debt,
    (4) future labor negotiations, and
    (5) internal resource allocation decisions.

All of these factors can have real costs associated with them and may be incentives for management to reduce health care costs.

Somewhat less likely in our opinion, is the possibility that managers reduced their health care costs because they feared the market reaction to the accounting recognition and disclosure. This is not necessarily inconsistent with the efficient market hypothesis as it is possible that even though the market is efficient, managers may not perceive it to be so. However, in this case, prior disclosure requirements (SFAS 81) and the long gestation period of the exposure draft, comment period and standard may have taken some of the surprise out of the actual accounting.

The third explanation is the most likely. Under this view, the benefit curtailments were not caused by new accounting standards. Rather, both events were influenced by the same underlying factor--the explosion of health care costs in recent years. The growth in these costs was a major factor that triggered the FASB project that resulted in new accounting standards. Similarly, the higher costs induced firms to reduce the health care benefits offered to employees. Thus the coincidence of these events is an example of *association and correlation not causation*.

C. One would not expect to see any market reaction to the survey as companies had already been disclosing the effect of the new standard. As far as reaction to the accounting rule itself and subsequent disclosures, any market reaction observed and its direction (positive or negative) would result from one of three factors:
    (1) the disclosure requirement itself,
    (2) the curtailment of benefits, or
    (3) the level and trend of health care costs.
    Under the efficient market hypothesis, *ceteris paribus*, one would not expect to see any market reaction to the rule itself or the subsequent balance sheet disclosures unless the market (analysts) had previously done a poor job of estimating the level of a firm's health care liabilities. Then the actual disclosure may contain surprises ("good" and "bad") triggering market reaction.

    Under the "economic consequences" hypothesis one would expect to see market reaction, primarily at the time of the adoption of the new rule. The direction would presumably be negative, unless it is assumed that the market anticipates that the disclosure rule will force firms to curtail future benefits. The curtailment may be perceived as being positive as it lowers future costs.

Under any approach, the results must be understood in the context of rising health care costs. Any results indicating that firms that have a higher burden of health care costs perform poorly relative to firms whose health care costs are not as high may be measuring reaction to rising health care costs rather than to the new accounting and disclosure requirement. This point would be especially relevant if the research did not focus on the period (days) immediately surrounding the new disclosure requirement.

9.{L} A. To determine abnormal returns, one must abstract from general market conditions as well as industry factors. Overall market indices rose by 1% to 2%, much less than the increases in Amgen (6.3%) and Deere (5.2%) and, in the opposite direction, the 16.9% decline in Dell. Thus, ignoring industry factors all three firms could be said to exhibit abnormal returns.

When we consider industry factors, the answers become more complicated. As the index for computer stocks increased slightly, it would be safe to argue that the decline in Dell is firm-specific and would qualify as an "abnormal" return. To a lesser extent, a similar argument can be made for Deere as the overall industry index for heavy machinery increased by only 2.9%; Deere's increase was substantially higher. However, this conclusion would depend on Deere's "beta" relative to the industry index. If it was very high then Deere's high return would be considered industry rather than firm related.

For Amgen, it would seem that its increase of 6.3% was industry-specific (rather than firm-specific) as the biotechnology index increased by a similar 5.4%. However, the industry index may itself be affected by firm-specific events (see Part E to this problem). Amgen is a component of the biotechnology index. Thus the change in that index may reflect the firm-specific change in Amgen rather than industry wide factors. To remedy this problem, an industry index without Amgen would have to be constructed and used. Additionally, to the extent that news about one firm provides information about other firms in the industry, it is difficult to argue that the market reaction was not related to Amgen simply because it affected the shares of other firms in the same industry. Similar arguments can, of course, be made for the other industry indices.

B. The efficient market hypothesis does not hold that the market is omniscient; only that it correctly and rapidly processes available information. If the information about Amgen's earnings was not known earlier, then the negative reaction at the time of the announcement would be totally consistent with the efficient market hypothesis. Only if there existed prior public information,[2] in the form of lower orders for example, that could have permitted the market to anticipate the earnings disappointment, would the lack of anticipation be an example of market inefficiency.

For Dell, the question of market inefficiency seems to be more relevant. Only a month earlier, Dell had hit an all-time high of approximately $50. This raises the first question: how did this happen? What news (seemingly completely contrary to present news about the firm) did the market react to then? Since then, the stock had declined by about 30% prior to February 24. Obviously, the market had wind of the negative news prior to the February 24th announcement. The question now becomes: why wasn't the full reaction immediate? Why did the decline take over a month? To answer these questions, more information would be required as to the pattern of news relating to Dell appearing in the last month.

C. The existence of abnormal returns would be an indicator of reaction to firm-specific news. Thus, as argued in part A, it appears that Dell's market reaction was related to the news item.

---

[2]We are ignoring the strong form of the efficient market hypothesis, that holds that even nonpublic information is reflected in prices as insiders trade on it. In Amgen's case, one would have to know when the insiders became aware of the disappointing earnings expectation and whether they had the time or opportunity to trade on it.

However, the strongest argument can be made for Amgen. The reaction was over a very short time horizon (one half-hour) *after* the normal market close, it immediately followed the release of the news item, and it was in the opposite direction to the stock's movement prior to the news release.

D. It is difficult to determine the "cause" of the market reaction because there are confounding news items:

    (i) the reduction of the long-term profit goal; and
    (ii) the withdrawal of the stock issue.

Which of these items is "responsible" for the market reaction is difficult if not impossible to determine.

E. (i) In this part, we assume that the Amgen effect is not large enough to significantly affect the Biotechnology index.

    The actual change in Amgen occurred after the market closed on February 24. On that day the biotechnology index was positive, and as we argued in part C, Amgen's reaction is surely a result of the news item. However, by using February 25 as the announcement date, when the index was negative, a researcher may erroneously conclude that the reaction was industry related.

    (ii) The evidence about the components of the index clearly indicate that the index was significantly affected by Amgen. The assumption made in (i) does not hold. However, since the index is affected by Amgen, by using the index to abstract industry wide effects, the researcher would erroneously conclude that the Amgen effect was industry related when the correct conclusion was the reverse. The industry effect was caused by Amgen! (Also see discussion earlier for questions 4 and 9A.)

F. One would expect to see little or no market reaction after the financial statements are released as all the information was anticipated by then. The market reaction will depend on how the actual earnings report compares with that expected (not just with prior year earnings).

This does not mean that financial statements in general are irrelevant. As discussed in previous questions (see #2), relevance should not be based on one statement but rather on the whole system of accounting reports. After all, the market reacted to a forecast of a number produced by that system. It is difficult to argue then that financial statements are irrelevant. Moreover, the detailed income statement will contain the components of earnings and may explain why earnings were disappointing (were gross margins too low, was selling expense too high, did research expense increase, did the tax rate rise, etc.). Taken together with the balance sheet (e.g. inventory levels) and cash flow statement (cash from operations) the statements may contain data that help the market forecast future earnings and cash flows. [At times, the market may first react to an earnings release in one direction, then reverse direction when details of the earnings report become available, casting new light on the results.]

G. Changes in production (and demand) ultimately affect profitability. Financial statements are useful in determining how such changes affect profitability. They provide information about a firm's operating and financial leverage, and provide a historical record of how previous changes in volume affected profitability.

10.{M} This question is based on the notion that, as there are market incentives to disclose financial data, market forces will result in rational managers providing such information.

Beaver's approach to this question is based on the concept of information as an economic good and explores three potential reasons why market forces alone will not provide the "sufficient" or "right amount" of information. The reasons offered attempt to explain why market forces by themselves do not result in the "appropriate" amount of information being produced.

These reasons, however, do not necessarily mean that levels of disclosure mandated by regulation result in an optimal amount of information production and disclosure. Beaver's three reasons follow:

(1) An economic commodity will be produced so long as the benefits from the commodity outweigh its production cost (marginal cost equal marginal benefits). This holds so long as those who benefit from a good also bear its cost. Information, however, is a *public good*. Access to it cannot be [and perhaps should not (see (2) below)] be limited. Thus, there will be some who benefit from disclosure without having to pay for it. Two examples are given:

   (i) Competing firms who obtain information from annual reports without bearing the cost of information production; and

   (ii) Investors who, based on the information provided, decide *not* to invest in the company. They obtain the benefit without paying any of the cost.

   This so-called *free rider problem* reduces the incentive to disclose, as those bearing the cost are not fully compensated.

(2) The second reason is usually couched in terms of equity or fairness. Without regulation, there may be selective disclosure and uneven distribution of information. Some investors will be better informed than others.[3] Regulation is needed to "protect" the uninformed from the informed.

(3) There exists *information asymmetry* as managers are better informed about the firm than investors.

---

[3]One can debate, as does Beaver, whether this is inherently unfair. Presumably, those who are better informed have paid for more information. The only thing stopping others from becoming as well informed is their unwillingness to pay (or lack of funds). This may be unfortunate but, as with any other good, it is a fact of life. Should all goods be distributed equally? Certainly some have put forth this argument. Its ramifications are clearly beyond the scope of this text.

Moreover, managers have incentives to suppress (unfavorable) information. As investors know that some firms suppress information but do not know which firms are doing so, they will treat all firms in some "average" fashion. Hence, poorer performing (below average) firms will be priced "too high" and better (above average) firms will be priced "too low". Poorer (better) performing firms will want to offer more (fewer) shares to investors as a result. To combat this, managers of better performing firms may offer warranties on their information (audited statements) and other guarantees to investors to distinguish themselves. The result may be that managers of "better" firms absorb too much risk leading to an inefficient sharing of risk in the economy. Regulation is designed to mitigate this information asymmetry.

11.{S} A. The actual reserve additions should not result in any market reaction, assuming that the market knew about the potential losses. However, the rule change itself could cause market reaction, not so much from the actual requirement to recognize losses, but from the associated *requirement that increased the level of required reserves.* This tightening up would increase the risk of a firm becoming "technically insolvent".

B. This article would probably not result in any market reaction. Any reaction (as described in part A) would occur at the time of the announcement of the rule change itself.

C. Positive accounting theory views a firm and its environment as consisting of a "nexus of contracts". The terms of these contracts, in many cases, are determined by accounting based numbers. RAP rules are a perfect example of this concept. Regulators set the rules for the contract between the firm and its environment. RAP rules determine not only the amount of profits that regulators (the environment) allow the firm to report but also the terms (net worth requirements) permitting the firm to operate at all.

12.{S} *The arguments summarized below are based on Christopher Farrell "The 'Efficient Market' was a Good Idea - and Then Came the Crash", Business Week (February 22, 1988), page 140.*

More than ten years after the October 1987 market "crash", there is considerable divergence of opinion regarding the implications of that crash for the Efficient Market Theory (EMT). Detractors of the EMT cite the crash as evidence that the theory is not a good description of financial markets. They argue that there was no significant news prior to the crash, certainly not sufficient news to justify a 25% decline in New York Stock Exchange prices. The market reacted, they contend, to sharp declines experienced the previous two days. Thus panic set in, there was no rationality and a herd instinct took over.

Defenders of the EMT, on the other hand, say that the crash does not invalidate the EMT. Market volatility had increased in the weeks prior to the crash. Then when a sell-of began, the exchanges broke down. The computers could not keep up with the flow of orders and specialists panicked. Thus, institutional factors helped turn a normal decline into a panic.

Chapter 6 - Solutions

Overview:
Problem Length   Problem #s
  {S}   *1-3, 8-9, 13, 15-18, and 20-21*
  {M}   *4-5, 12, 14, 19, and 22-23*
  {L}   *6, 7, 10, and 11*

1.{S}A.   Start with the basic inventory relationship

$$BI + P = COGS + EI$$

Opening inventory	400 units @ $20	$ 8,000
Purchases	1,000	25,000
Total	1,400 units	$33,000

(i)   Under FIFO, ending inventory consists of 600 units:

100 purchased in second quarter at $24	$2,400
300 purchased in third quarter at $26	7,800
200 purchased in fourth quarter at $28	5,600
600 units total	$15,800

(ii) Under LIFO, ending inventory consists of 600 units:

400 inventory at January 1 at $20	$8,000
200 purchased in first quarter at $22	4,400
600 units total	$12,400

(iii) Under average cost, ending inventory consists of 600 units with an average cost of $33,000/1,400 = $23.5714 per unit or $14,142.84 total.

B.   COGS for the year equals the $33,000 total of opening inventory plus purchases, less closing inventory under the method chosen:

(i)   FIFO: $33,000 less $15,800 = $17,200
(ii) LIFO: $33,000 less $12,400 = $20,600
(iii) Average cost: $33,000 less $14,142.84 = $18,857.16

C.   (i)   Reported income is highest under FIFO (lowest COGS) and lowest under LIFO (highest COGS). Average cost is in between FIFO and LIFO.

      (ii) Stockholders' equity is highest under FIFO (highest inventory and retained earnings) and lowest under LIFO (lowest inventory and retained earnings), with average cost in between.

2.{S}(i)   Net income is lower under LIFO than under FIFO because cost-of-goods-sold is higher.

(ii) Cash from operations is higher under LIFO than under FIFO because income tax paid is lower.

(iii) Inventory balances are lower under LIFO than under FIFO because cost-of-goods-sold is higher.

(iv) Working capital is lower under LIFO than under FIFO because inventory balances are lower, despite partial offset from higher cash balances (because of lower tax payments).

(v)   Cost-of-goods-sold is higher and inventory balances lower under LIFO than under FIFO. Both factors increase the inventory turnover ratio.

3.{S}Using FIFO instead of LIFO when prices are rising has the following effects:

(i)   Gross profit margins are higher under FIFO than under LIFO because revenues at higher current prices are matched with cost-of-goods-sold measured using older (lower) prices.

(ii) Inventory turnover is lower under FIFO than under LIFO because cost-of-goods-sold is lower and inventory balances higher. Both factors decrease the inventory turnover ratio.

(iii) The debt-to-equity ratio is lower under FIFO than under LIFO because equity is higher, reflecting higher retained earnings.

4.{M}A.   Start with the basic inventory relationship

$$BI + P = COGS + EI$$

Since opening inventory is zero, both BI and P (purchases) are identical under FIFO and LIFO; the difference in COGS equals the difference in ending inventory. That difference can be computed as follows:

Total purchases in units = (3 x 100,000) + (3 x 125,000) + (3 x 150,000) + (3 x 200,000) = 1,725,000

Total sales in units = (6 x 100,000) + (6 x 150,000)
= 1,500,000.

Therefore units in ending inventory =
1,725,000 - 1,500,000 = 225,000

(i) Purchases are identical; there is no difference between methods.

(ii) Closing inventory under FIFO uses the latest costs of $15; under LIFO uses the earliest costs of $25; the difference is $10/unit x 225,000 = $2,250,000 (LIFO higher).

(iii) COGS is $2,250,000 lower under LIFO, as the total of COGS and ending inventory is identical.

(iv) As a result of lower COGS, LIFO pretax income is $2,250,000 higher.

(v) Income tax expense is higher under LIFO by

.40 x $2,250,000 = $900,000

(vi) Net income is higher under LIFO by

.60 x $2,250,000 = $1,350,000

(vii) Since income tax is higher under LIFO, cash flow from operations is lower by $900,000 (assuming taxes paid in same year).

(viii) From (ii) ending inventory is higher by $2,250,000, but from (vii) cash is lower by $900,000. Therefore, LIFO working capital is higher by $2,250,000 - $900,000 = $1,350,000

The problem illustrates that, when prices are declining, LIFO results in higher inventory and higher net income than FIFO. This solution would, however, be modified in practice as all inventory must be reported at the lower of cost or market. Thus inventory would have to be written down to market value for financial reporting purposes (but not for tax).

B. If all inventory units were liquidated, FIFO and LIFO would be identical in all respects.

5.{M}We start by computing total inventory available for sale, using the second part of the identity BI + P = COGS + EI. Using the average cost amounts provided, the total must be $10,500 + $3,500 = $14,000. We also know that Metro purchased:

On February 1, 1,000 units @ $2 $ 2,000
On April 1, 2,800 units @ $3   8,400
Total $10,400

We can now infer that the August 1 purchase must be for $3,600 ($14,000 less $10,400).

A.   The unit price for the August 1 purchase must be $3,600/1,000 = **$3.60**.

B.   First, we need to determine the number of units in ending inventory. From the average cost data, 25% of costs ($3,500/$14,000) remain, implying 25% of the 4,800 units purchased. Thus 1,200 units remain in ending inventory.

     [Alternate solution: as the average cost is $2.9167, 3,600 units ($10,500/$2.9167 were sold.]

     Under LIFO, these 1,200 units must be those *first* purchased:

     1,000 units purchased February 1 @ $2 $2,000
       200 units purchased April 1 @ $3   600
     1,200 total $2,600

     Therefore COGS must be $14,000 less $2,600 = **$11,400**

     Under FIFO, these 1,200 units must be those *last* purchased:

     1,000 units purchased August 1 @ $3.60 $3,600
       200 units purchased April 1 @ $3   600
     1,200 total $4,200

     Therefore COGS must be $14,000 less $4,200 = **$9,800**

6.{L}A.   This problem tests the interrelationships among accounting methods and differentiates between the flow of units and the flow of costs. Keep in mind that some factors are affected by the choice of accounting method but others are not.

Opening inventory (in this problem), purchases, and actual inventory turnover are not a function of accounting method. *Actual* turnover is based on units while *reported* turnover is based on dollars and is affected by the choice of accounting method. Thus the accounting method can only approximate the actual turnover.

Opening inventory is $500 for all methods. Since the firm replenishes inventory every month, its *actual* inventory turnover is 12. Thus, in units, its cost of goods sold is 12 times its inventory level. That is, 12 months of inventory were sold; one month remains.

The solution begins with the weighted average method:

Cost-of-goods sold = units sold x average cost = $12,000

As closing inventory = units in inventory x average cost, and, units sold are 12 times units in inventory; then closing inventory equals $1,000.

We can now solve for purchases:
Opening Inventory + Purchases = COGS + Closing Inventory
    $500   +   ?   = $12,000 + $1,000

Therefore, purchases equal $12,500.

Reported turnover = COGS/Average Inventory = $12,000/$750 = 16.

Under the LIFO method:

Since inventory in units does not change:

Closing Inventory = Opening Inventory = $500

Therefore, Cost of Goods Sold = Purchases = $12,500

Reported turnover = COGS/Average Inventory = $12,500/$500 = 25.

Under the FIFO method:

First, note that under the weighted average method, closing inventory is greater than opening inventory. As cost changes were only in one direction, they must have gone up during the year. Therefore, use of FIFO must result in higher net income (lower COGS) and higher income taxes. Since the cash flow difference is $400 (all attributable to taxes), the income/COGS difference must be $1000. Therefore, $COGS_{FIFO}$ is $11,500 and Closing Inventory is $1,500.

Reported turnover = COGS/Average Inventory = $11,500/$1,000 = 11.5.

The completed table is:

	FIFO	Weighted Average	LIFO
Opening Inventory	$ 500	$ 500	$ 500
Purchases	12,500	12,500	12,500
Cost of Goods Sold	11,500	12,000	12,500
Closing Inventory	1,500	1,000	500
Inventory Turnover (Reported)	11.5X	16.0X	25.0X
Inventory Turnover (Actual)	12.0X	12.0X	12.0X

B. Reported turnover under the FIFO method most closely approximates the actual physical turnover whereas LIFO is farthest away. It is interesting to note that the weighted average method, using COGS/closing inventory (rather than average inventory) yields the actual turnover of 12.

C. The choice of method affects reported income, income taxes paid, and (therefore) the change in cash. The LIFO method reports the lowest net income but highest cash flow from operations (because of lower tax payments). Neither cash for investment nor cash for financing are affected. Thus LIFO reports the highest net cash flow. The FIFO method reports the lower cash from operations and, therefore, the lowest net cash flow. The average cost method is halfway between the other two methods.

7.{L}A.   The first step is to obtain FIFO cost-of-goods-sold:

Pretax income = sales - COGS - other expenses

$5,000 = $25,000 - COGS - $12,000

Solving: COGS = $8,000

Purchases are equal to COGS + Closing Inventory
= $8,000 + $10,000 = $18,000.

The key to this problem is to distinguish between the flow of units and the flow of costs. Purchases are independent of the accounting method used.

Since half the units were sold, half remain in inventory. Under LIFO, therefore, the cost allocations to inventory and COGS are the reverse of those allocated under FIFO. That is, under LIFO, COGS = $10,000 and Closing Inventory = $8,000.

Under the weighted average method, as total purchases equal $18,000, the allocation between COGS and closing inventory will be equal: COGS = Closing Inventory = $9,000.

The rest of the table can now be filled in by recalling that pretax CFO depends on purchases, not COGS.

	FIFO	Weighted Average	LIFO
Sales	$25,000	$25,000	$25,000
Cost of Goods Sold	8,000	9,000	10,000
Other Expenses	12,000	12,000	12,000
Pretax Income	5,000	4,000	3,000
Tax Expense	2,000	1,600	1,200
Net Income	3,000	2,400	1,800
Retained Earnings	3,000	2,400	1,800
Cash from Operations[1]	(7,000)	(6,600)	(6,200)
Cash Balance[2]	3,000	3,400	3,800
Closing Inventory	10,000	9,000	8,000
Purchases	18,000	18,000	18,000

[1] Cash from Operations = Sales - Other Expenses - Purchases - Tax Expense.
[2] Cash Balance = $10,000 + Cash from Operations

B.   M & J Company
     Balance Sheet, December 31, 19X0

	FIFO	Weighted Average	LIFO
Cash	$ 3,000	$ 3,400	$ 3,800
Inventory	10,000	9,000	8,000
Total Assets	$ 13,000	$ 12,400	$ 11,800
Common Stock	$ 10,000	$ 10,000	$ 10,000
Retained Earnings	3,000	2,400	1,800
Total Equities	$ 13,000	$ 12,400	$ 11,800

C.   The advantages of LIFO are that it results in the highest
cash flow (by reducing income taxes) and it best measures
net income by matching the cost of sales with most recent
costs to replace inventory sold. The disadvantage of LIFO
is that inventory on the balance sheet is understated.
     The advantage of FIFO is that inventory is measured
at most recent costs. Its disadvantages are the reduced
cash flow and overstatement of reported income.
     Average cost has the disadvantage of misreporting
both the balance sheet inventory and net income. Income
taxes are higher than under the LIFO method (but lower
than under FIFO). The "advantage" of average cost is that
it is "less wrong" than LIFO on the balance sheet and
"less wrong" than FIFO on the income statement.

8.{S}(i) Ending inventory:

   FIFO: $39 + $43 = $82   LIFO: $35 + $39 = $74

(ii) Gross profit:

   FIFO: $65 - $35 = $30   LIFO: $65 - $43 = $22

(iii)Unrealized holding gain equals replacement cost minus
     ending inventory:

   FIFO: (2 x $46) - $82 = $10   LIFO: (2 x $46) - $74 = $18

(iv) Comprehensive income = gross profit + unrealized holding
     gain:

   FIFO: $30 + $10 = $40   LIFO: $22 + $18 = $40

The two are identical. As comprehensive income measures total changes in economic well being it is independent of the accounting method and must, by definition, be equal for all methods.

9.{S}A. The number of units in inventory at December 31, 1994 = 475 (100 + 500 - 125). Total purchases equal $25,000 ($4,400 + $8,600 + $12,000). How that amount is allocated between ending inventory and cost-of-goods-sold (COGS) depends on the inventory method.

(i)	FIFO cost equals:	175 units @ $43	$ 7,525
		300 units @ $40	12,000
	Total cost	475 units	$19,525
(ii)	LIFO cost equals:	100 units @ $44	$ 4,400
		200 units @ $43	8,600
		175 units @ $40	7,000
	Total cost	475 units	$20,000

B. Cost of goods sold equals purchases less ending inventory:

FIFO: $25,000 - $19,525 = $5,475

LIFO: $25,000 - $20,000 = $5,000

Therefore, FIFO pretax income is $475 lower and income taxes are lower by $190 (40% of $475).

C. As the market price is now $40, the lower of cost or market (LOCOM) rule applies, and inventory with a cost exceeding $19,000 ($40 x 475) must be written down to that amount.

(i) FIFO: Inventory must be written down by $525, increasing COGS, decreasing pretax income and income taxes.

(ii) LIFO: Inventory must be written down by $1,000, increasing COGS. But as LOCOM writedowns are not permitted for tax purposes when LIFO is used, income taxes are not affected by the writedown.

10.{L}A. Adjusting Zenab to FIFO:

Since the LIFO reserve increased by $1,500, the LIFO effect is $1,500. Under FIFO, COGS is $1,500 lower at $59,800 ($61,300 - $1,500). Pretax income is $1,500 higher at $6,500.

A comparison of both companies on a FIFO basis is presented below:

	Zenab	Faybech
Sales	$ 92,700	$ 77,000
Cost of goods sold	59,800	52,000
Gross profit	$ 32,900	$ 25,000
Selling and general expense	26,400	21,500
Pretax income	$ 6,500	$ 3,500

B. Adjusting Faybech to LIFO/Current Cost is more complicated. The first step is to calculate an implied inflation rate using Zenab's statements. On a FIFO basis, Zenab's inventories are $24,900 + $3,600 = $28,500 at the beginning of the year. Of that inventory, 70% or $19,950 (.70 x $28,850) are carried on LIFO. The increase in the LIFO reserve implies a specific inflation rate of $1,500/$19,950 = 7.52%. Therefore, Faybech's COGS (pretax income) on an LIFO/current cost basis increases (decreases) by .0752 x $22,300 = $1,675. This decrease in pretax income is close to 50%.

A comparison of both companies on a LIFO basis is presented below:

	Zenab	Faybech
Sales	$ 92,700	$ 77,000
Cost of goods sold	61,300	53,675
Gross profit	$ 31,400	$ 23,325
Selling and general expense	26,400	21,500
Pretax income	$ 5,000	$ 1,825

Note that this solution is incomplete as Faybech is 100% on LIFO while Zenab is only 70% on LIFO. To complete the solution, convert the remaining 30% of Zenab's inventories to LIFO using the same inflation rate:

Thirty percent (30%) of Zenab inventory is FIFO (.30 x $28,500) or $8,550. Applying the same inflation rate of 7.52% increases COGS (reduces pretax income) by $643. The comparison now becomes:

	Zenab	Faybech
Sales	$ 92,700	$ 77,000
Cost of goods sold	61,943	53,675
Gross profit	$ 30,757	$ 23,325
Selling and general expense	26,400	21,500
Pretax income	$ 4,357	$ 1,825

C. It depends on the purpose of the comparison. There are three possibilities:

(1) Comparison of firms' operations.
(2) Comparison of firms' operations and tax policy.
(3) Analysis of firm's "economic" status.

If the purpose is a comparison of a firm's operations with another firm's, then the adjustment should be "as if" and a tax adjustment should be made. If the purpose is to compare operations and tax policy, then no tax adjustment should be made. Finally, for evaluation of the economic status no tax adjustment should be made unless liquidation is considered to be imminent.

11.{L}A.

Year	Zenab (LIFO) 19X5	Zenab (LIFO) 19X6	Faybech (FIFO) 19X5	Faybech (FIFO) 19X6
Current ratio	2.89	2.65	3.24	3.24
Inventory turnover		2.45		1.98
Gross profit margin		.339		.32
Pretax income/sales		.054		.045

B. Faybech's liquidity (as measured by the current ratio) appears to be better. Its inventory turnover is lower, however, implying lower efficiency. Faybech appears to be slightly less profitable as well.

C. (i) Using the FIFO income statements from problem 10, we compute the following ratios:

Year	Zenab (FIFO) 19X5	19X6	Faybech (FIFO) 19X5	19X6
Current ratio[1]	3.20	3.04	3.24	3.68
Inventory turnover[2]		2.03		1.98
Gross profit margin		.355		.32
Pretax income/sales		.070		.045

[1] 19X5 = ($33,500 + $3,600)/$11,600
     19X6 = ($33,600 + $5,100)/$12,700

[2] $$\frac{\$59,800}{(\$25,200 + \$5,100 + \$24,900 + \$3,600)/2}$$

(ii) Using the LIFO income statements from problem 10 (using the Zenab statement after conversion to 100% LIFO), we compute the following profitability ratios:

Year	Zenab (100% LIFO) 19X6	Faybech (LIFO) 19X6
Gross profit margin	.332	.303
Pretax income/sales	.047	.024

Balance sheet adjustments are not possible for Faybech and the 30% of Zenab inventories on FIFO. Thus adjusted current and inventory turnover ratios cannot be computed.

(iii) The current cost method of computing the inventory turnover ratio uses the FIFO measure of inventory and the LIFO measure of COGS. The ratios are:

	Zenab	Faybech
LIFO cost of goods sold	$61,943	$53,675
FIFO average inventory	29,400	26,300
Inventory turnover ratio	2.11X	2.04X

D. Balance sheet values are most meaningful when FIFO is used. For the income statement, however, LIFO should be used. Therefore for the current ratio, we use the FIFO amounts. For the gross profit margin, and pretax/sales we use the 100% LIFO amounts. For the inventory turnover ratio, the current cost approach is preferred. However that ratio and the FIFO based ratio are similar in this case:

| | Zenab | | Faybech | |
Year	19X5	19X6	19X5	19X6
FIFO current ratio	3.20	3.04	3.24	3.68
FIFO inventory turnover Current cost turnover		2.03 2.11		1.98 2.04
LIFO gross profit margin LIFO pretax income/sales		.332 .047		.303 .024

Notice that, based on these ratios, Zenab is clearly more profitable than Faybech. The inventory turnover ratios are, however, virtually identical. While Faybech still has a higher current ratio, the difference is smaller than it appears based on the reported balance sheet data.

12.[M]A. The LIFO Reserve increased by $4,000. If the company used FIFO, its pretax income would be $4,000 higher. After-tax income would be higher by .65 x $4,000 = $2,600.

B. Inventory turnover is COGS/average inventory:

LIFO $3,800,000/[.5($748,000 + $696,800)] = 5.26X
FIFO $3,796,000/[.5($794,000 + $746,800)] = 4.93X

C. Since the firm's ROE is 4.6% and net income is $340,000, then average equity = $340,000/.046 = $7,391,304

If the company used FIFO, equity would be higher by the amount of the LIFO reserve adjusted for taxes. The average LIFO reserve is $48,000. Therefore, average equity should be higher by $48,000 or $31,200 (.65 x $48,000) aftertax.

FIFO average equity = $7,391,304 + $31,200 = $7,422,504
ROE_{FIFO} = $342,600/$7,422,504 = 4.62%

The adjustment of ROE is insignificant in this case because the increase in the numerator (income) and denominator (equity) are proportionate.

D. There are two reasons to make adjustments for accounting methods:

1. To obtain a more accurate measure of the firm's operations
2. To facilitate comparisons of different firms on the same basis

For inventory turnover, the adjustment results in a more accurate measure of performance. However, the main purpose of the LIFO to FIFO adjustment is for comparative purposes. It enables the analyst to compare Zeta Corp. to other firms that use FIFO.

E. The current cost method (inventory and equity at FIFO, COGS and net income at LIFO) should be used for both inventory turnover and ROE. For inventory turnover, this method better approximates the actual (physical) turnover. The argument for ROE is that FIFO equity better reflects the Company's current value, while LIFO income reflects the current operating profit earned on that equity. For the Zeta Corporation, these adjustments offset. In some cases, however, the current cost method ratios are quite different.

13.[S]A. January 1, 19X3 inventory = $2,700,000 ($2,000,000 + $700,000).

B. To maintain its inventory balance at $2,700,000, Jofen would have had to increase its purchases by $1,000,000 ($700,000 + $300,000); $300,000 is the difference between the LIFO and FIFO inventory cost. The choice of inventory method does not affect purchases which reflect actual prices paid.

C. Ignoring taxes and any change in accounts payable, reported cash flow from operations increased by $1,000,000 due to lower purchases.

D. COGS should be increased by $300,000 to exclude the effect of the LIFO liquidation.

E. The LIFO liquidation is not an operating activity. Excluding that income makes net income more useful for evaluating operating performance (net income and cash from operations) and forecasting future performance.

14.{M}A. Inventory turnover equals cost-of-goods-sold/average inventory

	1992	1993	1994
(i) LIFO COGS	$28,389	$28,914	$$28,962
Average inventory	4,947.5	4,199	3,852
Turnover ratio	5.74	6.89	7.52
(ii) FIFO COGS	$28,185	$28,735	28,765
Average inventory	6,857.5	5,917.5	5,382.5
Turnover ratio	4.11	4.86	5.34

Note that COGS has been decreased for the FIFO calculation by the decline in LIFO reserve. GE's financial statements indicate that these declines are a combination of both LIFO liquidations and reserve declines (see chapter for the distinction). A better calculation would exclude the LIFO liquidation from the COGS adjustment. In this case, the effect is not material.

B. When sales is used instead of cost-of-goods-sold:

	1992	1993	1994
Revenues	$37,906	$37,777	$39,543
(i) LIFO Average inventory	4,947.5	4,199	3,852
Turnover ratio	7.66	9.00	10.27
(ii) FIFO Average inventory	$6,857.5	$5,917.5	$5,382.5
Turnover ratio	5.53	6.38	7.35

C. The ratios that are closest to the GE ratios are those derived from sales and average inventory at FIFO, shown in B (ii). [A member of GE's financial management confirmed that GE used sales as the numerator when calculating inventory turnover.]

D. The preferred measure of inventory turnover uses the current cost method:

COGS (LIFO)/Average inventory (FIFO)

As the turnover ratio is intended to measure the relationship between goods sold during the period and the stock of goods held for sale, COGS should be the numerator. Using sales in the denominator inflates the turnover ratio as sales always exceed COGS. In addition, when sales is the numerator, the ratio is affected when COGS fluctuates relative to sales.

COGS should be at LIFO to measure it at current cost.

FIFO inventory should be the denominator as LIFO inventory understates the inventory on hand. As discussed in the chapter, using LIFO inventory to compute turnover results in a ratio that is too high and that systematically increases over time.

Current cost method	1992	1993	1994
Turnover ratio	4.14	4.89	5.38

Under any measure, GE's turnover ratio increased over the 1992-1994 period. Management's chosen method shows a higher turnover ratio than the preferred method. Comparisons with other firms are misleading when turnover ratios are computed differently.

The point of this problem is that ratios reported by management cannot be used blindly (especially for comparisons with other firms). The analyst must determine how management calculates its ratios and ensure that those calculations accord with calculations made by other firms and, most important, by the analyst.

15.{S}A. ($ millions)

	1990	1991	Change
LIFO Inventory	$46,315	$40,844	$(5,471)
LIFO Reserve	7,882	3,619	(4,263)
FIFO Inventory	$54,197	$44,463	$(9,734)

Since the LIFO reserve dropped by $4,263, $COGS_{FIFO}$ would be higher (and pretax income lower) by $4,263 million.

B. The decline would have been $9,734 million rather than the $5,471 million reported (see above table).

C. Newsprint and magazine paper prices declined during 1991. These declines would reduce inventory at FIFO and the LIFO reserve (the difference between inventory at FIFO and inventory at LIFO) but would not reduce inventory at LIFO.

   The most likely explanation is that the firm sold a segment or a portion of a segment, eliminating related inventory.

16.{S}The last sentence in the statement is patently absurd. The accounting method for inventory should have nothing to do with a company's pricing strategy. Pricing should be based on current market conditions. Companies that ignore the cost of replacing inventory when setting prices will suffer from poor cash flows and, in some cases, will fail.

17.{S}A. The 1990 inventory decline can be explained by:

    (i)   Price decreases despite unit inventories that are steady or even increasing

    (ii) Production cutbacks due to poor demand; this would not explain the work in process increase

    (iii) Depleted inventory levels due to excess demand. This is consistent with lower finished goods but higher work in process as the company increases production as a result of higher sales.

B. Any one of these reasons reduces the desirability of LIFO. Declining prices and potential inventory liquidations lessen the tax advantages of LIFO.

C. For new products, startup expenses are reduced; subsequent cost-of-goods-sold is increased as the capitalized costs are amortized. The net effect depends on the timing of new product introductions.

18.{S}A. For service companies, inventory is an insignificant component of assets and COGS an insignificant cost. The main inputs of service companies are capacity and people. Thus inventory turnover is not a useful measure for such companies.

B. Capacity utilization is an important measure of operating efficiency for firms with fixed capacity. The fixed cost of such capacity means that utilization is an important determinant of profitability. An airline seat, rental car, or hospital bed that goes unused generates no revenue; the variable cost saved may be very low. This phenomenon explains why airlines sell discount tickets; as long as the marginal revenue exceeds the variable cost, such sales are profitable.

It is also important to measure costs in relation to either capacity or utilization. As revenues are subject to competitive and regulatory constraints, lower costs are important to profitability. Thus an airline's costs relative to available seat-miles (or to passenger revenue miles) measures the efficiency of its operations.

19.{M} Contracts can provide strong incentives that affect the choice of inventory method. However different contracts may provide incentives for different choices. The following discussion assumes rising prices.

The management compensation plan provides a mixed incentive. Use of LIFO reduces income but increases cash from operations. Assuming a tax rate t, and a LIFO effect L, net income decreases by $(1-t)L$ while cash from operations increases by tL. The net effect $(2t-1)L$ is positive only at tax rates above 50%. Thus management contracts argue against use of LIFO.

Bond covenants also argue against LIFO. Working capital is reduced by the LIFO reserve less taxes saved. The annual amount is $(t-1)L$ which is always negative. Retained earnings are also lower under LIFO.

Union employee profit sharing payments are lower under LIFO, assuming that profits would exceed the minimum level. This would seem to argue for LIFO, to reduce compensation paid.

However, there are also second and third order effects that must be considered. Lower profit sharing payments, for example, increase net income (and cash from operations), increasing management compensation and easing the effect of bond covenants. These effects require complex calculations and are highly firm-specific.

Some effects are non-quantitative. Lower profit sharing payments may result in higher wage demands from workers. For management, use of FIFO may raise questions about why they failed to obtain tax savings by using LIFO.

Thus, while we can identify many of the factors that motivate the choice of inventory method, the controller's choice will depend on how these factors affect Sechne; there is no simple answer.

20.{S}A. (i) Reported earnings are reduced by the obsolescence charges disclosed in the footnote.

(ii) Tax return earnings are unaffected by the obsolescence charges as the LIFO method of tax reporting does not permit such charges. While not disclosed by the company, we can assume that reported earnings reflect a deferred tax asset for the difference.

(iii) Cash from operations are also unaffected by the obsolescence charges. Inventory writedowns have no cash effect and, in this case, there is no income tax effect either.

B. The disadvantage to Monarch of using the LIFO method is that, when inventories are obsolete, there is no cash offset to the financial statement writedowns. Reported earnings and net worth (book value) are both reduced but cash flow is unaffected.

C. Changing to FIFO would allow Monarch to obtain the tax benefit of its inventory writedowns. But it would also have to pay tax on its (much larger) LIFO reserve. Thus, despite the answer to B, Monarch still derives a significant net benefit from using the LIFO method for tax reporting.

21.{S}A. Deere's gross margin percentage, using reported data:

	1991	1992	1993
Sales	$5,848	$5,723	$6,479
Gross margin	954	832	1,104
GM percentage	16.3%	14.5%	17.0%

B. Excluding the LIFO liquidation increases COGS and decreases gross margin by the same amounts:

	1991	1992	1993
Reported COGS	$4,894	$4,891	$5,375
LIFO liquidation	128	65	51
Adjusted COGS	$5,022	$4,956	$5,426
Adjusted gross margin	$826	$767	$1,053
Adjusted GM percentage	14.1%	13.4%	16.3%

Excluding the LIFO liquidation, the GM percentage still declines in 1992, and increases in 1993. However, the 1993 level using adjusted data exceeds that of 1991 by a much larger amount.

22.{M}A. To compute FIFO COGS, we must deduct the LIFO effect (change in LIFO reserve) for each year:

	1993	1994
LIFO (reported) COGS	$21,624	$21,977
LIFO effect	421	(53)
FIFO (adjusted) COGS	$22,045	$21,924

B. In 1993, there was a LIFO liquidation of $50 million that must be added back to reported COGS:

(i)   Reported COGS $21,624
      LIFO liquidation   50
      Adjusted LIFO COGS $21,674

(ii) No effect on FIFO COGS

C. Inventory purchases are derived from the identity:

$$BI + P = COGS + EI$$

Using reported data for 1993:

$$\$4,401 + P = \$21,624 + \$3,818$$

$$P = \$21,041$$

Similarly, for 1994:

$$\$3,818 + P = \$21,977 + \$3,969$$

$$P = \$22,128$$

D. To avoid a LIFO liquidation. duPont would have had to increase 1993 purchases by the sum of the reduction in inventory (at LIFO) and the LIFO liquidation:

$$(\$4,401 - \$3,818) + \$50 = \$ 633$$

Purchases required = $21,041 + $633 = **$21,674**

E. (i) Using reported data, with the 1993 LIFO liquidation excluded:

	1993	1994
Sales	$37,098	$39,333
COGS	21,674	21,977
Gross profit margin	$15,424	$17,356

(ii) Using the current cost method of computing inventory turnover:

	1993	1994
COGS	$21,674	$21,977
Average FIFO inventory	5,086	4,686
Turnover ratio	4.26	4.69

(iii) Comparing the change in LIFO reserve (excluding the liquidation effect) with the opening FIFO inventory:

	1993	1994
Opening FIFO inventory	$5,588	$4,584
Change in LIFO reserve	(371)	53
% change in price level	- 6.6 %	1.2 %

F. The LIFO reserve at each year end should be added to stated book value to restate inventories to current cost. As it is unlikely that this reserve will ever be taxed, no tax adjustment is required. Exhibit 17-1 in the text shows this and other adjustments to duPont's book value.

23.{M}A.   (All data in $ thousands)

	1990	1991
FIFO Inventory	$11,480	$16,141
LIFO Inventory	7,166	10,491
LIFO Reserve	$4,314	$ 5,650

The LIFO reserve increased by $5,650 - $4,314 = $1,336. On the opening current cost (FIFO) inventory of $11,480, the price level increase is $1,336/$11,480 = 11.6%.

B. The price level increase calculated from the Commodity Price Index is (134.3/126.8) - 1 = 5.9%. Even at its highest point (July) the rate of (136.9/126.8) - 1 = 7.96% is still below the inflation rate for Pope & Talbot computed in part A.

C. The calculation in part A assumes that the increase in the LIFO Reserve was all due to the effect of price changes on opening inventory. The company increased its inventory during 1991 and, therefore, part of the increased LIFO reserve is due to the added layer for the current year. As a result, the part A calculation is overstated. However, even if the inventory increase was early in the year (resulting in the largest 1991 LIFO effect) this factor explains less than half of the difference between the rates calculated in parts A and B.

D. The mostly likely explanation for the different estimates is that Pope and Talbot's product mix differs from that used to compute the Lumber and Wood Products Index. That index may, for example, include products at a more advanced stage of processing whose prices rose less rapidly than the prices of raw materials. Such products would include costs that change little over time, diluting the effect of increases in lumber prices.

The lesson here is that, when commodity prices are used to estimate the effect of price changes on company inventories, care must be taken to ensure that product mixes between index and inventories are similar.

Case 6-1 Solution

Estimated solution time: three hours
Note: The calculations required for this case are shown in Exhibit 6CS-1, and appear in question order. The calculations are explained in the solution. All data are in $thousands.

1. Gross margin equals sales less cost-of-products-sold (COPS). The adjusted COPS is derived by reducing the reported amount by the change in the LIFO reserve during the year. As the LIFO reserve declined in 1991 and 1992 (due to declining prices), FIFO COPS exceeds LIFO COPS for those years.

2. Over the 1990-1995 period, gross margins rose, declining only in 1991. GM as a percent of sales also rose over the period, despite a significant decline in 1991 and a marginal decline in 1995.

   Adjusted (to FIFO) gross margins also rose substantially over the period. Adjusted GM are more volatile relative to sales than the reported amounts, as price changes magnify operating changes. Not surprisingly, prices rose in periods of strong demand growth (and profitability). The contrast between reported and adjusted amounts is particularly striking in 1991 vs. 1990 (the FIFO decline is much higher) and 1993 versus 1992 (the FIFO increase is much higher). The exclusion of price effects under LIFO affects profitability trends.

3. The adjustment to gross margins must be carried down to pretax income, and then to net income. The final step, multiplying the pretax adjustment by $(1-t)$, requires the marginal tax rate t, provided in Exhibit 6C-1.

   The net income (and earnings per share) trends are similar to those of gross margins. The reported (LIFO) amounts are lower in all years except 1991 and 1992, and are more stable as they exclude the price effects. The reported EPS show a slightly higher growth rate.

4. The effect of LIFO on cash from operations (CFO) is the tax effect, equal to the LIFO effect (change in LIFO reserve) multiplied by the tax rate t. When the cash effect is removed, FIFO CFO is lower in all years except 1991 and 1992 (when prices declined).

   Over the entire six year period, the LIFO reserve increased $50 million, resulting in tax savings of approximately $17 million. The year-to-year changes in CFO are significantly affected, especially 1991 versus 1990 and 1993 versus 1992.

Case 6CS-1. INVENTORY ANALYSIS OF NUCOR, ADJUSTMENT FROM LIFO TO FIFO
Years Ended December 31 (data in $millions)

		1989	1990	1991	1992	1993	1994	1995
	Sales		1,481,630	1,465,457	1,619,235	2,253,738	2,975,596	3,462,046
	COPS		1,293,083	1,302,744	1,417,376	1,965,847	2,491,760	2,900,168
1	Reported gross margin		188,547	162,713	201,859	287,891	483,836	561,878
1	% of sales		12.7%	11.1%	12.5%	12.8%	16.3%	16.2%
	Pretax income		111,215	95,816	117,326	187,110	356,933	432,335
	Net income		75,065	64,716	79,226	123,510	226,633	274,535
	Earnings per share		$ 0.88	$ 0.75	$ 0.92	$ 1.42	$ 2.60	$ 3.14
	Change in LIFO reserve		7,180	(13,695)	(7,577)	37,497	14,534	12,270
	Adjusted COPS		1,285,903	1,316,439	1,424,953	1,928,350	2,477,226	2,887,898
1	Adjusted GM		195,727	149,018	194,282	325,388	498,370	574,148
1	% of sales		13.2%	10.2%	12.0%	14.4%	16.7%	16.6%
	Adjusted pretax		118,395	82,121	109,749	224,607	371,467	444,605
	Tax rate		34%	34%	34%	35%	35%	35%
3	Adjusted net income		79,804	55,677	74,225	147,883	236,080	282,511
	Adjusted EPS		$ 0.94	$ 0.65	$ 0.86	$ 1.70	$ 2.71	$ 3.23
	Cash from operations		214,330	173,396	205,409	271,793	424,946	447,160
	Tax effect of LIFO		2,441	(4,656)	(2,576)	13,124	5,087	4,295
4	FIFO CFO		211,889	178,052	207,985	258,669	419,859	442,866

LIFO inventory	139,450	136,644	186,075	206,405	214,015	243,027	306,773
LIFO reserve	43,723	50,903	37,208	29,631	67,128	81,662	93,932
FIFO inventory	183,173	187,547	223,283	236,036	281,143	324,689	400,705
Stockholders' equity	584,445	652,757	711,609	784,231	902,167	1,122,610	1,382,112
LIFO reserve	43,723	50,903	37,208	29,631	67,128	81,662	93,932
Adjusted equity	628,168	703,660	748,817	813,862	969,295	1,204,272	1,476,044
Book value per share	$ 6.83	$ 7.59	$ 8.23	$ 9.04	$ 10.36	$ 12.85	$ 15.78
5 Adjusted BVPS	7.34	8.18	8.66	9.38	11.13	13.78	16.85
Current assets		312,637	334,293	381,517	468,232	638,701	638,701
Current liabilities		202,789	229,166	271,972	350,491	382,465	382,465
Working capital		109,848	105,127	109,545	117,741	256,236	256,236
6 Current ratio		1.54	1.46	1.40	1.34	1.67	1.67
Adjusted CA		363,540	371,501	411,148	535,360	720,363	732,633
Adjusted WC		160,751	142,335	139,176	184,869	337,898	350,168
6 Adjusted CR		1.79	1.62	1.51	1.53	1.88	1.92
6 Return on equity		12.1%	9.5%	10.6%	14.6%	22.4%	21.9%
6 Adjusted ROE		12.0%	7.7%	9.5%	16.6%	21.7%	21.1%
7 LIFO turnover		9.37	8.07	7.22	9.35	10.90	10.55
7 FIFO turnover		6.94	6.41	6.20	7.46	8.18	7.96
7 CC turnover		6.98	6.34	6.17	7.60	8.23	8.00

5.   The adjustment to Nucor's book value per share (BVPS) is simply the LIFO reserve. As elsewhere in the text and problems, we make this adjustment pretax as there is little possibility that the LIFO reserve will be liquidated. (Nucor's rapid sales growth reduces this likelihood further.) The adjusted BVPS is computed using the same number of shares Nucor uses to report (unadjusted) BVPS.

     The adjustment increases BVPS each year, although the percentage adjustment is lower for years when the LIFO reserve declines. The adjustment slightly reduces the growth rate of BVPS (using 1990 as the base year). Given the variability of the LIFO reserve, the effect on BVPS varies with the choice of base and ending years.

6.   LIFO reduces the carrying value of inventory, lowering working capital and the current ratio. The adjusted amounts are, therefore, higher as the LIFO reserve is added (pretax) to current assets. The adjusted current ratio is always higher.

     The adjusted amounts are, however, more volatile, as they include the effect of price changes on Nucor's inventory. Note the greater 1991 and 1992 declines in the adjusted current ratio (prices fell, reducing the adjustment). In 1993, when prices rose, the reported current ratio fell but the adjusted ratio increased.

     LIFO also affects return on equity. Adjustments to FIFO always increase the denominator (equity); the effect on return (net income) varies. The most striking differences are in the period 1991 to 1993. In 1991 and 1992, when prices declined, the adjusted ROE is significantly lower; the effect reverses in 1993.

7.   The inventory turnover ratios calculated in exhibit 6CS-1 vary, as expected, with the inventory method. The LIFO ratios are always higher as the ratio denominator (average inventory) is understated by the LIFO reserve. The FIFO and current cost ratios are similar, as discussed in the text.

     The current cost method, using LIFO COPS in the numerator and FIFO inventory in the denominator, is the best measure of economic turnover. By this measure, Nucor's inventory turnover improved over the 1991 to 1995 period, rising from 6.98 to 8.00. While both inventory and COPS increased, reflecting Nucor's rapid sales growth, the inventory growth rate was slightly lower. As discussed in the chapter (see Economic order quantity on page 278), inventory turnover can be expected to increase as volume increases. As Nucor has grown by building new plants as well as expanding existing ones, the effect should be smaller than if all growth came from existing facilities.

8. The major advantages to Nucor of using the LIFO method are:

- Reduced volatility of reported gross margin and income (answers 2 and 3 above)
- Higher cash flow due to tax savings (answer 4)

The major disadvantages of the LIFO method are:

- Reduced reported income in most years (answer 3)
- Lower reported stockholders' equity (answer 5) Ratios that use equity (such as the debt-to-equity ratio) are understated.
- Lower current ratio (answer 6). Ratios that use total assets are also understated.

9. (a) Birmingham's ratios are:

Inventory turnover = $723,558/($132,459 + $173,053)/2 = 4.74

Gross profit margin = $885,553 - $723,558 = $161,995 or 18.3 % of sales

Gross margin return on average equity = $161,995/($439,049+$459,719)/2 = 36%

Inventory turnover is far lower than Nucor's reported ratio of 10.55.

Gross profit margin exceeds Nucor's 16.2%.
GMROE is far lower than Nucor's 45% ($561,878/$1,252,361)

(b) As prices rose during 1995, we should convert Birmingham's results to LIFO. We start by using Nucor data to estimate the inflation rate:

$$\frac{\text{Change in LIFO Reserve}}{\text{FIFO Opening Inventory}} = \frac{\$12,270}{\$324,689} = 3.8\%$$

Birmingham's 1995 LIFO effect is estimated by applying this percentage to its opening inventory:

3.8% x $132,459 = $5,033

Thus LIFO COGS is estimated at $723,558 + $5,033 = $728,591

Recomputing Birmingham's ratios:

Inventory turnover = $728,591/($132,459 + $173,053)/2 = 4.77 using the current cost method. Nucor's current cost ratio of 8.00 is still much higher, but the gap is smaller than when reported data are used.

Gross profit margin = $885,553 - $728,591 = $156,962 or 17.7 % of sales. While this ratio still exceeds Nucor's, the gap is smaller.

Gross margin return on average equity = $156,962/($439,049+$459,719)/2 = 34.9%.

Now the difference from Nucor's 45% ratio is even larger. However, we have not adjusted Birmingham's equity, as we do not have the data to compute the LIFO effect for prior years. Such an adjustment would reduce equity, increasing the gross margin return. Thus the ratios are still not comparable. We can, however, use adjusted (FIFO) equity to compare the firms, analogous to the current cost method of computing inventory turnover. This method effectively calculates ROE on a current cost basis for both firms:

Birmingham: $156,947   =   34.9%

                $449,384

Nucor: $561,878   =   41.9%

                $1,340,158

Nucor's gross margin ROE is still higher than Birmingham's. However, the difference is smaller.

This illustrates the difficulty of comparing firms using different inventory methods. Reported data cannot be compared without adjustment. Some adjustments can be made simply; others are difficult or impossible given lack of data. Some ingenuity may be required to obtain meaningful comparisons. Once reported data have been made comparable, the analyst can focus on real operating differences.

Chapter 7 Solutions

Overview:
Problem Length   *Problem #s*
   {S}   *1, 2, and 4*
   {M}   *3, 5, 6, 7, 8, and 10*
   {L}   *9*

1.{S}Effect of capitalizing versus expensing costs, for a firm
     growing at a variable growth rate, on:

   (i)   CFO: Capital expenditures are components of investing
         cash flows and never affect CFO. Firms that expense
         such outlays report them as operating cash flows.
         Therefore, CFO will be higher for the capitalizing firm
         and the cumulative difference will increase over time.

   (ii) ROA: Reported assets will be lower for the expensing
         firm as it has fewer recorded assets. The variable
         growth rate results in a volatile numerator for the
         expensing firm. Initially, ROA will be lower for the
         expensing firm, but eventually it will be higher than
         that reported by a capitalizing firm, as the
         denominator effect will dominate the ratio.

2.{S}Effect of capitalizing versus expensing costs on a firm's:

   (i)   Assets: Capitalizing increases reported assets. For a
         growing firm the balance will reflect a rising trend.

   (ii) Equity: Expensing firms report lower equity balances
         because they deduct all capital expenditures resulting
         in lower income and equity. Net assets or equity is
         lower as well since such firms record fewer assets.

3.{M}   (i)   Interest Payable

	Debt ($000s)	Interest Rate (%)	Interest ($000s)
Development loan	$ 6,000	11.0%	$ 660
Mortgage debt	10,000	9.0	900
Debentures	40,000	10.0	4,000
Interest Payable			$5,560

(ii) Capitalized Interest

	Debt ($000s)	Interest Rate (%)	Interest ($000s)
Development loan[1]	$ 6,000	11.0%	$ 660
Debentures[2]	4,000	10.0	400
Capitalized Interest			$1,060

[1] Development loan assumed to be related to the office building.
[2] Mortgage debt is assumed to be related to specific projects and the problem does not state that it is related to the office building; the remaining balance is assumed to be financed by debentures.

(iii) Interest expense =
Interest payable - capitalized interest
$5,560,000 - $ 1,060,000 = **$4,500,000**

B.   The coverage ratio should be based on interest payable, not on interest expense. The capitalization of interest is an accounting requirement and does not affect the leverage of the firm. Interest coverage should be computed as:

(Pretax income + interest expense) / (interest payable)

C.   Capitalization of interest reduces the comparability of the interest coverage ratio, CFO, and profitability ratios. Capitalization of interest improves all of these indicators for affected firms. Among the factors that affect capitalization are:

1. The availability of internally generated funds limits the firm's ability to capitalize interest; it can be capitalized *only* on external borrowings. Thus, a firm with excess cash and/or a lower debt/equity ratio will be able to capitalize less interest than a firm that must borrow, even if they are otherwise identical.

2. Firms with lower borrowing costs will be able to capitalize less interest than (riskier) firms that must pay higher interest rates.

3. Capitalized interest becomes part of the carrying amount of the asset and is amortized (depreciated) over time. Different firms may use different depreciation methods (accelerated versus straight-line) and lives (short or longer) for similar assets. Firms that use accelerated methods and shorter lives will report lower profitability (and interest coverage) in the years following the construction of the asset. Amortization does not, however, affect cash from operations as it is a noncash expense.

The computation of ratios and other performance measures should, therefore, be based on data that excludes the effect of capitalized interest. Such measures will reflect the actual leverage and cost of capital of the firm and will not be affected by the differences discussed above.

4.{S}A. The increase in pretax income equals interest capitalized less amortization of capitalized costs (S millions):

1987	1988	1989
$11 - $5 = $6	$16 - $7 = $9	$20 - $8 = $12

B. Increase in CFO (decrease in CFI) is equal to the amount of interest capitalized. Amortization has no impact on cash flow components.

	1987	1988	1989
Increase in CFO:	$11	$416	$20
Decrease in CFI:	11	416	20

C.   Times interest earned = EBIT / interest expense

As reported = ($251 + $39) / $39 = 7.44X
Adjusted   = ($239 + $59) / $59 = 5.05X

5.{M}
A.   Brand names are clearly an asset. However, it is not clear that these assets should be shown on corporate balance sheets.

One advantage of recognizing brand names on a firm's balance sheet is that it makes the balance sheet more complete; a balance sheet that ignores major firm assets is of limited use for analysis. Another advantage is that the cost of acquiring or developing a brand name should be recorded as an investment (asset) in order to properly match revenues and expenses.

The major disadvantage of brand name recognition is the difficulty of proper measurement. As each brand name is unique, market transactions are not available to value the brand. Thus, the value recognized is subjective; differences across firms may reflect either real differences in the value of the brands or different measurement decisions.

One approach involves capitalization of the acquisition cost (for purchased brands) or the advertising and other development costs (for internally developed brands). In the latter case, it is unlikely that the value of the brand will be equal to the cost of development. A successful brand will be worth much more than the cost of its development; an unsuccessful brand may have no value at all.

Further, the value of brands changes over time. Despite the quotation from Laing, brands can also become "dilapidated" if they are neglected, if the advertising is poor, or if the products are defective. The value of brands will also be affected by changes in market conditions, e.g., pricing decisions and the inroads made by generic products.

From the point of view of financial analysis, therefore, it is not clear that reporting management's estimate of brand value would be helpful. The "proof of the pudding is in the eating" and a valuable brand should be highly profitable. The evaluation of that profitability might be better left to the marketplace.

B.   The advantage of amortization is that the income statement should reflect all expenses that help produce income. If profitability is due to the brand name, the amortization of its acquisition cost should be an element of expense.

On the other hand, given the subjectivity of brand name valuation, the amortization amount (also affected by the choice of method and life) may be a poor measure of the expired cost. In addition, brand names may not decline in value over time; any decline is likely to be irregular.

For purposes of analysis, therefore, the amortization of brand name intangible assets should be excluded from income. The evaluation of profitability, however, should consider the role of brand names.

6.{M}A.
   (i)   The deferral of development costs increased pretax income by $4,710,000 in 1991 as these costs would otherwise have been included in operating expense.

   (ii)   The deferral of development costs increased cash from operations by $4,710,000. Cash outflows for investment were increased by the same amount. Net cash flow was unchanged.

   (iii) When the project becomes operational, the deferred costs will increase the depreciation or amortization of the investment in the project. If the commercial viability of the project becomes doubtful, the remaining, unamortized deferred costs will be written off and will reduce income in the year of the writeoff.

   (iv)   Future year cash flows will not be affected by the cost deferral. If the project is successful, depreciation will be a noncash expense; if the project is noncommercial, there will be a noncash writeoff. Thus, the decision to capitalize development costs shifts the expenditures from operating to investment cash flows; that shift will never be reversed.

B. (i)
The initial effect of the cost deferral is an increase in net income and, therefore, equity. The debt-to-equity ratio declines (improves).

The decline will be reversed gradually by amortization of the deferred costs and immediately if they are written off. Thus, the debt-to-equity ratio was reduced in 1991 but will, in future years, approach the ratio based on immediate expensing of the development costs.

(ii)
Return on assets increased in 1991 because of the cost deferral. Both profits and assets were increased by the same amount; the effect on profits had a greater effect on the ratio.

However, the cost deferral will tend to reduce the future trend of ROA. The higher asset level will reduce the ROA produced by any level of income. In addition, future amortization or writeoff of the deferred costs will reduce both income and assets, tending to depress ROA.

The deferral of development costs, therefore, improved both ratios for 1991 at the expense of future ratios.

7.{M}A. Income before extraordinary item and cumulative accounting change
= $2,770.0 - $1,720.5 = $1,049.5. ($ 000s)

B. The difference $ (8,449) - $ (9,280) = $ 781 ($000s) represents the amount applicable to prior years.

C. The 1991 cash outlay was not expensed, increasing income. This increase was partially offset by higher amortization of prior years' capitalized outlays.

D. CFO includes changes in costs under both methods.

E. $4,092 - $1,739 = $2,353 ($000s)
The $2,943 represents outlays made in 1991. The net increase of $2,353 consists of the 1991 outlays less amortization of previous years' outlays, that can be deduced as $590 ($2,943 - $2,353).

F. The increase in 1991 net income was $2,703,000, the sum of the 1991 increase of $1,720,500 and the cumulative effect of $983,000. The footnote shows $737,500 ($1,720,500 - $983,000) as it incorrectly subtracts the cumulative effect from the 1991 effect.

8. (M)
A. Neither the net change in cash nor cash from financing is affected by the switch in the accounting method; they remain at $6 and $(30) respectively. Successful efforts (SE) will report lower CFO balanced by lower cash outflows from investing than full costing (FC) as the outflow for dry holes is classified as operations not investment. FC will have higher amortization as the cost of dry holes is also amortized.

The effect on income depends on whether the decrease in dry hole expense for FC is offset by increased amortization. In Sonat's case, the decrease in expense of $21 ($382 -$361) is offset by higher amortization of $7 ($200 - $193) resulting in increased income of $14 which is approximately equal to the difference of $16 shown (All data in millions). (Note that Sonat restated 1990 results for discontinued operations and also reclassified some financial statement data making an exact reconciliation impossible.)

Therefore, the table should read ($ millions):

	SE	FC
Cash flow from operations	$ 361	$ 382
Cash flow from investing	(325)	(346)
Cash flow from financing	(30)	(30)
Net change in cash	$ 6	$ 6
Net income	$ 94	$ 110
Depreciation, depletion, & amortization	193	200

B. Decreases in the price of oil and gas may reduce the value of reserves to amounts below their carrying costs. FC (SE) firms must write down properties whose carrying costs exceeds the present value (undiscounted future cash flows) of the proved reserves. Note that the amortization of previously capitalized cost will decline. It is possible that Sonat wanted to avoid writedowns and was willing to accept lower and more volatile income under the less onerous SE method.

9.{L}A.   Exhibit 7S-1A depicts the oil and gas reserves by four geographic regions during the 1992 to 1994 period. Overall both oil and gas reserves have declined over the period with the latter falling more. Oil reserves would have fallen further without the 1992 and 1993 increases in reserves in Africa. With the exception of France (1992-94) and the rest of the world group in 1993, revisions have been positive. African reserves sport the longest, albeit declining lives. Both France and the rest of Europe show declining reserve lives.

Gas reserves show a significant decline in France over the 1992-1994 period. However, reserves in Africa jumped considerably in 1992. This increase arose equally from both revisions and discoveries. It also significantly affects the reserve life in 1992 relative to other years. Again, France and the rest of Europe report declining reserve lives.

In general, the firm reports declining oil and gas reserves. The exhibit shows increases in oil reserves in 1992 and 1993; gas reserves rose in 1992 only to decline in subsequent years. Reported BOE Equivalents increase through 1993 falling only in 1994. The firm's most significant increase in reserves has come from a purchase of an interest in a Nigerian property. The declines in reserves and the decrease in exploration and development activities reflect a decrease in investment in the oil and gas business.

B.   Finding costs for new reserves equal:

Total expenditures for exploration
BOE equivalent of reserves found

Computations for 1992 to 1994 are shown in exhibit 7S-1B. Finding costs are obtained from table 4 (page 360). We must be careful to exclude development costs as we are comparing the reserves found (both developed and undeveloped) with the costs of finding those reserves.

Reserves found are shown in tables 1(b), p. 358 (oil) and 2(b), p. 359 (gas). The gas total is converted to BOE using a ratio of 6:1 and then added to the oil total to compute BOE found.

The finding cost per BOE over the three year period is erratic, as might be expected, even for a large company like Elf. The low 1994 finding cost may well be due to luck; even the best firm varies in its success rate. The three year total is a better measure than any single year.

Exhibit 7S-1

Exhibit 7S-1A: Elf Aquitaine Reserve Analysis

	Oil Reserves (millions of barrels)					Reserve life in years		
	France	Rest of Europe	Africa	Rest of World	Total	France	Rest of Europe	Africa
1/1/92	68	690	1,655	34	2,447			
12/31/92	64	663	1,680	61	2,468	7.11	11.84	12.26
12/31/93	58	603	1,834	40	2,535	7.25	9.42	12.48
12/31/93	47	622	1,643	47	2,359	5.22	8.08	10.27

	Natural Gas Reserves (billions of cubic feet)					Reserve life in years		
1/1/92	1066	4,667	228	113	6,074			
12/31/92	879	4,568	796	84	6,327	8.45	14.93	88.44
12/31/93	801	4,297	783	89	5,970	7.49	13.30	60.23
12/31/93	665	4,256	698	96	5,715	6.52	12.06	43.63

Exhibit 7S-1B: Elf Aquitaine Finding Costs

Millions of FF	1992	1993	1994	Total
Property acquisition	602	3,326	1	3,929
Exploration	4,557	3,669	2,903	11,129
Total finding costs	**5,159**	**6,995**	**2,904**	**15,058**

Oil (millions of barrels)				
Extensions and discoveries	154	39	108	301
Reserve acquisitions	3	242	–	245
Total	157	281	108	546

Gas (BCF)				
Extensions and discoveries	432	42	362	836
Reserve acquisitions	33	7	–	40
Total	465	49	362	876
Gas (BOE)	78	8	60	146

	1992	1993	1994	Total
Total BOE	**235**	**289**	**168**	**692**
Finding cost/BOE (FF)	22.00	24.19	17.25	21.76

C. The year-to-year changes are shown in Table 7 (page 363) while the annual computations are shown in Table 6, p. 362.

The standardized measure (SM for convenience) varies considerably over the three year period, although the net increase from 1-1-92 to 12-31-94 is only 14%. The following observations can be made:

1. Sales net of production costs are large relative to the SM. Development costs are large. Together, they suggest that Elf's reserves are largely undeveloped. This is confirmed by Tables 1(b) and 2(b) which show that proved reserves are less than half of the total. As measurements of undeveloped reserves are less certain than for proved reserves, Elf's total reserve calculations should be viewed with caution.

2. Quantity revisions were significant in all three years, not surprising given observation #1. The net revision was negative, although the 1994 adjustment was positive. It is surprising that Tables 1(b) and 2 (b) do not show significant negative revisions. This discrepancy would be a good question to pose to Elf management.

3. Price changes are another significant variable, decreasing the 1993 SM but increasing the 1994 SM. DuPont had similar effects (see text page 1144) as 1993 oil and gas prices fell, with a recovery in 1994.

4. Elf made significant reserve acquisitions in 1993 and dispositions in 1994. From Table 1(b) we see that these activities mainly related to oil reserves in Africa.

5. The largest single change, however, was income taxes. Despite a small negative effect in 1994, taxes increased the SM by nearly FF32 billion over the three year period.

    Some income tax changes are offsets to other changes, as the other SM changes are pretax. However the large positive tax effect over the three year period despite an increase in the SM suggests that there was a more fundamental change.

While we cannot disaggregate the tax effects
due to each other change in the SM, we can gain
some insight into the effect of taxes on the SM.

Referring to table 6, we can compute the
implied tax rates for each geographic area. As
neither France nor "rest of world" is significant,
we show the data only for "Rest of Europe" and
Africa. All data are in FF millions.

	1992	1993	1994
Rest of Europe			
Future tax expense	37,029	24,287	27,342
Future net cash flows	40,832	33,989	37,201
Pretax cash flows	77,861	58,276	64,543
Implied tax rate	47.6%	41.7%	42.4%
Africa			
Future tax expense	62,877	35,818	45,127
Future net cash flows	31,011	25,410	30,514
Pretax cash flows	93,888	61,228	75,641
Implied tax rate	67.0%	58.5%	59.7%

The data show a sharp drop in the implied tax
rate for both areas in 1993. This drop accounts
for much of the large addition to the SM in that
year. The explanation for these declines would
have to come from management. The more important
question would be the likelihood of changes
affecting future years, when these reserves are
produced and contribute to reported income.

D.   The data provided in Exhibit 7P-2 can be used to adjust
     Elf's equity for the difference between the present
     value of its oil and gas reserves and the carrying cost
     reported on the balance sheet. This adjustment brings
     us closer to the market value of Elf's net assets than
     the reported historical costs.

     As can be seen from a comparison of carrying costs
     (table 3) with the SM (table 7), carrying costs are far
     above the SM. The adjustment to book value would be
     negative for both years. The 1994 adjustment would be:

Carrying cost	FF 63,572 million
Standardized measure	44,491
Adjustment	FF (19,081) million

Some allowance, however, should be made for the carrying cost of unproved properties. As Elf does not separately disclose the accumulated depreciation, depletion, and amortization for these properties, their net carrying amount is unknown. If we arbitrarily assume a 50% ratio, using duPont as a guide, then the 1994 adjustment would be reduced by approximately FF4.4 million.

E.   (i)   Costs incurred are comparable across firms and not affected by accounting methods because firms disclose total exploration and development costs incurred during the period.

(ii) Capitalized costs are affected by the accounting method used. As the FC method capitalizes both successful and dry wells whereas the SE method expenses dry hole costs, capitalized costs are higher under the FC method.

(iii) There will no difference in discounted future net cash flow. The estimates of future cash inflows and expenses are not affected by the accounting method used for financial reporting.

10.{M}A. (i)   The revaluation has no effect on cash flow or reported income (except for any "decrements" charged to income). Return on equity is, however, reduced when assets are revalued and the increment flows to equity.

(ii) There is no effect on cash flow or reported income in the following years excluding the impact on income of downward revisions in revalued amounts. As these assets are not amortized, the revaluation has no impact on reported income. ROE, however, remains depressed by higher reported equity.

(iii) When the assets are sold, gain or loss should be measured against the revalued amounts, rather than the original cost. As a result, gains on sales of these assets will be smaller (or losses will be reported). Cash flow from operations is not affected by sales of assets.

B. Revaluation facilitates disclosure of the true value of the firm's assets. This disclosure allows the financial statement user to measure operating results against the real investment in these assets rather than an obsolete cost. This permits the user to evaluate the "opportunity cost" of using the assets in operations rather than selling them.

However, revaluations are subjective by their nature. Management can manipulate revaluations and provide a misleading indication of the value of the firm.

C. Amortization may not be appropriate for all broadcast licenses and newspaper titles. The value of these assets may not decline with the passage of time, but reflects economic trends and management performance.

For films, television programs, and books, however, the case against amortization is weaker. While some assets of this type may not diminish in value over time (for example, the value of a classic film may increase over time), other titles may have little value after initial distribution (the value of initial broadcast rights relative to syndication rights varies for different television programs).

The footnote data in Exhibit 7P-3 are insufficient to answer the question of whether amortization is appropriate, as it depends on the specific assets included in the balance sheet categories.

D. (i) Net income would be reduced by revaluation as amortization would be based on higher, revalued amounts for these assets.

(ii) Cash from operations would not, however, be affected as amortization is a noncash expense.

Case 7-1 - Solution

Estimated time to complete this case is 2½ hrs

Overview

The case demonstrates that the financial statement effects of the capitalization versus expensing decision depend on patterns of expenditures. Digital Equipment's expenditures for Software development and R&D for the 1987-1995 are listed below.

Expenditures ($ millions)

	1987	1988	1989	1990	1991	1992	1993	1994	1995
Software[1]	35	44	51	57	46	86	73	55	35
R&D[2]	1009	1294	1498	1577	1605	1690	1461	1233	981
Total	1044	1338	1549	1634	1651	1776	1534	1288	1016

[1] Calculated in Part 1   [2] Calculated in Part 5

Note that for 1987-1992 (except for a dip in 1991 Software expenditures) software and R&D expenditures rose. From 1993-1995, however, they declined.

The effects of the capitalization versus expensing decision are summarized below. Reported income reflects the capitalization of software and the expensing of R&D. Income adjusted by expensing software reflects results of all costs being expensed. Income adjusted by capitalization of R&D reflects results of all costs capitalized.

Operating Income ($ millions)

	1987	1988	1989	1990	1991	1992	1993	1994	1995
Adjusted by Expensing of Software Development Costs[1]	1578	1603	1312	543	509	(658)	(241)	(777)	132
Reported	1612	1635	1336	563	511	(636)	(237)	(790)	108
Adjusted by Capitalization of R&D[2]	1900	2082	1795	873	660	(506)	(400)	(1142)	(375)

[1] Calculated in Part 4   [2] Calculated in Part 5

Note that for the 1987-1992 period, income with all items capitalized is highest whereas income with all items expensed is lowest. In 1994 and 1995 the situation has reversed with income with all items capitalized the lowest and income with all items expensed the highest. In 1993, (the year expenditures began declining), the results are in "transition". Income with all items capitalized is lowest whereas reported income is still higher than income with all items expensed as the shift in rankings depends on whether or not expenditures are higher or lower than the amortization of previous years' costs. The relationship between the patterns of expenditures and the effects on the differences in income are demonstrated in the following graphs. As expenditures rise (decline), capitalization (expensing) results in higher income.

R&D and Software Expenditures

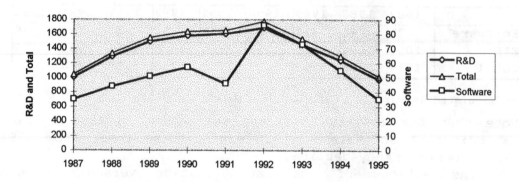

Operating Income

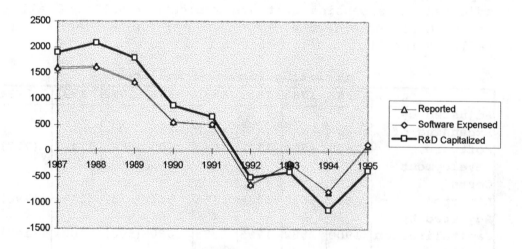

1. **Software Expenditure = Amortized expense + Δ in unamortized cost**

	1986	1987	1988	1989	1990	1991	1992	1993	1994	1995
Unamortized Cost	$ 0	$ 34	$ 66	$ 90	$110	$112	$134	$138	$125	$101
Δ in Unamort. Cost		34	32	24	20	2	22	4	(13)	(24)
Amortization expense		1	12	27	37	44	64	69	68	59
Software Expenditure		35	44	51	57	46	86	73	55	35

2.   Generally, it is approximately one year: 1988 amortization = approximately 1/3 of 1987 expenditure. Similarly 1989 amortization = approximately 1/3 of (1987 + 1988) expenditures. For 1991-1993, however, the lag appears to be shorter; amortization expense is higher than expected and in 1995 the lag appears to be longer as amortization expense is lower than the expected 1/3 of 1992-1994 expenditures implied by a one-year lag.

3.(a) Research and engineering costs may be difficult to link to specific products while computer software costs can be attributed to specific computers or programs. This distinction may justify the capitalization of the latter but the expensing of the former.

(b)   The ratio of research and engineering to computer software costs for 1987 was 28.9; for 1992 the ratio was 20.3 ($1754/$86). Had this trend continued, Digital would capitalize and amortize more of its product development costs, increasing its reported profitability and solvency ratios. Both the level and trend would improve as the ratio declines. However, for 1994 and 1995 the trend reversed as the ratio of research and engineering to computer software costs increased to 23.6 and 29.7 respectively. This reversal caused deterioration in profitability and solvency ratios as the next part demonstrates.

4.   Adjusted operating income is lower in the years 1987-1992 as software development costs (except for 1991) grew. Adjusted ROA & ROE decline as the numerator effect of lower operating income overwhelms the denominator effect of lower assets and equity. However, starting in 1993, software development costs declined. In 1994 they were below amortization expense resulting in higher (adjusted) operating income. For 1995 the effect of the higher income in the numerator combined with the lower assets and equity in the denominator result in a reversal of the trend occurring when software costs were growing. Adjusted ROA and ROE are greater when software costs are declining.

4. **As reported (all data in $ millions):**

	1986	1987	1988	1989	1990	1991	1992	1993	1994	1995
Research & eng. costs		$1,010	$1,306	$1,525	$1,614	$1,649	$1,754	$1,530	$1,301	$1,040
Operating income		1,612	1,635	1,336	563	511	(636)	(237)	(790)	108
Total assets	$7,173	8,407	10,112	10,668	11,655	11,875	11,284	10,950	10,580	9,947
Equity	5,728	6,294	7,510	8,036	8,182	7,624	4,931	4,885	3,280	3,528
ROA		20.7%	17.7%	12.9%	5.0%	4.3%	(5.5%)	(2.1%)	(7.3%)	1.1%
ROE		26.8%	23.7%	17.2%	6.9%	6.5%	(10.1%)	(4.8%)	(19.4%)	3.2%

Adjusted to expense computer software costs (all data in $ millions):

	1986	1987	1988	1989	1990	1991	1992	1993	1994	1995
Operating income[1]		$1,578	$1,603	$1,312	$543	$509	$(658)	$(241)	$(777)	$132
Total assets[2]	$7,173	8,373	10,046	10,578	11,545	11,763	11,150	10,812	10,455	9,846
Equity[2]	5,728	6,260	7,444	7,946	8,072	7,512	4,797	4,757	3,155	3,427
ROA		20.3%	17.4%	12.7%	4.9%	4.4%	(5.7%)	(2.2%)	(7.3%)	1.3%
ROE		26.3%	23.4%	17.1%	6.8%	6.5%	(10.7%)	(5.0%)	(19.6%)	4.0%

[1] Decrease reported operating income by change in unamortized cost calculated in Part 1.
[2] Decrease assets and equity by unamortized cost.

5   Adjusted to capitalize and amortize research and engineering costs as well as software development costs (all data in $ millions):

(Years)	1986	1987	1988	1989	1990	1991	1992	1993	1994	1995
Oper. income (reported)		$1,612	$1,635	$1,336	$ 563	$ 511	$ (636)	$ (237)	$ (790)	$ 108
Adjustments to oper. income:										
Capitalization of research & engineer-ing costs[1]		1,009	1,294	1,498	1,577	1,605	1,690	1,461	1,233	981
Amortization of capital. costs[2]		(721)	(847)	(1,039)	(1,267)	(1,456)	(1,560)	(1,624)	(1,585)	(1,464)
Net effect of capi-talization		$ 288	$447	$459	$ 310	$ 149	$ 130	$(163)	$(352)	$(483)
Oper. income (adjusted)		1,900	2,082	1,795	873	660	(506)	(400)	(1,142)	(375)
Increase in assets & equity[3]	$1,502	$1,791	$2,238	$2,697	$3,007	$3,156	$3,286	$3,123	$2,777	$2,295
Total assets (adjusted)	8,675	10,198	12,350	13,365	14,662	15,031	14,570	14,073	13,357	12,242
Equity (adjusted)	7,230	8,085	9,748	10,733	11,189	10,780	8,217	8,008	6,057	5,823
ROA		20.1%	18.5%	14.0%	6.2%	4.4%	(3.4%)	(2.8%)	(8.3%)	(2.9%)
ROE		24.8%	23.4%	17.5%	8.0%	6.0%	(5.3%)	(4.9%)	(16.3%)	(6.3%)

[1] Research and engineering costs less amortization of computer software costs.

[2] One-third of sum of capitalized costs over previous three years

[3] Increase equals capitalized costs less amortization. 1992, for example, equals 1992 costs plus 2/3 x 1991 costs plus 1/3 x 1990 costs.; i. e. 3286 = [1690 + (2x1605/3) + (1577/3)] . {Note that research and engineering costs for 1984-1986 are found in Exhibit 7C-1. }

Note that adjusted operating income is higher as growing research costs exceed their amortization until 1992. From 1993 the situation reverses and adjusted income is lower. The effect of capitalization on ROA and ROE varies; in some years the numerator effect is more powerful but in others the denominator effect dominates.

6   The capitalization of research or software costs increases cash from operations (and increases cash outflow for investment). In part 4 the effect of expensing software costs would be minimal as CFO would be reduced by $73, $55, and $35 million respectively.

The effect of capitalizing engineering costs in part 5 however, is highly significant due to their large size. CFO would increase by more than 30 fold in 1993 and increase by approximately three fold in 1994 and 1995 as CFO would increase by $1,461, $1,240, and $981 million respectively.

Chapter 8 Solutions

Overview:

Problem Length	*Problem #s*
{S}	*1, 2, 3, 4, 5, 6, 7, and 9*
{M}	*8, and 10*

1.{S}Acquisition cost (AC) = $ 20,000
    Economic Life (N) = 5 years
    Salvage value (SV)= $ 2,000

    (i)   Straight-line depreciation = (AC - SV) X (1/N) =
          ($20,000 - $2,000) X 0.2 = $3,600 per year.
          Depreciation expense will be $3,600 in year 1 as well
          as year 5.

    (ii) 150% declining balance = (AC-accumulated depreciation)
          X (150% X (1/N)).

ear	A Acquisition Cost	B Accumulated depreciation	C = (A -C) Depreciable cost	D Depreciation rate	E = C * D Depreciation expense
1	20,000	-0-	20,000	0.30	$ 6,000
2	20,000	6,000	14,000	0.30	4,200
3	20,000	10,200	9,800	0.30	2,940
4	20,000	13,140	6,860	0.30	2,058
5	20,000	15,198	4,802	0.30	1,440

Note: Firms may switch to straight-line during year 3 or
year 4 resulting in reported depreciation expense of $2,600
or $2,430 respectively, per remaining year. Carrying amount
must be reduced to salvage value by end of year 5.

(i)   Sum-of-years' digits

Year	C = (A -C) Depreciable Cost	D Depreciation Rate	E = C * D Depreciation Expense
1	$ 18,000	5/15 = 0.33	$ 6,000
2	18,000	4/15 = 0.2667	4,800
3	18,000	3/15 = 0.20	3,600
4	18,000	2/15 = 0.1333	2,400
5	18,000	1/15 = 0.0667	1,200

2.{S}

    (i)   Straight-line methods report constant depreciation expense throughout the life of the asset. Accelerated methods result in higher depreciation expense initially, but a declining trend thereafter. The effect on total depreciation expense depends on the growth rate of capital spending (whether the effect of higher depreciation expense on new assets offsets the impact of declining depreciation expense on old ones). Using the same economic life, accelerated methods will report higher depreciation expense than the straight-line method during the early years and lower expense thereafter.

    (ii)   The effect on net income is the reverse of the above. Net income is lower initially. Its reversal will depend on the level and growth of capital expenditures in the future.

    (iii) Accelerated depreciation methods report lower net income (higher depreciation expense), lower assets, and lower equity (higher accumulated depreciation) than the straight-line method. The numerator effect may dominate, producing lower return ratios. For a growing firm with increasing capital expenditures, the early years' depreciation expense difference will persist, resulting in lower return ratios.

    (iv) For financial reporting purposes, the choice of method has no effect on reported cash flows, as depreciation is a noncash expense. However, for tax purposes, the use of accelerated methods rather than the straight-line method will generate higher tax savings.

3.{S}

    (i)   **Depreciation expense: 19X3**   **19X4**

        Sum-of-years' digits: depreciable cost = \$8,000 (\$9,000 - \$1,000), SYD = 15
            5/15ths = \$2,666.67   4/15ths = \$2,133.33

    (ii)   Double declining balance: Year 1 depreciable cost = \$9,000, rate = 40% (2x20%)

            .40 x \$9,000 = \$3,600   .40x\$5,400* = \$2,160

        * Balance at end of 19X3 (\$9,000 - \$\$3,600)

    (iii) Straight line: depreciable cost = \$8,000 (\$9,000 - \$1,000), rate is 20%

            .20 x \$8,000 = \$1,600   (same) \$1,600

4.{S}

    (i)   ($9,000 - $1,800) / 8 = $ 900

    (ii)   ($9,000 - $1,800) / 9 = $ 800

    (iii) ($9,000 - $1,080) / 8 = $ 990

    (iv) ($9,000 - $1,080) / 9 = $ 880

5.{S}A.   The present value of the cash flows, discounted at 10%, is $60 for each asset.

    B.   **Asset A**

Year	Net Asset	Cash Flow	Depreciation Expense	Income	ROA
1	$ 60	$ 36	$ 30	$ 6	10%
2	30	23	20	3	10%
3	10	11	10	1	10%

Asset B

Year	Net Asset	Cash Flow	Depreciation Expense	Income	ROA
1	$ 60	$ 26	$ 20	$ 6	10%
2	40	24	20	4	10%
3	20	22	20	2	10%

    C.   The pattern for Asset A is the sum-of-the-years' digits method. The pattern for Asset B is the straight-line method.

6.{S}A. $(14) - $27 - $19 = $(60) [No cumulative effect and 1991 earnings increase would not have occurred.]

    B.   We can infer that the level of production in all three years was lower than the "normal" level at which the accounting change would make no difference. At higher levels of production, pro forma net income would be lower as depreciation expense would be higher under the units-of-production method.

    C.   The change in deprecation method had no effect on cash flow in 1991 as depreciation is a noncash expense.

    D.   The change in method should tend to stabilize Cummins' net income in future years, as depreciation expense has become a variable cost rather than a fixed cost.

7.{S}A. The accounting change applied only to newly acquired property so no restatement of prior year depreciation was required.

B. The trend of depreciation expense will be lower because depreciation expense on older property (accelerated methods) will be declining while depreciation expense on new property (straight-line method) will be lower than it would have been under accelerated methods. The net effect will be to increase reported net income.

8. (M) (A) Buildings

Ratio /Year	1991	1992	1993	1994
Relative Age = Accum Depr. / Gross Assets	525/1,942 = 27.03%	715/2,320 = 30.82%	865/2,551 = 33.91%	921/2,544 = 36.20%
Average depreciable life = Gross Assets / Deprec. Exp.	1,942/68 = 28.6 years	2,320/80 = 29.0 years	2,551/92 = 27.7 years	2,544/20 = 21.2 years
Average age = Accum. Depr. / Deprec. Exp.	525/68 = 7.7 years	715/80 = 8.9 years	865/92 = 9.4 years	921/120 = 7.7 years

Machinery

Ratio / Year	1991	1992	1993	1994
Relative Age = Accum. Depr. / Gross Assets	1,830/3,337 = 54.84%	2,750/4,513 = 60.94%	3,326/5,130 = 64.83%	3,385/5,019 = 67.44%
Average depreciable life = Gross Assets / Deprec. Exp.	3,337/348 = 9.6 years	4,513/381 = 11.9 years	5,130/479= 10.7 years	5,019/491 = 10.2 years
Average age = Accum. Depr. / Deprec. Exp.	1,830/348 = 5.3 years	2,750/381 = 7.2 years	3,326/479 = 6.9 years	3,385/491 = 6.9 years

B. Relative age indicates whether a firm's fixed asset base is old or new. If the firm is using straight-line depreciation, relative age is a good indicator of asset age as a percentage of depreciable life. It is not affected by changes in asset mix or the timing of purchases. However, this measure is affected by changes in depreciable lives and estimated salvage values. Atlas Copco's machinery shows an increasing relative age suggesting an aging fixed asset base that may need to be replaced.

The average depreciable life is affected by changes in asset mix and when assets are placed into service. Declining capital expenditures, writeoffs, newer assets with shorter lives, or special (extra) depreciation may have contributed to the significant decline in 1994.

The computation of average age is affected by changes in asset mix and acquisitions & divestitures. In 1994, the average age in years declined for buildings. However, this may be due to lower capital expenditures, writeoffs, or extra depreciation.

However, all measures are useful in comparing a firm with its competitors and enable analysts to better forecast capital expenditures.

9. {S}

A.   There are no cash flow consequences as it is a noncash charge and the tax benefits will be received only when the output of these properties is sold.

B.   1995 income was reduced relative to reported 1994 income because of the impairment charge. 1996 income will increase relative to 1994 and 1995 because the charge reduces the depreciable base and may include any operating gains that occur in that year (1996).

C.   (i)Future returns on assets will be higher because lower depreciation expense will result in higher income and the impairment charge reduced asset balances. (ii)Similarly, future asset turnover ratios will increase because of lower asset balances.

D.   It is likely that prior years' depreciation expense was understated leaving higher unrecoverable costs on the balance sheet.

10.{M}A.

	Average Age = Accumulated Depreciation/Depreciation Expense	Average Depreciable Life = Gross Investment/ Depreciation Expense
1990	3,599 / 488 = 7.38 years	7,585 / 488 = 15.54 years
1991	3,741 / 548 = 6.83	7,790 / 548 = 14.22
1992	3,888 / 591 = 6.58	7,842 / 591 = 13.27
1993	4,138 / 598 = 6.92	7,965 / 598 = 13.32
1994	4,454 / 588 = 7.57	8,230 / 588 = 14.00
1995	4,659 / 580 = 8.03	8,303 / 580 = 14.31

B. The interpretation is affected by the firm's use of accelerated depreciation methods because depreciation expense is high in early years, declining with asset age. As a result, both ratios are depressed in early years. It is further complicated by the declining capital expenditures (and depreciation expense as the average age of assets rises) as explained in part C.

C. Declining capital expenditures lower the depreciation expense over time. Increasing depreciation expense is observed during 1990 - 1993 followed by decreases in reported depreciation expense. Accelerated depreciation methods resulted in high depreciation in the early years with a sharp decline in later years. The sharp decline in capital expenditures exacerbates this effect.

D. Straight-line depreciation would have resulted in a longer lasting rising trend of depreciation expense as the effect of prior year capital expenditures persists longer.

Case 8-1 Solution

Approximate time to complete: 1 hour 45 minutes.

1. See Exhibit 8CS-1 for computations of:

    (i)   Average Age %
    (ii)   Average Depreciable Life in Years
    (iii) Average Age in Years

2.   Exhibit 8CS-1 also reports capital expenditures for each firm for the 1992-1994 period.

    Machinery & Equipment (M&E)
    The relative age computations for SCA and Stora show the gradual aging of M&E. MoDo shows a significant increase in 1993 due to an increase in accumulated depreciation. MoDo also reports a substantial decline in both gross investment and accumulated depreciation accompanied by a modest decrease in depreciation expense. MoDo reports the lowest depreciation expense and is out of line unless assets are really different. Both Stora and MoDo report declining depreciation expense in 1994. These firms also use higher depreciable lives and have older assets than SCA; their reported depreciation expense may not be adequate.

    In 1993, Stora reports a material increase in gross investment, accumulated depreciation, and depreciation expense reflecting higher than normal capital expenditures or an acquisition. These increases are followed by declines in 1994.

    Expected capital expenditures: Stora has the oldest M&E in terms of average age % and MoDo the oldest in years. SCA reported the largest increase in gross investment over the 1992-1994 period.

    Buildings
    Average age: The three firms report a rising trend and similar average age. MoDo appears to be using longer depreciable life and has the oldest buildings of the three firms. Both SCA and Stora have reported declines in gross investment and depreciation expense in 1994.

    Expected capital expenditures: MoDo has the oldest buildings and SCA the youngest. Generally, all three firms report low capital expenditure compared to depreciation expense.

3. See (2) above for a comparison of the Swedish firms. Exhibit 8-8 provides data and the analysis of U.S. firms. The average depreciable life measures suggest that the SCA, Stora, Georgia-Pacific and Mead use shorter lives. Using Westvaco as a guide, the Swedish firms appear to be using shorter depreciable lives for buildings. Except for MoDo, they may also be using shorter lives for M&E.

4. (i) With the exception of Westvaco, the U.S. firms do not provide a breakdown by asset class. The measures computed for U.S. firms are therefore a composite of equipment and buildings. The accounting policies, past capital expenditures, and asset mix may differ across firms in the two countries, further limiting the comparison.

(ii) Additional data on the accounting policies, past capital expenditures, financing methods used, and product mix of the various firms would improve comparisons and the validity of the conclusions drawn from the analysis.

Swedish Forest Products Industry Comparison

Machinery & Equipment

	SCA 1992	SCA 1993	SCA 1994	STORA 1992	STORA 1993	STORA 1994	MoDo 1992	MoDo 1993	MoDo 1994
Gross Investment	22,151	23,438	24,920	44,587	49,043	46,995	21,708	21,761	22,017
Accumulated Depreciation	9,971	11,199	12,599	22,638	26,263	25,997	8,771	10,503	11,206
Net Investment	12,180	12,239	12,361	21,949	22,780	20,998	12,937	11,258	10,811
Depreciation Expense	1,453	1,498	1,569	2,611	2,884	2,749	982	1,078	1,033
Capital Expenditures		1,557	1,691		3,715	967		(601)	586

Buildings

	SCA 1992	SCA 1993	SCA 1994	STORA 1992	STORA 1993	STORA 1994	MoDo 1992	MoDo 1993	MoDo 1994
Gross Investment	5,492	5,570	5,381	10,753	11,304	10,412	3,494	3,475	3,680
Accumulated Depreciation	1,608	1,768	1,865	4,484	5,043	4,987	1,643	1,775	2,013
Net Investment	3,884	3,802	3,516	6,269	6,261	5,425	1,851	1,700	1,667
Depreciation Expense	216	220	207	414	440	394	126	134	137
Capital Expenditures		138	(79)		432	(442)		(17)	104

Average Age %

	Machinery & Equipment SCA	Machinery & Equipment STORA	Machinery & Equipment MoDo	Buildings SCA	Buildings STORA	Buildings MoDo
1992	45.01%	50.77%	40.40%	29.28%	41.70%	47.02%
1993	47.78%	53.55%	48.27%	31.74%	44.61%	51.08%
1994	50.56%	55.32%	50.90%	34.66%	47.90%	54.70%

Average Depreciable Life in Years

	Machinery & Equipment SCA	Machinery & Equipment STORA	Machinery & Equipment MoDo	Buildings SCA	Buildings STORA	Buildings MoDo
1992	15.25	17.08	22.11	25.43	27.73	
1993	15.65	17.01	20.19	25.32	25.93	
1994	15.88	17.10	21.31	26.00	26.86	

Average Age in Years

	Machinery & Equipment SCA	Machinery & Equipment STORA	Machinery & Equipment MoDo	Buildings SCA	Buildings STORA	Buildings MoDo
1992	6.86	8.67	8.93	7.44	10.83	13.04
1993	7.48	9.11	9.74	8.04	11.46	13.25
1994	8.03	9.46	10.85	9.01	12.66	14.69

Chapter 9 - Solutions

Overview:

Problem Length	*Problem #s*
{S}	*1-4, 6, 7, and 10*
{M}	*5, 8, and 12*
{L}	*9 and 11*

1. {S} Deferred taxes can be found in all of the categories listed. Examples are:

    (i)   Deferred tax liabilities arising from an installment sale with cash payment expected within one year.

    (ii)   Deferred income tax resulting from use of accelerated depreciation for tax purposes and straight line for financial reporting.

    (iii) Deferred tax offset to valuation allowance for marketable equity securities or to currency translation adjustment.

    (iv) Deferred tax asset (debit) due to accrued compensation with cash payment expected within one year.

    (v)   Deferred tax assets (debits) recognized, such as for postretirement benefits or restructuring costs, that will not be funded within one year.

2. {S} (i) Correct: Under SFAS 109, changes in tax law must be reflected in the deferred tax liability in the period of enactment.

    (ii) Correct: Answer to (i) also applies to deferred tax assets.

    (iii) Correct: The tax consequences of events that have not been reflected in the financial statements (such as future earnings or losses) are not recognized.

    (iv) Incorrect: This statement is true of the deferral method but is false under the liability method of SFAS 109. See answers (i) and (ii) above.

    (v)   Incorrect: Changes in deferred tax assets and liabilities are included in income tax expense except for those charged or credited directly to stockholders' equity.

3. {S} Permanent differences are items of income or expense that affect *either tax return income or financial income, but not both*. Examples include:

- Tax-exempt interest income (not reported on tax return)

- Interest expense on amounts borrowed to purchase tax-exempt securities (not deductible on tax return)

- Amortization of non-tax deductible acquisition goodwill (not reported on tax return)

- Tax or other nondeductible government penalties (not reported on tax return)

- Statutory mineral depletion in excess of cost basis depletion (not reported in financial statements)

- Premiums on key-person life insurance policies (not deductible on tax return)

- Proceeds from key-person life insurance policies (not reported on tax return)

Permanent differences, depending on their nature, either increase or decrease the firm's effective tax rate from the statutory rate.

4. {S} A. (i) If the deferred tax liability is not expected to reverse, there is no expectation of a cash outflow and the liability should be considered as equity.

(ii) If the deferred tax liability is the result of a temporary difference that is expected to reverse, with consequent tax payment, it should be considered a liability.

B. The amounts and timing of tax payments resulting from the reversal of temporary differences are uncertain. Given this uncertainty, excluding deferred tax liabilities from both debt and equity (treating them as contingencies) may be appropriate.

C. The portion of the deferred tax liability that represents expected payments should be treated as debt (and discounted to present value). Accounting-based (timing) differences that are not expected to reverse should be treated as equity.

5.{M}Before answering the specific questions in this problem, we must determine the cost of each asset. We can use the information about asset L to do this:

Year 2 depreciation under the sum-of-the-years' digits method with a five year life is 4/15ths. Therefore the depreciation base (cost - salvage value) must be $12,000/(4/15) = $45,000 and cost must be $48,000 ($45,000 + $3,000).

This information can be used to prepare a depreciation schedule under each of the three methods:

Depreciation Expense

Year	Asset K Straight Line[1]	Asset L SYD[2]	Asset M DDB[3]
1	$ 9,000	$ 15,000	$ 19,200
2	9,000	12,000	11,520
3	9,000	9,000	6,912
4	9,000	6,000	4,147
5	9,000	3,000	3,221
Total	$ 45,000	$ 45,000	$ 45,000

[1] Base = $45,000 (cost - salvage value); expense = $45,000/5
[2] Base = $45,000; expense = 5/15ths, 4/15ths, 3/15ths, etc.
[3] Base = $48,000 (salvage value ignored); rate = 40%
  Year 1 expense = .40 x $48,000 = $19,200, leaving $28,800
  Year 2 expense = .40 x $28,800 = $11,520, leaving 17,280
  Year 3 expense = .40 x $17,280 = $ 6,912, leaving 10,368
  Year 4 expense = .40 x $10,368 = $ 4,147, leaving   6,221
  Year 5 expense = $3,221 to leave salvage value of   3,000

A. Double declining balance method is used on the tax return for all three assets; year two depreciation expense under that method is $11,520.

B. Financial statement depreciation expense in year two is:
Asset K (straight line) $ 9,000
Asset M (double declining balance)   11,520

C. (i) At the end of year two, accumulated depreciation equals (from expense table):

Asset K (straight line) $ 18,000
Asset L (SYD)   27,000
Asset M (DDB)   30,720

Tax Return (DDB)   30,720

Therefore the deferred tax liability is:

Asset K: .34 ($30,720 - $18,000) = $4,324.80
Asset L: .34 ($30,720 - $27,000) =   1,264.80
Asset M: no deferred tax as method is the same

(ii) At the end of year five, accumulated depreciation is the same under all methods and there is no deferred tax asset or liability.

6.{S}A. Assuming that Mother Prewitt continues to buy machines in the future, the depreciation timing difference will never reverse and there is no expected cash consequence. In this case the deferred tax liability can be treated as equity.

Assuming that the installment sale is not expected to recur, the tax on the sale will be paid in 1997 and will require cash. For that reason, the $27,200 of deferred taxes should be considered a liability when calculating liquidity, solvency and leverage ratios.

On the other hand, for many companies installment sales recur. When the installment method is permitted for tax purposes, such sales are no different from the depreciation example. The cash consequences of deferred tax items depends on their probability of reversal, not on their nature.

B. (i) Under the deferral method, no adjustment is made; only when the timing differences reverse are the new rates reflected in the financial statements (tax expense includes the difference between the balance sheet liability and the amount paid). (See the discussion of the gross change method in Exhibit 9A-1 on page 471.)

(ii) Under SFAS 109 (liability method), enacted changes in tax rates are reflected and the deferred tax liabilities restated to their amounts based on the 40% tax rate. The incremental liability is recorded as part of income tax expense regardless of when (or if) paid.

C. A valuation allowance would be required if it were deemed "more likely than not" that some or all of the deferred tax asset would not be realized.

7.{S}A. The 1993 deferred tax liability reflects the excess of tax depreciation over financial statement depreciation. Glatfelter, as most firms, uses more accelerated methods for tax reporting to minimize income tax payments.

B. The writedown reduces the carrying amount of the impaired fixed assets for financial reporting but has no income tax effect. Therefore the difference between the tax and book carrying amount of these assets is reduced, decreasing the deferred tax liability.

C. The impairment writedown of $189 million should reduce the book/tax difference by that amount, decreasing the deferred tax liability by

$$\$189 \times .35 = \$66.15 \text{ million}$$

D. The deferred tax liability at year-end 1994 reflects not only the effect of the impairment writedown but 1994 depreciation expense. The difference between tax and book depreciation also affects the liability. The $71 million reduction in the liability suggests that book depreciation exceeded tax depreciation for that year.

An alternative explanation is that the deferred tax liability includes state taxes. Thus a tax rate higher than 35% must be used to compute the effect of the impairment writedown on the deferred tax liability.

8. {M}A.   Not providing deferred income tax on the undistributed earnings of foreign subsidiaries

  (i)   Reduces income tax expense

  (ii) Has no effect on income tax paid

  (iii) Reduces the effective tax rate as income tax expense is lower

  (iv) Increases earnings per share as income tax expense is lower

  (v)   Increases book value per share as retained earnings are higher

B.   If Brown-Forman remitted prior year earnings on which no deferred tax had been provided, in that year

  (i)   Pretax income would not change.

  (ii) Income tax expense would increase reflecting current income taxes payable on the remitted earnings.

  (iii) Income tax paid would be higher as tax is paid on the remitted earnings.

  (iv) The effective tax rate would be higher as income tax expense increases and pretax income is unaffected.

  (v)   Earnings per share decline due to higher income tax expense.

  (vi) Book value per share declines due to income tax paid (the additional income tax expense).

C.   If there is no expectation that the undistributed earnings will be remitted, then no adjustment is required. If financial distress or the need for funds held overseas (for debt repayment or an acquisition) suggest that repatriation is likely, then a liability of $20.173 million should be established, reducing equity.

D.   The liability suggests that Brown-Forman expects to repatriate earnings (not included in the footnote amount) from some foreign subsidiaries and therefore has recognized the expected tax payments.

9.{L}*The calculations required are shown in Exhibit 9S-1, in the order required by the questions. The calculations are explained in the solution.*

A.   The first step is to convert the tax rate reconciliation to a pretax income-based reconciliation following the format of Exhibit 9-6 on page 451.

(i)   Exhibit 9S-1 shows that lower foreign tax rates reduced PepsiCo's income tax expense by $95 million, $80 million, and $144 million in 1992 to 1994.

(ii)   To compute foreign income tax expense, multiply foreign pretax income by the statutory rate and subtract the answer to (i). (We assume that the "other effects" apply to U.S. income.) For example, the 1992 calculation is (.34 x $702) – $95 = $144.
        When we compare the result to foreign pretax income, the effective tax rate on foreign income ranges from 19% (1994)to 24.9% (1993).

(iii) Subtracting foreign tax expense from pretax produces foreign net income.

(iv)   Subtracting foreign tax expense from the total yields U.S. tax expense and the effective rate. This analysis reveals that the U.S. tax rate rose over the 1992 to 1994 period.

(v)   Subtracting U.S. income tax expense from U.S. pretax income produces U.S. net income.

B.   (i)   Foreign pretax income rose by 12.5% in 1993 and 14.2% in 1994. U.S. pretax income increased 36.4% in 1993 and 7.9% in 1994.

(ii)   Aftertax foreign income increased by 6.2% in 1993 and 23.1% in 1994. Aftertax U.S. income rose by 33.7% in 1993 and 6.2% in 1994.

Exhibit 9S-1

Exhibit 9S-1
PepsiCo Tax Analysis

	1992	1993	1994
Statutory rate	34.0%	35.0%	35.0%
Foreign rate effect	-5.0%	-3.3%	-5.4%
Other effects (net)	2.4%	2.8%	3.4%
Effective tax rate	31.4%	34.5%	33.0%

Pretax income

	1992	1993	1994		
United States	$ 1,197	$ 1,633	$ 1,762		
Foreign	702	790	902		
Total	$ 1,899	$ 2,423	$ 2,664		

A

		1992	1993	1994	B: % Increase	
					1993	1994
	Tax @ statutory rate	$ 646	$ 848	$ 933		
(i)	**Foreign rate effect**	(95)	(80)	(144)		
	Other effects (net)	46	68	91		
	Total tax expense	$ 596	$ 836	$ 879		
	Foreign pretax	$ 702	$ 790	$ 902	12.5%	14.2%
	Foreign tax expense	(144)	(196)	(172)	36.6%	-12.5%
(iii)	**Foreign net income**	$ 558	$ 593	$ 730	6.2%	23.1%
(ii)	**Foreign tax rate**	20.5%	24.9%	19.0%		
	U.S. pretax	$ 1,197	$ 1,633	$ 1,762	36.4%	7.9%
	U.S. tax expense	(452)	(639)	(707)	41.3%	10.6%
(iv)	**U.S. net income**	$ 744	$ 994	$ 1,055	33.5%	6.2%
(v)	**U.S. tax rate**	37.8%	39.2%	40.1%		

C.   Changes in the tax rate distorted the income trend. For
      foreign income the effect was considerable. The pretax
      data show that the 1994 percentage increase was only
      slightly higher than that for 1993. The lower tax rate
      for 1994 made the percentage gain in net income much
      greater than for 1993. For U.S. income, the tax rate
      increase over this period changed the pretax trend only
      slightly.

D.   (i) The "other effects" increased tax expense each
           year. What are these effects and what factors will
           determine their future impact? The answer to these
           questions can help an analyst to forecast future
           effective tax rates and, therefore, future net
           income more accurately.

      (ii) Foreign effective tax rates depend on the "mix" of
           earnings from jurisdictions with different tax
           rates. Which foreign jurisdictions apply tax rates
           that are higher (lower) than the average, and how
           have mix changes affected the effective foreign
           tax rate over the 1992 to 1994 period? The answers
           to these questions also help earnings forecasts.
           In particular, they help the analyst forecast the
           aftertax impact of assumed changes in pretax
           income from major foreign subsidiaries.

10.{S}A. Debt can generate deferred tax effects if there is a
          difference between tax and financial reporting when the
          imputed interest expense is deducted. A deferred tax
          asset must mean that financial reporting deductions
          exceed tax deductions. The zero coupon debt must have
          been incurred in a tax jurisdiction where an interest
          deduction is not available until the bonds mature.

     B.   The deferred tax asset can be expected to increase each
          year by the amount of imputed interest expense
          multiplied by the marginal tax rate for that tax
          jurisdiction. When the debt matures, and the full
          amount of the accrued interest is paid (and deducted),
          the deferred tax asset becomes zero.

11. {L} *The calculations required are shown in Exhibit 9S-2, in the order required by the questions. The calculations are explained in the solution.*

A. The first step is to take the effective tax rate analysis provided in Exhibit 9P-1 and convert it to a pretax income-based reconciliation following the format of Exhibit 9-6 on page 451. Exhibit 9S-2 shows the results for each year and a three year total.

B. The pretax gain on the sale of Honda's investment in Rover was 14,654 million yen. At the statutory tax rate of 52%, the tax would be 7,620. Deducting the 6,034 reduction shown in the effective rate reconciliation (Exhibit 9S-2) results in a net tax of 1,586 million yen and an effective tax rate of 10.8%.

C. The reconciliation in Exhibit 9S-2 shows the following:

    (i)   Income tax expense was increased by 6,744 million yen due to nondeductible expenses.

    (ii) Changes in the valuation allowance increased income tax expense by 17,255 (21,543 - 4,288) million yen over the three year period. However the effect was greatest in 1993, declining in 1994 and 1995.

    (iii) Tax law changes increased income tax expense by 552 million yen over the three year period. A large 1994 increase was offset by decreases in 1993 and 1995.

D. The reconciliation in Exhibit 9S-2 shows the following:

    (i)   The reduction in income tax expense decreased each year, with the 1994 decrease especially large.

    (ii) As tax rates outside of Japan are lower than those on Japanese income, the proportion of Honda's income earned within Japan must have increased over the 1993-1995 period.

Exhibit 9S-2
Honda Tax Analysis
Reconciliation of Effective and Statutory Rates

Years ended March 31 (Yen millions except percentages)	1993	1994	1995	Total
Pretax income	88,564	46,890	94,287	229,741
Statutory tax rate (Japan)	52.0%	52.0%	52.0%	52.0%
Nondeductible expenses	2.2%	5.0%	2.6%	
New valuation allowance	10.9%	14.9%	5.2%	
Reduced valuation allowance		-0.9%	-4.1%	
Non-Japanese tax rates	-5.1%	-3.6%	-1.4%	
Tax law changes	-0.7%	2.7%	-0.1%	
Gain on Rover sale			-6.4%	
Other	0.8%	1.8%	-0.2%	
Effective tax rate	60.1%	71.9%	47.6%	57.4%

Income tax expense				
At statutory rate	46,053	24,383	49,029	119,465
Effects of:				-
Nondeductible expenses	1,948	2,345	2,451	6,744
New valuation allowance	9,653	6,987	4,903	21,543
Reduced valuation allowance	-	(422)	(3,866)	(4,288)
Non-Japanese tax rates	(4,517)	(1,688)	(1,320)	(7,525)
Tax law changes	(620)	1,266	(94)	552
Gain on Rover sale	-	-	(6,034)	(6,034)
Other	709	844	(189)	1,364
Income tax expense	53,227	33,714	44,881	131,821

Unrealized gain equities			89,134	
Deferred tax liability			46,350	
Effective tax rate			52.0%	

E.   The unrealized gain on equity securities was 89,134 million yen at March 31, 1995. The reported deferred tax liability was 46,350, making the effective tax rate 52%. As this is the statutory Japanese tax rate, these investments are almost certainly held in a Japanese subsidiary (or the parent company).

F.   Forecasting Honda's effective tax rate for 1996 requires consideration of the following:
     - the mix of Japanese and foreign pretax income
     - the impact of nondeductible expenses
     - changes in the valuation allowance
     - possible tax law changes
     - transactions with unusual tax rates (such as the Rover sale)

     While the analysis in this problem (and the chapter) does not provide all answers, it does help the analyst to ask the right questions, and break down the effective tax rate forecast to manageable steps.

12.{M}A.

	1991 Tax Rate	1992 Tax Rate
Q1 Q2 Q3	25.5% 24.0 26.1	20.7% 25.1 (594.9)

B. Using a tax rate of 17% for 1992 Q3 alone, tax expense would have been $16,660. The actual tax expense for Q3 was $583,000 (income) for a difference of $600,000

C. On a pretax basis, 1992 Q3 declined by 97% from 1991 Q3 ($98 vs. $3,244). Net income, however, declined by only 72% ($681 vs. $2,396) because 1992 Q3 included the tax benefit of revising the tax rate on earnings already reported for the first two quarters of 1992.

D. (i) One possibility is to make comparisons only on a pretax basis, thus avoiding any distortion from changes in the estimated tax rate.

Case 9-1 Solution

Approximate time to complete: 3 hours.

1. (i)   Difference between the benefits accrued and amounts deducted for taxes for the years
1993: $625/.35 = $1,786
1994: $673/.35 = $1,923
In both years, the firm has deducted less on its tax return than it accrued on its financial statements.

   (ii)   The deferred tax liability implies a higher deduction on the tax return (lower taxable income) compared to the expense recognized (higher pre-tax income) on the financial statements. Dow may have purchased annuities or made payments for supplemental unemployment, disability and similar benefits prior to accruing these expenditures on the income statement.

   (iii) The decrease in deferred tax may be due to either higher contributions in 1995 compared to the expenses accrued for postretirement benefits or payments for severance benefits as a result of work force reduction programs announced in 1993 (See Note B, p. 1154).

2. Decreases in the valuation allowance suggest that the firm expects to realize future sources of taxable income making it more likely that recorded deferred tax assets will be realized. The declines in the valuation account must be recognized in and as an increase in income from continuing operations. The declines will also increase CFO in the future, as tax payments will decline.

3. (i)-(iii) See Exhibits 9CS-1 and 9CS-2 for the three effective
        tax rates for Dow and ICI for the 1992-1994 period.

    (iv) ICI uses partial allocation, i.e., it does not recognize
        deferred taxes for timing differences that are not
        expected to reverse. However, both duPont and Dow use
        comprehensive allocation. In order to compare the three
        firms we need to adjust ICI's reported deferred taxes
        for the difference between partial and comprehensive
        allocation. Alternatively, we could adjust duPont and
        Dow to partial allocation.
            Exhibit 9C-1 and Footnote 9 in Appendix C reconcile
        deferred taxes accounted for in the balance sheet
        (partial allocation) to the full potential deferred
        taxes (comprehensive allocation) that would have been
        recognized if comprehensive allocation was used.

(Amounts in £ millions)

	1992	1993	1994
Accounted for at balance sheet date	55	88	90
Not Accounted for at balance sheet date	-8	-18	22
Full potential deferred tax	47	70	112
Change in deferred taxes not accounted for at balance sheet date		-10	40

Exhibit 9CS-2a computes effective tax rates using data
provided by Exhibit 9C-1 and Footnote 9 in Appendix C.

4. Dow reported effective tax rates above the statutory rate
    because it amortized nondeductible intangibles. In 1992 and
    1993, it also paid higher taxes in some foreign
    jurisdictions. However, in 1992, these two effects were
    overshadowed by "Other-net" (unexplained) differences, which
    lowered the effective tax rate below the statutory rate.

5. The increase in deferred tax assets in 1992 and 1993
    reflects the 1992 pretax asset write-downs of $433 million
    and the 1993 pretax charge of $180 million. The decline in
    1994 reflects the completion of restructuring activities and
    the recognition of losses (disposal or sale of assets) and
    deductions (severance payments) for tax purposes.

6.

(i) The increases in property related deferred tax liabilities were $43 million [($732-$94)-($683-$88)] in 1993 and $78 million [($799-$83)-($732-$94)] in 1994. Therefore, the additional tax deduction recorded in these two years was:

1993: $43/.35 = $123 million for a total tax depreciation expense of $1,675 ($1,552+$123).

1994: $78/.35 = $223 million for a total tax depreciation expense of $1,748 ($1,525+$223).

(ii) Dow must use shorter useful lives and lower or no salvage value for tax purposes.

7. Inventories: The deferred tax asset balance reflects higher cost of goods sold on the financial statements than tax deductions and may be due to inventory writedowns (due to the lower of cost or market rule) for financial reporting. This writedown is not available for tax returns. The deferred tax liability balance suggests the use of different LIFO pooling techniques on the financial statements than the tax return resulting in higher tax deductions than cost of goods sold recognized on the income statement. The increasing deferred tax liability may be due differences in expense under the two pooling methods.

Long-term debt: The deferred tax asset balance may be due to accrual of interest between coupon dates, amortization of debt discount (Footnote I reports a decrease in unamortized debt discount from $106 to $84 million), or recognition of interest expense on bonds issued at a discount. The deferred tax liability balance represents capitalization of interest on the financial statements reducing interest expense relative to interest paid and deducted on the tax return.

Effective Tax Rates - Dow Chemical Company

	1992	1993	1994	1992-1994
Taxes Payable	$ 569	$ 582	$ 745	$ 1,896
Deferred Tax Expense	(295)	24	34	(237)
Income Tax Expense	$ 274	$ 606	$ 779	$ 1,659
Income Tax Paid[1]	$ 439	$ 454	$ 257	$ 1,150
Pretax Income	$ 872	$ 1,525	$ 2,052	$ 4,449
Statutory Tax Rate	34%	35%	35%	34.7%
(i) Tax Expense/Pretax	31.4%	39.7%	38.0%	37.3%
(ii) Tax Payable/Pretax	65.3%	38.2%	36.3%	42.6%
(iii) Tax Paid/Pretax	50.3%	29.8%	12.5%	25.8%
Taxable Income	$ 1,740	$ 1,456	$ 1,955	$ 5,151

[1] See Footnote R, p. 1165

Effective Tax Rates: Imperial Chemical Industries PLC (ICI)
Millions of £

	1992	1993	1994	1992-1994
Taxes Payable	230	206	179	615
Deferred Tax Expense	(47)	(17)	(15)	(79)
Income Tax Expense	183	189	164	536
Income Tax Paid [1]	98	144	98	340
Pretax Income	(384)	360	408	384
Statutory Tax Rate	33%	33%	33%	33.0%
Tax Expense/Pretax	-47.7%	52.5%	40.2%	139.6%
Tax Payable/Pretax	-59.9%	57.2%	43.9%	160.2%
Tax Paid/Pretax	-25.5%	40.0%	24.0%	88.5%
Taxable Income	(242)	412	453	623

[1] See p. 1171

Effective Tax Rates - Imperial Chemical Industries PLC (ICI)
Millions of £

	1992	1993	1994	1992-1994
Taxes Payable	230	206	179	615
Deferred Tax Expense	(47)	(17)	(15)	(79)
Adj. to comp. allocation	–	(10)	40	30
Income Tax Expense	183	179	204	566
Income Tax Paid	98	144	98	340
Pretax Income	(384)	360	408	384
Statutory Tax Rate	33%	33%	33%	33.0%
Tax Expense/Pretax	-47.7%	49.7%	50.0%	147.4%
Tax Payable/Pretax	-59.9%	57.2%	43.9%	160.2%
Tax Paid/Pretax	-25.5%	40.0%	24.0%	88.5%

Chapter 10 - Solutions

Overview:
Problem Length   *Problem #s*
   {S}   1-4, 6, 11-13, 16, and 19-20
   {M}   5, 7-10, 14-15, 17-18, and 21-22

1.{S}(i) When full-coupon debt is issued, interest paid reduces cash from operations (CFO). When zero-coupon debt is issued, however, no cash interest is paid. CFO is unaffected, and is therefore higher than when full-coupon debt is issued. In addition, when imputed interest on zero-coupon debt is tax deductible, CFO is further increased by the tax benefit.

   (ii) When full-coupon debt is issued, the proceeds are included in cash from financing (CFI). When that debt matures, the amount paid reduces CFI. Assuming the debt is issued and redeemed at par, the net effect on CFI is zero over the life of the debt.

        Zero-coupon debt is issued at a discount; CFI is below the full-coupon case. However at maturity the full face amount is paid (same as full-coupon case). The net amount of CFI (outflow) is therefore greater than when full-coupon debt is issued.

  (iii) Net income is unaffected by the choice of debt assuming that the interest rate is the same. However interest on the zero-coupon bond rises each year as the carrying amount rises, increasing the base on which each year's interest expense is computed.

2.{S}(i) Net income declines as interest expense increases, reflecting the higher level of interest rates.

   (ii) The market value of the firm's debt should remain unchanged. As the interest rate adjusts to changes in market rates, investors will pay the face amount for the debt, assuming no change in credit risk.

3. {S} (i) Market values should be used to compute leverage ratios as they better measure what the firm would have to pay to retire the debt.

   (ii) Firm A will have the lower leverage (debt-to-equity) ratio when market values are used. The market value of its debt will be lower than the market value of Firm B's debt because the interest rate is lower.
      When book values are used, the leverage ratio is identical for both firms.

4. {S} The difference between the book amount of the debt and the amount paid to retire it must be recognized as a gain (if book value is higher) or loss (if amount paid is higher). The gain or loss is treated as an extraordinary item (SFAS 4) unless resulting from normal sinking fund repurchase.

5. {M} A.

	American Airlines		Eastern Airlines	
	1987	1988	1987	1988
Current assets	$2,146.3	$2,615.0	$1,022.4	$ 999.9
Current liabilities	2,071.0	2,795.6	1,192.7	1,153.8
Net working capital	$ 75.3	$ (180.6)	$ (170.3)	$ (153.9)
Current ratio	1.03X	0.94X	0.86X	0.87X
Quick ratio	0.84	0.76	0.67	0.69
Cash ratio	0.49	0.46	0.28	0.35

B. Unlike other payables, the air traffic liability will not require cash outlays (other than low marginal costs); instead this obligation is satisfied as customers use their tickets on flights. The air traffic liability should therefore be excluded from computations of short-term liabilities.

C. **Adjusted Computations:**

Current liabilities	$2,071.0	$2,795.6	$1,192.7	$1,153.8
Air traffic liability	(577.0)	(800.0)	(390.5)	(302.4)
Current liabilities	$1,494.0	$1,995.6	$ 802.2	$ 851.4
Net working capital	652.3	619.4	220.2	148.5
Current ratio	1.44X	1.31X	1.27X	1.17X
Quick ratio	1.17	1.06	0.99	0.94
Cash ratio	0.68	0.64	0.41	0.47

As expected, all of American Airlines' liquidity measures improve when the air traffic liability is removed from current liabilities.

D. Eastern's short-term liquidity position is weaker than American's over the two-year period shown. Eastern's ratios appear to improve slightly in 1988. However, the improvement in the current and quick ratios evaporates when the air traffic liability is eliminated. This liability declined from $390.5 million to $302.4 million due to reduced advance purchases by customers. Other liability categories increased proportionately and current assets (except cash) declined. The higher cash balance may have been required to meet potential reductions in credit availability.

E. The decline in air traffic liability indicates that fewer customers were willing to purchase tickets in advance, presumably due to the deterioration in Eastern's financial position. In contrast, American's air traffic liability increased, although the growth should be compared to past fluctuations and to growth for the rest of the industry.

6.{S}(i) Interest expense = Interest paid + change in bond
                                              discount
          $8,562   = $7,200   + $1,362

   (ii)   = Market rate x [face value - discount]
                     =   .12   x [face value - $8,652]

        Therefore, face value = ($8,562/.12) + $8,652 = **$80,000**

   (iii)Coupon rate   = interest paid/face value
                      = $7,200/$80,000 = **9%**

7.(M}A. Proceeds equal $100,000/(1.12)^5 = **$56,742**

     B.

	1996	1997	1998	1999	2000
EBIT	$50,000	$50,000	$50,000	$50,000	$50,000
CFO before interest & taxes	60,000	60,000	60,000	60,000	60,000
Interest expense	6,809	7,626	8,541	9,566	10,714
CFO	60,000	60,000	60,000	60,000	60,000
Times interest earned	7.34	6.56	5.85	5.23	4.67
Times interest earned (cash basis)	[Infinite, since no interest is paid. In 2000, the bond will be retired and the payment reported as a financing cash outflow.]				

C.   For a full-coupon bond, annual interest expense paid in cash would be $56,742 x .12 = $6,809

	1996	1997	1998	1999	2000
EBIT	$50,000	$50,000	$50,000	$50,000	$50,000
CFO before interest & taxes	60,000	60,000	60,000	60,000	60,000
Interest expense	6,809	6,809	6,809	6,809	6,809
CFO	53,191	53,191	53,191	53,191	53,191
Times interest earned	7.34	7.34	7.34	7.34	7.34
Times interest earned (cash basis)	8.81	8.81	8.81	8.81	8.81

D.   Cash flow from operations is higher when zero-coupon bonds are issued because interest is never reported as an operating cash outflow. [Note the infinite cash-basis coverage ratio.] Interest coverage, however, is lower after the first year, and declines as interest expense increases over time, reflecting the steadily increasing principal amount. Full-coupon bonds (if sold at par) result in a constant cash outflow from operations and constant interest expense. Given the Null Company's "steady state," the interest coverage ratio is constant on both accrual and cash flow bases.

E.   Given the tax deductibility of accrued but unpaid interest on zero-coupon bonds, cash flow from operations will be higher for both cases. The reported cash flow differences will remain unchanged. For the zero-coupon case, cash flow from operations is even more misleading as the firm must generate sufficient cash from operations to repay the debt at maturity. The obligation must be repaid, regardless of its cash flow classification.

8.{M}A. Adding principal and interest payments:

```
PV of $20 million, payable in 10 years¹ =    $ 9,127,800
+ PV of 20 payments of $1 million each² =     13,590,330
Financing cash inflow = proceeds =           $22,718,130
```

[1]PV factor (n=20, r=.04) = .45639 x $20,000,000 = $ 9,127,800
[2]PV factor (n=20; r=.04) = 13.59033 x $1,000,000 = $13,590,330

On January 1, 1994, cash and debt liability are each
increased by $22,718,130

Years Ended December 31	1994	1995
Long-term debt	$22,626,855	$22,433,206
Accrued interest	905,074	897,328
Total liability	$23,531,929	$23,330,534
Interest expense	$ 1,813,799	$ 1,798,605
Cash from operations	$(1,000,000)	$(2,000,000)

Calculations:

Interest expense (income tax ignored)
Year ended December 31, 1994:
July 1: $22,718,130 x .04 = $908,725
Interest payment of $1,000,000 (no impact on expense)
Reduction of bond premium = $1,000,000 - $908,725 = $91,275
Liability balance on July 1 = $22,718,130 - $91,275 =
$22,626,855

December 31: $22,626,855 x .04 = $905,074 interest expense,
shown as accrued interest on December 31, 1994 balance sheet

January 1, 1995:
Interest payment of $1,000,000 (no impact on expense)
Interest payment of $1,000,000 (no impact on expense)
Reduction of bond premium = $1,000,000 - $905,074 = $94,926
Liability balance on January 1 = $22,626,855 - $94,926 =
$22,531,929

Year ended December 31, 1995:
July 1: $22,531,929 x .04 = $901,277 interest expense
Interest payment of $1,000,000 (no impact on expense)
Reduction of bond premium = $1,000,000 - $901,277 = $98,723
Liability balance on July 1 = $22,531,929 - $98,723 = $22,433,206

December 31: $22,433,206 x .04 = $897,328 interest expense, shown as accrued interest on December 31, 1995 balance sheet.

January 1, 1996:
Interest payment of $1,000,000 (no impact on expense)
Reduction of bond premium = $1,000,000 - $897,328 = $102,672
Liability balance on January 1 = $22,433,206 - $102,672 = $22,330,534

Operating cash outflow
1994: One interest payment on July 1, 1994, $1,000,000
1995: Two interest payments of $1,000,000 each, on January 1 and July 1, $2,000,000

Balance sheet impacts

1994: effect of bond issuance
      reduction of bond premium at July 1
      interest payable at December 31
      interest expense reduces equity

1995: reduction of interest payable and bond premium at January 1
      reduction of bond premium at July 1
      interest payable at December 31
      interest expense reduces equity

B. The purchase price must be equal to the face amount since the market interest rate is equal to the coupon rate.[3]
    The carrying amount of the bonds on July 1, 1997 will be $21,997,050.[4] The gain from repurchase is the difference between the purchase price and carrying amount: $20,000,000 - $21,997,050 = $1,997,050. It is a gain because a liability has been extinguished for a lesser amount of assets. Because of the change in interest rates since the bonds were issued, Derek has captured the remaining bond premium. The journal entry would be:

```
Bonds payable                20,000,000
Premium on bonds payable      1,997,050
      Cash                                   20,000,000
      Gain on extinguishment                  1,997,050
```

[3] This can be shown, as well, by using present values: purchase price = present value of $20,000,000, to be repaid in 6.5 years: PV factor (n=13, r=.05) = .53032 x $20 million = $10,606,400 plus PV of 13 payments of $1,000,000 each: PV factor (n=13, r=.05) = 9.39357 x $1,000,000 = $9,393,570; total is $20,000,000.

[4] Present value of $20,000,000, to be repaid in 6.5 years: PV factor (n=13, r=.04) = .60057 x $20 million = $12,011,400 plus PV of 13 payments of $1,000,000 each: PV factor (n=13, r=.04) = 9.98565 x $1,000,000 = $9,985,650; total = $21,997,050. The carrying amount could also be determined by extending the analysis in part A (reducing the bond premium at the time of each interest payment) to July 1, 1997.

C. The gain is not a component of continuing, operating income but should be considered nonrecurring. It is a consequence of the change in interest rates rather than the firm's operating activities, and cannot be expected to recur.

D. 1. The gain provides a one-time increase in reported net income.

   2. The decrease in leverage (as a lower amount of higher coupon debt is issued to replace the lower coupon debt) may help the firm avert or delay technical default on bond covenants. The repurchase may also allow the firm to eliminate limiting covenants on this specific debt issue. Thus even if new debt must be issued to raise the funds needed for repurchase, the firm may wish to retire the bond issue.

9.{M}A.   (i)   Debt $662 million
                Equity   337
                Debt-to-equity ratio   1.96

          (ii) Debt $ 87 million
                Equity   912
                Debt-to-equity ratio   0.10

    B.   With the conversion price so far above the current
          market price of Conners common shares, the bonds are
          very unlikely to be converted and should be treated as
          debt.

    C.   With the market price of Conners common at $24, the
          6.50% bonds have a high probability of conversion and
          should be classified as equity, especially if
          completion of the merger would increase the price of
          Conners' shares further. The 6.75% bonds should still
          be treated as debt, subject to further changes in the
          price of Conners (or Seagate shares).

    D.   Debt $317 million
          Equity   682
          Debt-to-equity ratio   0.46

10.{M}A. and B. Balance sheet liability at 12/31/1991 =
$268/(1.0725) = **$249.9 million.**

1992 interest =.0725 x $249.9 = **$18.1 million.**

1993 interest = 2.5/12 x .0725 x $268 = **$4 million.**

C.   The $4 million interest for 1993 increases the liability to the redemption amount of $272 million. Thus, there is no gain or loss at redemption.

D.   (i)   Zero coupon notes have no effect on cash from operations (CFO) at any time; interest expense on conventional bonds affects CFO every year. When income taxes are considered, the zero-coupon notes generate an annual tax benefit despite the absence of any interest payment. Thus CFO is always higher when zero coupon notes are issued rather than full coupon notes. Cash for financing (CFI) in 1992 is zero for both zero-coupon and conventional notes.

(ii) The 1993 CFO effects are the same as 1992. CFI equals the redemption amount of $272 million for both zero-coupon and conventional notes.

(iii) Over the life of the notes, CFO is negative for the conventional notes but positive (due to tax benefits) for the zero-coupon notes.
          For both conventional notes and zero coupon notes, cash from financing includes the proceeds from issuance and the amount paid for redemption. These amounts are approximately the same for conventional notes (the difference being any premium or discount and the cost of issuance). The net amount over the life of the issue is approximately zero.
          For zero coupon notes, however, the redemption amount includes *all accrued interest* from the time of issuance. As a result the net effect over the life of the note issue is to increase the cash outflow from financing activities.

11.{S}A. (i) $$\frac{\text{Debt}}{\text{Equity}} = \frac{\$\ 4,000,000}{\$28,000,000} = \mathbf{0.14}$$

When the preferred shares are nonredeemable, they should be considered stockholders' equity.

(ii) $$\frac{\text{Debt}}{\text{Equity}} = \frac{\$21,500,000^{1}}{\$10,500,000^{2}} = \mathbf{2.05}$$

[1] $4,000,000 + $16,000,000 [redemption value of preferred stock] + $1,500,000 [preferred dividends in arrears (2 x 100,000 x $7.50)].

[2] $28,000,000 - $16,000,000 [redemption value of preferred stock] - $1,500,000 [dividends in arrears]

When the preferred shares are redeemable at the option of shareholders, they should be treated as debt, and stated at their redemption value. The dividend payments in arrears should also be included as they must be paid before common shareholders can receive any distributions.

B. Book value per common share:

(i)   ($28,000,000 - $15,000,000)/200,000 = **$65**

(ii) $12,000,000/200,000 = **$60**

C. Redeemable preferred shares should be considered as debt in computing solvency ratios since they constitute a fixed preference in liquidation and the dividend payments are fixed and often cumulative. Many redeemable preferred issues have the equivalent of "sinking-fund" provisions that also suggest their treatment as debt. Note that the SEC requires that redeemable preferred shares be reported separately from stockholders' equity.

12.{S}A. 1. To ensure that dividend payments can continue to be made.
2. To enhance the borrowing capacity of the firm.

B. Given the constraints discussed on text pages 511-12, the issuance of new equity was certainly a possibility. The only question would have been the market valuation of NorAm's shares relative to management's view of their intrinsic value.

C. The answer depends on the shareholder's view of the market price of NorAm's shares. Issuance of new shares to maintain the current dividend makes no sense given finance theory which states that the two are equivalent. In an imperfect world, however, NorAm's shares may be fully valued but the shareholder does not wish to sell and incur capital gains taxes. If NorAm has attractive investment opportunities not reflected in its stock price, then issuing new shares to increase the firm's borrowing capacity would be desirable.

13.{S}A. **The convertible debt should be treated as debt.** As the conversion price of $35.89 is three times the current market price of $12, conversion is very unlikely.

B. Fair value approximated book value as:
1. The interest rate on the revolving credit, two-thirds of total debt, is most likely variable.
2. The nonconvertible debt has short maturities.
3. While the interest rate on the convertible debt is low, the conversion feature has value despite the fact that it is far above current market.

14.{M}A. The March, 1993 U.S. Government intermediate rate was 5.41%. Glatfelter's rate of 5.875% was 46 basis points (.46%) higher.

B. At December 31, 1994, the U.S. Government intermediate rate was 7.76%. Glatfelter's rate would be 46 basis points higher, or 8.22%.

Alternatively, we can assume a constant *percentage* spread between Glatfelter and the intermediate U.S. Government bond. Under this assumption, the December 31, 1994 spread for Glatfelter would be:

(.46/5.41) x 7.76 = .66 and the rate would be 7.76 + .66 = 8.42%.

C. Glatfelter is "long" a bond with seven remaining payments of interest on $50 million at 5.875%. Each semiannual payment equals $587,500 ($50 million/2 x .05875). Seven payments of $578,500 equal $4.112,500; discounted at the current interest rate of 8.22%, the present value equals nearly $3.7 million. Cancellation fees might account for the difference from $4 million.

Under the alternative assumption, the present value would be approximately $10,000 lower.

15.{M}A. The data needed to calculate the ratios for each of the three options follows ($ thousands):

Financing Method Number		1 Preferred Shares	2 Convent. Bond	3 Zero Coupon
CFO before interest		$ 390	$ 390	$ 390
Interest paid[1]	Given	$ 200	$ 200	$ 200
	New	0	100	0
Total		$ 200	$ 300	$ 200
Preferred dividends	Given	$ 0	$ 0	$ 0
	New	100	0	0
Total		$ 100	$ 0	$ 0
Long-term debt[2]	Given	$2,000	$2,000	$2,000
	New	0	1,000	1,100
Total		$2,000	$3,000	$3,100
Tangible fixed assets	Given	$5,000	$5,000	$5,000
	New	1,000	1,000	1,000
Total		$6,000	$6,000	$6,000

[1] Note that no interest is paid on the zero coupon bond (see note 2).
[2] Unpaid interest on the zero coupon bond increases the liability.

Times interest earned (cash basis):

$\dfrac{\text{CFO Before interest}}{\text{Interest paid}}$ 1.95   **1.30**   1.95

Fixed charge coverage (cash basis):

$\dfrac{\text{CFO Before interest}}{\text{Interest paid + preferred dividends}}$ **1.30**   **1.30**   1.95

Debt to gross tangible assets:

$\dfrac{\text{Long-term debt}}{\text{Gross tangible fixed assets}}$ 0.33   0.50   **0.52**

The resultant ratios for each of the three options are shown above, with ratios that violate the applicable covenant in boldface. Note that each of the options violates at least one of the covenants and the conventional bond violates two.

    The zero-coupon bond seems to be the "best" as its coverage ratios are high (no cash interest payment) and the debt to assets limit is barely violated. It violates this covenant because debt increases to reflect the unpaid interest.

B.   The best approach is to combine the zero coupon bond, which violates only the debt/assets covenant, with another financing method that brings down that ratio without lowering either of the other ratios excessively. Preferred stock dominates conventional bonds as it has a lower debt/assets ratio and its coverage ratios are at least as high. Thus the optimal choice is a combination of preferred stock and zero coupon bonds. Because the times interest coverage ratio is identical at 1.95 for both we need only consider the last two ratios:

CFO/(interest + preferred dividends) must exceed 1.80.

Long-term debt/gross assets must be less than 0.50.

If P dollars are raised via preferred shares and Z dollars via zero coupon bonds, then P + Z = $1,000,000. For the zero coupon bonds, the amount of debt at year end is 1.1Z because of the accrual of unpaid interest. These constraints reduce to the following equations
    ($ thousands):

I: $390/($200 + $100p) > 1.80 where p = P/$1,000,000

II: $\dfrac{\$2,000 + \$1,100\,(1-p)}{\$6,000} < 0.50$

These reduce to the following constraints:

I: .167 > p   II: p > .091

    Thus, .167 > p > .091

One possibility would be to issue 85% zero coupon bonds and 15% preferred (p = .15):

CFO = $390 (neither issue reduces CFO)

Interest paid = $200 (neither issue creates interest payments)

Preferred dividends = $15 ($150 x 10%)

Long-term debt = $2,935 [$2,000 + ($1,100 x .85)]

Tangible fixed assets = $6,000 (same for both choices)

Times interest earned ($390/$200) = 1.95

Fixed charge coverage ($390/$215) = 1.81

Debt to tangible fixed assets ($2,935/$6,000) = .489

Another possibility would be 90% zero coupon bonds and 10% preferred (p = .10):

CFO = $390

Interest paid = $200

Preferred dividends = $10 ($100 x 10%)

Long-term debt = $2,990 [$2,000 + ($1,100 x .90)]

Tangible fixed assets = $6,000 (same for both choices)

Times interest earned ($390/$200) = 1.95

Fixed charge coverage ($390/$210) = 1.86

Debt to tangible fixed assets ($2,990/$6,000) = .498

Thus there is a tradeoff between the two ratios. As p increases, Sleepman reduces its debt ratio but also its coverage ratio. At the extremes (p = .167 and p = .091), the firm will be right on the edge of violating one covenant. The decision would be based on management's view of which ratio has the lower risk of being violated (or which ratio the lender considers more significant). Note, however, the zero coupon bond increases in amount as interest accrues and (all other things being equal) puts increasing pressure on the debt-to-fixed-assets ratio over time.

16.{S}A. In March 1993, interest rates were low, with an interest rate of 5.41% on intermediate term U.S. Government securities (Exhibit 10P-1). Interest rates were higher in 1991.

B. The notes were issued at a spread over U.S. Government intermediates of 49 basis points (.49%) [5.90% less 5.41%]. Using the December, 1994 U.S. Government rate of 7.76% and the same spread, Illinois Tool Works would have to pay 8.25% [7.76% + .49%].

C. In our calculations we make the simplifying assumption that payment dates are July 1 and January 1.

For the 7½% bond we assume the first payment is 7/1/1995 and the last payment 1/1/1998.

Therefore; the 7½% bond has 8 semi-annual payments of .075/2 x $125 million = $4.6875 million left. The present value of that stream plus the principal payment at the end, discounted at 8.25%, equals $122 million.

For the 5 7/8% bond we assume the first payment is 1/1/1995 and the last payment 1/1/2000. Therefore; the bond has 11 semi-annual payments of .05875/2 x $125 million = $3.6719 million left; the first of which is immediate and need not be discounted.

The present value of the interest payment stream plus the principal payment at the end, discounted at 8.25%, equals $117 million.

The combined market value of the two bonds = $122 + $117 = $239 million or $11 million less than the carrying value, not far from the company's calculated difference of $14 million.

17. {M}   *Note: Problem 11-17 is an extension of this problem, incorporating adjustments for off-balance-sheet debt.*

A.   Current debt $ 43,963
      Long-term debt   200,000
      Total debt $243,963

      Stockholders' equity   368,983

      Debt-to-equity ratio   .66

B.   Pretax income $ 32,848
      Interest expense   22,238
      EBIT $ 55,086

      Times interest earned   2.48

C.   The interest rate on debt rated BBB at 12/31/1994 is 9.47% (Exhibit 10P-1), just slightly below the coupon rates on Ashland Coal's long term debt (see note 7). If Ashland Coal debt had a BBB rating, market value and carrying value would be approximately equal. Note 16, however, reports that the fair value of Ashland's long term debt was $13,000 or 7.5% higher than its carrying value. Thus, the market is discounting the debt at an interest rate lower than 9.47%, implying a rating higher (better) than BBB.

18. {M}A.   Given the current market price of FF732, bonds convertible into common at FF990 should be classified as debt obligations. Only when the market price of PSA shares approaches the conversion price would conversion be considered likely.

B.   The cash payment on January 1, 1995 equals FF15.7 x 4 million = **FF62.8 million.**

      However, interest expense is based on the yield-to-maturity of 5%. For the nine months ended December 31 (ignoring any interest for March), interest expense equals 9/12 x 5% x FF3,960 = FF148.5 million. Thus the carrying amount of the debt must increase by FF148.5 - FF62.8 = **FF85.7 million.**

C. (i) At maturity, the carrying value per bond will equal FF1,234 (FF990 + FF234) reflecting the accrual of the excess of interest expense over interest paid. The carrying amount per bond can be approximated by carrying out the calculations from part B for the entire period (all amounts in FF):

Year	Opening Balance	Interest Expense	Cash Interest	Liability Increase	Closing Balance
1994	990.0	37.1	15.7	21.4	1,011.4
1995	1,011.4	50.6	19.8	30.8	1,042.2
1996	1,042.2	52.1	19.8	32.3	1,074.5
1997	1,074.5	53.7	19.8	33.9	1,108.4
1998	1,108.4	55.4	19.8	35.6	1,144.1
1999	1,144.1	57.2	19.8	37.4	1,181.5
2000	1,181.5	59.1	19.8	39.3	1,220.7

The computed amount is slightly lower than the actual amount due to our assumption that no interest is paid in March 1994 and because we computed interest annually rather than quarterly (which would compound interest faster).

(ii) For the entire bond issue, the redemption amount is FF4,896 million (4 million x FF1,234); the premium equals FF936 million. This can be approximated by calculations similar to those in part (i),(amounts in FF millions):

Year	Opening Balance	Interest Expense	Cash Interest	Liability Increase	Closing Balance
1994	3,960.0	148.5	62.8	85.7	4,045.7
1995	4,045.7	202.3	79.2	123.1	4,168.8
1996	4,168.8	208.4	79.2	129.2	4,298.0
1997	4,298.0	214.9	79.2	135.7	4,433.7
1998	4,433.7	221.7	79.2	142.5	4,576.2
1999	4,576.2	228.8	79.2	149.6	4,725.8
2000	4,725.8	236.3	79.2	157.1	4,882.9

As for the single bond, the computed amount is slightly below the actual amount.

(iii) As the carrying amount and redemption amounts will be equal, the redemption premium for financial reporting purposes equals zero. The premium is recognized as interest expense over the life of the bond.

(iv) The redemption premium will be included in cash outflow for financing (CFF).

D. (i) The advantage of convertible debt over straight debt is the lower interest rate and the possibility that the debt will be converted to common shares rather than requiring cash at maturity.

   The advantage of convertible debt over debt plus warrants is that none of the proceeds of issue need be allocated to the warrants. Such allocation (required for debt-plus-warrants) would increase reported interest expense as the reduced amount allocated to debt is amortized.

(ii) The advantage of discount debt is that CFO is increased; the portion of interest expense paid at redemption is never included in CFO.

19. {S}A. Future redemption depends on conditions in the credit markets at each "reset" date. Investors would choose redemption if more attractive SFR investments were available. That would be the case, for example, if PepsiCo's credit rating had declined.

   PepsiCo would redeem bonds if alternative financing sources are available or if Swiss franc debt is no longer desirable. The latter depends on PepsiCo's exposure to SFR assets at that time or, if the debt was swapped for debt in another currency, conditions in the swap market at that time.

B. The obligations should be classified as debt. One might argue that, because there is no stated maturity date, these bonds are "permanent" capital and should be considered equity. However the periodic reset provisions suggest that, at some point, either PepsiCo or investors will choose the redemption option. As investors can force redemption, the bonds should be classified as debt.

20.{S}A. (i)   SFR150/1.48 = $101.35
          (ii) SFR150/1.31 = $114.50

   B. Note 19 (text page 1125) states that the debt issuance
       proceeds were swapped for a U.S. dollar obligation.
       Thus, assuming that the swap counterparty does not fail
       to perform, duPont's obligation does not vary with the
       exchange rate. The increased dollar equivalent of the
       SFR obligation is not recognized in duPont's financial
       statements.

21.{M}

Amounts in millions	*12/31/93*		*12/31/94*	
A.	*$US*	*SFR*	*$US*	*SFR*
(i) Gross debt	1,000	1,480	1,000	1,310
(ii) Unamortized discount	278	411	245	321
(iii) Net debt	722	1,069	755	989

   B.

(i) Discount amortization	33
% of opening net debt	4.57%
(ii) Effective interest rate*	9.42%

       * 4.57% + 3.5% x
       1,000/722

   C. (i) Convertible debt would be shown at the full $1
           billion issue amount rather than the allocated
           $639 million for the bonds ex-warrants. The latter
           increases each year by the amortized discount.
           [Roche reports the SFR equivalent of these dollar
           amounts.]

      (ii) Interest expense on the convertible bonds would be
           (the SFR equivalent of) 3.5% of $1 billion, or $35
           million each year.
               When the proceeds are allocated between debt
           and warrants, interest expense is computed at the
           higher effective rate of 7.62% computed in B(ii).
           That rate is applied to the ever increasing
           carrying amount of the debt. Interest expense is
           (in $US) $55 million for 1994 (7.62% x $722
           million) and increases to $57.5 million for 1995
           (7.62% x $755 million).

(iii) Cash from operations is identical; actual interest paid reduces CFO. The only possible difference would be the consequence of different tax treatment for the two cases.

Cash from financing is also identical. In the year of issuance, an inflow of 1 billion is recorded. If the bonds are redeemed, a $1 billion outflow will be recorded in both cases.

If the warrants are exercised, there is no cash flow effect assuming that the bonds are delivered in payment.

The reported cash flow statement, therefore, is unaffected by the accounting choice of allocating the proceeds of convertible bonds between the bond and warrant portions.

22.{M}A. The market price of PepsiCo shares declined 13%, while debt increased. Thus, the market debt-to-equity ratio rose. As reported equity increased by more than debt, the book value ratio declined.

B. The market value debt-to-equity ratio is much lower than the book value ratio. The market price of PepsiCo shares must be far higher than book value as debt is at book value in both measures.

C. The market value of PepsiCo's equity reflects the financial markets' assessment of PepsiCo's future earnings and cash flows. It is these cash flows that will service the company's debt, making the market value ratio a superior measure of debt burden.

In addition, PepsiCo could sell additional equity if it wished, using the proceeds to reduce debt. Therefore, the market value of equity is a better measure of the company's ability to repay debt from this source.

D. On the other hand, market values can change, sometimes very quickly. The book value-based ratio compares PepsiCo's net assets with its debt burden.

Case 10-1 Solution

Approximate time to complete: 1 hour 45 minutes.

Comparative analysis of the financing liabilities of duPont, Dow Chemical, and Imperial Chemical Industries (ICI)

1. Interest expense related to discontinued operations should be excluded when measuring interest coverage applicable to continuing operations. Neither the debt nor the related interest charges remain obligations of the firm when the discontinued operations are sold or disposed of. However, if ICI has guaranteed the obligations of the discontinued unit, the interest coverage ratio calculation should include the interest expense related to discontinued operations.

2. (a) Market yield-to-maturity (YTM) of 8.00%.
    Annual coupon of Eurodollar issue is 8.55%.

    The market YTM is the rate at which the present value of the coupon and principal payments is equal to the 12/31/94 market price of 99.250. If we assume that three interest payments each of $4 million are made on 7/1/95, 12/31/95, and 7/1/96 with the return of principal of $100 million on 7/1/96, the YTM is 8.55%.
    If we assume one coupon payment of $8 million will be made on 12/31/1995 and a semi-annual payment of $ 4 million plus the principal repayment will be made on 7/1/1996, the present value of these two payments will be equal to 99.25 at 8.55%.
    The same rate results if we assume that a semi-annual payment of $ 4 million will be made on 7/1/1995 and an annual payment of $8 million plus the principal repayment will be made on 7/1/1996.

    (b) Exhibit 10CS-1 contains the market value computations for ICI's debt at December 31, 1994.

    (c) On December 31, 1994, Exhibit 10P-1 reports average yields of 8.52% for AA rated and 8.90% for A rated industrial and utility bonds with average maturities of 20 years. Maturities of the U.S. dollar debt issues of ICI range from 27 months for the 7.625s of 3/15/1997 to nearly 12 years for the 8.875s of 11/15/2006. The YTMs for these issues range from 8.31% to 8.60%. Yields of A+ rated bonds would be expected to fall between the AA and A rated bond yields and given their shorter maturities, yields on ICI debt issues are consistent with data provided by Exhibit 10P-1.

3.

    (a)   Exhibit 10P-1 tells us that the average yield on 'A' rated industrial bonds with 20 years to maturity was 8.90% on December 31, 1994. Dow's longest bond matures in the year 2010 (16 years) and yields 8.77% for a difference of 13 basis points (8.90%-8.77%). The short-term (2-4 years) U.S. government securities yielded 7.55% and the intermediate term (6-9 years) U.S. government securities yielded 7.76% on that day compared to 8.00% for 8.25% issue that matures in 1996. Dow's issues maturing in 8 to 9 years yield 8.40% or 50 basis points less than 'A' rated bonds. The difference is due to shorter maturities and low coupons (7.38% and 7.13%).

            The yields appear to be reasonably consistent with data in Exhibit 10P-1. The two exceptions are the 5.75% convertible and the 9.35% issue. These are discussed in 3(b).

    (b)   The 5.75% convertible issue bonds are convertible into shares of Magma Power Company (Magma) at $37.50 per share and on December 31, 1994, Magma shares were trading at $37 per share. During 1994, $135 million of these bonds were exchanged for shares of Magma. The low YTM reflects the value of the conversion feature.

            The 8.73% YTM of the 9.35% issue with seven years to maturity stems from the high coupon (shorter duration) and short remaining term to maturity.

    (c)   During 1994, Dow retired $526 million of long-term debt. The issues retired must have carried higher coupons and new debt must have been issued at lower rates lowering the average interest rate of remaining debt. Debt retired included $261 million at a weighted average rate of 6.42% and $350 million at a weighted average rate of 8.93% for an overall weighted average of 7.86%; new debt issues carry coupons of 7%.

    (d)   During 1994, the A rated bond yield rose from 7.91% in January to 8.98% in November closing the year at 8.90%. In 1993, yields began the year at a high of 8.48% and fell to 7.83% at the end of the year. Government bond yields show similar changes. The fair value of debt has declined because market rates have risen.

4. (a) During December 1994 AA bonds yielded 8.52% whereas the 8.125% issue maturing in 2004 traded at a YTM of 8.28% just below the AAA YTM of 8.30%. Reasons include the shorter maturity and improving credit position of duPont.

   (b) Note: The average interest rates used in this question relate to medium-term notes due 1995-2005 (See Footnote 19, page 1125). The firm did not report the average interest on total long-term debt. However, Footnote 19 shows that average interest rates on industrial development bonds and on other loans (various currencies) were 6.1% and 7.3% at December 31, 1994 and 6.0% and 7.4% at December 31, 1993.

   The remaining debt listed in Footnote 19 suggests a decline in average rates. Finally, the firm has used interest rates swaps that may be costly if rates rise as suggested by Exhibit 10P-1. However, according to Footnote 19 the effect in 1994 was insignificant.

   (c) See 3(d).

5. The relative sensitivity of the market values of debt and interest expense to changes in interest rates is a function of firm size, D/E ratio, interest rate risk management, and ratings. We cannot compare these two firms to ICI since we do not have 1993 data for ICI. However, Exhibit 10CS-1 shows a negligible decline in market value for ICI's U.S. dollar denominated debt. DuPont has more debt and its decline in market value is greater (11.5% decline compared to 7.5%) than that reported by Dow. In addition, after the interest swaps (see p. 1131), duPont debt is mostly fixed rate. Thus, the market value of duPont's debt is more sensitive to changes in interest rates. Its interest expense will largely remain constant.

EXHIBIT 10CS-1, Imperial Chemical Industries PLC (ICI)
Market Valuation of Long Term Debt at December 31, 1994

Coupon	Maturity	BV	FV	MP	MV	YTM

Debt for Which Market Prices Are Available
$U.S. Debt

7.625%	March 15 1997	225	225	98.63	221.91	8.31%
9.500%	November 15 2000	300	300	104.50	313.50	8.51%
8.750%	May 1 2001	250	250	101.25	253.13	8.49%
7.500%	January 15 2002	200	200	95.63	191.25	8.33%
8.875%	November 15 2006	250	250	102.00	255.00	8.60%

Eurodollar Debt

8.000%	July 1 1996	100	100	99.25	99.25	8.55%
	Subtotal	$1,325	$1,325		$1,334.03	

Debt for Which Market Prices Are Not Available

All secured loans	263	263	100.00	262.50
All unsecured loans[1]	1,073	1,073	100.00	1,073.40
Subtotal	£1,336	£1,336		£1,335.90

[1] This category includes the 7.83 to 8.9% medium-term notes and all debt
denominated in foreign currencies.

Chapter 11 Solutions

Overview:
Problem Length   *Problem #s*
  {S}   *1, 2, 3, 4, 9, 12, and 13*
  {M}   *5, 8, 11, 14, 15, 16, and 18*
  {L}   *6, 7, 10, 17, and 19*

1. (S) First year effects, capitalized versus operating lease method:

   (i)   Current ratio will be lower when the lease is capitalized as current liabilities now include the current portion of the capitalized lease obligation.

   (ii) The debt-to-equity ratio will be higher because the present value of the minimum lease payments must be reported as debt. Also, at the end of the first-year, reported equity may decline because capitalization reduces net income (see part iv).

   (iii) Operating income will be higher under capitalization. It is decreased only by depreciation. Under the operating lease method it is decreased by the full amount of the lease payment. [Depreciation is almost always lower, even when an accelerated depreciation method is used.] The interest component of lease expense (capital lease method) is a non-operating expense.

   (iv) Net income in the first year is lower under the capital lease method as total lease expense (the sum of depreciation and interest expense) exceeds the annual rental (lease expense under the operating lease method).

   (v)   Cash flow from operations is higher when leases are capitalized as only a portion (interest component) of the annual rental payment is reported as an operating cash outflow; the remainder is considered a financing cash outflow.

2.{S}   **Effect of choice of interest rate on lessee:**

		9% versus 10%	
		First Year	Lease Term
(i)	Interest expense: Lower interest rate reduces interest expense.	Lower	Lower
(ii)	Amortization expense: Lower interest rate increases present value of minimum lease payments, creating higher asset amount to be amortized over lease term.	Higher	Higher
(iii)	Total lease expense: The net effect for the first year depends on the lease amounts; over the lease term, however, total expense equals total lease payments regardless of the choice of interest rate.	Indeter minate	Equal
(iv)	Cash from operations: Lower interest rate shifts expense from interest to amortization (see i and ii); as cash from operations is decreased only by interest expense, a decrease in interest expense increases CFO, both in the first year and over the leas term.	Higher	Higher
(v)	Average assets: Lower interest rate increases present value (see ii) resulting in higher average assets, both in first year and over lease term.	Higher	Higher
(vi)	Average liabilities: Lower interest rate increases present value recognized as liability, both in first year and over lease term.	Higher	Higher

3.{S}A.   Present value of 10 annual payments of $2,400 plus the present value of a single payment of $4,000 due 10 years hence, both discounted at 9% is:

($2,400 x 6.4177) + ($4,000 x .4224) = $17,092

B.   Interest expense (.09 x $17,092)   = $1,538
+ Depreciation expense ($17,092-$4,000)/10   =   1,309
Total lease expense   = $2,847

C.   Total lease expense will decline over the lease term. Interest expense will fall as a fixed interest rate is applied to a declining liability. Depreciation expense remains constant as Dale uses the straight-line method. Total lease expense would decline faster if the firm used an accelerated depreciation method.

4.{S}A.   Pallavi must capitalize the lease because the lease
          agreement contains a bargain purchase option. Note that
          the lease also meets two other capitalization criteria:
          The lease term of 15 years is at least 75% of the
          economic life of the equipment, and the present value
          of minimum lease payments exceeds 90% of the fair
          market value of the equipment (see B for computations).

     B.   The fair market value of the asset is $125,000. The
          present value of the MLPs is $128,392 (at 8%, the lower
          of the lessee and lessor rates); the asset must be
          capitalized at the (lower) fair market value.

     C.   The existence of the bargain purchase option requires
          depreciation over the estimated economic life of the
          asset rather than the (shorter) lease term.

     D.   The option creates the presumption that the asset will
          be held past the expiration date of the lease.
          Otherwise it must be assumed that use of the asset will
          revert to the lessor at expiration, requiring the
          lessee to depreciate the leased asset over the
          (shorter) lease term.

5.{M}A.   The following states the effects of Tolrem using the
          capital lease method as compared with the operating
          lease method.

          (i)   Cash from operations is higher as only the
                interest portion of lease expense is deducted from
                operating cash flows; total lease expense is
                deducted for operating leases.

          (ii) Financing cash flow is lower for capital lease, as
                part of lease rental is treated as amortization of
                liability and classified as financing cash
                outflow.

          (iii) Investing cash flow is not affected by the lease
                treatment. However, the firm will report capital
                leases in the statement of cash flows (or a
                footnote) as noncash investment activities.

          (iv) Net cash flow is the actual rental payment and is
                unaffected by the financial reporting treatment of
                the lease.

(v)   Debt/equity ratio is higher for capital lease, as
       it records the present value of minimum lease
       payments as debt *and* reduces net income (and
       therefore equity) in first year.

(vi)   Interest coverage ratio is usually (not always)
       lower for capital lease method, which reports
       interest expense but also higher EBIT, see (vii).
       For coverage ratios well above 1.0, the ratio will
       decline. If the increase in interest expense
       exceeds the increase in EBIT, the ratio will
       decline even for firms with very low coverage
       ratios.

(vii) Operating income is lower for operating lease; for
       capital lease, interest portion of lease expense
       is nonoperating.

(viii) Net income is higher for operating lease; total
       lease expense (interest plus depreciation) is
       higher for capital lease.

(ix)   Deferred tax assets are higher for capital lease;
       as lease treatment for tax purposes is unaffected
       by accounting choice, capital lease will generate
       a deferred tax asset as taxable income (operating
       lease) exceeds pretax income (capital lease).

(x)   Taxes paid are unaffected by choice of method.

(xi)   Pretax return on assets is higher for operating
       leases as pretax income is higher and no assets
       are reported as the result of the lease; a capital
       lease reduces income and reports lease assets.
       Post-tax return on assets is higher for the same
       reasons.

(xii) Pretax return on equity: both pretax income and
       equity are higher for operating than for capital
       leases. The higher pretax income should increase
       the ratio in all but exceptional cases. Post-tax
       return on equity should be higher for same reason.
       However as increase in post-tax income equals (for
       first year) increase in equity, there may be more
       exceptional cases.

B.   Net income (viii) will be lower for the operating lease
     after the "crossover" point. As total net income over
     the life of the lease is unaffected by the accounting
     choice, higher net income (operating lease) in the
     early years must be offset by lower net income in later
     years.

C.   Consistent use of the operating lease method in place
     of capitalization will not change the direction of the
     effects shown in part A, but will increase their
     magnitude. In aggregate, new leases will keep Tolrem
     from reaching the crossover point for net income,
     keeping net income and return ratios higher than if the
     leases were capitalized.

6.{L}A. and B.

	Caramino	Aglianico	Difference
Operating income	$ 20,000	$ 20,000	$ None
Depreciation expense[1]	(8,624)		(8,624)
Lease rental expense		(10,000)	10,000
EBIT	$ 11,376	$ 10,000	$ 1,376
Interest expense[2]	(2,650)		(2,650)
Earnings before tax	$ 8,726	$ 10,000	$ (1,274)
Income tax expense	(3,490)	(4,000)	510
Net income	$ 5,236	$ 6,000	$ (764)

[1] The present value of the minimum lease payments is $43,121
    ($10,000 + 4 payment annuity of $10,000 per year at 8%).
    Assuming zero residual value, depreciation = $43,121/5 =
    $8,624.
[2] Interest expense = 8% x ($43,121-$10,000) = $2,650

Caramino's EBIT $1,376 higher; Aglianico reports rental
expense but no depreciation expense since it does not
record an asset. Because total lease expense
(depreciation plus interest) is higher than the lease
rental, Caramino's EBT is lower by $1,274. After a
deferred income tax offset of $510, Caramino's net
income is $764 lower.

Caramino's deferred tax debit (asset) results from the
difference between financial reporting (capital lease)
and tax reporting (operating lease). The $1,274 timing
difference results in a deferred tax debit of $1,274 x
.40 = $510

C. and D. Comparison of Cash Flow Statements

	Caramino	Aglianico	Difference
Net income	$ 5,236	$ 6,000	$ (764)
Addback:			
Depreciation expense	8,624		8,624
	$ 13,860	$ 6,000	$ 7,860
Other adjustments:			
Deferred taxes	(510)		(510)
Interest payable	2,650		2,650
Cash from operations	$ 16,000	$ 6,000	$ 10,000
Investment cash flow	-0-	-0-	-0-
Financing cash flow	(10,000)	-0-	(10,000)
Net cash flow	$ 6,000	$ 6,000	$ -0-

Note: We assume that all revenues generated by the firm have been collected by the end of the year.

Caramino reports higher cash from operations by $10,000. Since the tax rate is 40%, Aglianico (operating lease firm) reports aftertax operating cash *outflow* of $6,000. Caramino (capital lease firm) pays no interest but, since it uses the operating lease method for taxes, receives a tax deduction of $4,000 for the annual payment of $10,000. Caramino's aftertax operating cash *inflow* is $4,000.

The difference ($6,000 + $4,000 = $10,000) is recorded by Caramino as a *financing* cash outflow; this is the amount of the lease payment considered a reduction of the capitalized lease liability for 1993. [Note that the lease payment made on January 1, 1993 has no interest component; there is no accrued interest as the lease has just begun. Interest accrued during the year will be paid January 1, 1994.]

E.   There is no impact on investing cash flow for either firm. Caramino would report the present value of the capital lease as a noncash investment activity.

F.   The net cash outflow for each firm is the lease payment of $10,000 less the tax deduction of $4,000 (40% tax rate). Only the classification of cash flow components is affected by the lease method used.

G.   By using the capital lease method, Caramino reports higher debt and lower income. However the firm also reports higher cash from operations. The choice of method may reflect different debt covenants or simply a preference among financial characteristics.

7.{L}A.   The adjustment involves the addition of the interest
           component of minimum lease payments to stated interest
           expense. The adjustment reflects a partial, *de facto*
           capitalization of operating leases.

Unadjusted Ratio of Earnings to Fixed Charges:

Pretax earnings	$ 744,343
Interest on indebtedness	65,381
Earnings before interest and taxes (EBIT)	$ 809,724
Fixed Charges:	
Interest on indebtedness	$ 65,381
Unadjusted Ratio of Earnings to Fixed Charges	12.38X

The unadjusted ratio is more than three times the
adjusted ratio. Note, however, that the SEC rule that
governs this calculation assumes that the interest
component of the MLP is one-third. As can be seen from
part B, the interest component is higher, reducing the
coverage ratio further.

B.   The Limited, Inc.
      1994 Working Capital Position and Capitalization Table

	Reported	Adjusted
Cash from operating activities	$ 361,078	$ 670,337[1]
Working capital	1,750,111	1,440,852[2]
Capitalization:		
Long-term debt	650,000	650,000
Add: Capitalized lease payments		3,811,099[3]
Adjusted long-term debt		$4,461,099
Deferred income taxes	306,139	306,139
Shareholders' equity	2,760,956	2,760,956[4]
Total capitalization	$3,717,095	$7,528,194

[1] Addback of difference between rental expense and interest component:
($614,147 - (.08 x $3,811,099), where $3,811,099 is the present value
calculated in note 3 below. The net amount, $309,259, would be included
in cash flow from financing.

These calculations use the same MLP data that The Limited uses for
its adjusted coverage ratio. The minimum lease payment in the footnote
($617,645) is higher, perhaps because of definitional differences.

[2] Working capital is reduced by the principal component of the 1995 MLPs
(calculated in note 2 above). No adjustment is made here for the
deferred tax asset that would be reported on capitalization.

[3] Present value of MLPs using an interest rate of 8%. The "thereafter"
MLPs are spread equally over the 6 years ending in 2005.

[4] At year-end, equity will be reduced by capitalization as it reduces
net income.

The Limited: Measures of Liquidity and Capital Resources

	Reported	Adjusted
Debt-to-equity ratio (long-term debt divided by shareholders' equity)	24%	162%
Debt-to-capitalization ratio (long-term debt divided by total capitalization)	17%	59%
Interest coverage ratio (income before interest, depreciation, amortization, and income taxes divided by interest expense)	16X	3.65X[a]
Cash flow to capital investment (net cash provided by operating activities divided by capital expenditures)	113%[b]	210%[c]

[a] The reported interest coverage ratio of 16X implies income before interest expense, depreciation, amortization, and income taxes of $1,046,096 (16 * interest expense of $65,381). The adjusted coverage ratio is computed by adding interest of $304,888 on capitalized leases (.08 * $3,811,099) to reported interest. The adjusted coverage ratio is ($1,046,096 + $ 304,888) / ($65,381 + $ 304,888) = 3.65X.

[b] Implied capital expenditures are $ 319,538.

[c] $670,337/$319,538 using adjusted CFO.

Comparison of Reported and Adjusted Capitalization Table and Ratios: The adjusted capitalization shows the significantly higher leverage of the firm. Adjusted debt is seven times reported debt. This is evident in both debt and coverage ratios. However, the adjusted coverage ratio (3.76X) reported in The Limited's 10-K captures most of the effect of these off-balance sheet transactions. This example illustrates the importance for financial analysis of capitalizing leases used by retail firms.

The ratio of CFO to capital expenditures nearly doubles when operating leases are capitalized. This counterintuitive result is discussed on text page 540.

8.{M}A. Comparison of Reported CFO and Ratios

Three Months Ended	4/2/95	4/2/94
CFO	$ 34,649	$ 6,747
Current Ratio	1.64	2.10
CFO/Current Liabilities	0.52	0.10

The Wackenhut Corporation appears to have reported a significant improvement in its CFO and the CFO/Current Liabilities Ratio. However, the current ratio deteriorated during the same period as current assets declined with a slight increase in current liabilities.

B. Comparison of Adjusted CFO and Ratios

Three Months Ended	4/2/95	4/2/94
CFO	$ 5,709[1]	$ 6,747
Current Assets	137,295[2]	137,645
Current Liabilities	95,135[2]	65,570
Current Ratio	1.44	2.10
CFO/Current Liabilities	0.06	0.10

[1] Reported CFO of $34,649 minus $28,940, cash received on securitization of receivables.

[2] $28,940,000 of securitized receivables have been added back to both current assets and current liabilities.

The securitized receivables are added back to current assets and current liabilities to restore comparability; the firm has retained the same risk of credit loss as if the receivables had not been sold. We treat the securitization as a collateralized borrowing transaction. The increase in CFO and the CFO/current liabilities ratio disappear when the accelerated cash collection due to securitization is eliminated. Similarly, current assets and liabilities are increased, reflecting the deterioration in liquidity.

9.{S}A. The cash outflow of $25.6 million represents the decrease in the balance of sold but uncollected receivables ($192.8 - $167.2). It represents net collections (by Arkla as the firm continues to service the receivables) of receivables sold; amounts collected from previously sold receivables were paid to the purchasers of those receivables.

B. Receivables sold but uncollected as of 12/31/93 can be deduced to be:

Outstanding 3/31/94	$118.7 million
Decrease during quarter	107.7
Outstanding 12/31/93	$226.4 million

C. The required adjustments to Arkla's CFO for quarters ended:

	March 31, 1994	March 31, 1995
Cash outflow	107.7	25.6

These amounts are the decrease in receivables sold during the respective quarters. The adjustment is required because the cash flow was recognized when the receivables were sold rather than when customers paid. This adjustment produces a measure of CFO based on when the receivables were collected.

10{L}A. Since December 1991, Morrison Knudsen has sold receivables. Assuming that there was no gain or loss on these sales and that proceeds were used to repay debt, the sold receivables should be added back to the receivables (see below), current assets, and short-term debt (current liabilities).

	1990	1991	1992	1993
Reported Accounts Receivable	$182,283	$135,253	$160,196	$231,021
Sold Receivables	-0-	66,976	87,264	75,937
Adjusted Receivables	$ 182,283	$202,229	$247,460	$306,958
Average Receivables: as reported		158,768	147,725	195,609
adjusted		192,256	224,845	277,209

		1990	1991	1992	1993
Current Assets	Reported	$645,440	$658,200	$681,412	$793,221
	Adjusted	645,440	725,176	768,676	869,158
Current Liabilities					
	Reported	$404,795	$379,121	$608,730	$689,534
	Adjusted	404,795	446,097	695,994	765,471

		1992	1993
Current ratio	Reported	1.12	1.15
	Adjusted	1.10	1.14
Receivables turnover	Reported	15.47	13.92
	Adjusted	10.16	9.82
Days Receivables	Reported	24	26
	Adjusted	36	37

1993 Computations:
Current ratio: Reported = $793,221/ $689,534 = 1.15
            Adjusted = $869,158/ $765,471 = 1.14
Receivables turnover: Reported = $2,722,543/$195,609 = 13.92; days receivables
= 365/13.92 = 26
        Adjusted = $2,722,543/$277,209 = 9.82; days receivables = 365/9.82 = 37

The cash cycle equals days of receivables plus days of inventories less days of payables. Neither the inventories nor the payables are affected by sales of receivables. Therefore, the receivables sales improved the cash cycle. However, the adjusted data show that the receivables are actually outstanding longer and the firm's cash cycle increased.

B.	1992	1993
Total debt		
Reported	$ 6,214	$ 47,006
Adjustment	87,264	75,937
Adjusted	$ 93,478	$122,943
Equity	375,771	406,967
Debt-to-equity		
Reported	0.02	0.12
Adjusted	0.25	0.30
Total capital		
Reported	$381,985	$453,973
Adjustment	87,264	75,937
Adjusted	$469,249	$529,910
EBIT	36,690	66,075
Return on total capital		
Reported	9.6%	14.6%
Adjusted	7.8%	12.5%

Including the sold receivables increases the debt-to-equity ratio significantly for both years. The higher denominator reduces return-on-total-capital. Note that EBIT should be adjusted for interest on sold receivables; however, no information on interest expense or interest rates has been provided.

C.

	1990	1991	1992	1993
Receivables sold				
Closing		$66,976	$ 87,264	$ 75,937
Opening		-	66,976	87,264
Change		$66,976	$ 20,288	$(11,327)
Cash flow from operations				
Reported	$72,679	94,652	173,905	(64,302)
Adjustment	-	(66,976)	(20,288)	11,327
Adjusted	$72,679	$27,676	$153,617	$(52,975)

The sale of receivables increases the cash flow from operations. In the absence of sales of receivables, the firm would have reported lower CFO in 1991 and 1992. In 1993, the reduced amount of sold receivables reduced CFO. Sales of receivables distort reported CFO in each year as well as year-to-year comparisons.

11.{M} A. First, we compute data required to solve the problem.
($ in millions)

		1993	1994
Accounts receivable	Reported	$ 546.0	$ 742.0
Sold receivables		263.8	296.8
Adjusted receivables		$ 809.8	$1,038.8
Average receivables	Reported		644.0
	Adjusted		924.3
Current assets	Reported	2,078.0	2,229.0
	Adjusted	2,341.8	2,525.8
Current liabilities	Reported	1,993.0	2,232.0
	Adjusted	2,256.8	2,528.8
Total debt	Reported	1,707.0	1,530.0
	Adjusted	1,970.8	1,826.8

The ratios can be computed as follows:

		1994	Computations
Current ratio	Reported	1.00	$ 2,229 / $ 2,232
	Adjusted	1.00	$2,525.8/$2,528.8
Receivables turnover	Reported	7.91	$ 5,093 / $ 644
	Adjusted	5.51	$ 5,093 / $ 924.3
Days receivables	Reported	46	365 / 7.91
	Adjusted	66	365 / 5.51

The cash cycle equals days of receivables plus days of inventories less days of payables. Neither the inventories nor the payables are affected by sales of receivables. Therefore, sales of receivables, by increasing days of receivables from a reported 46 days to an adjusted 66 days, increases the cash cycle by the same number of days.

B.

	1994	Computations
Debt to equity ratio: Reported	1.02	$1,530.0/$1,505.0
Adjusted	1.22	$1,826.8/$1,505.0
Return on total capital: Reported	8.18%	$ 249 / $ 3,045
Adjusted	7.47%	$ 249/ $ 3.331.8

The adjusted leverage ratio is higher and the adjusted return lower than the reported ratios.

C.

	1994
CFO - as reported	$ 454.0
Sold receivables	(33.0)
Adjusted CFO	$ 421.0

The firm reported an increase of 87% in CFO. However, the increase in receivables sold inflated CFO by recognizing the proceeds of sale sooner than if the receivables had been collected in the normal course of business. To compare with 1993 CFO, we would need to know the change in receivables sold during that year as well.

12. {S} Aluminum producers that have take-or-pay contracts for energy and/or bauxite have converted significant variable costs into fixed costs. Therefore, their marginal costs are much lower than if these contracts had not been entered into. Under these conditions, aluminum producers will continue production as long as revenue exceeds *marginal costs*, even though they lose money based on *total costs*.

13. {S} A. If the bonds were converted, Alleghany would record a gain of $31,418,000, the difference between the face amount of the bonds and the carrying amount of the shares. [Note that conversion of the bonds would require Allegheny to surrender virtually all of its American Express shares; 59,600 x 22.8833 = 1,363,844 shares.]

   B. Dividend income is 1,366,000 shares @ $.94 = $1,284,000 or $1,197,000 after the effective tax rate of 7.2% [.20 x 36%] on dividend income. Interest expense is $59,600,000 x .065 = $3,874,000 or $2,479,000 after 36% tax. The net cost is therefore, $1,282,000 per year or 2.15% of the face amount of bonds.

   C. By issuing exchangeable bonds rather than selling its American Express shares, Allegheny avoided the payment of capital gains taxes. When the bonds are exchanged, Allegheny will receive a higher price than if it had sold the shares (exchangeable bonds are sold with an exchange price above current market). In the meanwhile, Allegheny enjoys the use of the funds at a low net cost.

14.{M} A. Debt should be increased by:

$ 20 million   (present value of operating lease)
   5   (guarantee)
   7   (present value of take-or-pay agreement)
$ 32 million

There is no effect on equity as each obligation is offset by a corresponding asset:
    Leased assets for operating lease
    Receivable for Crockett's obligation to repay debt
    Supply agreement

The recomputed debt-to-equity ratio is: ($12 + $32)/$20 = 2.2X as compared to .6X before adjustment

B. Additional interest expense is:

Lease (effective interest rate is about 18%)
                        .18 x $20 = $ 3.6 million
Bond guarantee   .10 x   5 =   0.5
   Total $ 4.1 million

Before adjustment, the interest expense is $1.0 million and the times interest earned ratio is 5.0, implying EBIT of $5.0 million.

After adjustment, the ratio is:
($5.0 + $4.1)/($1.0 + $4.1) = 1.78 X

No adjustment has been made for the take-or-pay contract as it does not affect 1993 interest expense. Adjustments in future years will be based on the implicit interest rate of 21%.

C. Reasons for entering into off-balance-sheet obligations:

1. Avoidance of or mitigation of the risk of violating debt covenant restrictions.
2. Leased assets revert to lessor after eight years, limiting risk of obsolescence.
3. Guarantee of Crockett's debt may lower interest costs, increasing profitability of investment.
4. Contract with PEPE secures source of supply and possibly advantageous pricing.

D.   Additional information needed for full evaluation:

   1.   (Lease) Useful life of leased assets; conditions under which lease can be canceled; nature of leased assets.
   2.   (Guarantee) Financial condition of Crockett; bond covenants.
   3.   (Take-or-pay) Alternate sources of supply; quantity to be purchased relative to total needs; price provisions of contract.

Problems 15 and 16 may be assigned separately or together. If assigned together, the two problems would take 75 - 90 minutes.

15 (M)A. (i) Computation of implicit interest rate using 1995 interest expense:

Year ending December 31, 1995 ($ in millions)

Minimum lease payment (MLP) for operating leases	$ 20
Less: Current portion of lease obligation	8
Equals: Interest component	$ 12
Present Value of minimum lease payments	94

Therefore, Interest rate = $12 / $94 = **12.77%**

   (ii) Computation of implicit interest rate using the minimum lease payments over the lease term:

Reported MLPs	
1995	$ 20
1996	16
1997	11
1998	11
1999	11
Remainder	104
Total	$173
PV of MLPs	$ 94

From the year 2000 on, we assume that the MLPs equal the 1999 MLP of $11 million. You may use a declining rate assumption. However, note that the 1997-1999 payments are stable at $11 million a year. Also, the Box 11-2 illustration of AMR Corp.'s operating leases shows that the use of the declining rate produced a difference of only 3% in computed present values.

   The   constant   rate   assumption   implies   an

11-16

additional 9 payments of $11 million each and a final payment of $5 million for the last year. This payment pattern and the reported present value of $94 million suggest an interest rate of 10.12%. Footnote 20 includes executory costs of $7 million in the total MLPs of $173 million. The implicit interest rate is 9.29% if we gross up the reported present value of $94 million to account for the executory costs.

B.   Interest rate implicit in the capital leases based on:

(i) 1995 interest expense   12.77%

(ii) MLPs over the life of the lease   10.12%   (or 9.29%, see part (A))

Using 1995 interest expense ignores the steep decline in MLPs over the lease term. Footnote 20 shows a decline of 25% from $20 million to $16 million in 1996 and a decrease of more than 31% in 1997 followed by equal payments in 1998 and 1999. When first year MLPs are significant, the timing of lease payments can distort these computations. Use of a declining rate assumption and consideration of executory costs would produce a lower interest rate.

C.   Operating Leases

Reported MLPs	
1995	$ 290million
1996	224
1997	182
1998	156
1999	124
Remainder	673
Total MLPs	$ 1,649million

The constant rate assumption gives us five more payments equal to the 1999 payment of $124 million and a final payment of $ 53 million. The present value of the operating lease MLPs at 12.77% is $980 million.

D.   Exhibit 4.7 (page 164) contains the 1990-1994 duPont
      long-term debt and solvency analysis. Summarized 1994
      data follow:

Capitalization Table

	Reported	Adjusted
Reported total debt	$ 7,668	
PV of operating lease		980
Adjusted total debt		$ 8,648
Reported total equity	12,822	
Total capital	20,490	21,470
EBIT	4,941	5,066 (4,941+125)
Interest expense	703 Includes capitalized interest	828 (703+125)
Interest on PV of operating leases		125 (.1277 x 980)
Ratios		
Debt to equity	**0.60** (7,668/12,822)	**0.67** (8,648/12,822)
Debt to capital	**0.37** (7,668/20490)	**0.40** (8,648/21,470)
Times interest earned	**7.03** (4,941/703)	**6.12** (5,066/828)

The addition of the PV of operating lease payments shows the
higher leverage and lower interest coverage relative to reported
data.

16.{M}DuPont

	Reported	Adjusted
Reported total debt	$ 7,668	
PV of operating lease		$ 980
Pro rata interest in affiliates' debt		1,220
Adjusted total debt		$ 9,868
Reported total equity	12,822	
Total capital	20,490	22,690
EBIT	4,941	5,176 (4,941+125+110)
Interest expense	703 includes capitalized interest	938 (703+125+110)
Interest on PV of operating leases		125 (.1277x980)
Interest on affiliates' debt		110 (.09x1,220)
Ratios		
Debt to equity	**0.60** (7,668/12,822)	**0.77** (9,868/12,822)
Debt to capital	**0.37** (7,668/20,490)	**0.43** (9,868/22,690)
Times interest earned	**7.03** (4,941/703)	**5.52** (5,176/938)

The addition of the PV of operating leases and DuPont's pro rata share of affiliates' debt results in much higher leverage and lower interest coverage relative to reported data.

17.{L}Extension of Problem 10-17, Ashland Coal, Inc.

A.

1994 Capitalization Table and Leverage Analysis ($ in thousands)

	Reported	Adjusted
Total debt	$243,963	
PV of fixed charges of Dominion[1]		31,781
PV of operating leases[2]		31,804
PV of leased mining equipment[3]		41,701
Adjusted total debt		$349,249
Reported total equity	368,983	
Total capital	612,946	718,232
EBIT	55,086	64,561 (55,086+2,862+ 2,860+3,753)
Interest expense	22,414	31,889 (22,414+2862+ 2,860+3,753)
Interest on PV of operating leases		2,862 (.09x31,804)
Interest on affiliates' debt		2,860 (.09x31,781)
Interest on leased equipment		3,753(.09x41,701)
Ratios		
Debt to equity	**0.66** (243,963/ 368,983)	**0.95** (349,249/368,983)
Debt to capital	**0.40** (243,963/ 612,946)	**0.49** (349,249/718,232)
Times interest earned	**2.46** (55,086/ 22,414)	**2.02** (64,561/31,889)

[1] PV of 21 payments of $3,000 each and one payment (22 years hence) of $26,000. Alternatively, you may use 17.5% of $132,800 or ($23,240) of financing costs.

[2] PV of operating lease payments from Note 19 (page 580).

[3] PV of payments on mining equipment under sale-leaseback: $10,500 in 1995, $2,500 in 1996, and guaranteed residual value of $35,600.

B. Ashland Coal is a highly leveraged firm employing several off-balance sheet techniques. The adjustments computed in Part A enable us to evaluate its actual leverage and risk more completely than the picture presented by the financial statements.

C.

Adjusted Exhibit 11-8
Ashland Oil, Inc.
ADJUSTED LONG-TERM DEBT AND SOLVENCY ANALYSIS
ADJUSTED CAPITALIZATION

	9/30/94
Total debt	$1,697
Stockholders' equity (BV)	1,639
Total capital (BV)	$3,336
Stockholders' equity (MV)	2,504
Total capital (MV)	$4,201
Adjustments to Debt:	
50% of Arch Mineral noncurrent liabilities	357
39% of Ashland Coal liabilities and OBS[1]	136
20% of LOOP and LOCAP's debt	105
38%-50% of other noncurrent liabilities	36
Capitalization of operating leases	296
Adjusted total debt	**$2,627**
Adjusted total capital (BV)	**4,266**
Adjusted total capital (MV)	**5,131**
Debt	
to equity (BV)	1.04
to capital (BV)	0.51
Debt	
to equity (MV)	0.68
to capital (MV)	0.40
Adjusted Debt	
to equity (BV)	**1.60**
to adjusted capital (BV)	**0.62**
Adjusted Debt	
to equity (MV)	**1.05**
to adjusted capital (MV)	**0.51**

[1] See Part A

D. Additional data on transactions with and obligations of Dominion terminal Associates, Coal's pension and other postemployment benefits, and the terms of the convertible preferred issue would be useful in assessing the financial and operational impact of Coal's off-balance sheet obligations on Coal and Ashland.

18.{M}

		1st Year	**9th Year**
(i)	Assets	Higher	Higher
(ii)	Revenues	Higher	Lower
(iii)	Expenses	Higher	Lower
(iv)	Asset turnover ratio	Higher	Lower
(v)	Interest income	Higher	Higher
(vi)	Cost of goods sold	Higher	No effect
(vii)	Net income	Higher	Lower
(viii)	Retained earnings	Higher	Higher
(ix)	Taxes paid	No effect	No effect
(x)	Post-tax ROA	Higher	Lower
(xi)	Cash from operations	Higher	Lower
(xii)	Investment cash flow	Lower	Higher

Assets are higher because inventory is replaced with (higher) receivables because of the recognition of manufacturing profit. Assets remain higher throughout the lease term.

Revenues are higher in Year 1 as the sales-type lease recognizes a sale whereas the operating lease method does not. In later years, interest revenue from the sales-type lease should be lower than lease revenue for the operating lease. This effect is more pronounced over time; in year 9 interest income is low given the small remaining receivable. The revenue effect increases the asset turnover ratio in the first year. But the revenue effect reduces turnover in the ninth year.

Expenses are higher in year 1 due to the recognition of cost of goods sold. In later years, there is no expense for the sales-type lease; the operating lease method reports depreciation expense in every year, however.

Initial period income and income-related ratios are higher for the sales-type lease because the sale (and income) is recognized at the inception of the lease. In later years, however, income is higher for the operating lease.

Income taxes paid are the same since the lease cannot be considered a completed sale for tax purposes.

Cash from operations is higher for the first year due to recognition of the sale (the investment in the lease is classified as an investing cash outflow). In later years the operating lease method shows higher cash from operations as rental income exceeds the interest income recorded for the sales-type lease (income taxes paid are the same).

[See Exhibit 11A-1 and the accompanying text for further explanation of these effects.]

19.{L}A. The present value of the minimum lease payments receivable of $170,271 (at 10%, the lower of lessee and lessor rates) is more than 90% of the fair market value of $185,250. Therefore, the lessee, Baldes, should capitalize the lease. It would be useful to know whether the lessee has guaranteed the residual value of the leased asset.

B.
Leased assets	$ 170,271
Long-term lease obligation	167,298
Current portion of lease obligation	2,973
Total lease obligation	$ 170,271

Note that there are no income or cash flow statement effects at the inception of the lease.

C. (i) **Balance sheet effects of capital lease:**

	01/01/94	12/31/94	12/31/95
Leased assets	$170,271	$170,271	$170,271
Accumulated depreciation	0	(8,514)	(17,028)
Leased assets (net)	$170,271	$161,757	$153,243
Current portion of lease obligation	$ 2,973	$ 3,270	$ 3,597
Long-term portion of lease obligation	167,298	164,028	160,431
Total lease obligation	$170,271	$167,298	$164,028

No impact on balance sheet if operating lease method applied.[Deferred tax assets reflecting the difference between total expense under the two methods would also be reported.]

(ii) **Income statement effects of capital lease:**

Years ended December 31,	1995	1994
Interest expense[1]	$ 16,730	$ 17,027
Depreciation expense[2]	8,514	8,514
Total expense	$ 25,244	$ 25,541

[1] Interest expense for: 1994 = .10 x $170,271
                          1995 = .10 x $167,298
[2] Deprecation expense = $170,271/20 for each year
The income statement would show lease expense of $20,000 each year under the operating lease method.

11-23

(iii) **Statement of cash flow effects of capital lease:**

Years ended December 31,	1995	1994
Cash from operations	$(16,730)	$(17,027)
Financing cash flow	(3,270)	(2,973)

The operating lease method reports $20,000 cash outflow from operations for each year.

D.   As in part A, the PV of the MLPs is more than 90% of the fair market value, permitting capitalization. However, for the lessor to capitalize the lease, revenue recognition criteria must be satisfied as well. These conditions are:

(i)   Collectibility of MLPs is reasonably assured, and

(ii) There are no significant uncertainties regarding the amount of costs yet to be incurred by the lessor or other obligations under the provisions of the lease agreement.

To evaluate these issues, information would be needed regarding the financial condition of Baldes and any remaining obligations of Malbec.

E.   The operating lease method has no effect on Malbec's balance sheet at the inception of the lease since the lessor has merely entered into a rental arrangement - an executory contract.

F.   **Sales-type lease reporting by lessor:**

Malbec's gross investment in the lease:

MLPs ($20,000 x 20)	$ 400,000
Unguaranteed residual value	5,500
Gross investment	$ 405,500

Net investment:

Present value of 20 payments at 10%	$ 170,271
PV of $5,500, 20 periods hence at 10%	818
Net investment	$ 171,089

Unearned income: $405,500 - $171,089 = $ 234,411

```
Journal entry at inception (1/1/94):
Gross investment              $ 405,500
Cost of goods sold              149,182
     Sales revenue                        $170,271
     Inventory                             150,000
     Unearned income                       234,411
```

Balance Sheet Effects, January 1, 1994:

Inventory (reduction due to sale)	$(150,000)

```
Gross investment in sales-type lease     $ 405,500
Less: unearned interest income            (234,411)
Net investment                           $ 171,089
```

Income Statement Effects, Year Ended December 31, 1994:

```
Sales revenue                            $ 170,271
Cost of goods sold                        (149,182)
  Income effect                          $  21,089
```

G. **Balance Sheet Effects:**

	12/31/94	12/31/95
Sales-type lease:		
Net investment in lease, current	$ 3,180	$ 3,498
Net investment in lease, long-term	159,518	156,020
Operating lease:		
Assets under lease	$150,000	$150,000
Accumulated depreciation	(7,225)	(14,450)
Net assets	$142,775	$135,550

Income Statement Effects:

	12/31/94	12/31/95
Sales-type lease:		
Sales revenue	$ 170,271	$ ---
Cost of goods sold	(149,182)	---
Sales profit	$ 21,089	---
Interest income	17,109	$ 16,820
Pretax income	$ 38,198	$ 16,820
Operating lease:		
Rental income	$ 20,000	$ 20,000
Depreciation expense	(7,225)	(7,225)
Pretax income	$ 12,775	$ 12,775

Statement of Cash Flow Effects:

	12/31/94	12/31/95
Sales-type lease:		
Cash from operations:		
Sales profit	$ 21,089	$ ---
Inventory reduction	150,000	---
Interest income	17,109	$ 16,820
Cash from operations	$ 188,198	$ 16,820
Investment cash flow:		
Net investment in lease	$(171,089)	$ ---
Reduction in net investment	2,891	3,180
Investment cash flow	$(168,198)	$ 3,180
Net cash flow	$ 20,000	$ 20,000
Operating lease:		
Rental income	$ 20,000	$ 20,000
Cash from operations	$ 20,000	$ 20,000

Note: There is no effect on investment cash flow when the operating lease method is used.

Cash from operations - indirect method:

	12/31/94	12/31/95
Sales-type lease:		
Pretax income	$ 38,198	$ 16,820
Inventory reduction	150,000	---
Cash from operations	$ 188,198	$ 16,820
Operating lease:		
Pretax income	$ 12,775	$ 12,775
Depreciation expense	7,225	7,225
Cash from operations	$ 20,000	$ 20,000

Case 11-1 Solution

Estimated time to complete this case is 2½ to 3 hrs.

Overview:

This case demonstrates that in dealing with OBS activities, useful information can be obtained by going beyond footnote data.

Information about Texaco's affiliate Caltex can be estimated from Texaco's footnotes. However, by examining Caltex's own financial statements, a more accurate measure of Caltex's debt can be obtained. More importantly, by examining the affilate's financial statements, a "grandfather" situation can be analyzed. That is, the OBS debt of Caltex's affiliates can be added to Caltex's debt and consequently added to Texaco's share of the OBS debt of its affiliates.

Part 5 of the problem deals with this issue using data from the first four parts. Accordingly, as we go through the first four parts we will indicate in square brackets [] which information we will need for part 5.

1 a. & b.
Texaco Capitalization Table and Selected Ratios

Capitalization, December 31,	1992	1993	1994
Current portion of debt		$ 669	$ 917
Long-term debt & Capital leases		6,157	5,564
Total Debt		6,826	6,481
Stockholder's equity		10,279	9,749
Total Capitalization		$ 17,105	$ 16,230
Total Debt/equity		**0.66**	**0.66**
Total Assets	$25,992	$26,626	$25,505
Average Assets		26,309	26,066
Pretax income		$1,172	$1,204
Interest expense		459	498
EBIT		$1,631	$1,702
ROA (EBIT/Average Assets)		**6.20%**	**6.53%**
Times interest earned		**3.55**	**3.42**

2. (a) and (b) Based on information provided in exhibit 11C-1, adjustments to Texaco's liabilities (and assets) must be made in the following areas
    - (i) share of affiliate debt
    - (ii) operating leases
    - (iii) guarantees
    - (iv) throughput agreements

As the discussion will indicate, a number of assumptions are needed to make appropriate calculations.

Texaco Adjusted Capitalization and Debt/Equity

Capitalization, December 31,	1993	1994
Current portion of debt	$ 669	$ 917
Long-term debt & Capital leases	6,157	5,564
Total debt as reported	$ 6,826	$ 6,481
Share of affiliates debt	1,876	1,969
PV of operating leases	900	900
Guarantees	154	176
Throughput agreements	590	561
Total Adjustments to debt	$ 3,520	$ 3,606
Total adjusted debt	10,346	10,087
Stockholders' equity	10,279	9,749
Total Capitalization	$ 20,625	$ 19,836
Adjusted Debt/equity	**1.01**	**1.03**

(i) *share of affiliate debt:* Note 6 in Exhibit 11C-1 provides information on an aggregate basis as to the composition of the balance sheets of Texaco's affiliates. However, the portion of current and noncurrent liabilities which is debt is not provided. We will assume that the noncurrent liabilities are (primarily) debt and therefore increase Texaco's debt by $1,876 and $1,969 in 1993 and 1994 respectively.
[We note for future reference (see part 5) that of the $1,969, $926 is due to Texaco's share of Caltex's noncurrent liabilities; i.e. 50% of $1,853]

(ii) *operating leases (Note 9):* From the capital lease payment stream and the present value of $149, we find an implicit interest rate of approximately 12%. Applying this rate to the operating lease payments[1] yields a present value of approximately $900. No data is provided for 1993 so we assume the same level.

(iii) *guarantees:* see note 16

(iv) *throughput agreements (Note 16):* We have used the "net" exposure of $590 and $561 in 1993 and 1994 although a conservative measure would use the "gross" exposure.

Adjusted Times Interest earned

The OBS debt carries with it an implied) interest cost which must be computed to better measure the times interest earned ratio.[2] Other than for leases, we do not know the rate of interest to apply to the debt. We assume that 9% is the appropriate average rate for all the debt.[3] This yields additional interest expense of $317 and $325 in 1993 and 1994 respectively. These amounts must be added to interest expense *and* to EBIT as they were not treated as interest expense when calculating reported EBIT.

Texaco: Adjusted Times Interest Earned

	1993	1994
Total Adjustments to debt	$ 3,520	$ 3,606
Adjustment to interest at 9%	317	325
Interest expense reported	459	498
Adjusted interest expense	$ 776	$ 823
EBIT as reported	$ 1,631	$ 1,702
Adjustment for interest	317	325
Adjusted EBIT	$ 1,948	$ 2,027
Adjusted Times interest earned	**2.51**	**2.46**

[Again for purposes of part 5 we note that the adjustment for interest expense for Caltex is equal to .09 x $926 = $83]

---

[1] The payment stream on operating leases is erratic. Based on the payment in year 5 of $52, there is an implied lease term of 13 years. However, fully 71% of the payments of $1,424 are payable in the first five years; thus, assumptions as to payment patterns after the initial five years are not crucial.

[2] For example, the affiliates must pay interest on their debt. The reported times interest earned ratio ignores that interest; it does, however, include Texaco's share of affiliate income in the numerator, thus biasing the ratio.

[3] This assumption can be justified as follows. The interest rate on leases is approximately 12%. The interest rate on the other debt is approximately 8%. The 8% is arrived at by comparing the interest expense of $498 reported on the income statement with the total debt of $6,481 reported on the balance sheet.

Adjusted ROA

The off-balance sheet data also imply adjustments to Texaco's assets. Taking the present value of leases implies capitalizing the operating leases; similarly for the throughput agreements. Finally, just as we recognize Texaco's share of its affiliates' debt, we should also reflect Texaco's share of its affiliates' total assets as these assets generated Texaco's share of affiliate income; at present Texaco is only carrying (its share of) the net assets of these affiliates (under the equity method). (Where data is unavailable for 1992, we assume the same levels as 1993)

Texaco: Adjusted ROA

	1992	1993	1994
Total Assets on B/S	$25,992	$26,626	$25,505
Adjustments:			
PV of operating leases	900	900	900
Throughput agreements	590	590	561
Affiliates (see data Ex11C-1 P.565)			
Current assets	1,826	1,637	1,711
Noncurrent Assets	5,463	5,888	6,453
less net assets	(3,468)	(3,741)	(3,906)
	$ 3,821	$ 3,784	$ 4,258
Adjusted Assets	31,303	31,900	31,224
Avg Adjusted Assets		31,602	31,562
Adjusted EBIT		1,948	2,027
Adjusted ROA		**6.16%**	**6.42%**

[Again we note for future reference (part 5), that of the $4,258 adjustment for affiliate assets, $2,539 is due to Texaco's share of Caltex's net assets calculated as follows:.5 x {$2,421 + 7,389] = 4,905 share of assets less $2,366 (=.5 x $4,733) net assets carried on Texaco's B/S]

2. (c) Texaco's reported and adjusted ratios for 1994 are reported below:

Texaco Ratios 1994	Reported	Adjusted for OBS
Debt/equity	.66	1.03
Times Interest Earned	3.42	2.46
ROA	6.53%	6.42%

Taking into consideration Texaco's OBS debt raises the debt/equity ratio by 50% from about .66 to 1.03 The adjustments to interest expense (added to both numerator and denominator) reduce the times interest earned ratio. ROA declined slightly as the increase in assets was offset for the most part by the increase in EBIT.

3. (a) & (b)

Caltex Capitalization Table & Selected Ratios

Capitalization, December 31,	1993	1994
Notes Payable & cur por of LTD		$ 1,386
Long-term debt & Capital leases		715
Total Debt		2,101
Stockholder's equity		4,733
Total Capitalization		$ 6,834
Total Debt/equity		**0.44**
Total Assets	$ 8,389	$ 9,810
Average Assets		9,100
Pretax income		$ 1,111
Interest expense		101
EBIT		$ 1,212
ROA (EBIT/Average Assets)		**13.32%**
Times interest earned		**12.00**

[Note (for purposes of part 5) that these data imply Texaco's share of Caltex

Debt	=	*.5 x $2,101 = $1,052*
Interest expense	=	*.5 x $ 101 = $ 52*
1994 Assets	=	*.5 x $9,810 = $4,905]*

4. The adjustments for Caltex's OBS activities are similar to those of Texaco.
   (i) *share of affiliate debt:* We assume that the other liabilities are primarily long-term debt requiring an adjustment of $1,776.
   (ii) *operating leases:* Using an assumed rate of 12%, the present value of Caltex's operating leases is approximately $240 million.
   (iii) *purchase commitment (similar to throughput agreement):* The present value of these payments is relatively small at $7 million.

Caltex Adjusted Capitalization Table and Debt/Equity

Capitalization, December 31,	1994
Current portion of debt	$ 1,386
Long-term debt & Capital leases	715
Total debt as reported	$ 2,101
Share of affiliates debt	$ 1,776
PV of operating leases	240
Throughput agreements	7
Total Adjustments to debt	$ 2,023
Total adjusted debt	4,124
Stockholder's equity	4,733
Total adjusted Capitalization	$ 8,857
Adjusted Debt/equity	**.87**

Caltex Adjusted Ratios -- Times Interest Earned

	1994
Total Adjustments to debt	$ 2,023
Adjustment to interest at 9%	182
Interest expense reported	101
Adjusted interest expense	$ 283
EBIT as reported	$ 1,212
Adjustment for interest	182
Adjusted EBIT	$ 1,394
Adjusted imes interest earned	**4.93**

Caltex Adjusted Ratios -- ROA

	1993	1994
Total Assets on B/S	$ 8,389	$ 9,810
Adjustments:		
PV of operating leases	240	240
Throughput agreements	7	7
Affiliates (see data Ex11C-2 P.568)		
Current assets	2,316	2,651
Noncurrent Assets	2,975	3,858
less net assets	(1,796)	(2,370)
	$ 3,495	$ 4,139
Adjusted Assets	12,131	14,196
Avg Adjusted Assets		13,164
Adjusted EBIT		1,293
Adjusted ROA		**9.82%**

[Note (for purposes of part 5) Texaco's share of Caltex adjustments for its OBS activities equals

Debt	=	.5 x 4,124 =	2,062
Interest expense	=	.5 x 283 =	142
1994 Assets	=	.5 x 14,196 =	7,098]

Caltex Adjusted Ratios -- Summary

Caltex Ratios 1994	Reported	Adjusted for OBS
Debt/equity	.44	.87
Times Interest Earned	12.00	4.92
ROA	13.32%	9.82%

All of Caltex's ratios worsen as a result of including Caltex's OBS activities. The effects of the adjustments are much more pronounced than they were for Texaco.

5. The results accumulated throughout the problem are summarized below:

Texaco's share of Caltex based on information available in:	Texaco's footnotes (part 2)	50% of Caltex's reported data (part 3)	50% of Caltex after adjusting for Caltex's OBS activities (part 4)
Debt	$ 926	$ 1,051	$ 2,062
Interest Expense	83	51	142
1994 Assets	4,905	4,905	7,098

As our information about Caltex becomes more refined our estimate of Calex's debt and assets increase larger. The only surprise in the data is the interest expense. From our initial estimate of $83, it drops to $51 indicating perhaps that the interest rate of 9% used was too high or that year end levels of debt are atypically high.

We can now compare Texaco's 1994 ratios using the various levels of OBS information available. For comparative purposes we also show Texaco's ratios as reported ignoring all OBS activities:

```
Debt to equity:                          Debt/Equity
 (from part 1) as reported ignoring OBS : $6,481/9,749  = .66

 (from part 2) using Texaco's footnotes : 10,087/9,749  =1.03
 (from part 3) using Caltex's financials:
      add increase in Caltex debt
                 (1051-926)              125
                                         10,212/9,749   =1.05
 (from part 4) including Caltex's OBS:
      add increase in Caltex debt
                 (2062-1051)             1,011
                                         11,223/9,749   =1.15
```

The debt/equity steadily deteriorates as we explore (Texaco's and) Caltex's OBS activities.

```
Times Interest Earned:                                 EBIT/Interest
(from part 1) as reported ignoring OBS : $1,702 / 498   =3.42


(from part 2) using Texaco's footnotes :   2,027 / 723  =2.80
(from part 3) using Caltex's financials:
  adjust for change in Caltex interest
                (51-83)                      (32)   (32)
                                           1,995 / 691  =2.89

(from part 4) including Caltex's OBS:
adjust for increase in Caltex interest
                (142-51)                        91     91
                                           2,086 / 782  =2.67
```

Overall the times interest earned ratio also declines as we add OBS debt.

```
ROA:                                                   EBIT/Assets
(from part 1) as reported ignoring OBS : $1,702/$26,066 =6.52%


(from part 2) using Texaco's footnotes :   2,027/ 31,562 =6.42%
(from part 3) using Caltex's financials:
  adjust for change in Caltex
 interest (51-83) and assets (0)             (32)      0
                                           1,995/ 31,562 =6.32%

(from part 4) including Caltex's OBS:
 adjust for change in Caltex
 interest (142-51) and assets(7098-4905)     91    2,193
                                           2,086/ 33,755 =6.18%
```

At each level, ROA declines.

6. It would be useful to know whether Caltex's affiliates, in turn, have their own off-balance-sheet liabilities. It would also be helpful to know more about transactions with Texaco (and with the other 50% stockholder, Chevron) to obtain a better idea of the role that Caltex plays. Caltex appears to be more than an investment; how much more we can't tell from the data provided.

Chapter 12 - Solutions

Overview:
Problem Length   *Problem #'s*
  {S}   *1,2,5,10,12,14,15,16*
  {M}   *3,4,6,8,9,11,13*
  {L}   *7*

Problems 1-5 deal with Deere's pension footnote. If they were assigned together, they would require approximately 1.5 to 2 hrs of work.
Problems 10-12 deal with IBM's postretirement benefits. If they were assigned together, they would require approximately 1 hour to 1 hour and 15 minutes of work.

1.{S} A. Interest rates fell in 1993 and rose in 1994. To calculate the PBO (and ABO) at the end of any year, current interest rates are used. The discount rate of 8% (7.25%) is therefore used to calculate the PBO in 1994 (1993).

   Interest cost for 1994 is calculated on the basis of the opening PBO. For that purpose, *the interest rate in effect at the time when the PBO was calculated is used*. As the opening PBO was calculated using the rate of 7.25%, that rate is used to calculate expenses in 1994. In 1993, an 8% interest rate was used to calculate interest cost as that rate was used to compute the PBO at the end of 1992.

   B. (i) The lowering of the discount rate for expenses to 7.25% will raise 1994 service cost. In 1995, the discount rate for expenses will be based on the 8.0% currently used to estimate the PBO. Therefore, in 1995 service costs will decrease.

   (ii) As noted in part A, interest cost in 1994 will be based on the lower rate of 7.25% and thus interest cost will be lowered. However, for 1995 as the higher rate of 8% was used to calculate the PBO obligation at the end of 1994, that rate will be used to calculate 1995 interest cost and therefore it will be higher.

   (iii) For 1994, since the effect of interest rate changes was to lower both service and interest costs, net pension cost will also be lowered. For 1995, (assuming interest rate stay the same), the effect of the interest rate changes in 1994 was to lower service cost and raise interest cost. The net effect will depend on which effect is larger. Given that Deere's plan is "mature" with interest cost approximately 4x service cost, it is most likely that the interest cost effect will dominate and overall net pension cost will increase.

(iv) PBO was be decreased in 1994 as a result of the interest rate increase to 8%.(1995 depends on the year end rate)

C.　　Opening PBO = $2,027 + $1,986 =　　$4,013
　　　times interest rate　　　　　　　　　 7.25%
　　　=　　Interest Cost　　　　　　　　　 $ 291

which is approximately equal to $286

2.{S} A.　(i)　An increase in the assumed ROA would increase the ROA recognized and therefore lower pension cost.

(ii) Actual plan status is based on the PBO and market value of plan assets and thus a change in the assumed rate would not affect the plan status.

(iii)As noted in part (i) above, the higher assumed ROA lowers pension cost recognized. Consequently, the net balance sheet liability (asset) would be decreased (increased).

B.　Investment gains were not as high in 1994 as in the past. 1995's reported pension cost would be affected as the assumed rate multiplied by the market value of plan assets is used to calculate current pension cost. In the future, to the extent accumulated investment gains/losses are being amortized, the effect would be to raise reported pension cost. The actual plan status will not be as high as it could have been as a result of the poor investment performance and will remain that way until the market recovers.

C.　Opening plan assets = $1,510 + $1,805　=$ 3,315
　　times assumed ROA　　　　　　　　　　 .097
　　　　　　　　　　　　　　　　　　　 $　321
　　As the actual gain was　　　　　　　　 86
　　　Deferred loss should be　　　　　　 $　235

Deferred loss recognized was $218; a discrepancy of $17.

3.{M}A. The minimum liability provision ensures that the balance sheet liability recognized is at least equal to the ABO minus Plan Assets. For a firm that has many plans, this adjustment must be calculated for each plan separately.

B. For those plans where the "Accumulated Benefits Exceed Assets", use the data from exhibit 12P-1 to calculate what the balance sheet liability would have been without the minimum liability adjustment.

	1994	1993
PBO in excess of plan assets	$(216)	$(476)
less Unrecognized		
Net loss	415	373
Prior service cost	154	176
Transition asset	(10)	(13)
Asset without minimum liability	$343	$ 60

Without the minimum liability provision the company would have shown an asset of $343 and $60 in 1994 and 1993 respectively. For those years the ABO exceeded plan assets by:

	1994	1993
ABO	$(1,963)	$(1,965)
Plan Assets	1,767	1,510
Required minimum liability	$ (196)	$ (455)

To convert the assets of $343 and $60 to the minimum liability of $196 and $455 requires an adjustment of (343 + 196 =) $539 and (60 + 455 =) $415 for 1994 and 1993 respectively.

Note: there is an unexplained discrepancy in 1994 of $6 between the required minimum liability and hence the minimum liability adjustment we calculate and the one shown by Deere.

C. The minimum liability increases the balance sheet liability. The offset is an decrease in equity and/or an increase in an intangible asset. The equity decrease is net of taxes as a deferred tax asset is recorded. In Deere's case the net effect of the 545 minimum liability was (see footnote)

Increase	Intangible asset	$158
Decrease	Equity	248
Increase	Deferred Tax asset	139
		$545

The minimum liability does not effect the cash flow or income statements.

D. On a going concern basis, the actual plan status should be measured by the difference between the PBO and plan assets. For 1994:

PBO - Plan Assets (see Exhibit 12P-1)
                          is a liability of   (179 + 216 =) $ 395
Deere recognized a B/S liability of   (208 + 202 =)   410

Thus the liability is overstated by $15 and should be reduced accordingly.

Additionally, the intangible asset of $158 recorded when the minimum liability was recognized must be eliminated.

The offset to both of these is equity. Thus, on a pretax basis, the following B/S adjustments should be made:

Equity   (decreases)   143
Pension Liability   (decreases)   15
    Intangible Asset   (decreases)   158

For *liquidation* analysis, the actual plan status would be measured via the difference between the ABO and the plan assets. For 1994

ABO minus Plan Assets is an *asset* of
        [(1,595 + 1,963) - (1,756 + 1,767)] $35
Deere recognized a B/S liability of (208 + 202 =)   (410)

Thus the pension liability should be eliminated and replaced by an pension asset of $35.

The intangible asset of $158 set up when the minimum liability was recognized however must still be eliminated.

The offset to both of these is equity. Thus, on a pre-tax basis, the following B/S adjustments should be made:

Pension Liability   (decrease)   410
Pension Asset   (increase)   35
    Intangible Asset   (decrease)   158
    Equity   (increase)   287

4.{M} To make the required calculations, the data in Exhibit 12P-1 must be aggregated for each year.

	1994	*1993*
PBO	(1935)+(1983)=$**(3918)**	(2027)+(1986)=$**(4013)**
Plan Assets	1756 + 1767 = **3523** _	1805 + 1510 = **3315**
PBO > Plan assets	(179)+(216) = **(395)**	(222)+(476) = **(698)**
less Unrecognized		
Net loss	35 + 415 = **450**	114 + 373 = **487**
Prior service cost	9 + 154 = **163**	3 + 176 = **179**
Transition asset	(73)+ (10) = **(83)**	(83)+ (13) = **(96)**
Asset pre min. liab.	**135**	**(128)**
Minimum liability	**(545)**	**(515)**
B/S liability	(208)+(202)=$**(410)**	(188)+(455)=$**(643)**

A. Contributions = Pension Cost + Δ in B/S asset (liability)

To make the calculation the balance prior to the minimum liability adjustment is used. Therefore
Contributions = Pension Cost + change in B/S asset
   $367   = $104   +   [135-(128)]

Balance Sheet Asset/Liability

Opening Balance(Liability)	$(128)
Pension Cost	(104)
Contributions	**367**
Close Balance Asset	$ 135

```
              Balance Sheet
              Asset/Liability
                        |128 Open
                        |104 Pension
Contributions 367|           Cost
Close           135|
```

B. Pension benefits = ROA + Contributions - Δ in plan assets
   $245   = $86 + $367   - [3,523-3,315]

Plan Assets

Opening Balance	$3315
ROA	86
Contributions (from A)	367
less benefits paid	**(245)**
Close Balance	$3523

```
              Plan Assets
Open          3315|
ROA             86| 245 Benefits
Contributions  367|
Close         3523|
```

C. Gross Pension Cost = Benefits paid + change in PBO

PBO

Opening Balance	$4013
Gross Pension Cost	**150**
<u>less benefits (from B)</u>	<u>(245)</u>
Close Balance	$3918

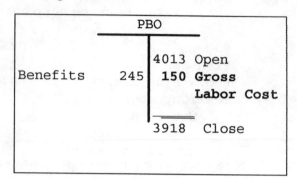

Therefore,

Service cost	$ 79
Interest cost	<u>286</u>
Recurring cost	**365**
Actuarial gains/losses +	
Prior service costs	<u>(215)</u> Plug
Gross Pension cost	**150**
ROA	<u>(86)</u>
Nonsmoothed pension cost	**$ 64**

D. The difference between the recurring and gross costs is due to actuarial gains/losses and/or prior service costs. In Deere's case the evidence suggests an actuarial gain resulting from the increase in the discount rate from 7.25% to 8.00%.

Total amortization was $43; from the transition asset there was an amortization of [(96)-(83)=] $(13) bringing the amortization from net gains/losses and prior service cost to $56. The change in unamortized prior service cost was $16. Given its magnitude we can assume it to be and amortization bring amortization of net gains/losses to be 40. Now we reconcile:

Net Gains and Losses:	
Opening balance	$487
Investment loss deferred in 1994	218
Actuarial gain	(215) PLUG
Amount amortized	<u>(40)</u>
Close balance	$450

5.{S}*Service Cost* increased by 17% in 1993 but only 7% in 1994. The difference in the rate of increase despite a lower discount rate suggests a low labor force growth. Thus, given a higher discount rate for 1995 which should lower service cost (see 1.B.(i)), we forecast that service cost will remain basically unchanged at 80.

Interest Cost for 1995 will be based on the rate of interest (8%) used to determine the PBO at the end of 1994. Therefore interest cost is forecasted to be 8% x 3$,918 = $313.

Expected ROA is equal to plan assets times 9.7% or $3,523 x 9.7% = $342.

Net Amortization increased considerably in the last two years from $18 to $32 to $43. Looking to the future however, the 1994 amount(s) to be amortized (i.e. unamortized net gains/losses; prior service cost and the transition asset) have not changed dramatically from the previous year. So we assume that for 1995 net amortization will remain $43.

Projected 1995 pension cost is therefore:

Service cost	$ 80
Interest cost	313
Expected ROA	(342)
Net amortization	43
	$ 94

6.{M} A.(i) Contributions = Pension Cost - change in B/S liability
$3,430 = $19,875 - [61,583-45,138]

Balance Sheet Liability

Opening Balance	$45,138
Pension Cost	19,875
less Contributions	**(3,430)**
Close Balance	$61,583

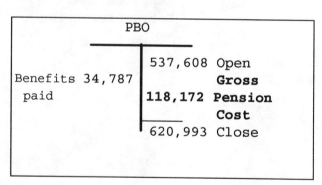

```
              Balance Sheet
              Asset/Liability
                          45,138  Open
                          19,875  Pension
Contribution 3430                 Cost
                          61,583  Close
```

(ii) Benefits = ROA + Contributions - Δ in plan assets
$245 = $35,720 + $ 3,430 - [588,182-583,819]

Plan Assets

Opening Balance	$583,819
ROA	35,720
Contributions (from i)	3,430
less benefits paid	**(34,787)**
Close Balance	$588,182

```
              Plan Assets
Open       583,819
ROA         35,720   34,787  Benefits
Contribution 3,430            Paid
Close      588,182
```

B. Gross Pension Cost = Benefits paid + change in PBO
$118,172 = $34,787 + [620,993-537,608]

PBO

Opening Balance	$537,608
Gross Pension Cost	**118,172**
- benefits paid (A(ii))	(34,787)
Close Balance	$620,993

```
                    PBO
                        537,608  Open
Benefits 34,787                 Gross
 paid              118,172  Pension
                               Cost
                        620,993  Close
```

Therefore,

	Service Cost	$14,459
	Interest Cost	50,009
(i)	**Recurring Cost**	**64,468**
	Actuarial Gain/Loss	
PLUG	& Prior Service Cost	53,704
(ii)	**Gross Pension Cost**	**118,172**
	ROA	(35,720)
(iii)	**Nonsmoothed Cost**	**$82,452**

(iv) Pension cost reported by the company is $19,875

12-8

C. (i) For liquidation we use the ABO-Plan assets to measure the economic status of the plan. On that basis, the firm has an asset of (588,182 - 520,065=) $68,117. As the firm's balance sheet shows a liability of $61,583; the following adjustment (pretax) is required:

    Pension asset (increase)   68,117
    Pension liability (decrease)   61,583
         Equity (increase)   129,700

(ii) For a going concern we use the PBO - Plan assets. On that basis, the economic status of the plan is a liability of $32,811. As the firm's balance sheet liability of $61,583 is greater by $28,772, the following adjustment (pretax) is required:

    Pension liability (decrease)   28,772
         Equity   (increase)   28,772

7 {L} A.(i) *To calculate the contribution, use the balance prior*
         to the minimum liability adjustment:
    Contributions = Pension Cost - change in B/S liability
       $94.0   = $96.3   - [137.5-135.2]

Balance Sheet Liability
(Pre Minimum Liability)
Opening Balance(136.6-1.4) $ 135.2
Pension Cost   96.3
less Contributions   **(84.0)**
Close Balance (151.2-3.7) $ 147.5

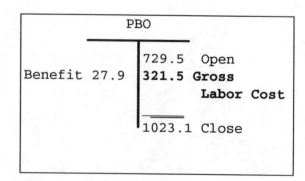

(ii) Benefits = ROA + Contributions - Δ in plan assets
       $27.9   = $121.3 + $84   - [677.1-499.7]

        Plan Assets
Opening Balance $499.7
ROA   121.3
Contributions (from i)   84.0
less benefits paid   **(27.9)**
Close Balance $677.1

B. Gross Pension Cost = Benefits paid + change in PBO
       $321.5   = $27.9   + [1023.1-729.5]

        PBO
Opening Balance $ 729.5
Gross Pension Cost   **321.5**
less benefits paid   27.9
Close Balance $1,023.1

Therefore,

	Service Cost	$ 72.6
	Interest Cost	69.8
(i)	**Recurring Cost**	**142.4**
	Actuarial Gain/Loss	
PLUG	& Prior Service Cost	169.1
(ii)	**Gross Pension Cost**	**321.5**
	ROA	(121.3)
(iii)	**Non-Smoothed Cost**	**$200.2**

(iv) Pension cost reported by the company is $96.3

C.   The first step is to adjust the amount reported on the B/S
     to reflect the actual economic status of the plan. The B/S
     shows a liability of $151.2; the actual economic status is a
     liability of $346. Therefore there should be an adjustment
     to increase the liability by $194.8 with a corresponding
     (pretax) decrease in equity.
     The second step eliminates the intangible asset of $3.7 by
     reducing the asset and equity by $3.7.
       Overall, the entry is
       Equity (decrease)   198.5
            Pension liability (increase)   194.8
            Intangible asset (decrease)   3.7

D.   Actual ROA   = $ 121.3
     Expected ROA = .098 x 499.7   =   48.7
     ROA deferred $ 72.6

     The amount deferred is included in the net amortization and
     deferral of $75.2.

E.   The discount rate was decreased by 1.4% in 1993 from 9.1%
     to 7.7%. This caused a large actuarial loss. From Part B,
     we know that the total of actuarial gains/losses and prior
     service costs was $169.1. Given that unrecognized prior
     service cost fell from $37.0 to $33.1 we can assume that
     the change was due to amortization; i.e. there was no new
     prior service cost. Thus, the change in the PBO was
     largely due to an actuarial loss of $169.1

F.   Amortization of transition liability   (21.0-19.7) $ 1.3
     Amortization of prior service cost   (37.0-33.7)   3.3
     Deferral of ROA   (see part D)   72.6
     Amortization of net gains/losses   (see below)   (2.0)
                                                         $ 75.2

     The amortization of net gains/losses can be inferred by
     reconciling the change in the unrecognized net gain/losses

     Opening balance $ 36.6
     Actuarial loss   (see part E)   179.1
     Deferral of ROA   (see part D)   (72.6)
     Amortization of net gains/losses   2.0 **Plug**
     Closing Balance $145.1

                              12-11

8 {M}A.
(i) Contributions = Pension Cost - change in B/S liability
$$\$197,183 = \$265,385 - [119,767-51,565]$$

Balance Sheet Liability
(Pre Minimum Liability)

Opening Balance	$ 51,565
Pension Cost	265,385
less Contributions	**(197,183)**
Close Balance	$119,767

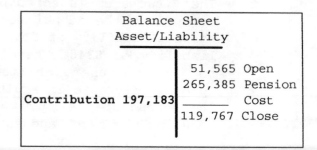

(ii) Benefits = ROA + Contributions - Δ in plan assets
$$\$123,589 = \$493,703+ \$197,183 - [4,350,316-3,783,019]$$

Plan Assets

Opening Balance	$3,783,019
ROA	493,703
Contributions (from i)	197,183
less benefits paid	**(123,589)**
Close Balance	$4,350,316

B. Gross Pension Cost = Benefits paid + change in PBO
$$\$602,691 = \$123,589 + [4,900,555-4,421,453]$$

PBO

Opening Balance	$4,421,453
Gross Pension Cost	**602,691**
- benefits paid(Aii)	(123,589)
Close Balance	$4,900,555

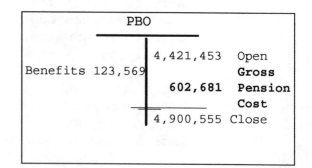

Therefore,

		Service Cost	$216,867
		Interest Cost	389,333
(i)		**Recurring Cost**	**606,200**
		Prior service Cost &	
PLUG		Actuarial Gains/Losses	(3,509)
(ii)		**Gross Pension Cost**	**602,691**
		ROA	(493,703)
(iii)		**Nonsmoothed Cost**	**$108,988**

C. The economic liability declined by 14% from $638 million to $550 million. Much of this decline was due to the actual ROA of $494 million earned on the plan assets. This actual ROA, however, was not recognized on the firm's financial statements as only the expected ROA was recognized. As a result the B/S liability did not report or show a similar decline -- it actually rose as the pension cost recognized was greater than contributions.

9. {M} A. The APBO is equal to :

	1994	1993
Retirees	$ 281.7	$ 315.4
Fully eligible active plan participants	24.7	26.2
Other active plan participants	38.3	40.4
APBO	**$ 344.7**	**$ 382.0**

B. Interest cost in 1994 is based on the discount rate used in 1993 to calculate the APBO. That rate was 7.4% yielding a estimate of interest cost of .074 x $382 = $28.3

C. Without plan assets, benefits are calculated as

$$\text{Benefits} = \text{Postretirement Cost} - \Delta \text{ in B/S liability}$$
$$\$25.5 = \$29.9 - [\$379.1 - \$374.7]$$

Balance Sheet Liability

Opening Balance	$374.7
Postretirement Cost	29.9
less Benefits	(25.5)
Close Balance ($1505+$182)	$379.1

Balance Sheet Asset/Liability		
		374.7 Open
Benefits	25.5	29.9 Cost
		379.1 Close

D. Gross postretirement benefit components resulted in a "benefit" of $11.8 as the calculation below indicates:

Gross Postretirement Benefits = Benefits paid + change in APBO

$$\$(11.8) = \$25.5 + [\$344.7 - \$382.0]$$

APBO	
Opening Balance	$382.0
Gross Cost (benefit)	**(11.8)**
less benefits paid	25.5
Close Balance	$344.7

```
            APBO
          ┌──────┬──────
          │      │382.0  Open
  Benefit 25.5   │
  Gross          │
  Cost     11.8  │
          │      │──────
          │      │344.7  Close
```

Therefore,

	Service Cost	$ 2.9
	Interest Cost	27.0
	Recurring Cost	**29.9**
PLUG	Actuarial Gain	(41.7)
	Gross Benefit Cost	**(11.8)**
	ROA	N/A
	Non-Smoothed Cost	**$(11.8)**

Gross benefit and nonsmoothed costs are identical as there is no ROA; the plan is unfunded.

E. Non-smoothed cost was ($11.8) whereas reported cost was $29.9 a difference of $41.7. As noted in the schedule in part D, the difference is due to an actuarial gain.

The actuarial gain was a result of raising the discount rate from 7.4% to 8.75%. Note that the unrecognized actuarial gain (loss) went from $(9.5) to $34.4 a change (gain) of $43.9, an amount consistent with the $41.7 actuarial gain.

The actuarial gain was reflected in the nonsmoothed costs but due to the "smoothing" provisions of SFAS 106 was not reported as part of periodic postretirement cost in 1994.

F.

	1994	1993
APBO	$ 344.7	$ 382.0
Balance Sheet liability	379.1	374.7
(under) over reported	$ 34.4	$ (7.3)

In 1994, the B/S liability should be reduced and equity increased by $34.4 (pretax). In 1993, the B/S liability should be increased and equity decreased by $ 7.3 (pretax).

G. Note that since the adjustments are in opposite directions the difference in the adjustments total $34.4 + $7.7 = $41.7. This is equal to the actuarial gain discussed in part E. It was reflected in the actual APBO not the balance sheet; hence the adjustment.

10. {S}A. Income taxes are the primary motivating factor. Contributions to pension plans are tax deductible and earnings generated by plan assets are not taxed. Both of these tax advantages are unavailable for nonpension plans, except in limited circumstances.

B. The answer to this question is not clear, as IBM could use the money to fund its own operations. However, it is a point well worth considering in evaluating IBM. Some possible reasons are listed below:

1. IBM may not have alternative investment opportunities providing a sufficient return.
2. The money may be invested to build up "financial slack."
3. Tax deductions are available for limited funding.
4. Given the volatility and the uncertainty associated with health costs, IBM may be attempting to hedge some of the risk by investing money in a "more stable" environment.
5. IBM has historically eschewed debt. Thus, as part of the corporate culture it may have wanted to minimize the debt associated with these benefits.

C. IBM does not offer these plans to its employees in its foreign subsidiaries. Countries outside of the U.S. generally have national health-plans that negate the need for company specific plans.

11.{M} A. Interest cost in 1994 is based on the discount rate used in 1993 to calculate the APBO. That rate was 7.25% yielding a estimate of interest cost of .0725 x $7,361 = $534 about 4% higher than the $512 reported by IBM.

B.
Opening plan assets	[.5 x (1,366 + 1,028)] =	$1232
Expected long-term ROA	=	9.5%
Expected ROA		$ 114

Actual ROA was a *loss* of 22 which is 136 less than the expected amount of 117. Thus based on our calculations the deferred amount should have been 136; 9% more than the 125 amount IBM deferred. It is possible they used an alternative averaging method to arrive at the expected return.

C.(i)

$$\text{Contributions} = \text{Postretirement Cost} - \Delta \text{ in B/S liability}$$
$$\$95.0 \quad = \quad \$422 \quad - \quad [\$5,719 - \$5,392]$$

Balance Sheet Liability
(Pre Minimum Liability)

Opening Balance	$5,392
Postretirement Cost	422
less Contributions	**(95)**
Close Balance	$5,719

```
                 Balance Sheet
                   Liability
                ┌──────────────
                │ 5392 Open
Contribution 95 │ 422 Cost
                │ 5719 Close
                │
```

(ii) Benefits = ROA + Contributions − Δ in plan assets

$$\$411 \quad = \quad \$(22) \quad + \quad \$95 \quad - \quad [\$1,028 - \$1,366]$$

Plan Assets

Opening Balance	$1,366
ROA	(22)
Contributions (from i)	95
less benefits paid	**411**
Close Balance	$1,028

```
                      Plan Assets
                  ┌──────────────────
Open      1366    │
                  │  22 ROA
Contribution  95  │  411 Benefit
Close     1028    │
```

D. IBM had a Gross benefit cost of

Gross benefit cost   = Benefits paid + change in APBO
$(442)   = $411   + [$6,508-$7,361]

APBO

Opening Balance	$7,361
Gross Pension benefit	**(442)**
less benefits paid	411
Close Balance	$6,508

```
+------------------------------------------+
|                  APBO                    |
|          -------------                   |
|                      | 7361  Open        |
| Benefit     411      |                   |
| Gross       442      |                   |
| Benefit Cost         |                   |
|                      --------            |
|                      6508 Close          |
+------------------------------------------+
```

Therefore,

	Service Cost	$ 51
	Interest Cost	512
(i)	**Recurring Cost**	**563**
	Actuarial Gain/Loss & Prior Service Cost	(1,005)
(ii)	**Gross benefit Cost**	**(442)**
	ROA	22
(iii)	**Nonsmoothed Cost**	**$(420)**

E.   IBM's B/S shows a liability of $5,719. The economic status is a liability of $5,480. Thus, the B/S liability should be reduced and equity increased by $239 million [$5,719 - $5,480].

F.   Plan assets declined as a result of the ROA loss of $22 coupled with benefits paid of $411. These outflows were offset by contributions of only $95.

      The decline in the APBO would seem to result from actuarial gains as the discount rate was increased from 7.25% to 8.25%. Further evidence of this can be seen when we analyze the unrecognized net loss account:

Unrecognized net loss	
Open	$ 1,431
Additional investment loss	125
	1,556
Close	(505)
Difference	$ 1,051

The difference is due to actuarial gains and amortization of old losses. As total net amortization is $(38); $(84) of which is a result of amortization of prior service cost[1] ($744-$828); that leaves $46 as amortization of losses. Thus $1,051 - $46 = $1,005 --- actuarial gains.

12. {S}
Service Cost: 1993 and 1992 levels are approximately the same following the 1993 curtailments. However as the discount rate at the end of 1994 was increased by 1% to 8.25%, service cost in 1995 will be reduced. Thus, we estimate a 10% decrease in 1995 service cost to $46.

Interest Cost: .0825 x $6,508 = $537

ROA: .095 x $1,028 = $98

Net amortizations: In 1994 amortization of unrecognized prior service cost was $(84) (see 11 - F). We assume this amount will continue in 1995.
Amortization of net losses was $46 (see 11 - F). However, as the balance in net losses decreased by close to two-thirds we will accordingly reduce the amortization to $15.
Thus, net amortization = $(84) + $15 = $(69)

Forecasted Pension Costs :
Service Cost	$ 46
Interest Cost	537
ROA	(98)
Net amortization	(69)
	$416

---

[1] Note that IBM has negative prior service cost, apparently due to the 1993 reduction in plan benefits.

13. {M} A. By taking the one-time charge in 1993 for the transition liability, 1994 pretax earnings were higher than if Deere had amortized the transition liability over 20 years. Deere avoided the amortization expense in 1994.

   1993 *net income* was lower due to the one time charge. However as the charge was taken as a one time expense -- accounting change; the effects were shown "below" the line. Had they amortized the transition liability over time, the change would have been above the line and pretax earnings would have been lower. Thus, pretax earnings before the effect of the accounting change were higher for both years.

   B. On a pay-as-you-go basis, the amount expensed is equivalent to the payments made to retirees. Without plan assets, that amount is calculated as

   Benefits = Total net cost - Δ in B/S liability
   $116 = $131 - [$1687-$1672]

Balance Sheet Liability

Opening Balance (1498+174)	$1,672
Postretirement Cost	131
less Benefits	**116**
Close Balance (1505+182)	$1,687

Balance Sheet Asset/Liability		
Benefits	116	1,672 Open
		131 Cost
		1,687 Close

   On a pay-as-you-go basis, Deere would have shown a pretax expense of $116 million or ($116 x .65) $75.4 million after tax.

   C. Deere's reported pretax pension cost was $131 million or ($131 x .65) $85.1 million after-tax. Thus, adoption of SFAS 106 increased cost by less than $10 million. This is considerably less than the $40 million estimated in 1992. Deere reports a prior service credit in 1993 and 1994. Thus, the difference may be due to the curtailment of health benefits which Deere imposed subsequent to (making the estimates in) 1992.

   Additionally, Deere may be paying it larger benefits than it expected. In 1992, they paid $86 million in benefits; in 1994 that amount was $116 million.

14.{S} A. Dow's pension plans funded status went from a liability of $168 million in 1993 to a liability of $337 million in 1994; a decline of $169 million.

| Funded status | 1994 | | | 1993 | | |
	Fully	Partial	**Total**	Fully	Partial	**Total**
PBO	(4,405)	(632)	**(5,037)**	(4,335)	(575)	**(4,910)**
Plan Assets	4,439	221	**4,660**	4,534	208	**4,742**
	34	(411)	**(377)**	199	(367)	**(168)**

B. The PBO increased only slightly in 1994. Dow increased its discount rate in 1994. That would lower the PBO and improve the funded status of the plan.

Plan assets decreased in 1994; Note O shows that, in 1994, Dow's actual ROA was only $93 million. This amount was considerably lower than the $494 million earned the previous year and $266 million lower than the long-term (expected) ROA. Thus, the decline in the funded status resulted from the poor investment performance, as the ROA (and contributions) did not keep up with the benefits earned and paid in 1994.

C. Dow's B/S showed an increase in liability from $101 million to $249 million; a change of $148 million.

Accrued pension asset(liability)
1994 $128 + $(377) = $(249)
1993 $140 + $(241) = $(101)

Due to the smoothing provisions of SFAS 87, the B/S amounts do not fully reflect the funded status of the pension plans. Thus of the $169 million change; only $148 million was reflected.

D. Dow shows a negative prior service costs because it (like many other companies) curtailed health benefits available to retirees. Dow amended its health benefit plans in October 1993 and April 1994. (See Note P)

E. (i) The balance sheet liability is $243 whereas the funded status is a liability of $377. This requires a (pretax) liability increase and equity decrease of $134.
   (ii) The balance sheet liability is $1,663 whereas the funded status (APBO - plan assets) is a liability of $1,124. This requires a (pretax) liability decrease and equity increase of $539.

12-20

15.{S}A.

	ICI Note 33	Chemical Industry '94 Average	Range
Discount Rate	8.7%	8.26%	7.0% - 9.0%
Rate of Compensation Increase	5.9%	5.25%	5.0% - 5.75%
Long-term ROA	8.8%	9.15%	8.5% -10.60%

The discount rate and compensation increase assumptions used by ICI are slightly above the industry averages reflected in Exhibit 12P-5. The long-term ROA, on the other hand, is slightly below the average. The differences may be explained by a higher inflation rate (higher interest rates) in the UK and stock market performance which has not been as strong as the US "bull" market. These factors, however, are not compelling as in all cases, the assumptions used by ICI are within the range used by the individual companies shown in Exhibit 12P-5.

B. Note 33 states that the pension plan assets of £5,747m were enough to cover 92% of the PBO. This implies a PBO of (5747/.92) =£6,247m and a "shortfall" of £500m.

The note also indicates that for its funded[2] plans the B/S shows

accrued pension liability	(£ 29m)
prepaid pension asset	69m
Net asset	£ 40m

Thus, the (pretax) adjustment is

Equity (decrease)	£540m
Prepaid asset (decrease)	£ 69m
Pension liability (increase)	£471m

C. Disclosure of the following items would be useful:
- components which make up pension costs (service; interest and actual ROA)
- year-to-year comparisons and changes in PBO and plan assets
- the ABO and the degree to which pensions are vested
- the unamortized portions of gains/losses and prior service cost

---

[2] The solution assumes that the £130m liability for unfunded plans is not related to the (funded) plans whose PBO totals £6,247m . If that assumption is incorrect, then, the adjustment would be

Equity (decrease)	£410m
Prepaid asset (decrease)	£ 69m
Pension liability (increase)	£341m

16.{S} A. The high discount rate assumption reduced the PBO and improved the funded status of duPont's plan.

B. (i) DuPont has the greatest spread. The spread is 4.0% with a discount rate of 9.0% and a rate of compensation increase of 5.0%.

(ii) The spread improved the funded status as higher discount rates and lower rates of compensation increases both tend to lower the PBO.

C. Air Products has the highest assumed ROA.
(i) The economic plan status is based on actual ROA, not the assumed rate. Thus the actual status is unaffected. The reported (B/S) status, however, is based on the assumed ROA and, as a result, the reported status improves with the higher expected ROA.

(ii) Reported pension cost declines as higher expected ROA offsets the labor components of pension cost.

(iii) If all competitors have similar actual ROA, Air Products is more likely to have actuarial losses as actual ROA does not keep up with expected ROA.

Case 12-1 Solution

Estimated solution time: 3 to 4 hours

Note: The calculations required for this case are shown in Exhibits 12CS-1, and 12CS-2. The calculations are explained in the solution. All data are in $millions.

(a) We must forecast each of the pension cost components:

Service Cost: GM's employee count has decreased in recent years. However rising wage rates and changes in the discount rate affect service cost, as seen in Exhibit 12C-4 (text page 653). As GM reduced the discount rate at December 31, 1992 to 8.6% (from 9.3% one year earlier), 1993 service cost will rise. Assuming an 11% increase (the same as the 1992 increase with a similar discount rate decline), **estimated 1993 service cost equals $954.6.**

Interest Cost: Estimated as the December 31, 1992 PBO multiplied by the discount rate at that date:

$$\$51,671.5 \times .086 = \mathbf{\$4,443.7}$$

Expected Return on Assets: Estimated as the December 31, 1992 plan assets multiplied by the 1993 estimated ROA. *Assuming that this rate is unchanged in 1993*:

$$\$39,571.6 \times .11 = \mathbf{\$4,352.9}$$

Amortization: We estimate 1993 amortization of

- deferred actuarial losses
- unrecognized prior service cost
- transition asset

For prior years (see text) we assumed no amortization of deferred actuarial losses which did not exceed 10% of the (larger of) the PBO and plan assets (corridor method). However the December 31, 1992 deferred losses of $8,178.8 are well in excess of 10% of the PBO (.10 x $51,671.5 = $5,167.1). Thus we must assume 1993 amortization of the excess ($8,178.8 - $5,167.1 = $3,011.7). If this excess is amortized over 15 years, the amortization equals

$$\$3,011.7/15 = \mathbf{\$200.8}$$

Estimated amortization of unrecognized prior service cost equals one-tenth of the December 31, 1992 balance. The discussion in Exhibit 12C-3 suggests that GM amortizes these amounts over ten years. Thus, 1993 amortization equals

$$\$4,494.2/10 = \$449.4$$

Amortization of the transition asset has approximated $59 each year. As that asset is fixed, 1993 amortization should be unchanged from the 1992 level of $59.8.

Total forecast amortization, therefore, is the sum of these three components:

Deferred actuarial losses	$200.8
Unrecognized prior service cost	449.4
Transition asset (credit)	(59.8)
Net amortization	**$590.4**

Putting all of the pension cost component estimates together, 1993 estimated pension cost equals:

Service Cost	$ 954.6
Interest Cost	4,443.7
Estimated ROA	(4,352.9)
Amortization	590.4
Net Pension Cost	**$1,635.8**

The computation of nonsmoothed pension cost is more difficult as it requires assumptions about 1993 economic events. We start with recurring cost, equal to service cost plus interest cost:

Recurring Cost = $954.6 + $4,443.7 = $5,398.3

The 1993 prior service cost can be expected to be significant. Reviewing the data in Exhibit 12C-4, we see large PSC every three years, corresponding to new labor contracts. The 1990 amount of $3.6 billion should be a minimum expectation.

Actuarial gains and losses result from changes in actuarial assumptions as well as deviations between expected and actual assumptions related to other factors. The most important factor is a possible change in the discount rate, which depends on 1993 changes in interest rates.

Interest rates also affect the actual ROA for 1993. As declining interest rates (resulting in actuarial losses as the discount rate falls) tend to increase ROA (bond and stock prices rise), we can assume these factors offset. If we assume no change in 1993 interest rates, then the ROA should be "normal" and equal to the expected ROA of 11% multiplied by 1992 year end assets (.11 x $39,571.6) = $4,352.9.

Putting all of these factors together, estimated 1993 nonsmoothed pension cost equals:

Recurring Cost	$5,398.3
Prior Service Cost	3,600
Return on Assets	(4,352.9)
Net Nonsmoothed Cost	$4,645.4

[Examining the actual data in Exhibit 12C-5 (p. 655), we find 1993 reported pension cost of $2,016.6 million, well in excess of our estimate. Three of the four cost component estimates were close; the major difference is that our forecast of expected ROA was too high.

In 1993, GM changed its ROA assumption from 11% to 10%, reducing the expected ROA component by $383 million. Had the ROA assumption remained unchanged, pension cost would have been $1,633.6 million ($2,016.6 - $383), within 1% of our forecast!

This exercise illustrates the use of pension disclosures to forecast future pension cost and that such forecasts can err due to the effect of assumption changes on pension cost.]

(b) Exhibit 12CS-1 updates Exhibit 12C-4 for the years 1993 to 1995. The final column contains aggregate data for those three years. The 1992 data are retained to facilitate comparisons. **Note that the data used exclude the minimum liability.**

Exhibit 12CS-2 applies the calculation method shown in Exhibit 12C-3 to 1993 to 1995 data. Again the 1992 data are repeated to facilitate comparisons.

Exhibit 12CS-1

General Motors - U.S. Pension Plans ($millions)

Pension Plan Status

	1992	1993	1994	1995	1992-1995 Change
Plan Assets	$ 39,571.6	$ 46,949.9	$ 50,407.6	$ 68,281.3	$ 28,709.7
PBO	51,671.5	65,428.0	59,751.9	71,284.1	19,612.6
Over(under)funded	$ (12,099.9)	$ (18,478.1)	$ (9,344.3)	$ (3,002.8)	$ 9,097.1

Computation of Pension Cost

	1992	1993	1994	1995	1993-1995 Cumulative
Service Cost	859.9	939.9	1,207.0	989.2	3,136.1
Interest Cost	4,089.9	4,258.9	4,466.6	4,916.4	13,641.9
					-
Actual Return	(2,770.9)	(7,159.0)	(1,161.3)	(12,156.3)	(20,476.6)
Deferred Return	(1,320.9)	3,329.1	(3,312.0)	6,624.7	6,641.8
Expected Return	$ (4,091.8)	$ (3,829.9)	$ (4,473.3)	$ (5,531.6)	$ (13,834.8)
Amortization of					
Gains and losses	-	200.8	434.6	251.5	886.9
Prior Service Cost	463.7	509.0	703.7	889.5	2,102.2
Transition Asset	(59.8)	(62.1)	185.2	(87.0)	36.1
Net Pension Cost	$ 1,261.9	$ 2,016.6	$ 2,523.8	$ 1,428.0	$ 5,968.4

Assumptions (%)

	1992	1993	1994	1995	Average
Discount Rate (Year-end)	8.6	7.1	8.5	7.0	7.5
Compensation Increase	4.9	5.0	5.2	5.1	5.1
Assumed ROA	11.0	10.0	10.0	10.0	10.0
Actual ROA	**7.1**	**18.1**	**2.5**	**24.1**	**14.9**

Alternative Measures of Pension Cost

	1992	1993	1994	1995	Cumulative
(1) Service Cost	$ 859.9	$ 939.9	$ 1,207.0	$ 989.2	$ 3,136.1
Interest Cost	4,089.9	4,258.9	4,466.6	4,916.4	13,641.9
(2) Recurring Cost	$ 4,949.8	$ 5,198.8	$ 5,673.6	$ 5,905.6	$ 16,778.0
Prior Service Cost	275.7	3,784.4	178.8	87.4	4,050.6
Actuarial (Gains)/Losses	3,552.7	8,413.6	(6,192.4)	10,288.8	12,510.0
(3) Gross Pension Cost	$ 8,778.2	$ 17,396.8	$ (340.0)	$ 16,281.8	$ 33,338.6
Actual ROA	(2,770.9)	(7,159.0)	(1,161.3)	(12,156.3)	(20,476.6)
(4) Nonsmoothed Pension Cost	$ 6,007.3	$ 10,237.8	$ (1,501.3)	$ 4,125.5	$ 12,862.0
(5) Contributions	891.3	3,859.6	7,695.5	10,467.0	22,022.1
(6) Benefits Paid	2,993.2	3,640.3	5,399.1	4,749.6	13,789.0

Exhibit 12CS-2

General Motors - U.S. Pension Plans ($ millions)

Calculation of Pension Costs and Cash Flows, 1993-1995

	1992	1993	1994	1995
Step 1: Calculate contributions made:				
Closing balance sheet (asset)	$ (284.8)	$ (2,127.8)	$ (7,236.5)	$ (16,275.5)
Opening balance sheet (asset)	(655.4)	(284.8)	(2,127.8)	(7,236.5)
Change	$ 370.6	$ (1,843.0)	$ (5,108.7)	$ (9,039.0)
Pension cost	1,261.9	2,016.6	2,523.8	1,428.0
Contributions made	$ 891.3	$ 3,859.6	$ 7,632.5	$ 10,467.0
Step 2: Calculate benefits paid:				
Closing pension assets	$ 39,571.6	$ 46,949.9	$ 50,407.6	$ 68,281.3
Opening pension assets	38,902.6	39,571.6	46,949.9	50,407.6
Change in plan assets	$ 669.0	$ 7,378.3	$ 3,457.7	$ 17,873.7
Contributions made (Step 1)	891.3	3,859.6	7,632.5	10,467.0
Return on assets	2,770.9	7,159.0	1,161.3	12,156.3
Benefits paid	$ 2,993.2	$ 3,640.3	$ 5,336.1	$ 4,749.6
Step 3: Calculate gross pension cost:				
Closing PBO	$ 51,671.5	$ 65,428.0	$ 59,751.9	$ 71,284.1
Opening PBO	45,886.5	51,671.5	65,428.0	59,751.9
Change in PBO	$ 5,785.0	$ 13,756.5	$ (5,676.1)	$ 11,532.2
Benefits paid (Step 2)	2,993.2	3,640.3	5,336.1	4,749.6
Gross pension cost	$ 8,778.2	$ 17,396.8	$ (340.0)	$ 16,281.8
Step 4: Calculate PSC and actuarial gains/losses:				
Total amortization	$ 403.8	$ 647.7	$ 1,323.5	$ 1,054.0
Closing unamort. trans. asset	(288.3)	(226.2)	(411.4)	(324.4)
Opening unamort. trans. asset	(348.1)	(288.3)	(226.2)	(411.4)
Amortization of trans. asset	$ (59.8)	$ (62.1)	$ 185.2	$ (87.0)
Amort. PSC and gains/losses	463.6	709.8	1,138.3	1,141.0
Opening unamortized loss	$ 3,305.2	$ 8,178.8	$ 13,062.5	$ 9,747.5
Less: Amortization	–	(200.8)	(434.6)	(251.5)
Plus: Deferred invest. (g)/l	1,320.9	(3,329.1)	3,312.0	(6,624.7)
New actuarial (g)/l	3,552.7	8,413.6	(6,192.4)	10,288.8
Closing unamortized loss	$ 8,178.8	$ 13,062.5	$ 9,747.5	$ 13,160.1
Opening prior service cost	4,682.2	4,494.2	7,769.6	7,244.7
Less: Amortization	(463.7)	(509.0)	(703.7)	(889.5)
Plus: New PSC	275.7	3,784.4	178.8	87.4
Ending prior service cost	$ 4,494.2	$ 7,769.6	$ 7,244.7	$ 6,442.6
10% of opening PBO	4,588.7	5,167.2	6,542.8	5,975.2
Excess opening unamort. loss	–	3,011.7	6,519.7	3,772.3
1/15 of excess	–	200.8	434.6	251.5

We start with Exhibit 12CS-2. Steps 1 through 3 replicate the analysis shown in Exhibit 12C-3. Step 1 shows that contributions rose sharply from prior year amounts. We discuss those contributions in part (d). Step 2 reveals a rising level of benefits, as more of GM's aging work force retires, and benefits increase following labor negotiations.

Step 3 calculates gross pension cost. Note the small negative cost in 1994. Rising interest rates resulted in an increased discount rate (from 7.1% to 8.5%), reducing the PBO and creating a large actuarial gain.

Step 4 is more complex than in Exhibit 12C-3. As we saw in part (a), the unamortized actuarial loss at December 31, 1992 exceeded the amount that could be deferred under the corridor method.

We start by removing amortization of the transition asset from total amortization. The 1992 and 1993 amounts are similar to prior years. The 1994 amortization is negative, an impossibility. Clearly the composition of this plan group changed, increasing the unamortized transition asset.

Next, we estimate amortization of the unamortized actuarial and investment loss. Calculation of the "excess" and amortization of that excess is shown farther down in the exhibit. The result is estimated actuarial losses in 1993 and 1995, but a gain in 1994. These results are consistent with the discount rate increase in 1993 and 1995 and the 1994 decrease.

Finally, we estimate amortization of unrecognized prior service cost indirectly by deducting amortization of the unamortized actuarial losses just computed from the total previously derived. For 1993, for example:

Total Amortization - Amortized Actuarial Loss =
                                      Amortized PSC

        $709.8 - $200.8 = $509.0

This indirect calculation results in estimated new PSC. Note the large 1993 increment, as predicted in part (a).

Turning to Exhibit 12CS-1, all of the data are derived either from Exhibit 12C-5 (text page 655) or from Exhibit 12CS-2.

(c) Using data from Exhibit 12C-5 (text page 655), replace the accrued pension cost with the economic status of the U.S. plans as measured by excess of the PBO over plan assets at December 31, 1995:

Accrued pension cost	$3,558.7
Less: excess PBO over plan assets	(3,002.8)
Pretax adjustment	$6,561.5
Less: deferred income tax at 37%	(2,427.8)
Required adjustment	**$4,133.7**

The accrued pension cost should be removed from GM's assets and the excess PBO added to liabilities. The $4,133.7 million adjustment reduces stockholders' equity. In addition, stockholders' equity must be reduced by the pension intangible asset created by the minimum liability (the $6.5 billion amount shown in Exhibit 12C-5 includes non-U.S. plans.

(d) The case conclusions (text page 654) suggest that GM's pension cost and contributions can be expected to rise from their 1992 levels.

The data in Exhibit 12CS-1 show that reported pension cost increased to more than $6 billion for the three years 1993 to 1995, exceeding total cost of $5.4 billion for the seven years ending with 1992. The prediction of rising costs based on the underfunded plan status at December 31, 1992 was accurate.

Exhibit 12CS-1 also shows rapid growth in GM's contributions. Such contributions totaled $22 billion over the 1993 to 1995 period, nearly five times the aggregate contributions for the seven years ended 1992. In 1995 alone, GM contributed $10.5 billion to its U.S. plans. These higher contributions were predictable.

(e)   Despite the increased contributions and excellent investment
      performance over the three years ending in 1995, GM's U.S.
      plans remained underfunded at December 31, 1995. As 1996 was
      a union contract year, another large prior service cost
      increment could be expected, further increasing the
      underfunded status.

          As shown in part (a), 1996 pension cost was expected to
      increase to more than $2 billion from the 1995 level of $1.4
      billion. Given the underfunded plan status, there is little
      prospect of that cost returning to the lower levels prior to
      1993.

          Plan contributions should also remain high relative to
      pre-1993 levels. While the large contributions in 1993 to
      1995 reduced the underfunded status significantly, periodic
      increases in the PBO due to labor contracts will tend to
      reduce the funded status further. Flat benefit plans, by
      their nature, defer recognition of probable benefit
      increases to future years.

          In summary, GM's U.S. pension plans can be expected to
      remain both a cash drain and a substantial earnings charge
      indefinitely.

Case 12-2 Solution

Estimated time to complete the case is 3 to 3½ hrs

1. and 2.

Year 1

The employees work one year. As a result, based on current salary scales, each will receive a pension of $1,000 per year for 15 years (age 66-80). At an assumed discount rate of 10%, the present value of the accumulated and projected pension liability for each employee and the total is computed as follows:

	ABO			PBO		
	JR	SR	Total	JR	SR	Total
Retirement Annuity	$1,000	$1,000		$1,500	$1,000	
Years Paid Out	15	15		15	15	
PV at retirement	$7,606	$7,606		$11,409	$7,606	
Years to retirement	25	2		25	2	
PV of Liability	**$702**	**$6,286**	**$6,988**	**$1,053**	**$6,286**	**$7,339**

Calculations:

Accumulated Benefit Obligation (ABO): Present value (at retirement) of a 15-year annuity of $1,000 per year = $7,606. For JR, we must discount this amount to find the present value at the end of year 1 (25 years prior to retirement): $7,606 x $(1.1)^{-25}$ = $702.

For SR, we must discount this amount to find the present value at the end of year 1 (two years prior to retirement);
$7,606 X $(1.1)^{-2}$ = $6,286.

Projected Benefit Obligation (PBO): Based on the projected salary at the time of retirement, JR will receive a pension of $1,500 per year, and SR will receive a pension of $1,000 per year. JR's PBO will be 1.5 times ($1,500/$1,000) as large (1.5 x $702 = $1,053) as the ABO, while SR's PBO will be the same as the ABO (because salary at retirement is the same as current salary).

Reconciliation of Change in ABO/PBO

	ABO			PBO		
	JR	SR	Total	JR	SR	Total
Opening Balance	$ -	$ -	$ -	$ -	$ -	$ -
Service Cost	**702**	**6,286**	**6,988**	**1,053**	**6,286**	**7,339**
Closing Balance	$ 702	$ 6,286	$ 6,988	$1,053	$ 6,286	$ 7,339

Since it is the first year of the plan, The changes in the ABO/PBO result from the *service cost* component which is equal to the benefit obligation at the end of the year.

Year 2

In year 2, both employees work another year. Each has expected benefits at retirement of $2,000 (2 x $1,000) annually based on current salary scales. Based on projected scales, the expected benefit is $3,000 (2 x $1,500) for JR and $2,000 for SR. The ABO and PBO are calculated as follows:

	ABO			PBO		
	JR	SR	Total	JR	SR	Total
Retirement Annuity	$2,000	$2,000		$3,000	$2,000	
Years Paid Out	15	15		15	15	
PV at retirement	$15,212	$15,212		$22,818	$15,212	
Years to retirement	24	1		24	1	
PV of Liability	**$1,544**	**$13,829**	**$15,373**	**$2,317**	**$13,829**	**$16,146**

Reconciliation of Change in ABO/PBO

	ABO			PBO		
	JR	SR	Total	JR	SR	Total
Opening Balance	$ 702	$ 6,286	$ 6,988	$1,053	$ 6,286	$ 7,339
Service Cost	772	6,914	7,686	1,159	6,914	8,073
Interest Cost	70	629	699	105	629	734
Closing Balance	$1,544	$13,829	$15,373	$2,317	$13,829	$16,146

Calculations:

The change in the ABO/PBO now has two elements. The *service cost* component is calculated as in year 1. It represents the (present value of) increase in benefits earned this year.

For JR it represents for the ABO (PBO), the present value of a 15 year annuity of $1,000 ($1,500) discounted 24 years;

For ABO: PV of 1,000 for 15 years = $ 7,606 x $(1.10)^{-24}$ = $ 772
For PBO: PV of 1,500 for 15 years = $11,409 x $(1.10)^{-24}$ = $1,159

For SR it represents for both the ABO and PBO, the present value of a 15 year annuity of $1,000 discounted 2 years; i.e.

PV of 1,000 for 15 years = $ 7,606 x $(1.10)^{-1}$ = $6,914

In addition, the amounts earned in previous years are one year closer to realization, requiring the accretion of interest on outstanding obligations. The resulting *interest cost* component is equal to 10% of the opening PBO and ABO.

Year 3

At the end of year 3, SR retires and she will start collecting her pension benefits of $3,000 per year ($1,000 x 3 years of service) next year. Also, as the actuaries have revised JR's life expectancy to 85 the calculations are now

	ABO			PBO		
	JR	*SR*	*Total*	*JR*	*SR*	*Total*
Retirement Annuity	$3,000	$3,000		$4,500	$3,000	
Years Paid Out	20	15		20	15	
PV at retirement	$25,541	$22,818		$38,311	$22,818	
Years to retirement	23	0		23	0	
PV of Liability	**$2,852**	**$22,818**	**$25,670**	**$4,279**	**$22,818**	**$27,097**

Reconciliation of Change in ABO/PBO

	ABO			PBO		
	JR	SR	Total	JR	SR	Total
Opening Balance	$1,544	$13,829	$15,373	$2,317	$13,829	$16,146
Service Cost	951	7,606	8,557	1,426	7,606	9,032
Interest Cost	154	1,383	1,537	232	1,383	1,615
Actuarial Loss	203	-	203	304	-	304
Closing Balance	$2,852	$22,818	$25,670	$4,279	$22,818	$27,097

Calculations:

The change in ABO and PBO now has three elements. *Interest cost* is 10% of opening balance.

Service cost calculations for JR are now based on a 20 year annuity;

For ABO: PV of $1,000 for 20 years = $ 8,514 x $(1.10)^{-23}$ = $ 951
For PBO: PV of $1,500 for 20 years = $12,770 x $(1.10)^{-23}$ = $1,426

For SR it represents for both the ABO and PBO, the present value of a 15 year annuity of $1,000. No discounting is required as SR reached retirement this year; i.e. PV of $1000 for 15 years = $ 7,606

In addition, because of the revised actuarial assumption, we assume that JR will receive the $2,000 ($3,000 using projected salary) annual pension for an additional five years. The increase in present value resulting from this change in assumption is the *actuarial loss* calculated as:

For ABO: Present value of 5 year $2,000 annuity = $7,582.
This amount must be discounted for 38 years (retirement in 23 years plus additional pension after 15 years).

Therefore actuarial loss = $7,582 x $(1.10)^{-38}$ = $203

For PBO: PV of 5 year $3000 annuity = $11,372 x $(1.10)^{-38}$ = $304

Year 4

The plan is amended to make the pension benefit 1.1 times the monthly salary for each year worked retroactive to the beginning of the plan for all workers still in the company's employ (JR). JR works one more year so that his estimated annual benefit is $4,400 ($1,000 x 4.4). SR receives the first year benefits of $3,000. The ABO and PBO calculations are now

	ABO			PBO		
	JR	*SR*	*Total*	*JR*	*SR*	*Total*
Retirement Annuity	$4,400	$3,000		$6,600	$3,000	
Years Paid Out	20	14		20	14	
PV at retirement	$37,459	$22,100		$56,189	$22,100	
Years to retirement	22	0		22	0	
PV of Liability	**$4,601**	**$22,100**	**$26,701**	**$6,902**	**$22,100**	**$29,002**

Reconciliation of Change in ABO/PBO

	ABO			PBO		
	JR	SR	Total	JR	SR	Total
Opening Balance	$2,852	$22,818	$25,670	$4,279	$22,818	$27,097
Service Cost	1,150	–	1,150	1,725	–	1,725
Interest Cost	285	2,282	2,567	428	2,282	2,710
Prior Service Cost	314		314	470	–	470
Benefits Paid	–	(3,000)	(3,000)	–	(3,000)	(3,000)
Closing Balance	$4,601	$22,100	$26,701	$6,902	$22,100	$29,002

Calculations:

The change in ABO and PBO now has four elements. *Interest cost* again is 10% of opening balance and the *benefits paid* represents the $3,000 received by SR.

To analyze the service cost and prior service cost we must examine, the $4,400 ($6,600) retirement annuity due JR.
Included are $3,000 ($4,500) = 3.0 x salary previously earned,
$\qquad\qquad$ $1,100 ($1,650) = 1.1 x salary for this year's service,
$\qquad$ and $ 300 (450) as adjustment for prior years' service

Service cost =
For ABO: PV of 20 year $1,100 annuity = $ 9,365 x $(1.10)^{-22}$= $1,150
For PBO: PV of 20 year $1,650 annuity = $14,054 x $(1.10)^{-22}$= $1,725

Prior service cost =
For ABO: PV of 20 year $ 300 annuity = $2,553 x $(1.10)^{-22}$= $314
For PBO: PV of 20 year $ 450 annuity = $3,829 x $(1.10)^{-22}$= $470

Four Year Summary Reconciliation: ABO and PBO

ABO

Year	1	2	3	4
Opening Balance	$ -	$ 6,988	$15,373	$25,670
Service Cost	6,988	7,686	8,557	1,150
Interest Cost	-	699	1,537	2,567
Actuarial Loss	-	-	203	-
Prior Service Cost	-	-	-	314
Benefits Paid	-	-	-	(3,000)
Closing Balance	$6,988	$15,373	$25,670	$26,701

PBO

Year	1	2	3	4
Opening Balance	$ -	$ 7,339	$16,146	$27,097
Service Cost	7,339	8,073	9,032	1,725
Interest Cost	-	734	1,615	2,710
Actuarial Loss	-	-	304	-
Prior Service Cost	-	-	-	470
Benefits Paid	-	-	-	(3,000)
Closing Balance	$7,339	$16,146	$27,097	$29,002

3.

Plan Assets

Year	1	2	3	4
Opening Balance	$ -	$ 7,280	$ 15,158	$ 24,690
Contributions	6,500	6,500	6,500	1,500
Actual Return	780	1,378	3,032	3,143
Benefits Paid	-	-	-	(3,000)
Closing Balance	$ 7,280	$15,158	$24,690	$ 26,333

4. (a) At the end of year 2, the fair value of plan assets (part 3) is $15,158, and the PBO (part 1) is $16,146. The difference is the transition liability of $988, which is to be amortized over 23 years (JR's remaining service life).[1]

---

[1] This calculation assumes that for years 1 and 2, DBP had expensed the exact amount it contributed each year to the pension plan, leaving no balance sheet accrual.

4. (b)   *Pension Plan Footnote*

The following table sets forth the components of pension cost:

		Year 3		Year 4
Service cost[1]		$9,032		$1,725
Interest cost[1]		1,615		2,710
Actual return[2]	(3,032)		(3,143)	
Less: deferred	433		0	
Expected return[3]		(2,599)		(3,143)
Amortization of:				
Losses(gains)[4]		-		(6)
Prior service cost[5]		-		21
Transition liability[6]		43		43
Net pension cost		$8,091		$1,350

The retirement plans' status and the pension liability recognized in DBP's balance sheet is presented below:

	Year 3	Year 4
ABO[1]	$25,670	$26,701
PBO[1]	27,097	29,002
Plan assets[2]	24,690	26,333
PBO in excess of plan assets	(2,407)	(2,669)
Less: unamortized portion		
Actuarial loss[4]	304	290
Excess returns[4]	(433)	(413)
Prior service cost[5]	-	449
Transition liability[6]	945	902
Pension liability[7]	$(1,591)	$(1,441)

Explanations (not provided in financial statements)

1 Part 1.
2 Part 3.
3 Expected return calculated by multiplying (plan assets + contribution) by 12%, the expected long-run rate of return. (See part 3). The difference between the actual return and expected return is deferred.
4 Deferred gain of $433 at end of year 3 is *amortized in year 4* over 22 years ($433/22 = $20), leaving $413 balance; actuarial loss of $304 (part 2) *is amortized in year 4*, over 22 years ($304/22 = $14), leaving $290 balance.
5 Prior service cost (Part 2) in year 4 of $470 is amortized over 22 years, assuming it originated at beginning of year: $470/22 = $21.
6 Amortization of transition liability of $988/$23 = $43.
7 This is equivalent to opening balance + pension cost - contributions. For year 3, 0 + $8,091 - $6,500 = $1,591; for year 4, $1,591 + $1,350 - $1,500 = $1,441.

5. i. Contributions = Pension Cost - change in B/S liability
       $1,500 = $1,350 - [$1,441-$1,591]

Balance Sheet Liability

Opening Balance	$ 1,591
Pension Cost	1,350
less Contributions	**(1,500)**
Close Balance	$ 1,441

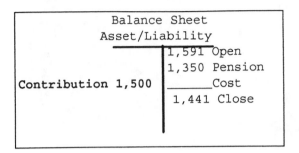

ii. Benefits = ROA + Contributions - Δ in plan assets
       $3,000 = $3,143 + $ 1,500 - [$26,333-$24,690]

Plan Assets

Opening Balance	$ 24,690
ROA	3,143
Contributions (from i)	1,500
less benefits paid	**(3,000)**
Close Balance	$ 26,333

Plan Assets

Open	24,690
ROA	3,143
Contribution	1,500
Close	26,333

3,000 Benefits Paid

Gross Pension Cost = Benefits paid + change in PBO
       $4,905 = $3,000 + [$29,002-$27,097]

PBO

Opening Balance	$27,097
Gross Pension Cost	**4,905**
- Benefits paid	(3,000)
Close Balance	$29,002

PBO

Benefits paid	3,000

27,097 Open	
Gross	
4,905 Pension	
Cost	
29,002 Close	

Therefore,

	Service Cost	$1,725
	Interest Cost	2,710
iii.	**Recurring Cost**	**$4,435**
	Actuarial Gain/Loss & Prior Service Cost	470
iv.	**Gross Pension Cost**	**$4,905**
	ROA	(3,143)
v.	**Nonsmoothed Cost**	**$1,762**

Chapter 13 Solutions

Overview:
Problem Length: Problem #s
  {S}   4, 8, 12, 14,
  {M}   1, 5, 6, 9, 15, 16
  {L}   2, 3, 7, 10, 11, 13,

1.{M}A.   (i) Dividend income:

          X: $10,000 (100,000 x $.10)
          Z: 0
          Total $10,000
          Dividends are not recorded as income for Y, but
          are included in "equity in income of affiliates"
          instead)

          (ii) Unrealized gains/losses included in stockholders'
               equity (all before deferred tax):

Firm	12/31/X0	X1 Change	12/31/X1
X	$(400,000)	$ 300,000	$(100,000)
Z	300,000	450,000	750,000
Total	$(100,000)	$ 750,000	$(650,000)

          Y: market value changes not recognized under
          equity method.

          (iii) Equity in income of affiliates:

          Y: .40 x $900,000 = $360,000

      B. The investments are accounted for as follows:

          Y using the equity method, as ownership exceeds 20%

          X and Z at market value under SFAS 115

      C. Dividend income $ 10,000
          Equity income   360,000
          Total income $370,000

D. X: 100,000 x $49 = $4,900,000
   Z: 150,000 x 30 = 4,500,000

   Y: carried at original cost plus equity in
   undistributed earnings subsequent to acquisition.

   Carrying amount at 1/1/X1 equals:

   Carrying amount at 1/1/X0: 800,000 x $35 = $2,800,000
   Plus 1990 undistributed earnings (data not available)
   Plus 19X1 earnings: .40 x $900,000 =   360,000
   Less 19X1 dividends: $.09 x 800,000 =   (72,000)

E. Mark to market returns for 19X1:

	Firm Dividends	+ MV Change	= Total Return
X	$ 10,000	$ 300,000	$ 310,000
Y	72,000	1,600,000	1,672,000
Z	0	450,000	450,000
Total	$ 82,000	$2,350,000	$2,432,000

For firms X and Z, the total return is reported in the
financial statements, but that return is reported primarily
as an adjustment to stockholders' equity.

F. (i) Under LCM, Bart's accounting for firm X is
         unchanged as market is below cost for both years,
         The shares of firm Z would be carried at cost
         under LCM as market value is higher for both
         years. Bart's reported income and the total return
         on the investments are unchanged.

    (ii) If consolidation were required for 40% ownership,
         Bart would consolidate firm Y. While consolidation
         does not change reported income, Bart's equity
         would be replaced by all revenues and expenses.
         Similarly, Bart's investment in firm Y would be
         replaced by all of the assets and liabilities of
         firm Y. The 60% of firm Y equity (and income) not
         owned by Bart would be shown as minority interest.

2.{L}A. The held-to-maturity fixed maturities are measured at amortized cost. The available-for-sale fixed maturities and equity securities are measured at market value.

B. 1995 Reported ROA by Portfolio Component ($ millions)

	Total Fixed Maturities	Equity Securities	Total Portfolio
Opening balance	$10,723	$ 642	$11,365
Investment income	844	116	960
Return on assets	7.87%	18.07%	8.45%

Note: Opening balances from Exhibit 13-3A (p. 680).
      Investment income includes realized gains

All returns exceed the corresponding reported 1994 returns shown in Exhibit 13-3C.

C. First, compute the mark-to-market returns, using the analysis on p. 684 as a guide.

1995 Change in MVA ($ in millions)

	Fixed Maturity Portfolios			
1995	Held-to-Maturity	Available for-Sale	Total	Equity Securities
Market value	$3,439	$9,374	$12,813	$588
Cost	3,229	8,891	12,120	493
MVA	$ 210	$ 483	$ 693	$ 95
1994				
Market value	$3,781	$6,954	$10,735	$642
Cost	3,768	7,128	10,896	610
MVA	$ 13	$ (174)	$ (161)	$ 32

Change in MVA
Fixed maturities	$693 - $(161) =	$854
Equity securities	$ 95 - $ 32 =	63
Total portfolio		$915

Calculation of 1995 Mark-to-Market Return

	Fixed Maturities	Equities	Total
Dividends and interest	$ 813	$ 16	$ 829
Realized gains (losses)	31	100	131
Reported income	$ 844	$116	$ 960
Change in MVA	854	63	917
Mark-to-market return	$1,698	$179	$1,877

13-3

Calculation of 1995 Mark-to-Market ROA

Fixed Maturities:

Opening balance	$10,735
Investment income	1,698
Return on assets	15.82%

Equity securities:

Opening balance	642
Investment income	179
Return on assets	27.88%

Total portfolio:

Opening balance	$11,377
Investment income	1,877
Return on assets	16.50%

These returns are quite different from the 1995 reported returns. Both the fixed maturity and equity portfolio returns are much higher, reflecting the 1995 rise in both the debt and stock markets. While Chubb realized capital gains in both portfolios, the realized gains were only a fraction of the market appreciation; Chubb "banked" the excess, which is available to smooth earnings in future years.

The 1995 mark-to-market returns also contrast with 1994, when both portfolio segments had negative returns.

These comparisons show that mark-to-market returns, while they report actual market results, are more volatile than reported returns that can be smoothed by management decisions.

D. The mark-to-market returns clearly report the effect of market performance on Chubb's investment portfolios. To fully evaluate the performance of Chubb's portfolios, we need benchmarks. For the bond portfolio, a weighted average of market returns (with weights equal to the proportion of U.S. government, corporate, tax-exempt, etc.) held in Chubb's portfolio. The benchmark should also be adjusted for any differences in duration, quality, or other bond characteristics.

The equity benchmark should also reflect the composition of Chubb's portfolio, reflecting such characteristics as type of stock (preferred vs. common), capitalization (large vs. small), and any international representation.

3.{L}A. Reported ROA by portfolio segment:

<u>1994</u>

Fixed maturities	$899 / $10,721 =	8.39%
Equity securities	92 / 910 =	10.11
Total portfolio	$991 / $11,631 =	8.52%

<u>1995</u>

Fixed maturities	$1,010 / $11,562 =	8.74%
Equity securities	81 / 855 =	9.47
Total portfolio	$1,091 / $12,417 =	8.79%

where return equals dividend and interest income plus realized gains or losses.

These data suggest that the return on the fixed income portfolio improved in 1995, partly offset by a reduced return on the equity portfolio.

B. First, compute the mark-to-market returns for 1994 and 1995, using the analysis on p. 684 as a guide.

1995 Change in MVA ($ in millions)

	Fixed Maturity Portfolios			Equity Securities
	Held-to-Maturity	Available for-Sale	Total	
1995				
Market value	$2,388	$11,928	$14,316	$1,119
Cost	2,045	10,856	12,901	598
MVA	$ 343	$ 1,072	$ 1,415	$ 521
1994				
Market value	$1,948	$9,509	$11,457	$ 855
Cost	2,053	9,608	11,661	565
MVA	$ (105)	$ (99)	$ (204)	$290
1993				
Market value	$11,966	---	$11,966	$910
Cost	10,721	---	10,721	513
MVA	$ 1,245		$ 1,245	$397

1995 Change in MVA

Fixed maturities	$1,415 - $(204) =	$1,619
Equity securities	$ 521 - $ 290 =	231
Total portfolio		$1,850

1994 Change in MVA

Fixed maturities	$(204)- $1,245 =	$(1,449)
Equity securities	$ 290 - $ 397 =	(107)
Total portfolio		$(1,556)

Calculation of 1995 Mark-to-Market Return

	Fixed Maturities	Equities	Total
Dividends and interest	$ 981	$ 45	$1,026
Realized gains (losses)	29	36	65
Reported income	**$1,010**	**$ 81**	**$1,091**
Change in MVA	1,619	231	1,850
Mark-to-market return	**$2,629**	**$312**	**$2,941**

Calculation of 1995 Mark-to-Market ROA

Fixed Maturities:

Opening balance	$11,457
Mark-to-market return	2,629
Return on assets	22.95%

Equity securities:

Opening balance	$ 855
Mark-to-market return	312
Return on assets	36.49%

Total portfolio:

Opening balance	$12,312
Mark-to-market return	2,941
Return on assets	23.89%

Calculation of 1994 Mark-to-Market Return

	Fixed Maturities	Equities	Total
Dividends and interest	$ 908	$ 44	$ 952
Realized gains (losses)	(9)	48	39
Reported income	**$ 899**	**$ 92**	**$ 991**
Change in MVA	(1,449)	(107)	(1,556)
Mark-to-market return	**$ (550)**	**$(15)**	**$(565)**

Calculation of 1994 Mark-to-Market ROA

Fixed Maturities:
     Opening balance $11,966
     Mark-to-market return   (550)
     Return on assets   (4.60)%

Equity securities:
     Opening balance $ 910
     Mark-to-market return   (15)
     Return on assets   (1.65)%

Total portfolio:
     Opening balance $12,876
     Mark-to-market return   (565)
     Return on assets   (4.39)%

These returns are quite different from reported returns. In 1995, both the fixed maturity and equity portfolio returns are much higher, reflecting the 1995 rise in both the debt and stock markets. While Safeco realized capital gains in both portfolios, the realized gains were only a fraction of the market appreciation; Safeco "banked" the excess, which is available to smooth earnings in future years.

The 1995 mark-to-market returns also contrast with 1994, when both portfolio segments had negative actual returns. Safeco realized capital gains (net) for the year, resulting in positive reported returns.

These comparisons show that mark-to-market returns, while they report actual market results, are more volatile than reported returns that can be smoothed by management decisions.

C.   The mark-to-market returns clearly report the effect of market performance on Safeco's investment portfolios.

D.   To fully evaluate the performance of Safeco's portfolios, we need benchmarks. For the bond portfolio, a weighted average of market returns (with weights equal to the proportion of U.S. government, corporate, tax-exempt, etc.) held in Safeco's portfolio. The benchmark should also be adjusted for any differences in duration, quality, or other bond characteristics.

The equity benchmark should also reflect the composition of Safeco's portfolio, reflecting such characteristics as type of stock (preferred vs. common), capitalization (large vs. small), and any international representation.

E.   (i)   The reclassification had no effect on reported income. However, stockholders' equity increased by $27 million less a 35% deferred tax provision.

(ii) A future reclassification would have the identical effect. It might also result in Safeco's auditor's questioning whether any fixed maturities can be classified as held-to-maturity.

(iii) The reclassified securities were most likely those that Safeco management may wish to sell prior to maturity. Reclassification reduces the probability that Safeco investment managers would be faced with a choice between holding securities they wish to sell, and risking loss of the ability to maintain some holdings as "held to maturity."

F.   (i)

	1994	1995
Reported pretax	$ 137	$ 141
Less: reported return	(991)	(1,091)
Plus: MTM return	(1,556)	2,941
Equals: adjusted pretax	$(2,410)	$1,991

(ii) Managements generally oppose mark-to-market accounting because of the resulting volatility of stockholders' equity and because, when only realized gains are reported, earnings can be managed as discussed in (iii). If MTM returns were included in reported income, return volatility would be transmitted directly to the income statement as well, as illustrated in (i) above.

(iii) When only realized gains and losses are included in reported earnings, management can smooth variations in operating earnings by varying the amounts of realized gains and losses. In good years, realized losses reduce total earnings. In poor operating years, realized gains augment reported earnings. Securities sold for earnings management purposes can be replaced with other (similar) securities.

G. We disagree with Safeco management. Analysts should look at corporate profits relative to the resources available to management. In the case of marketable securities, market value is a better measure of those resources than historical cost. If those resources cannot earn an adequate return in Safeco's insurance business, that suggests that assets should be returned to stockholders for reinvestment in other businesses with higher returns. Reducing the reported asset base inflates reported ROA and ROE, suggesting that the enterprise is more profitable than it really is.

4.{S}A. Carrying amounts at December 31, 1996:

(i)	Trading: 100 x $ 37 =	**$3,700**
(ii)	Available-for-sale:(same)	3,700
(iii)	Equity method:	
	$4,000 + 100 ($3.00 - $1.00) =	4,200

B. Investment income for 1996:

(i)	Trading: 100 x $1 - $300 =	**$(200)**
(ii)	Available-for-sale: 100 x $1 =	100
(iii)	Equity method: 100 x $3.00 =	300

C. Total income over holding period:

(i)	Trading: $(200)in 1996 + $200 gain in 1997 =	0
(ii)	AFS: $100 in 1996 - $100 loss in 1997 =	0
(iii)	Equity: $300 in 1996 - $300 loss in 1997 =	0

Over the entire holding period, all accounting methods report the same total return. The pattern of income recognition, however, differs.

5.{M}A.   19X0: Cost method, unless Burry can argue that it has "significant influence" over Bowman. SFAS 115 does not apply as Bowman shares are not marketable securities.

19X1: Equity method, unless Burry does not have "significant influence." If the equity method is appropriate, a retroactive restatement of the Investment in Bowman account and retained earnings is required.

B.   19X0: Income and Cash from Operations both equal the dividends received during the year: $152,000 (.19 x $800,000). Cash for investment equals $(10) million.

There is no effect on the carrying amount of Burry's investment in Bowman which remains at the acquisition cost of $10 million.

19X1: Because Burry acquired an additional 1% for a total share of 20%, a retroactive restatement of the investment account and retained earnings is required:

Acquisition cost:	$10,000,000
Less:	
Share of 19X0 loss (.19 x $600,000)	(114,000)
Dividends received (.19 x $800,000)	$ (152,000)
Restated carrying amount, 1/1/19X1	$ 9,734,000

NOTE: The $266,000 reduction is charged to retained earnings.

19X1 transactions and entries:

Restated carrying amount, Jan. 1, 19X1	$ 9,734,000
Plus: Additional acquisition cost	500,000
Share of 19X1 income (.20 x $2,000,000)	400,000
Less: dividends received (.20 x $1,000,000)	(200,000)
Carrying amount, December 31, 19X1	$10,434,000

Income equals Burry's proportionate interest in the earnings of Bowman: $400,000 (.2 x $2,000,000).

Cash from operations equals the amount of dividends received from Bowman: $200,000 (.2 x $1,000,000). Cash for investing equals $(500,000).

C. 19X0:   same as B

Income = $152,000 (.19 x $800,000)

No effect on investment

19X1: income equal to cash flow from dividend payments of $200,000 (.2 x 1,000,000).

The investment account would equal the total cost of $10,500,000 ($10,000,000 + $500,000) at the end of 19X1.

D. 19X0: Burry would recognize its proportionate share of Bowman's loss: ($114,000) = .19 x $(600,000)

Investment account would be $9,734,000 a decrease of $266,000 ($152,000 + $114,000) reflecting the share of loss and the dividends received. [See restatement in part B.]

[Alternate calculation: share of undistributed loss for 19X0 = .19 x [($600,000) - $800,000] = .19 x ($1,400,000) = $(266,000)]

Cash from operations equals $152,000. Cash for investment equals $(10,000,000).

19X1: Income equal to $400,000 (.2 x $2,000,000)

Cash from operations equal to $200,000 (.2 x $1,000,000). Cash for investing equals $(500,000).

Investment account equals $10,434,000, an increase of $700,000 including the $200,000 difference between income and cash flow and the additional investment of $500,000.

E. The answer depends on the relationship between Burry and Bowman. It is unlikely that the purchase of an additional 1% interest changed that relationship. Thus B, which uses different methods for the two years, does not provide useful information. The choice is between the cost method (C) and the equity method (D).

The advantage of the cost method is that Burry's income statement records only the cash flow (dividends) received. If Burry is a passive investor in Bowman, the cost method provides the best information.

The equity method is more appropriate when Burry is actively involved in managing Bowman and thus earning its share of the profits of Bowman. The payment of dividends may be discretionary on the part of the major shareholders.

6.{M}A. *Cost method is used for 19X6:*

No effect on sales.

Income recognized = dividends received of $10 (.01 x $1,000)

Cash from operations = dividends received	$ 10
Cash for investment = cost of shares	(100)
Net cash flow	$ (90)

Equity method is used for 19X7:

No effect on sales

Income recognized = proportionate share of earnings
                   = $660   (.30 x $2,200).

Cash from operations = dividends received	$360
Cash for investment = cost of shares	(3,190)
Net cash flow	$ (2,830)

B. 19X6
December 31, 19X6 (cost method) $ 100

19X7
The equity method must be applied retroactively to 19X6:

Initial acquisition cost	$ 100
Plus share of 19X6 earnings (1% of $2,000)	20
Less dividends received	(10)
Adjusted carrying amount, January 1, 19X7	$ 110

January 1, 19X7 shares purchased	$ 3,190
Equity in 19X7 earnings	660
Less: 19X7 dividends received	(360)
Carrying amount, December 31, 19X7	$ 3,600

C. The additional share purchases require that Potter consolidate San Francisco, for two reasons:

(i) It owns 100% of San Francisco's shares
(ii) It controls San Francisco.

Potter must use the purchase method of accounting (see Chapter 14) to reflect its ownership of San Francisco. Potter cannot use the pooling method because:

(i)   It owned 30% (more than the maximum allowed of 10%) of San Francisco prior to the acquisition of the controlling interest,

(ii) The combination was completed over a two year period, whereas pooling can be used only if the transaction is completed within one year, and

(iii) Potter used cash for its purchases not stock.

The assets and liabilities of San Francisco must be consolidated with those of Potter using fair market values at January 1, 19X8 (San Francisco only). Off-balance-sheet items (such as contingencies and postemployment benefits) may also be recognized. Information on fair values and off-balance-sheet items, as well as full financial statements for San Francisco, would be needed to evaluate the effect of the acquisition on Potter's 19X8 financial statements.

Problems 7 through 9 should require approximately 2-3 hours.

7.{L}   A. Disaggregate HP's earnings:

($ thousands)	1993	1994
Operating income[1]	$35,106 x .577 = $20,262	$24,381 x .662 =$16,148
Marketable securities[2]	$ 8,125 x .577 = 4,690	$ 5,918 x .662 = 3,919
Affiliates	(402)	904
Total	$24,550	$20,971

[1] Sales and other operating revenues less operating costs, multiplied by (1 - tax rate).

[2] Income from investments less interest expense, as debt is assumed to finance the investment portfolio.

B.   Disaggregate HP's assets:

($ thousands)	1992	1993	1994
Operating	$ 484,596	$ 516,881	$ 528,416
Short-term and marketable securities	81,188	74,769	75,668
Affiliates	19,720	19,285	20,743
Total assets	$ 585,504	$ 610,935	$ 624,827

Now, compute ROA on opening asset values, for each segment:

	1993	1994
Operations	4.2%	3.1%
Investments & marketable securities	5.8%	5.2%
Affiliates	(2.0%)	4.7%
Total	4.2%	3.4%

C.   Total return on assets declined in 1994. The disaggregated data show that the return on operating assets also declined; operating income fell approximately 20%. A positive swing from affiliate results helped moderate the decline in total returns as investment returns also fell.

D.
	1993	1994
(i) Dividends and interest	$6,136	$6,179

(Income from investments less realized gains)

(ii) Realized gains and losses	2,914	124

(iii) Unrealized gains and losses	9,512	(13,974)

[Change during year]

The market value adjustments (MVA) at each year-end are calculated below:

	Market		Cost		MVA	Change
1992:	$128,063	-	$68,060	=	$60,003	---
1993:	135,175	-	65,660	=	69,515	$ 9,512
1994:	122,212	-	66,671	=	55,541	(13,974)

E. The mark-to-market return equals dividend and interest income plus realized gains plus the change in MVA (from D (iii) above):

	1993	1994
Dividends and interest[d(i)]	$ 6,136	$ 6,179
Realized gains and losses [d(ii)]	2,914	124
Change in MVA [d(iii)]	9,512	(13,924)
Pretax mark-to-market return	**$18,562**	**$(7,671)**
Aftertax return [pretax x (1-t)]	**10,710**	**(5,078)**

Return on assets = MTM return/opening market value

1993: $10,710/($128,063+$13,128) = **7.6%**
1994: $(5,078)/($135,175+$9,109) = **(3.5)%**

F. We start with market value data:

		Change
9-30-92	$15,200	---
9-30-93	17,200	$ 2,000
9-30-94	22,800	5,600

The aftertax mark-to-market return is the aftertax change in value as a % of the opening value:

1993: $2,000(.577)/$15,200 = **7.6%**
1994: 5,600(.662)/ 17,200 = **21.6%**

G. HP reported portfolio returns of 5.8% in 1993 and 5.2% in 1994 (part B). The mark-to-market returns (parts E and F combined) are quite different: 7.6% for 1993 and a 0.8% ($1,370/$161,484) for 1994.

H.   The mark-to-market return is a better measure of the performance of Atwood shares over the 1992 to 1994 period. The equity method is an arbitrary accounting method. The market value measures the market's assessment of the worth of Atwood and is a better measure of the resource available to HP should it wish to sell its investment.

I.   The MVA at September 30, 1994 was $55,541 thousand (see part D). This amount was the pretax effect of adopting SFAS 115.

8.{S}A. Start with the carrying amounts on HP's balance sheet (see Exhibit 13P-2):

		Change
9-30-92	$19,720	---
9-30-93	19,285	$ (435)
9-30-94	20,743	1,458

Because Atwood paid no dividend, the change in carrying amount equals HP's share of the income (loss) of Atwood. As HP owns 23.8% of Atwood, Atwood's total pretax income (loss) must have been:

1993:	$(435)/.238 =	**$(1,828)**
1994:	1,458 /.238 =	**6,126**

B.   The tax rate can be computed by comparing HP's pretax and after-tax equity in Atwood's income:

Tax rate = [1 - (402)/(435)] =   7.6%

HP must have assumed that it would receive income in the form of dividends, mostly untaxed (see Box 13-2, p. 691-2).

C.   Tax rate = [1 - (904/1,458)] =   38.0%

In 1994, HP made the assumption that income from Atwood would be taxed at normal corporate tax rates. One possible reason for this changed assumption is that HP decided it would sell its investment in Atwood.

D.   The differing tax rate (dividends-received versus sale assumption) may be the reason for separate reporting; reporting equity earnings on a pretax basis would result in a distorted effective tax rate.

HP may also have reported its equity in Atwood's income on a separate line so that HP investors could see HP's results without distortion from the highly variable results of Atwood's operations.

9.(M)A.   Atwood Oceanics (carrying value) $ 22,495
          Other marketable securities (at market)   126,102
          Total shown on balance sheet   **$148,596**

B.   (i) The MVA at September 30, 1994 was $55,541 ($122,212 - $66,671).

     (ii) The MVA at September 30, 1995 must be $61,298 ($126,102 - $64,804).

     The 1995 change in unrealized gain = closing amount less opening amount:

     $61,298 - $55,541 (from Exhibit 13P-2) = **$5,757**

C.   1995 reported return = $10,846/($8,997+$66,671) = **14.3%** The adoption of SFAS 115 had no effect on these amounts. However, with marketable securities carried at market value, *future* calculations will be affected as the denominator of the ROA calculation will differ from cost.

D.   Mark-to-market return equals reported return plus the MVA change:

     $10,846 + $5,757 (part B) = $16,603

     With all assets at market, the ROA equals:

     $16,603/($8,997+$122,212) = **12.7%**

     The adoption of SFAS 115 had no effect on these amounts.

PROBLEMS 10 AND 11 SHOULD TAKE APPROXIMATELY 3 TO 4 HOURS.

10.{L}A. Exhibit 13S-1 presents the December 31, 19X8-X9 balance sheets for Moore Motors, using the equity method to account for Moore's investment in MMF.

B. Exhibit 13S-2 provides Moore Motor's income statement for the year ended December 31, 19X9 using the equity method for MMF.

C. **19X9 Ratios:**

	Consolidated	Equity Method
Gross profit margin	14.27	14.27
Return on assets	5.93	5.16
Return on equity	11.68	11.68
Receivables turnover*	1.16	6.06
Times interest earned	1.73	8.03
Debt-to-equity	2.55	0.18

*Average trade and finance receivables used in this ratio.

D. **Gross profit margin:** The consolidated and equity method statements report the same gross profit margin, as MMF has no operations other than financing.

Return on assets: The ratio based on consolidated statements is more useful; the equity method reports neither the total assets used by the parent and its affiliate nor the total interest expense.

Return on equity: Because net income and equity are the same under the equity method and consolidation, these methods report the identical ROE.

Receivables turnover: Consolidated statements are more informative for the parent's stockholders since they include all receivables generated by the firm, unlike the equity method wherein the receivables sold to MMF are excluded from the analysis. Note the large difference in the ratio due to this exclusion.

Times interest earned: Again, the parent's stockholders are better served by the consolidated ratio that reflects the total cost of amounts borrowed whether the debt is reported on MMF's books or those of the parent. The equity method excludes the subsidiary's interest expense as it reports only the parent's share of the net income of its subsidiary.

13-18

Debt-to-equity: The consolidated ratio is more informative as it reflects the debt of the parent as well as that of its affiliate, MMF. The equity method ratio is misleadingly low as it excludes the debt of MMF.

11.{L}A. The cash flow consequences of finance or credit receivable transactions are reported as components of investment cash flows. Because MMF's credit receivables are generated by the long-term financing it provides for Moore's customers, i.e., for Moore's essential operating activities, their cash flow consequences should be reported as components of cash flow from operations.

    The net cash flow impact of these transactions should be reported as operating cash flows. For the year ended December 31, 19X9, the reported operating cash flow of $13,006,000 should be reduced by $5,295,000 (cash inflow of $95,394,000 from liquidation of finance receivables less cash outflow for investment in finance receivables of $100,689,000) for an adjusted operating cash flow of $7,711,000 and adjusted investing cash flow of $9,710,000.

B. Interest payments of manufacturing and retailing firms should be components of financing cash flows because they reflect firms' leverage choices. The analysis of a firm's ability to generate cash from operations should not be confused by its financing decisions. Interest payments reported by Moore's manufacturing units should therefore be reflected in its financing cash flows (see Chapter 3). However, interest incurred by MMF is an operating cost and should be considered a component of its operating cash flow.

[Solution continues on page 13-21]

Exhibit 13S-1
Moore Motors-Equity Method
($ thousands)
Balance Sheets, December 31, 19X8-19X9

	19X8	19X9
Cash and cash equivalents	$ 6,909	$ 7,070
Accounts receivable--trade	4,541	5,447
--subsidiary	3,515	2,898
Finance receivables	13,246	13,235
Inventories	10,020	10,065
Fixed assets (net)	30,238	32,286
Investment in finance subsidiary	7,271	7,782
Miscellaneous assets	14,908	16,092
Total assets	$ 90,648	$ 94,875
Accounts payable--trade	$ 7,897	$ 7,708
--subsidiary	14,840	14,460
Bank debt	6,255	6,557
Accrued liabilities	21,054	23,847
Accrued income tax	4,930	5,671
Total liabilities	$ 54,976	$ 58,243
Stockholders' equity	35,672	36,632
Total liabilities and equity	$ 90,648	$ 94,875

Exhibit 13S-2
Moore Motors - Equity Method
Income Statement, Year Ended December 31, 19X9

Sales	$110,448
Equity in income of finance subsidiary	1,111
Interest income	1,980
Total revenues	$113,539
Cost-of-goods-sold	(94,683)
Selling and administrative expense	(6,386)
Interest expense	(849)
Depreciation and amortization	(5,664)
Total expenses	(107,582)
Pretax income	5,957
Income tax expense	(1,733)
Net income	$ 4,224

C.   Exhibit 13S-3 contains the 19X9 direct method cash
      flows of MMF and Moore's manufacturing operations.

D.   Cash flow from MMF to Moore's manufacturing operations
      $ thousands):

      Decrease in intercompany receivables $(380)
      Dividends paid   600
      Decrease in intercompany payables   617
      Total $ 837

      Note that this computation does not consider the cash
      flow effects of transactions involving the purchase of
      and payments for finance receivables. Data required to
      evaluate these transactions has not been provided in
      the problem.

E.   The segmentation allows the analyst to separately
      determine the leverage, profitability, and cash flows
      generated by the manufacturing unit and the finance
      operations and to understand the impact of each segment
      on the consolidated entity. Trends in these critical
      performance indices can be evaluated in the light of
      the industry and economic conditions that affect
      manufacturing operations and those (different)
      conditions that influence the financing business.

Indirect Method:

	Moore Motors Finance	Moore Motors (Equity Method)
Net income	$ 1,111	$ 3,713[1]
Depreciation and amortization	1,504	5,664
Δ accounts receivable	---	(906)
Δ inventories	---	(45)
Δ accrued liabilities	(366)	2,793
Δ accrued income taxes	---	741
Δ accounts payable	---	(189)
Δ intercompany receivables	380	(380)
Δ intercompany payables	(617)	617
Miscellaneous operating cash flow	---	(414)
Cash Flow from Operations	$ 2,012	$ 11,594
Net change in fixed assets[2]	(1,645)	(8,065)
Net change in finance receivables[2]	(4,889)	(406)
Cash Flow for Investment	$(6,534)	$ (8,471)
Net change in bank debt[2]	4,993	302
Repurchase of equity	---	(1,474)
New equity issued	---	173
Dividends paid	(600)	(1,963)
Cash Flow for Financing	$ 4,393	$ (2,962)
Net Cash Flow	$ (129)	$ 161

[1] Net income less equity in earnings of finance subsidiary plus dividends received.

[2] Only net entries possible from data provided.

Direct Method:

Sales	$ 110,448	
Δ accounts receivable	(906)	
Cash collections		$ 109,542
Cost-of-goods-sold	(94,683)	
Δ inventories	(45)	
Δ accounts payable	(189)	
Cash inputs		(94,917)
Selling and administrative	(6,386)	
Δ accrued liabilities	2,793	
Cash administration		(3,593)
Interest expense		(849)
Interest income		1,980
Dividend from MMF		600
Miscellaneous operating cash flow		(414)
Income tax expense	(1,733)	
Δ accrued income tax	741	
Income taxes paid		(992)
Δ intercompany receivable		(380)
Δ payables		617
Cash Flow from Operations		$ 11,594

Moore Motors Finance

Direct Method:

Finance Revenues	$ 14,504	
Δ finance receivables	(4,889)	
Cash collections		$ 9,615
Interest expense	(7,908)	
Cash inputs		(7,908)
Net cash collections		$ 1,707
Selling and administrative	(3,540)	
Δ accrued liabilities	(366)	
Cash administration		(3,906)
Income tax expense		(441)
Δ intercompany receivable		380
Δ intercompany payables		(617)
Cash Flow from Operations[1]		$ (2,877)

[1] Cash flow from operations reported under the indirect method is $2,012. The difference of $4,889 [$2,012 - ($2,877)] results from reclassification of the change in finance receivables from investment to operating cash flow.

12. {S} A. Under current U.S. GAAP, the increase in ownership from 25 to 33% would have no effect; Ford would continue to use the equity method to account for its investment in Mazda.

B. Under the proposed FASB standard, it is likely that Ford would have to consolidate Mazda as it now has management control (including substantial board representation. If there is no other significant shareholder, the presumption of control would be strengthened. Possible Japanese government restriction on control of Japanese firms by foreign firms would also have to be considered.

C. (i) Proportionate consolidation would replace Ford's investment in Mazda with its proportionate share of Mazda's assets and liabilities. The resulting balance sheet would give financial statement users a more complete picture of Ford's activities. Similarly, the income statement and cash flow statement would include Ford's share of Mazda's income, expenses, and cash flows.

(ii) Unless Ford is fully responsible for Mazda's debt, full consolidation would overstate the importance of Mazda to Ford.

13. {L} A. See Exhibit 13S-4A (page 13-25)

B. See Exhibit 13S-4B (page 13-26)

C. Mobil's equity method affiliates have financial characteristics that are different from those of Mobil itself. Consolidation of these affiliates has the following effects:

(i)   Increase in long term debt to equity ratio
(ii) Decrease in pretax profit margin
(iii) Lower effective tax rate
(iv) Decrease in pretax return on assets

Full consolidation has the greatest impact on these ratios. Proportionate consolidation results in ratios that are between the equity method ratios and those resulting from full consolidation.

MOBIL CORP. CONSOLIDATION
Year Ended December 31, 1995 ($ in millions)

Balance Sheet	Mobil	Affiliates	Eliminations	Consolidation
Current assets	$ 12,056	$ 8,345		$ 20,401
Investments	4,184	-	(2,417)	1,767
Other assets	25,898	12,220		38,118
Total assets	$ 42,138	$ 20,565	$ (2,417)	$ 60,286
Current liabilities	$ 13,054	$ 8,027		$ 21,081
Long-term debt	4,629	2,520		7,149
Other liabilities	6,504	2,122		8,626
Total liabilities	$ 24,187	$ 12,669		$ 36,856
Minority interest			5,479	5,479
Equity	17,951	7,896	(7,896)	17,951
Liabilities and equity	$ 42,138	$ 20,565	$ (2,417)	$ 60,286

Income Statement				
Sales revenues	$ 73,413	$ 31,324		$ 104,737
Other income	1,957		(397)	1,560
Total revenues	$ 75,370	$ 31,324		$ 106,694
Operating costs[1]	$ (51,960)	$ (29,964)		$ (81,924)
Operating taxes	(19,019)			(19,019)
Minority interest			691	691
Pretax income	$ 4,391	$ 1,360		$ 5,751
Income tax	(2,015)	(272)		(2,287)
Net income	$ 6,406	$ 1,088	$ (1,088)	$ 6,406

Ratios				
Current ratio	0.924	1.040		0.968
LT debt to equity	0.258	0.319		0.398
Pretax margin	0.060	0.043		0.055
Effective tax rate	0.459	0.200		0.398
Pretax ROA	0.104	0.066		0.095

[1] Difference between revenues and pretax income of affiliates
   assumed to be operating expense.

MOBIL CORP. PROPORTIONATE CONSOLIDATION
Year Ended December 31, 1995 ($ in millions)

Balance Sheet	Mobil	Affiliates	Eliminations	Consolidated
Current assets	$ 12,056	$ 2,678		$ 14,734
Investments	4,184	-	(2,417)	1,767
Other assets	25,898	3,735		29,633
Total assets	$ 42,138	$ 6,413	$ (2,417)	$ 46,134
Current liabilities	$ 13,054	$ 2,643		$ 15,697
Long-term debt	4,629	758		5,387
Other liabilities	6,504	595		7,099
Total liabilities	$ 24,187	$ 3,996		$ 28,183
Equity	17,951	2,417	(2,417)	17,951
Liabilities and equity	$ 42,138	$ 6,413	$ (2,417)	$ 46,134

Income Statement				
Sales revenues	$ 73,413	$ 9,835		$ 83,248
Other income	1,957		(397)	1,560
Total revenues	$ 75,370	$ 9,835		$ 85,205
Operating costs[1]	$ (51,960)	$ (9,369)		$ (61,329)
Operating taxes	(19,019)			(19,019)
Pretax income	$ 4,391	$ 466		$ 4,857
Income tax	(2,015)	(69)		(2,084)
Net income	$ 6,406	$ 397	$ (397)	$ 6,406

Ratios				
Current ratio	0.924	1.013		0.939
LT debt to equity	0.258	0.314		0.300
Pretax margin	0.060	0.047		0.058
Effective tax rate	0.459	0.148		0.429
Pretax ROA	0.104	0.073		0.105

[1] Difference between revenues and pretax income of affiliates
assumed to be operating expense.

14.(S}A. (All data in $ thousands) Nucor's minority interest rose by $18,607 ($124,048 - $105,441) in 1991. This increase must reflect the minority interest in income and capital contributions or distributions during the year. Given distributions of $7,507, the minority interest in 1991 income must be:

Change in minority interest = 1991 income - distributions
$18,607 = ? - $7,507

Therefore: ? = $18,607 + $7,507 = **$26,114**

This amount represents the 49% of the 1991 net income of the joint venture that accrues to the minority shareholder rather than to Nucor.

B. Dividing the data provided by .49 results in 100% of the 1991 net income and 1990 - 1991 equity of the joint venture:

1991 net income = $26,114/.49 = $ 53,294
12-31-90 equity = $105,441/.49 = $215,186
12-31-91 equity = $124,048/.49 = $253,159

1991 return on (average) equity equals:

$53,294/$234,172 = 22.8%

ROE can also be computed directly from the minority interest data:

$26,114/$114,744 = 22.8%

where $114,744 is the average minority interest.

C. The answer mainly depends on how the joint venturers are responsible for the liabilities of the venture. If each party is responsible only for its share of joint venture debt, there is a strong argument for reflecting only that portion of the debt on Nucor's balance sheet (and only its share of the assets as well).

D.   (i) From the point of view of Nucor management, proportionate consolidation has two advantages. First, it can hide the profitability of the joint venture, as the analysis is part B would no longer be possible. This may be a competitive advantage. The second advantage is that reported debt and debt-based ratios decline under proportionate consolidation. The only possible disadvantage is that reported sales and assets also decline under proportionate consolidation.

     (ii) From the point of view of a financial analyst, full consolidation is better in that the analysis in part A can determine the profitability of the joint venture and thus help the analyst understand the source of Nucor earnings.

15{M}A.   See Exhibit 13S-5 (page 13-29)

     B.   *Lumex Segment:*
          Modest but relatively stable operating profit margin
          No trend in ROA or asset turnover
          Capex rose from half of depreciation in 1992 to approximately equal for 1993/1994

          Cybex Segment:
          Erratic operating profit margin, declining in 1993-4
          Erratic ROA; negative in 1993
          Rising asset turnover but below Lumex segment
          Capex relative to depreciation over 1 and rising

     C.   Segment results are affected by allocation of parent overhead. Trends are affected by acquisitions and divestitures, price changes, and exchange rate changes.
          Comparisons with other companies are affected by the same factors. In addition, seemingly similar segments of different firms may have different customer bases, product mixes, or production processes that limit their comparability.

     D.   Improved segment analysis requires better understanding of the economic factors that affect segment sales and profitability, as well as the impact of acquisitions and divestitures, and price and exchange rate changes.

          [Solution continues on page 13-32]

Exhibit 13S-5

Lumex
Industry Segments
Ratio Computations, 1992 to 1994

	Years Ended December 31 ($000)		
Lumex Segment	1992	1993	1994
Sales	$ 50,038	$ 54,187	$ 60,764
Operating profit	3,445	3,881	4,012
Identifiable assets	24,297	24,756	28,659
Capital expenditures	603	1,481	1,532
Depreciation and amortization	1,142	1,283	1,568
Operating profit margin	6.9%	7.2%	6.6%
Return on ending assets	14.2%	15.7%	14.0%
Asset turnover	2.06	2.19	2.12
Capex-to-depreciation	0.53	1.15	0.98
Cybex Segment			
Sales	$ 53,850	$ 54,781	$ 70,420
Operating profit	3,690	(692)	2,218
Identifiable assets	31,452	32,117	37,087
Capital expenditures	1,550	1,736	2,047
Depreciation and amortization	1,382	1,523	1,671
Operating profit margin	6.9%	-1.3%	3.1%
Return on ending assets	11.7%	-2.2%	6.0%
Asset turnover	1.71	1.71	1.90
Capex-to-depreciation	1.12	1.14	1.23

Coca-Cola Company
Geographic Segments
Ratio Computations, 1993 to 1995

Years Ended December 31 ($millions)

United States	1993	1994	1995
Net operating revenues	$ 4,586	$ 5,092	$ 5,261
Operating income	782	869	840
Identifiable operating assets	2,682	2,991	3,384
Capital expenditures	165	252	285
Depreciation and amortization	127	128	146
Operating profit margin	17.1%	17.1%	16.0%
Return on ending assets	29.2%	29.1%	24.8%
Asset turnover	1.71	1.70	1.55
Capex-to-depreciation	1.30	1.97	1.95
Greater Europe			
Net operating revenues	$ 4,456	$ 5,047	$ 6,025
Operating income	1,029	1,173	1,300
Identifiable operating assets	3,287	3,958	4,301
Capital expenditures	366	330	383
Depreciation and amortization	120	160	180
Operating profit margin	23.1%	23.2%	21.6%
Return on ending assets	31.3%	29.6%	30.2%
Asset turnover	1.36	1.28	1.40
Capex-to-depreciation	3.05	2.06	2.13
Middle & Far East & Canada			
Net operating revenues	$ 2,957	$ 3,551	$ 4,162
Operating income	1,005	1,208	1,437
Identifiable operating assets	1,184	1,437	1,539
Capital expenditures	45	51	85
Depreciation and amortization	18	21	23
Operating profit margin	34.0%	34.0%	34.5%
Return on ending assets	84.9%	84.1%	93.4%
Asset turnover	2.50	2.47	2.70
Capex-to-depreciation	2.50	2.43	3.70

Exhibit 13S-6

Latin America

Net operating revenues	$ 1,683	$ 1,928	$ 1,920
Operating income	582	713	797
Identifiable operating assets	1,220	1,164	1,294
Capital expenditures	141	129	88
Depreciation and amortization	33	36	31
Operating profit margin	34.6%	37.0%	41.5%
Return on ending assets	47.7%	61.3%	61.6%
Asset turnover	1.38	1.66	1.48
Capex-to-depreciation	4.27	3.58	2.84

Africa

Net operating revenues	$ 255	$ 522	$ 595
Operating income	152	182	206
Identifiable operating assets	153	357	348
Capital expenditures	6	27	19
Depreciation and amortization	3	6	8
Operating profit margin	59.6%	34.9%	34.6%
Return on ending assets	99.3%	51.0%	59.2%
Asset turnover	1.67	1.46	1.71
Capex-to-depreciation	2.00	4.50	2.38

Consolidated

Net operating revenues	$13,963	$16,181	$ 18,018
Operating income	3,108	3,716	4,092
Identifiable operating assets	9,806	11,363	12,327
Capital expenditures	800	878	937
Depreciation and amortization	360	411	454
Operating profit margin	22.3%	23.0%	22.7%
Return on ending assets	31.7%	32.7%	33.2%
Asset turnover	1.42	1.42	1.46
Capex-to-depreciation	2.22	2.14	2.06

E.   Sale of the Lumex segment, with its stable profitability, left the company exposed to the volatile Cybex segment. The segment data permitted analysts to see that sale of the Lumex segment would force the firm to confront the operating difficulties of Cybex.

In early 1997, the company merged with a better managed company in the exercise equipment field, expecting that the combined firms would prove more profitable.

16.{L}A.   See Exhibit 13S-6 (pages 13-30 and 13-31)

B.   Operating profit margin was high and stable overall. However, different segments had quite different levels and trends. The Latin America and Africa segments, while small in size, had the highest margins, with margins rising sharply in Latin America.

ROA rose slightly from already high levels overall despite a decline in the U.S. ROA was highest in the less developed areas of Latin America, Africa, and Middle and Far East and Canada. A large increase in assets reduced the Africa ROA.

Stable asset turnover also disguises significant regional variations. Turnover is highest in the Middle & Far East segment, lowest in Greater Europe.

Capex is more than twice depreciation overall. The ratio is highest in the undeveloped market segments.

C.   Geographic segment results with companies are affected by allocation of parent overhead. Trends are affected by acquisitions and divestitures, price changes, and especially exchange rate changes.

Comparisons with other companies are affected by the same factors. In addition, geographic segments may be defined differently. Note, for example, that Coca Cola combines the Middle East, Far East, and Canada in one segment. It is unlikely that others firms would choose exactly the same combination of countries.

D.   Improved segment analysis requires better understanding of the economic factors that affect the sales and profitability of operations in different geographic areas. The impact of acquisitions and divestitures, and price and exchange rate changes must also be considered.

Case 13-1 Solution

Estimated time to complete this case is 3 to 3½ hrs.

Overview:
The "punch line" for this case is Exhibit 13CS-2. Selected ratios of Coca-Cola (Coke) as reported, with Enterprises on an equity basis are compared to ratios calculated with Enterprises consolidated on a full and proportional basis.

Enterprises' operations are heavily entwined with those of Coke. Carrying the affiliate on an equity basis results in only the net assets and bottom-line income being reported for the total entity. This serves to mask the actual liabilities of the total entity as well as the total assets and revenues required to generate the firm's income. As such, the firm's solvency and profitability ratios are distorted.

An additional consideration which should be noted is related to the nature and *quality* of Enterprises' assets. *Approximately two-thirds of Enterprises' assets are intangible;* an important consideration in any credit analysis. *Moreover, these intangibles result from bottling franchises granted by Coke to Enterprises.* On a consolidated basis, as one entity, a strong argument can be made that these assets *de facto* reflect a form of brand capitalization by Coke - a practice not permissible under GAAP[1].

1. Given Coke's 44% ownership of Enterprises, the board of directors representation, and the licenser/supplier relationship, clearly Coke is not a passive investor. Purchases from Coke account for over 40% of Enterprises' cost-of-goods-sold (Exhibit 13C-1). These close relationships suggest that either full consolidation or proportionate consolidation would be a more appropriate method of accounting, reflecting the effective control by Coke.

2. The solution to this problem is presented in Exhibit 13CS-1(a)-(c). Full consolidation requires the elimination of all intercompany transactions and the addition of 100% of the assets and liabilities of Enterprises to Coke's balance sheet and 100% of the revenues and expenses of Enterprises to Coke's income statement. However, since Coke owns only 44% of Enterprises, we must also recognize that 56% of the assets, liabilities, revenues, and expenses are owned by

---

1 If one were to make the argument that brand accounting is desirable, then one would have to justify the value placed upon it by Coke and Enterprises -- it would be hard to argue that the sale was "arm's length". Furthermore, at the very least, for comparison purposes with other firms which do not practice brand accounting, such assets should be ignored.

other stockholders. This is accomplished using "minority interest" accounts on the balance sheet and the income statement. On the former, the minority interest represents the 56% of the net assets of Enterprises owned by non-Coke stockholders.

As 44% of Enterprises common equity of $1,405 equals $618 and Coke carries the investment at $556, there is "negative goodwill" of $62 which is deducted from intangible assets.

For the income statement we eliminate the intercompany sales from sales and COGS. Additionally, we assume the marketing payments from Coke to Enterprises were recorded as revenues by Enterprises and adjust accordingly.

The cash flow eliminations [13CS-1(c)] are much simpler. The operating adjustments (intercompany sales and marketing payments) automatically offset as they are classified as CFO for both companies.

Consolidated net income, however, is equal to Coke's income. Thus, we must eliminate Enterprise's income of $82. The offset is minority interest of $46, a noncash item, and $36 which has previously been included in "Equity income, net of dividends."

Additionally, we need to adjust for the $3 dividends paid by Enterprises to Coke. These are recorded as CFO by Coke and CFF by Enterprises.

As Enterprises' CFO and CFI are virtually identical, consolidated cash flow is little different from the equity method cash flow statement.

3.   See Exhibit 13CS-2

4.   Virtually all of Coke's ratios are adversely affected by the consolidation of Enterprises. Enterprises is much more leveraged with a debt/equity ratio of 2.99 compared to Coke's ratio of .75. On a consolidated basis, Coke debt/equity ratio doubles to 1.53. A similar phenomenon occurs with the debt/assets ratio. The effects are more pronounced when we consider the debt to tangible assets and equity. Removing Enterprises' intangible assets from equity results in negative tangible equity.

Coke reports a healthy 16.9 for its times interest earned ratio. This ratio, however, is biased as it included Enterprises' income in the numerator but ignores its interest expense. On a fully consolidated basis, the ratio declines 50% to 8.4

Enterprises' income based ratios are also greatly inferior to those of Coke. ROA as well as return on sales are low for Enterprises as compared with Coke. As Enterprises' and Coke's income are affected to a great extent by the "transfer price" Coke charges Enterprises for its syrup, the relative profitabilities may be distorted and the lower levels reported on a consolidated basis are a better measure of overall profitability. Note that ROE is not affected by consolidation as income and equity are unchanged.

Interestingly, receivables turnover (sales/average trade receivables) is also worse after consolidation despite Enterprises higher ratio. The elimination of "double counting" explains this surprising result. After eliminations, Enterprises increases proportionately consolidated sales by only 24% but receivables by 30%, thus lowering the turnover ratio.

Overall, the consolidated statements are less favorable to Coke than those prepared using the equity method.

5. The calculations for the proportionally consolidated statements are presented in Exhibit 13CS-3(a)-(c). The calculations are similar to those carried out on a consolidated basis except that instead of all of Enterprises' assets/liabilities and revenues/expenses being added to Coke's only 44% are combined. This eliminates the need for a minority interest account. Eliminations and adjustments are also reduced proportionally.

The effect on the ratios is demonstrated in Exhibit 13CS-3. The ratios on a proportionally consolidated basis can be compared to those reported by Coke as well as to the consolidated ratios computed earlier. Overall, the effect of proportional consolidation is similar to that of full consolidation. Leverage ratios are worse as they become larger and profitability declines. However, as only a portion is consolidated the degree of decline is mitigated.

In the case of proportional consolidation, as only a portion of the intangibles are reduced, tangible equity remains positive allowing us to consider the effect of removing the intangible assets. Debt to tangible equity increases by more than three and a half times from .91 to 3.11.

The proportional consolidation cash flow statement [13CS-3(c)], like the income statement, includes 44% of the cash flows of Coke. Adjustments are similar to those of the fully consolidated cash flow statement (see question 2); the only difference being that there is no need for a minority interest adjustment to income. The proportional consolidation has eliminated that.

6. Data in Exhibit 13C-2 indicate the following profitability measures for Coke's other affiliates ($ in millions).
      Gross Profit $3,917/$11,563 = 34%
      Return on sales $ 355/$11,563 = 3%

Return on assets $ 355/$ 9,591 = 3.7%

As these measures are well below Coke's (as reported or on a (proportionally) consolidated basis), consolidating these other affiliates would lower Coke's profitability ratios even further. The size of the effect would depend on the degree of intercompany eliminations.

Coke's leverage ratios would also be affected negatively by consolidating these affiliates. These affiliates have total liabilities of over $5.8 billion. We do not know what portion of those liabilities are debt. However, even if we assume only 25% is debt, that would add approximately $1.5 billion to Coke's $8.2 billion consolidated debt (an 18% increase). As equity would not change, the debt to equity ratio would increase correspondingly.

7. The FASB's new standard calls for economic or effective control as the basis for consolidation policy. Such a standard would most likely require consolidation of Enterprises by Coke given the extensive operational and managerial influence wielded by Coke.

8. The difference between the methods is significant. The equity method (as argued in part 1) is inappropriate and misleading. Given the interdependence of the companies one must view their activities as a unified company with a number of divisions.

Under consolidation, the financial statements of Coke includes 100% of the assets, liabilities, revenues, expenses, and cash flows of its affiliates. The minority interest account shows the (net) interest in the equity and earnings held by the non-Coke stockholders of these affiliates. Proportionate consolidation, on the other hand, includes only approximately (44%-49%) of the assets, liabilities, revenues, expenses, and cash flows of the affiliates in the financial statements of Coke.

Full consolidation may, therefore, overstate the degree to which Coke is responsible for the liabilities of the affiliates. It also overstates the affiliates' contribution of revenues, expenses, and cash flows to the operations of the total entity. On the other hand, it is unlikely that Coke would allow such operationally significant affiliates to suffer financial distress.

Proportionate consolidation, on the other hand, may understate the influence of the affiliates. Like other stockholders, Coke is a residual owner. Before it can receive any return on its investment, *all* of the affiliates' liabilities must be satisfied. Coke's Statement of Cash

Flows reports its proportionate share of the cash flows generated by the affiliates. However, since creditors often have a senior claim on these cash flows, Coke's proportionately consolidated cash flow statement can be misleading.

Exhibit 13CS-1(a)
Coke and Enterprises - Consolidated Balance Sheet ($ millions)

	Coke	Enterprises	Adjustments Debit	Adjustments Credit	Full Consolidation
Cash & mrktble securities	$ 1,315	$ 8			$ 1,323
Accounts receivable	1,695	510	–	–	2,205
Amounts due from Coca Cola		6		6	–
Finance subsidiary receivables	55	–			55
Inventory	1,117	225			1,342
Prepaids and other	1,268	233			1,501
Current Assets	$ 5,450	$ 982			$ 6,426
Investment in Affiliates					
Coca Cola Enterprises	556	–		556	–
Coca Cola Amatil	682	–			682
Other	1,157	–			1,157
Cost Method investments	319	–		–	319
Finance subsidiary receivables	351	–			351
Marketable securities	1,246	–		–	1,246
	$ 4,311	0			3,755
Property, plant and equipment	4,336	2,158			6,494
Intangible assets	944	5,924		62	6,806
Total Assets	$15,041	$ 9,064			$ 23,481
Accounts payable	4,425	796	6		5,215
Notes payable & current debt	2,923	63			2,986
Current Liabilities	$ 7,348	$ 859			$ 8,201
Long-term debt	1,141	4,138	–	–	5,279
Other liabilities	966	600			1,566
Deferred taxes	194	2,032	–		2,226
	$ 2,301	$ 6,770			$ 9,071
Minority interest				787	787
Preferred equity		30			30
Common equity	5,392	1,405	1405		5,392
Total Liabilities & Equity	$15,041	$ 9,064			$ 23,481

Coke and Enterprises - Consolidated Income Statement ($ millions)

	Coke	Enterprises	Eliminations	Fully Consolidated
Sales	$ 18,018	$ 6,773	(2,424)	$22,367
C O G S	(6,940)	(4,267)	2,081	(9,126)
Gross Profit	$ 11,078	$ 2,506	(343)	$13,241
S G & A	(6,986)	(2,038)	343	(8,681)
Operating Income	$ 4,092	$ 468	0	$ 4,560
Interest Income	245			245
Equity Income	169	-	(36)	133
Other Income	94	3	0	97
EBIT	$ 4,600	$ 471	(36)	$ 5,035
Interest Expense	(272)	(326)	0	(598)
EBT	$ 4,328	$ 145	(36)	$ 4,437
Minority Interest			(46)	(46)
Income Taxes	(1,342)	(63)	0	1,405
Net Income	$ 2,986	$ 82	(82)	$ 2,986

Coke and Enterprises-Consolidated Cash Flow Statement ($ millions)

	Coke	Enterprises	Eliminations	Fully Consolidated
Cash Flow from operations				
Net Income	$ 2,986	$ 82	$ (82)	$ 2,986
Equity Income, net of dividends	(25)	---	33*	8
Minority Interest			46	46
Other Adjustments	154	562	---	716
	$ 3,115	$ 644	(3)	$ 3,756
Cash flow from investing	$ (1,013)	$ (620)		$(1,633)
Cash flow from financing				
Debt financing	$ 542	-		$ 542
Repurchase of stock	(1,710)	(31)		(1,741)
Dividends	(1,110)	(7)	3	(1,114)
	$ (2,278)	$ (38)	3	$(2,313)
Effect of Exchange Rate Changes	(43)	--		(43)
Change in Cash	$ (219)	$ (14)		(233)

* Sum of $36 (Equity share of Enterprise's Income) less $3 dividend

Exhibit 13CS-2

		Enterprises	C O	C A C O	L A
			As Reported Equity	Part 5. Proportional Consolidation	Part 3. Fully Consolidated
(a)	Current Ratio	1.14	0.74	0.76	0.78
(b)	Debt to Equity	2.99	0.75	1.10	1.53
(c)	Debt to Tangible Equity	NMF	0.91	3.11	NMF
(d)	Debt to Assets	0.46	0.27	0.32	0.35
(e)	Debt to Tangible Assets	1.34	0.29	0.40	0.50
(f)	Gross Profit	37%	61%	60%	59%
(g)	Return on Sales	1%	17%	15%	13%
(h)	ROA	1%	20%	16%	13%
(i)	Return on tangible assets	3%	21%	20%	18%
(j)	ROE	6%	55%	55%	55%
(k)	Return on Tangible Equity	NMF	67%	157%	NMF
(l)	Times Interest earned	1.4	16.9	11.5	8.4
(m)	Inventory turnover	19.0	6.2	6.5	6.8
(n)	Receivables Turnover	13.3	10.6	10.4	10.1

NMF : Not meaningful as ratio is negative

Coke and Enterprises - Proportional Consolidated Balance Sheet

	Coke	Enterpr -ises	44% of Enterpr -ises	Adjustments Debit	Credit	Proportional Consolidation
Cash & mktble securities	$ 1,315	$ 8	$ 4			$ 1,319
Accounts receivable	1,695	510	224	-	-	1,919
Amounts due from Coke		6	3		3	-
Finance subsidiary receivables	55	-	-			55
Inventory	1,117	225	99			1,216
Prepaids and other	1,268	233	103			1,371
Current Assets	$ 5,450	$ 982	$ 432			$ 5,879
Investment in Affiliates						
Coca Cola Enterprises	556	-	-		556	-
Coca Cola Amatil	682	-	-			682
Other	1,157	-	-			1,157
Cost Method investments	319	-	-			319
Finance subsidiary receivables	351	-	-			351
Marketable securities	1,246	-	-			1,246
	$ 4,311	0	0			$ 3,755
P P & E	4,336	2,158	950		-	5,286
Intangible Assets	944	5,924	2,607		62	3,488
Total Assets	$15,041	$9,064	$3,988			$ 18,408
Accounts payable	4,425	796	350	3		4,773
Notes Pyble & cur. debt	2,923	63	28			2,951
Current Liabilities	$ 7,348	$ 859	$ 378			$ 7,723
Long-term debt	1,141	4,138	1,821			2,962
Other Liabilities	966	600	264			1,230
Deferred taxes	194	2,032	894			1,088
	$ 2,301	$6,770	$2,979			$ 5,280
Preferred Equity		30	13			13
Common Equity	5,392	1,405	618	618		5,392
Total Lblties & Equity	$15,041	$9,064	$3,988			$ 18,408

Exhibit 13CS-3(b)
Coke and Enterprises - Proportional Consolidated Income Statement
($ millions)

	Coke	Enterprises	44% of Enterprises	Eliminations	Proportional Consolidation
Sales	$18,018	$ 6,773	$ 2,980	(1,067)	$ 19,932
C O G S	(6,940)	(4,267)	(1,877)	916	(7,902)
Gross Profit	$11,078	$ 2,506	$ 1,103	(151)	$ 12,030
S G & A	(6,986)	(2,038)	(897)	151	(7,732)
Operating Income	$ 4,092	$ 468	$ 206	-	$ 4,298
Interest Income	245		-		245
Equity Income	169	-	-	(36)	133
Other Income	94	3	1	-	95
EBIT	$ 4,600	$ 471	$ 207	(36)	$ 4,771
Interest Expense	(272)	(326)	(143)	-	(415)
EBT	$ 4,328	$ 145	$ 64	(36)	$ 4,356
Income Taxes	(1,342)	(63)	(28)	-	(1,370)
Net Income	$ 2,986	$ 82	$ 36	(36)	$ 2,986

Exhibit 13CS-3(c)
Coke and Enterprises-Proportional Consolidated Cash Flow Statement
($ millions)

	Coke	Enterprises	44% of Enterprises	Eliminations	Proportional Consolidation
CFO					
Net Income	$ 2,986	$ 82	$ 36	(36)	$ 2,986
Equity Income, net of dividends	(25)	---	-	33*	8
Other Adjustments	154	562	247	---	401
	$ 3,115	$ 644	$ 283	(3)	$ 3,395
CFI	$ (1,013)	$ (620)	$ (273)		$(1,286)
CFF					
Debt financing	$ 542	-	-		$ 542
Repurchase of stock	(1,710)	(31)	(14)		(1,724)
Dividends	(1,110)	(7)	(3)	3	(1,110)
	$ (2,278)	$ (38)	$ (17)	3	$(2,292)
Effect of Exchange Rate Changes	(43)	--			(43)
Change in Cash	$ (219)	$ (14)	$ (6)		(225)

* Sum of $36 (Equity share of Enterprise's Income) less $3 dividend

13C-10

Chapter 14 - Solutions

Overview
Problem Length   *Problem #s*
  {S}   *4*
  {M}   *1, 2, 5, 6, 11, and 12*
  {L}   *3, and 7 - 10*

1.[M]A. B. and D.   Acetar Combined Balance Sheet

| End of | Year 1 | | Year 2 |
	Pooling	Purchase	Purchase
Cash	$ 150	$ 150	$ 200
Inventory	1,300	1,330	1,400
Fixed assets (net)	4,000	4,050	4,145
Goodwill	0	320	312
Total assets	$5,450	$5,850	$6,057
Current liabilities	1,250	1,250	1,300
Equity	4,200	4,600	4,757
Total equities	$5,450	$5,850	$6,057

Under the pooling method, the balance sheets of Ace and
Tar are combined without adjustment. When Ace acquires
Tar, and the purchase method is used, the assets and
liabilities of Tar (but not Ace) are restated to fair
value. The excess of the purchase price ($1,500) over
the fair value of the net assets acquired ($1,180) is
recorded as goodwill ($1,500 - $1,180 = $320).

C.   Year 2 reported income under the purchase method is
$157, calculated as follows:

Reported income under pooling	$ 200
Less: increase in COGS due to write-up	
of Tar inventory	(30)
additional depreciation of Tar	
fixed asset write-up ($50/10)	(5)
goodwill amortization ($320/40)	(8)
Reported income under purchase method	$ 157

D.   Balance sheet shown above. Differences between last two
     columns (Year 2 changes) are:

     • Cash increased by change in cash
     • Inventory increase of $100 from pooling method cash
       flow statement less $30 additional COGS under
       purchase method.
     • Fixed assets increased by capital expenditures
       ($500) and reduced by depreciation ($405)
     • Current liabilities increased by accounts payable
       increase of $50 from cash flow statement
     • Equity increased by purchase method net income
       ($157).
     • Goodwill decreased by amortization ($8).

E.   Purchase Method Cash Flow Statement
     Indirect Method

     Net income $ 157
     Depreciation   405
     Goodwill amortization   8
     Change in inventory   (70)
     Change in accounts payable   50
          Cash from operations $550

     Capital expenditures   (500)
     Acquisition net of cash   (1,450)
          Cash from investing   (1,950)

     Shares issued for financing   1,500
          Cash from financing $1,500

          Net cash flow $ 100

     Alternatively, shares issued for financing would be
     shown as supplementary information and the acquisition
     cash flow would be shown as $50 (cash acquired),leaving
     the net cash flow unchanged.

2.{M}A.   For each balance sheet account, we use the difference between the sum of the 1-1-96 historical data and the 12-31-96 balance sheet amounts as well as the cash flow and additional information provided:

Accounts receivable: $550 - $500 = $50, equal to the cash flow change. Therefore fair value unchanged at $200.

Inventory: $1,600 - $1,500 = $100. As there was no cash flow change in inventory, the write-up must be $100 and fair value $400.

Goodwill: $390 increase all due to acquisition. As goodwill amortized over 40 years, original amount must have been $400 with 1996 amortization of $10 ($400/40).

Fixed assets: $6,400 - $5,500 = $900. Capital expenditures = $1,290 and depreciation $580 ($600 less goodwill amortization of $10 and discount amortization of $10), for a net increase of $710. Therefore write-up must be $190 and fair value $690.

Accounts payable: $1,700 - $1,500 = $200 equal to cash flow change. No write-up; fair value equals $500.

Long-term debt: $2,750 - $2,700 = $50. As debt issued was $100, and discount amortization was $10, there must be a $60 *writedown* with a fair value of $640.

Equity: $6,290 - $4,300 = $1,990 equal to stock issued of $550 + elimination of Dove equity of $(200) + net income of $1,240.

Thus, Dove's fair value balance sheet at the acquisition date must have been:

Cash	$ 0
Accounts receivable	200
Inventory	400
Fixed assets	690
Less:	
Accounts payable	(500)
Long-term debt	(640)
Net assets	$ 150

B. As the purchase price was $550, **goodwill of $400** ($550
    - $150) was recorded.

C. If the pooling method had been used, net income would
    be:

Purchase method net income $1,240

Adjustments:
Reduced depreciation[1]   10
No goodwill amortization[2]   10
Lower interest expense[3]   10
      Total adjustments $ 30
Income tax offset[4]   (7)
      Aftertax adjustment $ 23

Pooling method net income $1,263

[1] Average life approximately 20 years; $190/20 = approx. $10
[2] Computed in part A
[3] Debt discount of $60 under purchase method must be amortized
     over remaining life of 5 years. Amortization of $10 (later year
     amounts will be higher) increases interest expense
[4] Assumes 35% tax rate with goodwill not tax-deductible

D. Pooling Method Cash Flow Statement
    Indirect Method

Net income $ 1,263
Depreciation   570
Increase in accounts payable   200
Increase in accounts receivable   (50)
      Cash from operations $1,983

Capital expenditures   (1,290)
      Cash from investing   (1,290)

Debt issued   100
      Cash from financing   100

      Net cash flow $ 793

Cash flow under the purchase method is $7 higher
because of the tax reduction resulting from the tax
deductibility of the purchase method adjustments.

3. [L]A.   (i)   Column 3 of Exhibit 14S-1A (p. 14-6) shows the December 31, 1996 *pro forma* balance sheet and the resulting book value per share. Under the pooling method, the assets and liabilities of the two firms are aggregated without any adjustment.

          (ii) Column 3 of Exhibit 14S-1B (p. 14-7) shows the 1997 *pro forma* income statement and the resulting earnings per share. The estimated income statements are aggregated without adjustment.

   B.   (i)   Column 5 of Exhibit 14S-1A shows the December 31, 1996 *pro forma* balance sheet and the resulting book value per share. Under the purchase method, the assets and liabilities of the acquired firm (PSI) are restated to their fair market values. Column 4 shows the adjustments to fair value for each balance sheet category.
                In addition, the pro forma balance sheet recognizes goodwill of $1,400, equal to the excess of price paid ($3,000) over the sum of the preacquisition book value ($600) and fair value adjustment ($1,000).

          (ii) Column 5 of Exhibit 14S-1B shows the 1997 *pro forma* income statement and the resulting earnings per share. The increased expenses due to purchase method adjustments must be recognized:

                Depreciation = $1,000/10 = $(100)
                Goodwill amort. = $1,400/20 =   (70)
                Interest = .10 x $3 billion =   (300)
                Total additional expense $(470)
                Less: tax reduction = .4 x $400 =   160
                Equals: net income adjustment $(310)

   C.   (i)   As shown in Exhibit 14S-1A, the debt ratios are higher when Aspen acquires PSI for cash, financed with additional debt.

          (ii) As shown in Exhibit 14S-1B, interest coverage is reduced when Aspen acquires PSI for cash, financed with additional debt. Interest expense is higher and EBIT is lower (due to purchase method adjustments).

Exhibit 14S1-A

Aspen Pharmaceuticals, *pro forma* balance sheet
December 31, 1996 ($millions)

	(1)	(2)	(3)	(4)	(5)
	Historical Cost		Pooling	Purchase Method	
	Aspen	PSI	Pro Forma	Adjust.	Pro Forma
3A(i) 3B(i)					
Current assets	$ 4,500	$ 1,000	$ 5,500	$ -	$ 5,500
Property	5,000	200	5,200	1,000	6,200
Goodwill				1,400	1,400
Total assets	$ 9,500	$ 1,200	$ 10,700	$ 2,400	$ 13,100
Current liabilities	$ 3,500	$ 300	$ 3,800	$ -	$ 3,800
Long-term debt	1,000	300	1,300	3,000	4,300
Deferred taxes	1,000	-	1,000	-	1,000
Stockholders' equity	4,000	600	4,600	(600)	4,000
Total equities	$ 9,500	$ 1,200	$ 10,700	$ 2,400	$ 13,100
Shares outstanding	1,000	100	1,100		1,000
Book value per share	$ 4.00	$ 6.00	$ 4.18		$ 4.00
3C(i) Debt/total capital	0.20	0.33	0.22		0.52
3C(i) Debt/tangible equity	0.25	0.50	0.28		1.65

This exhibit is modeled after Exhibit 14-2A and B.
Under the pooling method, the balance sheets add without adjustment.
Under the purchase method, the balance sheet of PSI is adjusted to fair value.
Goodwill equals the excess of purchase price over fair value of net assets.

Exhibit 14S-1B

Aspen Pharmaceuticals, *pro forma* income statement
Year ended December 31, 1997 ($millions)

	(1)	(2)	(3)	(4)	(5)
	1997 Estimated		Pooling		Purchase Method
3A(ii)					
3B(ii)	Aspen	PSI	Pro Forma	Adjust.	Pro Forma
Sales	$ 10,500	$ 3,360	$ 13,860		$ 13,860
Cost of goods sold	(2,500)	(2,880)	(5,380)		(5,380)
Marketing/admin.	(2,700)	(110)	(2,810)		(2,810)
Depreciation	(200)	(20)	(220)	(100)	(320)
Interest	(100)	(20)	(120)	(300)	(420)
Research	(1,000)		(1,000)		(1,000)
Goodwill amortization				(70)	(70)
Pretax income	$ 4,000	$ 330	$ 4,330	$ (470)	$ 3,860
Income tax expense	(1,200)	(130)	(1,330)	160	(1,170)
Net income	$ 2,800	$ 200	$ 3,000	$ (310)	$ 2,690
Shares outstanding	1,000	100	1,100		1,000
Earnings per share	$ 2.80	$ 2.00	$ 2.73		$ 2.69
3C(ii) Interest coverage	41.00	17.50	37.08		10.19

This exhibit is modeled after Exhibit 14-4.
Under the pooling method, the income statements add without adjustment.
Under the purchase method, the adjustment of property to fair value and goodwill
are amortized over 10 and 20 years respectively. Interest expense on the new
debt must also be recognized. Income tax expense is reduced by 40% of the
increased depreciation and interest expense.

(iii) Reasons why Aspen would prefer a share-for-share exchange include:
- Transaction is tax-free to PSI shareholders, possibly reducing purchase price
- Higher earnings as purchase adjustments not required
- If Aspen sells some PSI assets, it will recognize gains as assets carried at historic cost which is below market value.
- Lower risk as additional debt and interest expense not required
- Higher reported book value per share and earnings per share
- Better debt and interest coverage ratios

(iv) Analyst criticisms of pooling method include:

a. Does not recognize true acquisition cost as assets and liabilities recorded at target's cost.
b. Fictitious gains if acquired assets are sold.
c. Income overstated as acquired assets are depreciated based on target cost.
d. Understated balance sheet and overstated income overstate returns on acquired firms.
e. Restatement of prior year financial statements creates fictitious corporate history.

4.{S}A. Purchase method acquisitions distort the trend of financial data for the following reasons:
- The purchased assets and liabilities are consolidated at fair value; other assets and liabilities are carried at historic cost.
- The sales and earnings of the acquired firms are included from their purchase date, creating a discontinuity. It is hard to distinguish internal growth from acquisition effects.

As a result, postmerger ratios are not comparable with premerger ratios.

B. Purchase method acquisitions hinder interfirm comparisons because:
- Acquisitions distort growth rates, making it hard to distinguish operating effects from acquisition effects.
- Acquired firm assets and liabilities restated to market value, distorting turnover and return ratios when compared with firm with all assets and liabilities at historic cost.
- Ratio distortions make interfirm ratio comparisons difficult.

C. (i) Purchase method reduces gross profit margin percentage because premerger inventories written up to market value and increased depreciation may be included in postmerger COGS.

(ii) Long-term debt to equity ratio lower under purchase method. Stock issued for acquisitions is valued at market (virtually always above book value) while debt is similar under both methods [Under purchase method, debt restated based on current interest rates.]

(iii) Pretax earnings are lower under purchase method because of amortization of property write-ups and new goodwill, as well as lower gross profit margins.

5. {M} Philip Morris would purchase Kraft for $10.8 billion ($90 x 120 million). This amount would be added to long-term debt, increasing interest expense by $1,188 million (11% x $10.8 billion). The excess purchase price over book value of Kraft would be treated as goodwill, and its amortization over forty years would be:

$$($10,800 - $1,920)/40 = $222 \text{ million annually.}$$

Interest expense would be tax deductible, reducing taxes paid by $499 million (using Philip Morris' tax rate of 42%). However, goodwill amortization would not reduce taxes paid. Cash flow from operations would be reduced by the additional interest expense less the associated tax reduction ($1,188 - $499 = $689 million).

The Merged Company *Pro Forma* ($ millions):

Common shares	234	[Kraft purchased for cash]
Long-term debt	$16,300	[$4,700 + $800 + $10,800]
Stockholders' equity	7,394	[Kraft equity eliminated]
EBIT	$ 4,914	[$4,340 + $796 - $222]
Interest expense	(1,744)	[$475 + $81 + $1,188]
Pretax income	$ 3,170	
Income tax expense	(1,403)	[$1,623 + $279 - $499]
Net income	$ 1,767	
Cash from operations	$ 2,892	[$2,974 + $607 -$1,188 + $499]
Capital expenditures	1,110	[$850 + $260]
Dividends paid	892	[No change]
Earnings per share	$ 7.55	[$1,767/234]
Debt to equity	2.20	[$16,300/$7,394]
Times interest earned	2.82	[$4,914/$1,744]

EPS and the debt/equity and TIE ratios all deteriorate as a result of the acquisition. EPS and TIE are lower because of higher interest expense and the amortization of goodwill. Leverage is increased by the additional debt of $10.8 billion. However, the combined firm generates significant cash flows from operations that mitigate the decline in the other indicators of financial quality. There are insufficient data to discuss the effect of the acquisition on Philip Morris' activity ratios.

6. (M}A.

[$ Millions]	Prior	Following
Debt	$ 800	$ 11,600
Equity [1]	1,920	100
Total capital	$ 2,720	$ 11,700
EBIT	796	574
Interest expense	81	1,269
Net income	436	(475)

    (i)   Debt-to-equity   .42   116.00

    (ii)   Return on total capita   1.29   .05
          (EBIT/total capital)

    (iii) Interest coverage ratio 9.83   0.45

    (iv) Net profit margin is reduced when the purchase method adjustments are pushed down into Kraft.

[1] We assume that Philip Morris put a nominal amount of equity capital into new Kraft. A different amount would not change the analysis meaningfully.

B. The comparison of Kraft data before and after the merger is affected by the economic effects (higher debt and interest expense) and the accounting effects (asset write-ups and income statement amortization) of the merger. While the business is unchanged, the financial statements and all ratios derived from them are radically different. While one can argue that the economic effects are "real" the accounting effects are less so. Unless the "accounting" effects generate cash flows (e.g. they affect income tax payments), they have no economic significance.

C. The comparability of Kraft financial data with that of firms that have not been acquired is also affected by the problems discussed in B. The accounting adjustments, in particular, make it difficult to tell whether interfirm differences are real or the result of accounting variations alone.

D. The push down adjustments replace the historical cost of Kraft's assets and liabilities with their fair value at the merger date. To the extent that certain assets and liabilities are not adjusted, we can infer that fair value does not exceed cost. The creation of goodwill implies that all assets have been written up to fair value and that Kraft has no "undervalued" assets following the merger.

14-11

In addition, the amortization periods may be an indication of the useful life that management ascribes to assets acquired.

E. The advantage of push-down accounting is that Kraft's financial statements fully reflect the merger transaction, including a write-up of assets and liabilities to fair market value. The disadvantage is that push-down limits the comparability of Kraft financial statements with those prior to the merger and with those of other companies.

7.{L}A. Pooling allowed Allwaste to report substantially higher revenues, net income, and return on equity for 1987-1989. However, the rate of increase in revenues and net income from 1987 to 1988 declines when the 1989 acquisitions are pooled. 1988 return on equity increases more under pooling as income increased faster than equity (the acquired firms had very high ROE). The 1987-1989 comparisons also show substantial declines when the pooled data are compared. Note the decline in ROE from 1988 to 1989, and 1989 relative to 1987.

1987-1989 (Pre-1989 poolings)

	1987		1988		1989
	Original Report	Pooled	Original Report	Pooled	Reported[#]
Revenues	$ 45,894	$86,771	$ 67,804	$125,584	$165,689
Net income	2,667	5,205	5,329	9,877	11,797
ROE[*]	18.3%	29.2%	22.0%	35.3%	27.3%[@]

[#] Pooled and reported amounts are identical in 1989.
[*] Year-end equity used in 1987; average used for 1988 and 1989.
[@] ROE is 26.1% when the average of pooled 1988 and reported 1989 amounts used in equity.

1987-1989 Percent Change

	1987-1988		1988-1989		1987-1989	
	Original Report	Pooled	Original Report	Pooled	Original Report	Pooled
Revenues	48%	44%	144%	32%	261%	91%
Net income	100%	90%	121%	19%	342%	127%
ROE	20%	21%	24%	(26%)	49%	(11%)

B. Note: If we assume that acquisitions were made at the end of the year, the purchase method would add the assets, liabilities, revenues, and expenses of the acquired companies only as of that date. We have instead assumed that the acquisitions occurred as of the beginning of the year, impacting sales and earnings for that year. Under either assumption, we must first adjust equity to reflect use of the purchase method rather than pooling.

Market value of shares issued for acquisitions	$ 70,000,000
Stockholders' equity of acquired companies[1]	(4,263,000)
Adjustment to stockholders' equity	$ 65,737,000
Reported equity at August 31, 1989 (pooling)	52,359,000
Adjusted equity at August 31, 1989 (purchase)	$118,096,000

[1] Difference in reported equity between equity reported in the restated 1988 balance sheet ($38,077,000) and that reported in the original 1988 balance sheet, ($33,814,000).

The adjustment to stockholders' equity is the excess of purchase price over the book value of the acquired firms (the goodwill recorded by Allwaste) that must be amortized over 40 years for an annual amortization expense of $1,643,000 ($65,737,000/40). Reported net income in 1989 under the purchase method would be $11,797,000 − $1,643,000 = $10,154,000.

C.   1987-1989 [Pooling versus Purchase]

	1987		1988		1989	
	Pooled	Purchase	Pooled	Purchase	Pooled	Purchase
Revenues	$86,771	$45,894	$125,258	$67,804	$165,689	$165,689
Net income	5,205	2,667	9,877	5,329	11,797	10,154
ROE*	29.2%	18.3%	35.3%	22.0%	26.1%	13.5%

* Year-end equity used in 1987; average used for 1988 and 1989.

1987-1989 Percent Change: Pooling versus Purchase

	1988-1989		1987-1989	
	Pooled	Purchase	Pooled	Purchase
Revenues	32%	144%	91%	261%
Net income	19%	90%	127%	281%
ROE*	(26%)	(39%)	(11%)	(26%)

* Year-end equity used in 1987; average used for 1988 & 1989.

Both net income and ROE are lower for 1989 when the purchase method is used as net income is reduced by amortization expense and equity is increased by the excess of the purchase price over book value of the acquired companies. However, the growth rates of sales and net income are significantly increased as amounts for the acquired firms are added only during the year of the acquisition, as compared to the retroactive adjustment of the pooling method. Because the purchase method recognizes the market value of equity used in the acquisitions, the decline in ROE is substantial. It now shows the cost of acquiring the earnings of other firms.

D. (i) Annual amortization expense would be $6,574,000 ($65,737,000/10) if a ten-year life were used. Income and ROE would be lower in the periods following the merger.

    (ii) Only half of the sales, net income, and amortization expense would be added to that of Allwaste in the year of the acquisition. The effect would be to "smooth" the reported growth resulting from the acquisitions as the full effect would be seen only in the following year.

E. (i) EPS increased from $.16/share (1987) to $.27/share (1988) before the 1989 poolings (an increase of 69%). The acquisitions increased EPS retroactively to $.22/share (1987) and $.35/share (1988), a lower growth rate (60%) than reported previously. The rate of increase in EPS was even less in 1989 (after pooling) as EPS rose to $.40/ share.

      We can compute marginal EPS from the acquisitions by dividing the increase in earnings from restatement with the shares issued:

1987: ($5,205 - $2,667)/8,616 = $0.29 per share
1988: ($9,877 - $5,329)/8,616 = $0.53 per share

For each year, the marginal EPS exceeded EPS prior to restatement, illustrating the "bootstrapping" technique discussed in the text. The purchase method, by reducing reported earnings from the acquisition and by precluding restatement, makes "bootstrapping" more difficult.

(ii) If the purchase method is used, 1989 EPS is $.34/share, compared to $.16/share in 1987 and $.27/share in 1988. While the level of EPS is reduced, the reported growth rate is higher.

(iii) The method changes the level and trend of EPS with the purchase method reporting lower EPS because it adds amortization expense, income, and shares from the date of acquisition as compared with the retroactive adjustment used in pooling.

Note the level and trend of ROE discussed in part C above. The impact of acquisitions on ROE is greater than the effect on EPS.

F.   (i) The pooling method retroactively restates the statement of cash flows for all years presented. The acquisition itself does not affect the statement as shares were issued. If cash were used, financing cash flow would be affected.

(ii) The purchase method would reflect a financing cash flow of $70 million, representing the issuance of equity to obtain the cash needed to purchase the acquired companies.

(iii) Under the purchase method, investing cash flow would report the assets acquired. Cash flow from operations would be affected if the firm changed its level of inventories or receivables following the acquisition.

(iv) Cash flows following the acquisition year are not affected by the accounting method used (ignoring any income tax effects). Under either method, reduced working capital needs may overstate reported cash flow from operations.

8.{L}A.   Derivation of Cole balance sheet at acquisition date:

	Balance Sheet Change	Cash Flow Change	Difference
Cash	$ 15,714	$ 15,714	$ 0
Marketable securities	72,981	72,476	505
Accounts receivable	43,393	39,999	3,394
Prepaid expenses	(5,696)	(7,925)	2,229
Property	43,466	30,701 [1]	12,765
Goodwill	1,033	(2,408) [2]	3,441
Total assets	$ 170,891	$148,557	$ 22,334
Accounts payable	$ 38,865 }	0	$ 0
Salaries	(5,013) }	34,269	2,231
Claims payable (short-term)	2,648 }	0	0
Income taxes payable	3,080	3,022	58
Dividend payable	1,139	(48,984)	50,123 [3]
Deferred income tax	(8,411) }	0	0
Future equipment repairs	2,749 }	(4,984)	4,052
Claims payable (long-term)	4,730 }	0	0
Total liabilities	$ 39,787	$(16,677)	$ 56,464
Additional capital	19,121 }	0	0
Treasury stock	14,699 }	18,693	15,127
Retained earnings	97,284 }	147,407	(50,123)
Total equities	$ 170,891	$149,423	$ 21,468
Assets less equities	0	(866)	(866)

[1] Reconciliation of property account:
   Net purchases $201,011   [$211,073 - $10,062]
   Depreciation   (170,287)   [$172,695 - $2,408 goodwill amort.]
   Loss on sale   (23)   [cash flow statement]
   Net change $ 30,701

[2] Reconciliation of goodwill account:
   Goodwill purchased $ 3,441   [Given]
   Balance sheet change (1,033)
   Amortization $ 2,408

[3] Note that change in dividends payable = discrepancy in retained earnings.

As the cash flow statement provides balance sheet changes that exclude the effects of the acquisition of Cole, the differences between the balance sheet changes and cash flow changes must be due to the acquisition. The differences tell us that Roadway acquired:

Assets of Cole	$ 22,334
Liabilities of Cole	(6,341)
Net assets acquired	$ 15,993

Roadway paid for Cole with:

Cash	$ 866
Roadway shares valued at	15,127
Total payment	$ 15,993

The cash paid for Cole equals the net cash flow change.

B.

Ratios	Cole	Roadway
Fixed asset turnover	1.49	3.73
Accounts receivable turnover	5.60	12.17
Equity to assets	0.72	0.60

C. Roadway's fixed asset and accounts receivable ratios are more than twice those of Cole. The higher ratios may be due to the advantages of size or to better management. In that case we would expect the differences to disappear as Cole in integrated into Roadway. The cash flow implications would be positive as higher turnover would reduce the investment in fixed assets and accounts receivable.

There are other possible explanations. Cole's fixed assets may be newer than Roadway's, understating the turnover ratio. Again this would imply lower future investment. The lower accounts receivable turnover might be due to the sale of receivables. This is a form of financing (see Chapter 11). If this practice were ended, the future *reported* cash flow of Roadway would be reduced.

D. If Roadway had significant foreign operations, the differences between balance sheet changes and cash flow changes could be due to changes in exchange rates. For this reason the methodology in part A could not be used to accurately derive the balance sheet of Cole.

E. Roadway purchased Cole for almost $16 million. The future earnings of Cole should be used to compute the return on this investment.

9.[L]A.   The first table was prepared from the U.S. GAAP data in
          Exhibit 14P-6:

Hanson Industries Goodwill (£ millions):

	1988	1989	1990	1991
Opening balance	£2,041	£1,811	£3,724	£3,550
Amortization	(50)	(56)	(97)	(95)
Disposal	(180)	(92)	(171)	(46)
New goodwill[1]	0	2,061	94	29
Closing balance	£1,811	£3,724	£3,550	£3,438

[1] Deduced; assumed to be zero for 1988 as opening balance not provided.

The amortization period appears to be in the range of
35 years in accordance with U.S. GAAP requirements.

The second table was prepared assuming a ten year
amortization period for goodwill and that new goodwill
and disposal goodwill are accounted for halfway through
each year.

Hanson Industries Adjusted Goodwill (£ millions):

	1988	1989	1990	1991
Opening balance	£2,041	£1,666	£3,370	£2,960
Amortization[2]	(195)	(265)	(333)	(295)
Disposal	(180)	(92)	(171)	(46)
New goodwill[3]	0	2,061	94	29
Closing balance	£1,666	£3,370	£2,960	£2,648

[2] (Opening balance + (new - disposal)/2)/10.

[3] Same as previous table; new goodwill depends on acquisitions made
and is unaffected by amortization method or period.

Note that disposal goodwill is unchanged. However
faster amortization would reduce the remaining balance
of goodwill at disposal. For simplification we omit
this complex calculation; extra credit should be
awarded to the reader who sees its necessity.

The effect of these adjustments on U.S. GAAP net income and stockholders' equity follows:

Net income[1]	£(145)	£(209)	£(236)	£(200)
Stockholders' equity[2]	(145)	(354)	(590)	(790)

[1] The increase in amortization reduces net income.
[2] The cumulative net income effects.

Adjusted net income and stockholders' equity (U.S. GAAP) are:

Net income	£ 735	£ 718	£ 714	£ 756
Stockholders' equity	3,816	4,471	6,042	6,303

B. Now compute return on (ending) equity under all three methods:

U.K. GAAP	51.1%	105.3%	35.3%	33.3%
U.S. GAAP	22.2	19.2	14.3	13.5
U.S. GAAP Adjusted	19.3	16.1	11.8	12.0

Net income is fairly constant under each of the three accounting methods. However the level is lower under U.S. GAAP (mainly due to goodwill adjustments) than under U.K. GAAP, and even lower when goodwill is amortized over a (shorter) ten year period.

Return on equity is vastly different depending on the method used. Under U.K. GAAP, with goodwill written off immediately, ROE appears very high, exceeding 100% for 1989. Under U.S. GAAP, with income reduced and equity increased, ROE is not particularly high, and decreases sharply from 1989-1992. After adjustment to a shorter amortization period, the level of ROE declines further. Note however that it increases in 1992 reflecting the reduced level of equity after several years of rapid goodwill amortization.

C. Profits on disposal are reduced when the associated goodwill is written off. Adjusted disposal profits are:

Unadjusted profit (U.K. GAAP)	£ 445	£ 288	£ 168	£ 115
Disposal goodwill	(180)	(92)	(171)	(46)
Adjusted profit (U.S. GAAP)	£ 265	£ 196	£ (3)	£ 69

Over the four year period, recognition of disposal goodwill reduces reported disposal profits by 48% (from £1,016 to £527). For 1990 the adjustment creates a reported loss on disposal.

D. The adjustments in part C (already reflected in the U.S. GAAP data) are one factor in the lower level of earnings and ROE (both before and after the adjustment for rapid amortization). As goodwill is already written off under U.K. GAAP, there is no effect on the ROE denominator; the reduction of reported earnings thus reduces ROE.

10.{L}A. Using only the data in Exhibit 14P-7A, we are limited to computations of net sales and operating income ($ thousands):

	1989	1990	1991
Coors (excluding ACX)			
Sales	$1,366,108	$1,477,271	$1,530,347
Operating income	71,081	100,662[*]	59,126

[*] Excluding special charge

	1989	1990	1991
ACX Technologies			
Sales	$ 324,595	$ 361,295	$ 387,075
Operating income	(25,906)	20,187	(19,463)

These data exclude corporate expenses as there is no basis upon which to allocate them between the two companies. Also excluded are interest expense, "other income," and income tax expense. To prepare more accurate pro forma income statements we would also need data regarding intercorporate transactions (especially purchases of aluminum and packaging by the beer business from the other segments) and the additional cost of having a second public company.

B. Using the data in Exhibit 14P-7B, we can compute ratios before and after the exclusion of ACX:

			Originally Reported	ACX	Pro forma
(i)	Long-term debt-to-equity	1989	.00	.07	.00
		1990	.10	.45	.10
		1991	.20	.63	.20
(ii)	Times interest earned	1989	19.9X	5.0X	NMF*
		1990	200.5	3.4	NMF*
		1991	36.8	1.0	NMF*
(iii)	Return on sales	1989	0.8%	1.1%	0.7%
		1990	2.1	0.7	2.7
		1991	1.2	0.2	1.6
(iv)	Return on equity	1989	1.2%	1.8%	1.0%
		1990	3.6	1.2	4.4
		1991	2.2	0.5	2.8
(v)	Book value per share	1989	$28.75	$7.77	$20.98
		1990	29.12	7.86	21.26
		1991	29.33	7.86	21.47
(vi)	Asset turnover	1989	1.10X	1.10X	1.10X
		1990	1.04	0.90	1.11
		1991	0.97	0.85	1.02
(vii)	Working capital ($ millions)	1989	$193.6	$78.9	$114.7
		1990	201.0	124.4	76.7
		1991	110.4	101.0	9.4
(viii)	1989-1991 growth:				
	Sales		13.4%	16.4%	12.2%
	Operating income		(35.7)	(40.2)	(32.2)
	Net income		82.1	(73.2)	178.7

*   This computation is not meaningful due to lack of information regarding intercorporate borrowings, short-term debt, and the capitalization of interest. Using data from Coors' 1992 annual report, in which ACX is treated as a discontinued operation, times interest earned is 20.4 (1990) and 2.3 (1991), much lower than the ratios originally reported. The ratios are even lower (less than 1.0 for 1991) if interest costs (before capitalization) are used in the denominator.

C. Pro forma data are subject to a number of limitations. Most important, they assume that the same operating results would have occurred under different managements. Second, they rely on sometimes arbitrary cost allocations and assumptions regarding intersegment pricing. Third, the ratios are based on incomplete data; for example short term debt is not reported.

D. (i)   The segment data for the non-beer segments could be aggregated, resulting in approximate balance sheet and income statement data for ACX.

    (ii) To complete the estimate, we would require details of the balance sheet (e.g. fixed assets, inventories, accounts payable) and income statement (COGS).

    (iii) Historic segment data, while useful indicators of how ACX performed during the periods shown, have limited usefulness as predictors of future results. The segment data include asset writedowns, for example, but details must be obtained elsewhere in the financial statements to estimate operating earnings. We also need to know about past capital expenditures, research and development spending, and any changes in operations made by the post-spinoff management.

E. (i)   ACX may have been viewed as a "turnaround" company. While past returns on sales and equity were nominal, future returns may be higher. The segment data show substantial capital expenditures in the non-beer segments, especially aluminum, over the 1989-1991 period. There is often some delay before new facilities become profitable, and investors may have seen the possibility of substantial profits. In addition, they may have believed that ACX would fare better as a separate company than as part of a major beer producer.

    (ii) The efficient market hypothesis suggests that the value of a firm should not be affected by its division into two parts. The value of the firm should be equal to the sum of the value of each part.

In reality, however, spinoffs may change investor expectations about one or both parts. While segment data provide an indication of how each segment performs, those data are highly summarized. When detailed information about a segment is released, those data may help investors to understand the firm operations. This is especially true when the spinoff is a small part of the firm.

Small segments are frequently "lost" in a big firm. Investors focus only on the prospects for the major business; the results of that business dominate the results of the pre-spinoff firm. When the smaller segment is separated, its operating results become significant to investors in the spinoff.

In addition, investors who had no interest in the beer business may have been attracted to the aluminum, packaging, and/or ceramics businesses. ACX shares, which initially sold at a price well below book value, may also have attracted investors who use book value (rather than reported earnings) to select investments.

While the performance of spinoffs appears to violate the EMH, there are some costs involved. Investors must spend time studying the spinoff firm's financial statements, interviewing management, etc. In addition the cost of preparing these data, and maintaining a second public company, reduce the profitability of the spinoff firm as compared to the period when it did not bear these costs.

F. If Coors had sold ACX (either to another company or through an initial public offering) it would have recognized a gain or loss measured as the difference between the equity of ACX and the proceeds of sale. Given the poor profitability of ACX, it seems likely that the assets would have been sold for less than their book value, resulting in a loss, and reducing the reported earnings of Coors. By spinning off ACX, no loss was recognized.

In addition, a buyer of ACX may have been unwilling to shoulder that company's large debt load. By spinning off ACX, Coors was able to eliminate virtually all of its long-term debt from its balance sheet.

Finally, Coors management may have anticipated that investors would be interested in ACX at its post-spinoff "bargain" price. They may have believed (based on their examination of other spinoffs) that their shareholders would benefit by having shares in two companies rather than one.

11.{M}A. Because Sandoz used the purchase method to account for its acquisitions, 1994 sales and income look better compared with 1993 levels than if the pooling method had been used (requiring restatement of 1993 data).

Charging goodwill directly to equity increases 1994 income which is not burdened with the amortization of that goodwill.

B. Reported ROE is overstated because

- operating income is overstated absent goodwill amortization
- equity is understated because goodwill has been written off at the acquisition date

C. (i) Recomputing 1994 data for 1994 acquisitions only, and assuming that goodwill is not tax deductible:

Net income = 1,734 - 4,827/10 =   SFR 1,251
Equity = 6,887 + $4,827 =   11,774
ROE = 1,251/11,774 =   10.7%

In comparison, reported ROE is more than double at 25.2% (1,734/6,887). Adjustment for 1993 goodwill would reduce ROE to 10.4% (1,240/11,889)

(ii) The adjusted ROE is superior because it includes the total cost of acquired companies, not just the portion allocated to tangible assets. A better measure, however, as discussed on page 780, would exclude goodwill amortization from the numerator:

ROE = 1,734/11,774 = 14.7%

12.{M}A. Two adjustments must be made:

- The restructuring reserves in each year must be added back to pretax income and the actual expenditures in each year subtracted from pretax income.
- Goodwill charged directly to equity must be restored and amortized over twenty years.

Exhibit 14S-2 (p. 14-26) shows the calculations required to make these adjustments. We assume a 20% tax rate.

(i)   Total assets are increased by the amount restored to income, and reduced by the actual restructuring expenditures and goodwill amortization, both aftertax. The net result is a small increase in 1992 assets but small decreases in 1993 and 1994.

(ii) As liabilities are unchanged, adjusted equity follows the same pattern; the equity adjustments are smaller as they are the *aftertax* asset increases.

(iii) Cash from operations is unchanged; the provisions and goodwill amortization are noncash charges. The actual restructuring expenditures reduce CFO regardless of accounting method.

(iv) Net income increases in 1992 as provisions exceed the sum of expenditures and goodwill amortization. However 1993 and 1994 net income are reduced.

B. Exhibit 14S-2 shows both adjustments.

C. (i)   While the trend of net income is similar after adjustment, the post-1992 decline in sharper.

(ii) EPS follows the same trend as net income.

(iii) No effect; see A(iii).

(iv) Return on equity is higher for 1992, lower for 1993 and 1994. After adjustment, the downward trend in ROE is accentuated.

Exhibit 14S-2

Exhibit 14S-2
Alcatel Alsthom acquisition adjustments
French francs in millions except per share data

Years ended December 31		1992	1993	1994
B(i)	Restructuring Reserve			
	New plans and adjustments	3,160	2,488	2,898
	Increase due to acquisitions	3,778	324	506
	Expenditures during year	(6,183)	(4,869)	(4,068)
	Adjustment to pretax income	755	(2,057)	(664)
B(ii)	Goodwill			
	Charged to equity	(2,974)	(6,305)	(1,024)
	Cumulative amount	(2,974)	(9,279)	(10,303)
	Amortization (20 years)	(149)	(464)	(515)
	Total pretax adjustment	606	(2,521)	(1,179)
	Aftertax adjustment	485	(2,017)	(943)
	Cumulative adjustment	485	(1,532)	(2,475)
C(I)	Reported net income	7,053	7,062	3,620
	Adjusted net income	7,538	5,045	2,677
C(ii)	Reported EPS	53.17	49.77	26.05
	Adjusted EPS	56.83	35.56	19.26
	Reported equity	49,895	57,844	59,784
	Adjusted equity	50,380	56,312	57,309
C(iii)	Reported ROE	14.14%	12.21%	6.06%
	Adjusted ROE	14.96%	8.96%	4.67%

14-26

Case 14-1 - Solution

Estimated solution time is 3 hours.

Case Overview: the objective of this case is to compare the purchase and pooling methods using the acquisition of Great Northern Nekoosa by Georgia-Pacific as an example. This case recasts a purchase method acquisition as a pooling. Case 14-2 reverses the process, recasting the pooling acquisition of Golden Valley by Conagra as a purchase.

1. (a) Under the purchase method, inventory is written up to fair value, which may be greater than FIFO cost. Thus the LIFO reserve may understate the required adjustment.

   (b) Goodwill can be amortized, under U.S. GAAP, over as long as forty years while property must be amortized (depreciated) over its remaining life. Thus, allocation to goodwill may reduce the annual amortization.

      In addition, if property expected to be sold is written up to an amount below its fair value, then the acquirer reports a gain on sale, increasing reported income.

   (c) Goodwill on the target's balance sheet has no fair value. The acquirer creates new goodwill equal to the excess of the price paid over the fair value of the target's assets net of liabilities.

   (d) When an acquisition is taxable, the tax and accounting basis of the acquired assets and liabilities is the same. Thus all timing differences have disappeared and no deferred taxes are required.

2. (a) Exhibit 14CS-1 (p. 14C1-2) shows the recast balance sheet. Most of the adjustments reverse those in Exhibit 14C-1 (p. 796), the adjustments to GNN's assets and liabilities under the purchase method. If the pooling method were used, the assets and liabilities of GNN would be added to those of GP without adjustment.

Georgia-Pacific Acquisition of GNN Recast as Pooling
December 31, 1990 (in $ millions)

	Purchase	Adjustments	Pooling
Cash	$ 58		$ 58
Accounts receivable	409		409
Inventories	1,209	(117)	1,092
Other current assets	90	–	90
Current assets	$ 1,766	$ (117)	$ 1,649
Timber and timberland	1,630	(98)	1,532
Property	6,341	(20)	6,321
Goodwill	2,042	482	
		(2,001)	523
Other assets	281	45	326
Total assets	$ 12,060	$ (1,709)	$ 10,351
Short-term debt	$ 1,444		$ 1,444
Payables and accruals	1,091		1,091
Current liabilities	$ 2,535		$ 2,535
Long-term debt	5,218	(3)	5,215
Deferred income tax	928	421	1,349
Other liabilities	404	(162)	242
Total liabilities	$ 9,085	$ 256	$ 9,341
Stockholders' equity	2,975	1,734 [1]	
		(3,699) [2]	1,010
Total equities	$ 12,060	$ 1,990	$ 14,050

[1] Historical equity of GNN

[2] Assumed reurchase (at market) of GP shares issued

However, an additional adjustment is required. As stated in the case, we now assume that GP issued stock to acquire GNN but then reacquired the shares issued for $3,699 million. One adjustment (footnote 1) records the GP shares issued to acquire GNN *at the historical equity of* GNN. The second adjustment (footnote 2) assumes repurchase of the same number of shares *at the current GP market* price. These adjustments create the same capital structure under both cases (purchase and pooling).

(b)
Ratio	Purchase	Pooling
Current	.70	.65
Debt-to-equity	2.24	6.59

The inventory writeup under the purchase method improves the current ratio. The debt-to-equity ratio is also better (lower) due to the higher level of equity (measured by the purchase price rather than GNN's historic equity).

(c) Tangible equity (reported equity less goodwill) equals $933 million under the purchase method versus $487 million under pooling. The major difference is the increased equity resulting from elimination of GNN's deferred tax liability under the purchase method.

3. (a) Georgia Pacific Sales Comparison ($millions)

	1990	1991	% Change
Reported sales	$12,665	$11,524	-9.0%
Pro forma sales	13,359	11,524	-13.7

GP's reported sales fell in 1991, but still exceeded sales reported for 1988 and 1989. When the effect of the GNN acquisition is considered, by comparing actual 1991 sales with 1990 *pro forma* sales, the sales decline is more severe.

(b) If the pooling method had been used, reported income would have differed because

- income prior to the acquisition date would have been restated to include GNN
- the purchase method adjustments would not have affected postmerger income

4. (a) GP Inventories:
        Opening balance $ 876 million
        Plus: GNN inventories acquired   388
        Plus: inventory cash flow change   (34)
        Equals: expected closing balance $1,230 million

    The discrepancy between the expected closing
    balance and the actual closing balance of 1,209
    million must be due to inventories sold (included
    in cash from investing) as part of postmerger
    restructuring. [The 1990 GP cash flow statement
    shows $204 million of proceeds from the sale of
    assets.]

    (b) GP Property:
        Opening balance $3,691 million
        GNN property acquired   2,480
        Capital expenditures   833
        Depreciation expense   (622)
        Expected closing balance $6,382

    The $41 million discrepancy between this amount
    and the actual balance of $6,341 million is, once
    again, most likely due to assets sold.

    (c) The difference is $448 million. The $484 million
    of GNN receivables added must be offset by $46
    million of receivables included in asset sales.

    (d) Reported CFO increased by $715 million in 1990.
    The receivables decrease of $929 million must have
    been an important component of this increase. But
    the sale of accounts receivable for $850 million
    is a financing transaction, not an operating
    change. When that sale is removed, the receivable
    decrease of $79 million ($929 - $850) is
    insignificant. Further, the CFO *increase* of $715
    million becomes a $135 million *decrease*.

Case 14-2 - Solution

Estimated solution time is 3 hours.

Case Overview: the objective of this case is to compare the purchase and pooling methods using the acquisition of Golden Valley Microwave by ConAgra as an example. This case recasts a pooling method acquisition as a purchase. Case 14-1 reverses the process, recasting the purchase acquisition of Great Northern Nekoosa by Georgia-Pacific as a pooling.

1. The journal entries required to eliminate the investment in Lamb-Weston and consolidate the joint venture are taken from Exhibit 14C-4, column 3:

Brands, etc.	$ 4,560	
Other current liabilities	667	
Common stock	53,255	
Retained earnings	51,608	
Investment account		$104,847
Other noncurrent liabilities		5,243

2. (a) Exhibit 14CS-2 (p. 14C2-2) shows the recast balance sheet. Exhibit footnotes explain the required adjustments.

    Goodwill is calculated as follows:

Purchase price [1]	$ 407 million
Less: Fair value of net assets [2]	(138)
Excess = goodwill	$ 269 million

    [1] 9,958,731 shares x $40.875 (market price)

[2]		
	Stated equity of Golden Valley	$108 million
	Adjustments to fair value (net)*	30
	Fair value of net assets acquired	$138 million

    * Adjustments shown in Exhibit 14CS-2

Exhibit 14CS-2
Conagra-Golden Valley
Purchase Method Pro Forma Balance Sheet
February 24, 1991 ($ in millions)

		Pooling	Adjustments	Purchase
	Cash and equivalents	$ 115		$ 115
	Receivables, net	1,450		1,450
(1)	Inventories	2,499	7	2,506
	Other current assets	396	-	396
	CURRENT ASSETS	$ 4,460	$ 7	$ 4,467
(2)	Property	2,093	10	2,103
(3)	Intangible assets	2,740	269	3,009
	Investments	117		117
	Other assets	267	-	267
	TOTAL ASSETS	$ 9,677	$ 286	$ 9,963
	Notes payable	915		915
	Current debt	433		433
	Other current	2,734		2,734
	CURRENT LIABILITIES	$ 4,082		$ 4,082
	Long-term debt	2,142		2,142
(4)	Deferred tax	-	(14)	(14)
(5)	Other liabilities	1,237	1	1,238
	Preferred equity	356		356
(6)	Common equity	1,860	299	2,159
	TOTAL EQUITIES	$ 9,677	$ 286	$ 9,963

(1) Write-up of Golden Valley inventories to fair value.
(2) Write-up of Golden Valley property to fair value.
(3) Goodwill = excess purchase price over fair value.
(4) Elimination of deferred tax liability of Golden Valley and
      50% of deferred tax liability of Lamb-Weston.
(5) Pension liability of Lamb-Weston (50%).
(6) Excess fair value of ConAgra shares over GV equity.

Conagra-Golden Valley
Purchase Method Pro Forma Income Statement
12 Months Ended February 24, 1991 ($ in millions)

		Pooling	Adjustments	Purchase
	Net sales	$ 21,249		$ 21,249
(1)	Cost of goods	(18,334)	(8)	(18,342)
(2)	Other expenses	(2,113)	(9)	(2,122)
	Interest expense	(374)		(374)
	Equity income	9		9
	Pretax income	$ 437	$ (17)	$ 420
(3)	Income tax expense	(189)	3	(186)
	Net income	$ 248	$ (14)	$ 234
	Preferred dividends	(24)		(24)
	Net for common	$ 224	$ (14)	$ 210
	Average shares	147.7		147.7
	Earnings per share	$ 1.52		$ 1.42

(1) Effect of inventory write-up and additional
    depreciation ($7+$1=$8).
(2) Amortization of goodwill ($269/30).
(3) Income tax reduction (35% rate);
    assumes goodwill not tax-deductible.

(b)   To accurately allocate the purchase price, we need the following information on Golden Valley as of the acquisition date:

1)   Fair value of inventories
2)   Fair value of accounts receivable
3)   Fair value of property
4)   Fair value of investment in Lamb-Weston
5)   Fair value of long-term debt
6)   Tax treatment of acquisition
7)   Funded status of any employee benefit plans
8)   Off-balance-sheet obligations

3.   Exhibit 14CS-3 (p. 14C2-3) shows the *pro forma* income statement under the purchase method of accounting. Footnotes explain the required adjustments.

4.   (a)   Ratios under both accounting methods:

	Pooling	Purchase
Debt-to-total capital	61.2%	58.1%
Return on ending common equity	12.0	9.7
Return on ending total capital	14.1	13.1
Net profit margin	1.17	1.10

Calculations:	*Pooling*	*Purchase*
Debt-to-total capital	$3,490/$5,706	$3,490/$6,005
Return on ending equity	$224/$1,860	$210/$2,159
Return on total capital [1]	$802/$5,706	$785/$6,005
Net profit margin [2]	$248/$21,249	$234/$21,249

[1] Numerator = pretax less equity income plus interest
[2] Numerator = net income before preferred dividends

(b)   Debt-to-total capital is *lower* under the purchase method because the common stock issued is valued at market rather than at the premerger equity of Golden Valley.

Return ratios are *lower* under the purchase method. The numerators are reduced and the denominators increased as compared with the pooling method. The effect on ROE is greater because of the high financial leverage of ConAgra.

Net profit margin is also *lower* under the purchase method because of the reduced income caused by the purchase method adjustments.

5. (a) We determine the effect of acquisition of Golden Valley on ConAgra's earnings per share by computing the "marginal earnings per share:"

Additional net income/shares issued

Under the pooling method, the result is:

Additional net income [1]	$22.21 million
ConAgra shares issued [2]	10.23
Marginal earnings per share	$2.16

[1] Difference between first and last columns of Exh. 14C-5.
[2] From Exhibit 14C-5, adjustments column

Under the purchase method, the additional net income is lower, resulting in:

Additional net income [3]	$ 8.21 million
ConAgra shares issued	10.23
Marginal earnings per share	$ .80

[3] Net income under pooling method less purchase method adjustments of $14 million (Exhibit 14CS-3)

(b) ConAgra's preacquisition earnings per share was $1.47. The acquisition of Golden Valley, using the pooling method, increased EPS as seen in Exhibit 14CS-5. The marginal earnings per share computation confirms that the acquisition was anti-dilutive (it *increased* EPS).

If the purchase method had been used, the acquisition would have diluted (reduced) ConAgra's EPS to $1.42 per share (Exhibit 14CS-3). The marginal EPS calculation shows an amount lower than ConAgra's EPS, confirming the dilution.

While there may have been sound business reasons for the acquisition apart from the initial effect on EPS, acquirers do consider the effect of potential acquisitions on reported earnings. If the pooling method were restricted, some acquisitions would not be made, or would be made at lower prices to reduce their dilutive effect.

Chapter 15 - Solutions

Overview:
Problem Length   *Problem #'s*
      {S}   1,4,8,9
      {M}   2,3,7,10-12
      {L}   5,6

1.{S}(i)   No effect; reported sales are translated at the average rate regardless of the choice of functional currency.

     (ii)   No effect; cash flow from operations is translated from local currency cash flows using the average rate for the period.

     (iii) When the local currency is the functional currency, translation gains and losses are based on the net investment in each local currency.

             When the dollar is the functional currency, translation gains and losses are based on net monetary assets or liabilities in each local currency.

     (iv)   When the local currency is the functional currency, translation gains and losses are accumulated in the cumulative translation adjustment component of stockholders' equity and do not affect reported income except when a subsidiary is sold or the decline in the currency is deemed permanent.

             When the dollar is the functional currency, translation gains and losses are included in reported net income for each accounting period.

2.{M}A.   Subtracting U.S. income of E&O, Erzi's income statement in dollars follows:

($ millions)	19X0	19X2	19X3
Revenues	$ 50.0	$ 60.0	$ 70.0
Operating expenses	25.0	27.0	29.0
Income taxes	7.0	9.4	11.8
Net income	$ 18.0	$ 23.6	$ 29.2
% Change: Sales		20%	17%
Net income		31%	24%

To remove the impact of exchange rate changes we convert the income statement to LC's (using the *average* exchange rate for each year):

	19X0	19X1	19X2
Exchange rate	1	1.5	0.75
Revenues	LC50.0	LC40.0	LC93.3
Operating expenses	25.0	18.0	38.7
Income taxes	7.0	6.3	15.7
Net income	LC18.0	LC15.7	LC38.9
% Change--operations:			
Sales		(20%)	133%
Net income		(13%)	147%

These data give the operating results of Erzi; year 2 operating performance declined whereas year 3 was a "boom" year.

Looking at the consolidated results of E&O, we can now disaggregate the effect of Erzi's operations and that of exchange rate changes for the 19X0-19X2 period:

	Sales	Net income
Erzi's operations[1]	$ 43.3	$ 20.9
Exchange rate effects[2]	(23.3)	(9.7)
Net change	$ 20.0	$ 11.2

[1]The dollar change in sales and income assuming that the exchange rate remained at the 19X0 level of 1.0.
[2]The effect of the decline in the LC on reported sales and net income (19X2 amounts x .25).

B. Sales were unaffected by the choice of functional currency as they were translated at the average rate for the year regardless of that choice.

Net income was affected by the functional currency choice. If the LC was the functional currency, translation adjustments did not affect net income; if the dollar was the functional currency, translation gains and losses were included in the determination of net income.

3.{M}A. With dollar as the functional currency, FI is translated using the temporal method.

	Ponts (Millions)	Exchange Rate (Ponts/$)	Dollars (Millions)
Balance Sheet:			
Cash	82	4.0	$ 20.50
Accounts receivable	700	4.0	175.00
Inventory	455	4.0	113.75
Fixed assets (net)	360	4.0	90.00
Total assets	1,597		$ 399.25
Accounts payable	532	4.0	$ 133.00
Capital stock	600	3.0	200.00
Retained earnings	465		132.86
Translation adjustment	---		(66.61)
Total liabilities and equities	1,597		$ 399.25
Income Statement:			
Sales	3,500	3.5	$1,000.00
Cost of sales	(2,345)	3.5	(670.00)
Depreciation expense	(60)	3.5	(17.14)
Selling expense	(630)	3.5	180.00)
Net income	465		$ 132.86

*Translation Adjustment = $600 \left\{ \frac{1}{3} - \frac{1}{4} \right\} = 600 \ (1/12) = \$(50.00)$

$+ \ 465 \left\{ \frac{1}{3.5} - \frac{1}{4} \right\} = 465 \ (1/28) = \underline{(16.61)}$

$\$(66.61)$

B.   (i) **Dollar:** Inventory and fixed assets translated at historical rates.

Pont: All assets and liabilities translated at current exchange rates.

Dollar: Translation gain (loss) computed on the basis of net monetary assets.

Pont: Translation gain (loss) computed on the basis of net investment (all assets and liabilities).

(ii) **Dollar:** All revenues and other expenses are translated at the average rate for the period; cost of sales and depreciation expense translated at historical rate.

Pont: All revenues and expenses translated at average rates for the period.

Dollar: Translation gain(loss) included in net income (volatility increased).

Pont: Translation gain(loss) reported in separate component of stockholders, equity. Net income is less volatile.

(iii) **Dollar:** Financial statement ratios skewed by translation effects.

Pont: Ratios in dollars are similar to ratios in ponts.

4.{S} A.&B. Remeasurement (temporal method) is the process under which local currency results are converted into the functional currency. Under the temporal method, nonmonetary assets and liabilities (mainly inventories and property) are translated using historical exchange rates. These rates are also used to translate cost-of-goods-sold and depreciation expense. Using FIFO inventory accounting results in a lag in recognizing price level changes.

(i) *Gross profit margin* percentage (gross profit/sales) is higher after remeasurement. With the local currency appreciating, sales (translated at the weighted average exchange rate) will rise (in FC) more rapidly than COGS. Thus, gross profits will generally increase after remeasurement.

(ii) *Operating profit margin* (operating profit/sales) is higher after remeasurement. In addition to the reason given in (i) above, depreciation expense is lower. Depreciation is lower because property (and, therefore, depreciation) remains at historical exchange rates. With an appreciating local currency, depreciation expense will rise more slowly than sales.

(iii) *Net profit margin* (net income/sales) may be higher or lower after remeasurement. Exchange rate gains and losses included in reported income under the temporal method may offset the effects discussed in (i) and (ii). The actual effect depends on the asset and liability composition of the particular company and exchange rate changes, including foreign subsidiary assets, liabilities, revenues, and expenses in currencies other than the local currency.

C. Translation is the process under which functional currency results are translated from the functional currency into the reporting currency. SFAS 52 requires using the all-current- rate method. All balance sheet items are translated at the current exchange rate; income statement items are translated at the average rate for the period.

(i) *Gross profit margin* percentage is not affected by translation. Pure income statement ratios are not affected because all elements are translated from the functional currency to the reporting currency at the same (average for period) exchange rate.

(ii) *Long-term debt to equity* is not affected by translation. Pure balance sheet ratios are not affected because all elements are translated from the functional currency to the reporting currency at the same (current) exchange rate.

5.{L}A.   The Swiss Franc (or another non-dollar currency) must
           have been the functional currency for the Swiss
           subsidiary. Use of the dollar as the functional
           currency for that unit would have reported translation
           adjustments as part of income, rather than accumulating
           them in the stockholders' equity account.

      B.   The deferred translation gains of $3,213,000 reflect
           appreciation of the functional currency of the Swiss
           subsidiary against the dollar; net assets of that
           subsidiary were translated into an increased dollar
           amount.

      C.   (i) The gain on liquidation did not result from
                operating activities but from the recognition of
                previously deferred exchange rate effects.

           (ii) The gain should not be considered 1991 income as
                it was generated over the life of the subsidiary
                and recognized in 1991 only because management
                chose to liquidate in that year.

      D.   Change in cumulative translation adjustment:

           1991 $ (6,405,000) [The $3,213,000 reduction in
                                  the CTA due to the liquidation
                                  must be excluded.]
           1990   13,246,000
           1989   (3,607,000)

           Because the liquidation of the inactive subsidiary was
           completed in the first quarter of 1991, the effect of
           exchange rate changes is captured by the decline of
           $6,405,000 on foreign net assets of $96,933,000 (net
           assets on October 31, 1990 of $100,146,000 less the
           $3,213,000 of deferred gains relating to the Swiss
           subsidiary):

                   $$\frac{\$(6,405,000)}{\$96,933,000} = (6.61\%)$$

           Thus, the functional currencies used by the firm
           declined by 6.61% against the dollar in 1991. The
           actual decline may be higher since the net assets of
           the Swiss unit should be deducted from the net assets,
           resulting in a lower denominator. However, that
           information is not available.

E. The cash flow statement reports that the 1991 effect of exchange rate changes on cash was $(2,075) million. Using the result of part D, the estimated cash balance in nondollar functional currencies at October 31, 1990 was:

$$\$(2.075)/.0661 = \$31.392 \text{ million.}$$

NOTE: This calculation ignores the effect of exchange rate changes on the increase in cash balances during 1991.

Commercial Intertech's total balance of cash and cash equivalents at October 31, 1990 was $12,049 million, making the estimate clearly wrong. We can conclude that the company kept cash balances in foreign currencies that depreciated by more than the functional currency average computed in part D. Given the size of the loss, an analyst might have questioned management about it.

F. First we must estimate inventories in nondollar functional currencies. One estimate would compare 1991 foreign sales to total sales (in $ millions):

$$\$229/\$437 = 52.4\%$$

The comparison of total foreign assets at October 31, 1990 to total assets would result in a 44.6% estimate.

Either of these percentages can be applied to total inventories at October 31, 1990 of $59,762 million to estimate foreign inventories. The result is then multiplied by the adjustment factor computed in part D to obtain the estimated effect of exchange rates on inventories in nondollar functional currencies:

$$.524 \times \$59,972 \times .0661 = \$2.07 \text{ million}$$
or $$.446 \times \$59,972 \times .0661 = \$1.77 \text{ million}$$

The actual effect can be estimated by comparing the balance sheet change in inventories with the cash flow change (data not provided in problem). This method, which assumes no acquisition or divestiture activity for the year, results in an estimate of $2.76 million.

As this estimate is somewhat higher than that arrived at by using the geographic segment data, it appears that the company has higher inventories relative to sales (lower inventory turnover) in its foreign subsidiaries. An alternative explanation would be higher inventories in weaker currencies (similar to part E).

G.   Reported foreign net assets:

    1991 $ 94,709,000
    1990   100,146,000
    Decrease $ 5,479,000

The net decrease of $5,479,000 was reported after a total decline in the CTA of $9,618,000 of which $6,405,000 was due to exchange rate changes and $3,213,000 stemmed from the liquidation of the Swiss subsidiary. Thus, the firm must have *increased* its local currency investments in its foreign subsidiaries.

H.   (i)   The percentage decline in foreign sales is significantly below the decline factor computed in part D. However the part D factor is based on comparison of exchange rates at fiscal year-ends. The effect on sales is based on average rates for the fiscal years, which might be quite different.

          Therefore, while the sales decline probably reflects weak foreign currencies, and should not surprise us, more data is needed to estimate the exchange rate impact on reported sales.

    (ii) The data needed would be average exchange rates for the fiscal year, preferably weighted by Commercial Intertech's sales in each foreign currency.

    (iii) Year to year sales comparisons are also affected by volume changes, price changes (in local currencies), and acquisition and divestiture activities. Removing exchange rate changes from the sales trend may permit better focus on these other effects.

6.{L} A.

	1991	1992	1993
CTA	$467.4	$(155.9)	$(494.4)
Change in CTA		(623.3)	(338.5)
Opening net assets		12,000	12,000
Change in exchange rate		-5.2%	-2.8%

The dollar has strengthened relative to the LC.
1992 exchange rate was LC 1 = $0.948 [(1-.052)x $1.00]
1993 exchange rate was LC 1 = $0.921 [(1-.028)x $0.948]

B. The first step is to convert non-US sales and income into units of LC's

	1991	1992	1993
Total Non-U.S. sales	$36,000	$38,000	$35,000
Exchange Rate LC 1 =	$1.00	$0.948	$0.921
Total Non-U.S. sales in LC's	36,000	40,084	38,002
Total Non-U.S. income	$2,600	$2,200	$2,200
Exchange Rate LC 1 =	$1.00	$0.948	$0.921
Total Non-U.S. income in LC's	2,600	2,321	2,389

Exchange rate effect on sales:
The exchange rate effect is equal to sales in LC's times the change in the exchange rate:

For 1992 = $40,084 x -.052 = -$2,084

For 1993 = $38,002 x -.028 = -$1,064

Note that the above reflects the exchange rate effect in 1993 relative to 1992. Using 1991 as a basis of comparison, we find the exchange rate effect to be
38,002 x -.079 = $2,002
where -.079 is the cumulative exchange rate change from 1991-1993 ($1.00-$0.921).

Exchange rate effect on income:
The exchange rate effect is equal to income in LC's times the change in the exchange rate:
For 1992 = $2,321 x -.052 = -$121

For 1993 = $2,389 x -.028 = -$67

Again, the above reflects the exchange rate effect in 1993 relative to 1992. Using 1991 as a basis of comparison, we find the exchange rate effect to be

$$\$2,389 \times -.079 = -\$189$$

where -.079 is the cumulative exchange rate change from 1991-1993 ($1.00-$0.921).

C. Disaggregation of operating and exchange rate effects of sales

	1992		1993	
Non-US sales	$38,000		$35,000	
Non-US sales - 1991	36,000		36,000	
Total change	2,000	5.55%	(1,000)	(2.77%)
less Exchange rate effect (part B)	($2,084)	(5.79%)	($3,002)	(8.34%)
Operations effect	$ 4,084	11.34%	$ 2,002	5.55%

Disaggregation of operating and exchange rate effects of income

	1992		1993	
Non-US income	$ 2,200		$2,200	
Non-US income - 1991	2,600		2,600	
Total change	(400)	(15.4%)	(400)	(15.4%)
less Exchange rate effect (part B)	(121)	(4.7%)	(189)	(7.3%)
Operations effect	$(279)	(10.7%)	$ (211)	(8.1%)

Note that the operations effect can be determined directly (in this case) as the change in LC sales and income (computed in part B) between a given year and the 1991 base year. This is possible since the base year, 1991, is assumed to have an exchange rate of LC 1 = $1:

	Sales		*Income*	
(in units of LC's)	1992	1993	1992	1993
Non-US	40,084	38,002	2,321	$2,389
Non-US - 1991	36,000	36,000	2,600	2,600
Operations effect	4,084	2,002	(279)	$(211)

D. *Points to consider:*

1. We have assumed that all subsidiaries use the all-current method. To the extent this is not true, the results may be incorrect.

2. We have ignored the timing of exchange rate changes. If the exchange rate increases and then decreases during the year, then depending on when the firms carry out certain

transactions, the results may not be correct. (See Case 15-1 for example). *More importantly, we have used the year-end change in exchange rates as a surrogate for the average rate.*

3. Our results are based on a composite measure for all foreign subsidiaries. Sales and income patterns, however, may not be uniform over all subsidiaries.

E. (i) We would expect to see a *negative* exchange rate effect on cash each year as the dollar strengthened.

   (ii) GM reports a *positive* exchange rate effect on cash each year, contrary to what we would expect. The possibility exists that GM has anticipated these effects and kept low LC cash balances in those countries where the dollar strengthened and higher LC cash balances in countries where the dollar was weak.

7. {M}
   A. & B. See Exhibit 15S-1. The local currency (LC) results are calculated by dividing sales in SEK by the average exchange rates.

   C. For most countries, the changes based in SEK's are higher than those in the local currency as the SEK weakened relative to (most) other currencies. The weakening of the SEK magnified the increase in LC sales. The exceptions (italicized), Italy, Norway and US/Canada, are countries whose currencies were weak relative to the SEK. Sales growth rates in SEK's and local currencies are within two percentage points for most countries. The exceptions are Belgium and Italy, where the differential are higher.

   D. Forest products are a commodity and extremely price sensitive. As products are easily imported and exported, changes in exchange rates often impact local currency prices. Otherwise, exchange rate changes would have large effects on trade volumes. Thus, a change in one country's exchange rate, which would *ceterus parabus,* make a product more expensive to international customers would lead to an offsetting price change in the local currency in order to remain competitive. Given these relationships, one cannot discuss operational effects and exchange rate effects as independent phenomena.

Exhibit 13S-1

| | S A L E S (SEK) | | | | Average Rate | | S A L E S (LC) | | | |
| | | | | | | | A. | | | B. |
	1993	1994	Change	% Change	1993	1994	1993	1994	Change	% Change
Germany	9,895	10,424	529	5.3%	4.7211	4.7717	2,096	2,185	89	4.2%
Sweden	7,577	8,017	440	5.8%	1	1	7,577	8,017	440	5.8%
Great Britain	4,694	5,564	870	18.5%	11.71	11.83	401	470	69	17.3%
France	4,045	4,469	424	10.5%	1.3805	1.3957	2,930	3,202	272	9.3%
Denmark	2,225	2,502	277	12.4%	1.2061	1.217	1,845	2,056	211	11.4%
Netherlands	1,943	2,422	479	24.7%	4.2038	4.2554	462	569	107	23.1%
Italy	1,709	2,100	391	22.9%	0.00495	0.0048	345,253	437,500	92,247	26.7%
Belgium	1,256	1,759	503	40.0%	0.2262	0.2316	5,553	7,595	2,042	36.8%
Norway	1,286	1,614	328	25.5%	1.0998	1.097	1,169	1,471	302	25.8%
US/Canada	2,359	2,378	19	0.8%	7.80	7.73	302	308	5	1.7%

8.{S}A.   Functional currency = hib means that local financial statements are prepared in hib and then translated into dollars.

First in First Out	Last in First Out
Cost of goods sold: Opening inventory hib 6,000 becomes COGS; translate at rate when sold ($1 = 6 hib) makes COGS $1,000	Purchases during the year of hib 7,500 becomes COGS; translate at rate when sold ($1 = 6 hib) makes COGS $1,250
Ending inventory: Purchases during the year of hib 7,500 translated at closing rate of $1 = 6 hib makes inventory $1,250	Opening inventory of hib 6,000 remains in inventory; when translated at the closing rate makes inventory $1,000

NOTE: COGS and ending inventory must total hib 13,500, the sum of opening inventory and purchases, regardless of inventory method.

B.   Functional currency = dollar means that calculations are made using dollars; temporal method rules apply.

First in First Out	Last in First Out
Cost of goods sold: Opening inventory of $1,500 (hib 6,000/4) becomes COGS	Purchases during the year of $1,500 (hib 7,500/5) become COGS
Ending inventory: Purchases during the year of $1,500 remain in inventory	Opening inventory of $1,500 remains in inventory

NOTE: COGS and ending inventory must total $3,000, the sum of opening inventory and purchases.

C.   The essence of LIFO is that (with rising prices) higher priced purchases become COGS, whereas lower priced goods remain in inventory; FIFO is the reverse, resulting in higher income (lower COGS) and higher inventory valuation.

15-13

The choice of functional currency interacts with the choice of inventory method. When the functional currency is the hib (local currency), the normal LIFO/FIFO effects are directly transmitted to the parent company financial statements. This accords with the objective of SFAS 52 of having parent results replicate subsidiary results.

However, the temporal method applies when the dollar (the parent or reporting currency) is used as the functional currency. Price changes are measured in dollars rather than hibs. In this case, the unit price in dollars has not changed. Purchases are at $15 (hib 75/5) which is unchanged from the cost of opening inventory (hib 60/4). Thus, in dollars there is no price change and LIFO = FIFO.

Generalizing, the choice of functional currency determines whether the effects of changing prices are determined in the local currency or the reporting currency. Depending on the interplay between price changes and currency exchange rates, the impact of LIFO versus FIFO can be quite different depending on the choice of functional currency.

9.{S} A. When the long-term liabilities denominated in a foreign currency are held by the parent then, under GAAP, the carrying value is converted using the current (year end) exchange rate and the gains and losses are recorded as part of income. The process is equivalent to remeasurement (temporal method). Therefore
(i)   *long-term monetary liabilities* will be equivalent to those shown by Suncor
(ii)   *net income* will be lower as under U.S. GAAP, the entire loss will be recognized immediately whereas under Suncor's policy the loss is amortized to income over the life of the debt.
(iii) *stockholder's equity* will also be lower under U.S. GAAP as a result of the differences in net income assuming that Suncor does not recognize the unamortized portion as a part of equity. If they do record the unamortized portion as equity then stockholder's equity will be equivalent.

B. When the long-term liabilities denominated in a foreign currency are held by a subsidiary whose functional currency is the currency the liabilities are denominated in, then the all-current method is used. The carrying value is converted using the current (year end) exchange rate and the gains and losses are recorded directly to the cumulative translation adjustment bypassing income. Therefore
(i)   *long-term monetary liabilities* will be equivalent to those shown by Suncor
(ii)   *net income* will be higher under U.S. GAAP as the loss never affects income whereas under Suncor's policy the loss is amortized to income over the life of the debt.
(iii) *stockholder's equity* will also be higher under U.S. GAAP as a result of the differences in net income assuming that Suncor does not recognize the unamortized portion as a part of equity. If they do record the unamortized portion as equity then stockholder's equity will be equivalent.

C. In this case the temporal method, remeasurement, is used. Since the subsidiary's functional currency is the Canadian dollar (the reporting currency), it is as if the subsidiary is an integral part of the parent and the answer is equivalent to that of part A.

10.{M}(a) The first step is to convert equity in income of affiliates from dollars to LC

	Base	**Year 1**	**Year 2**
Income in $	$ 100	$ 140	$ 225
Exchange Rate LC 1 = $1.00		$1.40	$1.50
Income in LC	LC 100	LC 100	LC 150

Year 1 : No change in operations as LC income remained at LC 100. The full increase of $40 is a result of exchange rate change.

Year 2 : Operations increased by 50%. Therefore, in *base year* dollars,[1] the transaction effect is $150-$100 = $50 and the exchange rate effect is $225-$150 = $75.

(b)

	(i) **LC**		(ii) **Dollars**	
	Year 1	**Year 2**	**Year 1**	**Year 2**
Opening value	1,000	1,200	1,000	1,680
Close value	1,200	1,300	1,680	1,950
Capital gain	200	100	680	270
Dividend	20	100	28	150
Return	220	200	708	420
Rate	22.0%	16.7%	70.8%	25.%

(c) (i)

	Year 1	**Year 2**
Opening balance	$1,000	$1,512
Equity income	140	225
Dividends	(28)	(150)
Subtotal	1,112	1,587
Exchange rate gain	400	108
Closing balance	$1,512	$1,695

Calculation of exchange rate gain =
Change in exchange rate x opening balance

Year 1	(1.4/1.0 - 1)	x	$1,000	= $400
Year 2	(1.5/1.4 - 1)	x	$1,512	= $108

---

[1] Note that the answer for year 2 will differ depending on whether the year 2 change is measured relative to the base year (as we do) or whether the change is measured relative to year 1.

(ii) The CTA at the end of year 1 is $400, the exchange rate gain for the year. At the end of year 2, the CTA is $508 ($400 + $108).

(iii) Given the equity income and investment in affiliates and dividends received, one could calculate the change in the CTA. That change divided by the opening balance in the investment account would yield the percentage change in the exchange rate.

Year 1: Δ in CTA=($1,512-$140+$28-$1,000)=$400

$\%$ Δ in exchange rate = $400/$1,000 = 40%

Year 2: Δ in CTA=($1,695-$225+$150-$1,512)=$108

$\%$ Δ in exchange rate = $108/$1,512 = 7.14%

11.{M} A. FX book value is $1,750 (LC 3,500/2) at time of merger. Since amount paid equals $2,000 the excess of $250 goes to net fixed assets.

	AMREK	FX	Merged
Cash	$2,000	$ 250	$2,250
Accounts Receivable	3,000	1,000	4,000
Inventory	1,500	250	1,750
Net fixed assets	5,500	750	6,250
	$12,000	$2,250	$14,250
LTD	$ 7,000	$ 250	$ 7,250
Equity	5,000	2,000	7,000
	$12,000	$2,250	14,250

B. Since the acquisition was effected by the issue of shares and the only cash was the $250 FX held at the time of the merger, the cash flow statement would report

Acquisition net of cash acquired = $250 as an inflow.[2]

C. Under pooling, the net assets would not be revalued upwards. Therefore depreciation would be lower and income higher.

D. Change in CTA =$ 200
Net Assets of FX at acquisition = $2,000
Exchange rate change = $200/$2,000 = 10%

That is from LC 1 = $0.50 to LC 1 = $0.55
  or $1.00= LC 2   to $1.00 = LC 1.82

E.

	A/R	Inventory
Opening balance	$3,000	$1,500
Acquisition	1,000	250
Exchange rate effect (10% of above)	100	25
Change on cash flow statement (plug)	**400**	**(275)**
Closing balance	$4,500	$1,500

---

[2] An alternative method (not recommended by GAAP but perhaps more informative from an analytic point of view) would be to recognize the implicit cash flows as

CFI: Acquisition net of cash acquired   ($1,750)
CFF: Issue of shares   2,000

12.{M}A. The exact amount of the equity *cannot **be*** determined. It will, however, be $500 less on a pooling basis as compared to purchase. In pooling the *book value* of COL's equity or net assets ($3,000) will be used rather than the amount used under purchase accounting; i.e. the price paid for COL's net assets ($3,500).

   B.   (i) Since Δ in CTA = $300 and for pooling, net assets are $3000, the Δ in exchange rate is $300/$3,000 =10%

        Therefore since the effect on cash is also 10%, cash acquired should be $20/.10 = $200.

        (ii) At acquisition there will be no effect as in pooling, the acquisition is not reflected in the SoCF. For 1995, the cash flows of COL will be added to those of AMREK.

   C.   (i) Under purchase the net assets are $3,500. Since the Δ in CTA = $300, the percent change in the exchange rate is $300/$3,500 = 8.6%.

        Therefore cash acquired = $20/.086 = $233

        (ii) At acquisition:[3]
             CFI:
             Acquisition net of cash acquired 233 (inflow)

             The issuance of shares for the acquisition would be reported in the section "Significant noncash investing and financing activities". For 1995, cash flows would be similar as the pooling method. The only difference would be tax consequences of the purchase method adjustments.

_____

[3] An alternative method (not recommended by GAAP but perhaps more informative from an analytic point of view) would be to recognize the implicit cash flows as

        CFI: Acquisition net of cash acquired   ($3,267)
        CFF: Issue of shares   3,500

D. Under the pooling assumptions, the change in exchange rate
was 10% resulting in an exchange rate of LC 1 = $1.10.
Therefore foreign sales were $33,000/1.10 = LC 30,000.

Estimate of future sales:

	1995		**1996**		**1997**
Foreign sales LC's	30,000	(x2/3=)	20,000	(x1.25=)	25,000
Exchange rate	1.10		1.65		1.32
Foreign sales $	33,000		33,000		33,000
Domestic sales	567,000		567,000		567,000
Total sales	$600,000		$600,000		$600,000

Under the purchase assumptions, the change in exchange
rate was 8.6% resulting in an exchange rate of LC 1 =
$1.086.   Therefore foreign sales were $33,000/1.086 = LC
30,387.

Estimate of future sales:

	1995		**1996**		**1997**
Foreign sales LC's	30,387	(x2/3=)	20,258	(x1.25=)	25,323
Exchange rate	1.086		1.65		1.32
Foreign sales $	33,000		33,426		33,426
Domestic sales	567,000		567,000		567,000
Total sales	$600,000		$600,426		$600,426

Case 15-1 Solution

Estimated solution time is 1 to 1 1/2 hours.

Case Overview: the objective of this case is to show the effect of exchange rate changes by examining a company with significant foreign operations in a single currency. Case 15-2 examines a multicurrency case, using IBM.

Note: the answers to the questions posed are supplemented by actual data from AFLAC's 1996 financial statements, shown in [square brackets].

1.   (a) The decline in the yen against the dollar should reduce revenue growth as Japanese revenues are translated into fewer dollars.

   [The average exchange rate for the yen versus the dollar was 107.67 for the second quarter of 1996, 21.6% below the 90.39 rate for the 1995 quarter. While yen revenues rose 9.7%, that growth was more than offset by the lower value of the yen.
   Corporate revenues declined 9.9% for the second quarter of 1996. This decline was caused by the lower yen and should not have surprised anyone.]

   (b) Pretax income is also affected by the yen/dollar exchange rate and would be expected to decline.

   [While AFLAC Japan's pretax income rose 9.8% (in yen), it fell in dollars. AFLAC's total pretax earnings declined 9.8%.]

   (c) When examining the change in the CTA for the first six months of 1996, we must consider the exchange rate change for the first half only. The rate was 110 at June 30, 1996 as compared with 102.95 at December 31, 1995. This 6.8% decline in the yen would be expected to produce a negative CTA, given AFLAC's yen exposure.

   [AFLAC's second quarter report, however, shows that the CTA rose to $221.3 million at June 30, 1996 from $213.3 million at December 31, 1995. The second quarter report does not provide an explanation for this surprising result.]

(d)   Asset growth for the first six months of 1996 should also be affected by the decline in the value of the yen, as assets at December 31, 1995 will be translated into fewer dollars at June 30, 1996.

[Total reported assets at June 30, 1996 were $24,671 million, slightly below the $25,022 million at December 31, 1995. Actual asset increases during the period were more than offset by the effect of yen weakness.]

2.   Shifting investments from yen to dollars increases the investment income of AFLAC Japan. Because dollar interest rates are higher, the same investments earn higher income when invested in dollar investments.
      This effect is compounded when the yen declines against the dollar. Dollar investment income translates into more yen, increasing investment income for AFLAC Japan even further.
      Both of these effects increase pretax income of AFLAC Japan (in yen).

[AFLAC's 1996 annual report states that AFLAC Japan's investment income grew 12.5% in yen even though interest rates in Japan declined, reducing the income on yen investments.]

      For the consolidated enterprise, the shift from yen investments to dollar investments again increases reported investment income. This shift also mitigates the effect of the weak yen on translated investment income (which is lower as the yen falls).
      This translation effect, however, disappears in consolidation, as exchange rate changes do not affect the investment income derived from dollar investments.
      The increase in investment income, therefore, offsets to some extent the effect of the 1996 decline in the yen.

[AFLAC's investment income fell slightly in 1996, after a large 1995 gain. Increased yen investment income and increased investment income from U.S. operations were more than offset by the effect of the weak yen on the translation of yen investment income to dollars. The average exchange rate for 1996 was 108.84, 13.5% below 1995. Consolidated pretax income also declined excluding nonrecurring income.]

3. If the U.S. dollar investments of AFLAC Japan were remeasured into yen, exchange rate changes would result in translation gains and losses that are included in reported income. [The yen is the functional currency for AFLAC Japan.]

    These translation gains and losses would be included in the net income of AFLAC Japan, and therefore would be included in the consolidated net income of AFLAC.

    Thus, the 1995 yen rise would have resulted in translation losses (as dollar investments are remeasured into fewer yen) that would have reduced the reported income of both the Japanese subsidiary (AFLAC Japan) and the parent (AFLAC). In 1996, both would have reported translation gains as dollar assets were remeasured into more yen as that currency declined.

Note: the FASB Emerging Issues Task Force (EITF) considered this issue in 1996 (Issue No. 96-15), indicating a difference of opinion among auditors as to the correct accounting treatment. The EITF reached a consensus that:

> *the entire change in the fair value of foreign-currency denominated AFS [available-for-sale] debt securities should be reported in stockholders' equity.*[1]

The EITF also agreed that gains and losses on hedges of such investments should be reported in the SFAS 115 component of equity [rather than with foreign currency gains and losses].

These conclusions would not apply to foreign-currency denominated debt securities designated as held-to-maturity.

---

[1] November 14, 1996 EITF Meeting Minutes, p. 35

Case 15-2 Solution

Estimated solution time is 3 to 4 hours.

Case Overview: the objective of this case is to illustrate the effect of exchange rate changes on a mutlinational company. While this is mostly a teaching case (most issues are considered within the case itself), the required questions extend the case to cash flow analysis.

For exchange rate information use the data provided in Exhibit 15-C6:

	1989	1990
Year-end rate	.937	.837
Average rate	.986	.891

1. (a) Balance sheet translated at *year-end rate*
          (millions of $US and LC)

	12/31/89		12/31/90	
	$US	**LC**	**$US**	**LC**
Cash (5% of CA)	$ 1,018	LC 954	$ 1,217	LC 1,019
Other current assets	19,343	18,124	23,120	19,351
Current liabilities	(12,124)	(11,360)	(15,917)	(13,323)
Net working capital	$ 8,237	LC 7,718	$ 8,420	LC 7,047
Net property	9,879	9,257	11,628	9,733
Investments	6,822	6,392	9,077	7,597
Total assets	$24,938	LC 23,367	$29,125	LC 24,377
Long-term debt	$ 3,358	LC 3,146	$ 5,060	LC 4,235
Other liabilities	2,607	2,443	2,699	2,259
Deferred taxes	1,814	1,700	2,381	1,993
Total liabilities	$ 7,779	LC 7,289	$10,140	LC 8,487
Net assets (equity)	17,159	16,078	18,985	15,890
Total equities	$24,938	LC 23,367	$29,125	LC 24,377

   (b) Income statement translated at *average rate* for year
        (millions of $US and LC)

	$US	**LC**
Revenues	$ 41,886	LC 37,320
Earnings before tax	7,844	6,989
Income tax expense	(3,270)	(2,914)
Net income	$ 4,754	LC 4,075

(c)
Net assets at December 31, 1989	LC 16,078
Net income for 1990	4,075
Subtotal	LC 20,153
Net assets at December 31, 1990	(15,890)
Discrepancy	LC 4,263

There must be dividends paid and/or share redemptions by IBM's foreign subsidiaries during 1990. It is possible that a small portion of the discrepancy is the result of valuation allowances included in equity.

2. Investments translated at *average rate* for the year.

	$US	LC
Investment in property	$ 3,020	LC 2,691
Net property at December 31, 1989		LC 9,257
Investment for 1990		2,691
Subtotal		LC 11,948
Net property at December 31, 1990		(9,733)
Difference		LC 2,215

This difference reflects depreciation expense for the year. We assume (lacking data) that there were no acquisitions or divestitures and there were no property dispositions during the year.

3. (a) Exhibit 15CS-1 uses the transactional analysis method to produce a summarized cash flow statement in LC units. Note that:

- Depreciation must be reclassified from CFO to CFI to properly compute those two components.

- Net cash flow should equal the change in cash to check our calculations.

- Net income equals the sum of all income statement components to ensure that none were omitted or incorrectly copied.

Exhibit 15CS-1

1990 Cash Flow Statement
IBM Non-U.S. Operations
Millions of LC

	Income Statement	Balance Sheet 12/31/89	12/31/90	Change	Cash Effect +	Cash Effect −
Pretax income	6,989				6,989	
Other current assets		18,124	19,351	1,227		1,227
Current liabilities		11,360	13,323	1,963	1,963	
Other liabilities		2,443	2,259	(184)		184
Depreciation expense	2,215				2,215	
Income tax expense	(2,914)					2,914
Deferred tax		1,700	1,993	293	293	—
Cash from operations						**7,135**
Depreciation expense	(2,215)					2,215
Net property		9,257	9,733	476		476
Investments		6,392	7,597	1,205		1,205
Cash for investment						**(3,896)**
Long-term debt		3,146	4,235	1,089	1,089	
Dividends paid [1 (d)]						4,263
Cash from financing						**(3,174)**
Net cash flow						**65**
[Net income]	4,075					

(b)   Translation of LC cash flow components to $US at the *average rate* for 1990 of .891 (data in millions):

	LC	$US
Cash from operations	7,135	8,008
Cash for investment	(3,896)	(4,373)
Cash for financing	(3,174)	(3,562)
Net cash flow	65	73

(c)   Percentage of consolidated cash flow obtained from non-U.S. operations ($ millions):

		Total	Non-US	Percent
i.	Cash from operations	$7,472	$8,008	107%
ii.	Cash from debt financing	2,958	1,222	41
iii.	Cash for investment	(7,144)	(4,373)	61

iv.   It appears that IBM's 1990 operating cash flow was derived *entirely* from its non-U.S. operations. These operations accounted for 61% of investment cash flow, similar to their proportion of operations (measured by revenues or assets). This suggests that IBM's U.S. operations had significant liquidity problems.

IBM's foreign operations were able to pay more than $4 billion in cash dividends to the parent company (part 1c).

The debt financing ratio (ii.) may not be meaningful. Much of IBM's debt is short-term and the short-term debt of the non-U.S. operations is not broken out. This problem also affects the computation of CFO. If the short-term debt (included in current liabilities) of IBM's non-U.S. operations rose, CFO has been overstated.

More analysis would be needed to understand whether these conditions were temporary or reflected longer term trends.

It must also be remembered that these conclusions are based on summarized data and simplifying assumptions. It is possible that more detailed data would modify these conclusions.

In sum, the data derived suggest that IBM's non-U.S. operations in 1990 were much healthier that domestic operations. The data could have been used to question management about these conditions.

(d) The effect of exchange rates on cash and cash equivalents:

	LC	Multiplier*	$ Effect
Beginning cash balance	LC 954	.1275	$122
Effects on:			
Cash from operations	7,136	.0724	517
Cash for investment	(3,896)	.0724	(282)
Cash for financing	(3,174)	.0724	(230)
Net effect			$ 127
Actual effect(Exhibit 15C-4)			$ 131

* The beginning cash balance was translated at the rate of .937 at December 31, 1989 but is now translated at the rate of .837. The effect on LC cash is [(1/.937)-(1/.837)] = .1275.
   Cash flows during 1990 are assumed to have originated at the average rate of .891 but are now translated at the year-end rate of .837. The effect on 1990 cash flows is therefore [(1/.837)-(1/.891)] = .0724.

Alternative method:

Cash balance at December 31, 1989: LC954/.937	$ 1,018
1990 increase in cash (net cash flow): LC65/.891	73
Subtotal	$ 1,091
Cash balance at December 31, 1990: LC1019/.837	(1,217)
Effect of exchange rates on cash	$ (126)

The difference between the computed and the actual effect is quite small, suggesting that our assumption that non-U.S. cash is 5% of current assets was approximately correct. Even if it were exactly correct, differences in the distribution by currency would introduce an element of error. Another possible source of error is the assumption that 100% of IBM's foreign operations uses local functional currencies.

The point of this exercise is that non-U.S. cash and cash equivalents can be estimated by estimating cash flows and reversing this process. Subtracting the effect of rate changes on cash flows from the total effect provides the impact on the beginning cash balance. As we know the exchange rate, we can estimate the beginning cash balance. Thus the actual effect, provided in the consolidated cash flow statement, provides the answer; the question is the amount of non-U.S. cash and cash equivalents.

Chapter 16 Solutions

Overview:

Problem Length	*Problem #s*
{S}	1, 5, and 6
{M}	2, 3, 4, and 7

Problems 1 through 4 together should require approximately 1 1/2 hours to solve.

1.{S}A. The market value of fixed rate debt increases (decreases) when interest rates decline (rise). Generally, the market value of variable-rate debt is affected by changes in interest rates only to the extent that the variable-rate adjustment lags changes in market rates.

        The fair-value of debt denominated in other currencies will depend on the changes in exchange rates over time. The appreciation of the dollar or the foreign currency will be reflected in the estimated fair value of debt.

   B. Long-term debt ($ millions)

	1994	1995
Fair value	$ 689,181	$ 604,537
Carrying amount	(669,157)	(557,595)
Excess fair value	$ 20,024	$ 46,942

The increase in the fair value of debt during a period of declining interest rates suggests that a significant portion of the Becton Dickinson debt must be fixed-rate obligations of intermediate or long maturity. The market values of variable rate debt and short-maturity debt are little affected by interest rate changes.

   C. Investments in marketable securities (non-current) $millions

	1994	1995
Fair value	$ 70,093	$ 43,509
Carrying amount	(71,527)	(44,400)
Excess fair value	$ (1,434)	$ (891)

The decline in interest rates had only a small effect on the fair value. As fair value remained slightly below carrying amount, the marketable securities are probably fixed rate (with low coupons) but with short maturities.

2.{M}A.   Becton Dickinson appears to use foreign currency hedges
          to manage its accounting exposure from monetary assets
          and liabilities denominated in currencies other than
          the functional currencies of the company and its
          subsidiaries. Exchange rate changes result in
          remeasurement gains and losses under the temporal
          method, adding volatility to reported earnings.
              In addition, BD uses interest rate swap and cap
          agreements to lower the volatility of interest costs on
          foreign currency denominated short-term debt. Fixed
          rates make interest costs more predictable; caps
          eliminate the risk of sharp rate rises.

      B. We expect the cumulative translation adjustment (CTA)
          to increase when foreign currencies rise against the
          dollar because local currency net assets are translated
          to more dollars.

          The 1995 decrease in CTA may be due to:

          i.   The hedging of non-functional currency monetary
                assets and liabilities discussed in part A.
                Hedging eliminates the positive effect of currency
                appreciation on those assets.

          ii.   BD's mix of assets and liabilities may not be
                uniform. It may have net assets in subsidiaries
                whose currency declined against the dollar despite
                the general decline of the dollar.

          iii. BD hedged a portion of its investment in a foreign
                subsidiary in which it contracted to sell French
                francs and buy U.S. dollars forward. The loss on
                this hedge would be reported as a component of the
                CTA.

      C. The foreign currency hedges disclosed in Note 9 are
          primarily commitments to purchase and sell foreign
          currencies and interest rate hedges. These are designed
          to hedge foreign currency transaction exposures. The
          only exception is the hedge of a portion of its net
          investment in a foreign subsidiary. BD may have decided
          to sell or liquidate that subsidiary and hedged its
          exposure to manage the impact on the income statement.

      D. The increase in CTA from a negative $109 million to a
          positive $38 million suggests that the local,
          functional currencies must have appreciated relative to
          the dollar.

E.   BD purchased three currency options:

German mark put, U.S. dollar call
Brazilian real put, U.S. dollar call
Italian lira put, German mark call

The first two option hedges may be related to expected future cash flows, such as dividends or debt service payments from the German and Brazilian subsidiaries. The options permit BD to fix the dollar amount of the cash flow at the time the cash flow is planned, even if the cash flow takes place some time later.
       The third option hedge may be intended to fix BD's margins on future foreign currency transactions. If it expects to receive revenue in Italian lira while incurring costs in marks, the option fixes the resulting profit margin.

3.{M}A.   BD's swap agreements reflect its objective of limiting the variability of interest costs on foreign currency denominated short term floating rate debt.

B   The interest rate swaps obligate BD to exchange fixed rate payments for variable rate receipts. At September 30, 1994 the outstanding interest rate agreements were:

	Notional Amount (000)	Fixed Rate	Average Variable Rate	Difference	Receipt/ (Payment) (000)
Francs	$18,886	8.16%	6.41%	(1.75)%	$(330.50)
Francs	18,886	5.00	6.80	1.80	339.95
Pounds	15,795	5.85	5.40	(0.45)	(71.08)
Yen	5,041	2.61	2.23	(0.38)	(19.16)
Yen	10,082	2.61	2.25	(0.36)	(36.30)
Total					$(117.01)

Under the assumption that none of these swaps expire before the end of the year, or rates change, BD will make net payments, that is, report additional interest expense of $117.01 million.

C.   The fair value of the swaps is higher than the carrying amount because BD is a fixed rate payer (variable rate receiver) and interest rates declined during 1995. The fact that the swaps increased 1995 interest expense would be consistent with either gains or losses on the swaps. [See Exhibit 10-6 (p.489) and the related text discussion for further explanation.

16-3

D.   As a result of an interest rate swap, at September 30, 1995 BD is a fixed rate (1.74%) payer and variable rate (1.05%) receiver on $9,023 of Japanese yen denominated short term debt. Thus, the company is exposed to fluctuating interest rates. BD has also negotiated an interest rate cap which limits BD's interest payments to 2%. The company would receive from a bank the amount by which its interest payments exceeded 2%.

4.{M}A.   (i)   If interest rates remain within the collar band, then the premium is "wasted" and interest expense is higher than if the collar had not been purchased.

(ii) At an interest rate of 6%, the collar increases interest expense by the amount of the premium paid and by the .5% excess of the collar minimum (6.5%) over 6%.

(iii) At an interest rate of 9%, the collar reduces interest expense by .5% (8.5% maximum less 9%) offset by the premium paid.

B.   (i)   First year interest expense would be higher by the amortized premium (case A(i) above). In year 2 (case A(ii)) interest expense is again higher. Over the two-year period, the loss is the premium plus the .5% loss in year 2.

(ii) First year interest expense would be higher by the amortized premium (case A(i) above). Second year (case a(iii) above) interest expense is lower. Over the two year period, the second year interest differential (gain of .5%) is offset by the premium paid for the collar.

C.   BD must have expected interest rates to rise. To protect against the effect of higher rates on interest expense. BD is willing to pay the premium and run the risk of a rate decline. [BD is willing to run that risk as the collar will have a lower premium than a cap because of option granted to the counterparty.]

5.{S}A. DuPont's change in functional currencies changes its exposure to foreign currency rate changes. When the dollar is the functional currency, exposure equals net monetary assets in each local currency (temporal method). When local currencies are functional currencies, the exposure is the net assets in each functional currency.

Thus, the change in functional currency changes duPont's exposures, requiring changes in its hedges of those exposures.

B. When exposure is measured by net assets, assets such as inventories and fixed assets are now exposed. Therefore, the exposure to exchange rate changes increases when the functional currency is changed from the dollar to local currencies.

6.{S}A. Alcoa uses futures and options contracts to protect against losses form future increases in prices of metals that it has agreed to provide under long-term contracts. These hedges are particularly necessary when the sales contracts are at fixed prices.

B. The deferred gains reflect unrealized gains from hedge contracts on raw materials needed for long-term contracts. As these gains will offset any increase in the purchase price of the metals, some might consider them to be a component of comprehensive income and stockholders' equity.

On the other hand, if Alcoa has committed to deliver metals at prices that are below current market, it has unrecognized losses (most contracts do not receive accounting recognition until cash flows take place). To the extent that deferred hedging gains merely offset unrecognized contract losses, they are liabilities rather than equity.

The resolution of this issue, therefore, requires more information about the nature of the long-term contracts.

C. Whether these deferred gains are realized has little bearing on their analytical treatment. As long as the other side of the transaction (delivery of metals under long-term contracts) is open (unrealized), these gains may or may not accrue to shareholders (see B above).

D. (i) Gains and losses from rolling hedges would have to be recognized in income during the hedge period. The volatility of reported income would be higher than if hedge accounting (deferral of unrealized gains and losses were allowed.

(ii) When the contractual commitments are met the final leg of the rolling hedge is closed out and the gain or loss recognized in that period. The resulting gain or loss will differ from the amount recognized if rolling hedges were permitted.

7. {M}A. Suncor's cash inflows depend on the price of oil after translation into Canadian dollars. Its cash outflows are all incurred in Canadian dollars. The two risks that Suncor is concerned with are fluctuations of the price of oil (in $ U.S.) and the exchange rate between the Canadian and U.S. dollars.

B. Suncor has hedged a portion of it exposure to the oil price and exchange rate as shown in the following table:

Year	Oil Price	Exchange Rate
1995	33%	8%
1996	3	33
1997	2	22

These calculations assume that revenues remain at $C1,001, which excludes excise taxes that are not affected by either risk. For example, the 1995 oil price hedge equals $326/$1,001 or 33%.

C. (i) If oil rises to $US30, the hedge reduces cash flow and earnings by depriving Suncor of the higher market price.

(ii) If oil falls to $US20, the hedge increases cash flow and earnings as Suncor receives the higher hedge price.

(iii) If the Canadian dollar rises to $US1.25, the hedge increases cash flow and earnings as Suncor receives the higher market rate of exchange.

(iv) If the Canadian dollar falls to $US1.45, the hedge decreases cash flow and earnings as Suncor must exchange its U.S. dollar revenues at the lower hedge rate of exchange.

CASE 16C-1

Estimated solution time is 3 hours

1. A. The reported unrealized gains and losses on derivatives are affected by new contracts for the period, restructuring of existing contracts, and the effects of price changes. Disclosure of these components would improve our understanding of the profitability of ECT's risk management services.

    The unrealized gains and losses on new contracts would inform users about the contribution of those contracts as compared with that of older contracts.

    Contracts may be restructured when the counterparty is financially distressed; disclosure of such restructurings would provide information about the credit risk of counterparties and ECT's risk assessment abilities.

    Price changes are the major contributor to unrealized gains and losses. More disclosure regarding those changes would help users understand the risks inherent in ECT's business and its sensitivity to price changes. It would also convey information about management's understanding of their markets and their ability to evaluate supply and demand conditions in their markets.

    B. The recognition of all unrealized gains increased ECT's earnings in each of the last three years (see last line of Exhibit 16C-2 on page 923). As the gains and losses on new contracts are not separately disclosed, we cannot discern their impact.

    As such gains and losses are volatile, the trend of ECT's earnings has also been affected by their inclusion. Immediate recognition of unrealized gains and losses increases the volatility of reported earnings as the impact of fluctuating interest and exchange rates and commodity prices is reflected in the earnings of each period as they occur.

C. Enron reports deferred tax liabilities because the unrealized gains are recorded in the income statement before they are reflected on the tax return, where they will be recognized only when the contracts are closed out.

The deferred tax liabilities will increase (decrease) with the level of unrealized gains and losses. They will decrease (increase) when profitable (unprofitable) contracts are closed out.

D. The growing deferred tax liability indicates low earnings quality as it reflects *unrealized* gains on highly volatile derivative contracts. These gains are an important component of reported income.

2. Note 2 shows that Enron is a fixed price receiver on gas contracts. When gas prices increase, Enron will continue to receive fixed prices for gas as it meets the conditions of these contracts. Because the price of natural gas fluctuates, Enron's operating margins will decline when prices rise and increase if they fall.

3. A. and B.
    As PGE is a generator and distributor of electricity, it is both a supplier and demander. As the electricity market deregulates, ECT may offer surplus PGE output to other electricity users. PGE may be a market for the output of other suppliers with whom ECT has contracts. The acquisition of PGE, by increasing both the supply and demand for electricity by ECT, will permit it to offer a more diverse array of derivatives in the energy sector as it will have greater control over price and quantities of the underlying product and its distribution.

    C. The expansion can be expected to increase the level of unrealized gains and losses and resulting deferred tax liabilities as the amount and types of derivative and hedge instruments increases.

4.   A.   Assets from Price Risk Management Activities
           ($millions)

	1994		1995	
Investment Grade/Total	1,422/1,608=	88.43%	1,532/1,984 =	77.22%
Below Investment Grade/Total	186/1,608 =	11.57%	452/1,984 =	22.78%
Credit Reserves/Total	130/1,608 =	8.08%	207/1,984 =	10.43%

In 1995, the proportion of ECT's risk management assets related to non-investment grade counterparties increased 97% from 11.57% at year-end 1994 to 22.78% at year-end 1995. There has been a significant increase in unrealized gains from transactions with energy marketers (from 3% to 12%) and a substantial decrease in assets from contracts with investment grade financial institutions (from 11% to 2%).

However, the credit reserves as a percent of risk management assets grew only 29% over the same period. ECT's counterparties are riskier but it may not have fully recognized the higher risk.

B.   The reported credit reserve reflects risk adjusted for collateral provisions and concentration of exposure. Separate disclosure of credit reserve by counterparties would allow the user to better assess adequacy of the level and trend in reserves for different segments of the market.

The collateral ranges from standby letters of credit, parent company guarantees, and property interests including oil and gas reserves. Knowledge of types of collateral would also improve our ability to evaluate the adequacy of reserves.

C. The increase in below investment grade counterparties can be expected to increase credit losses due to counterparty nonperformance, requiring higher credit reserves as discussed in part B.

However, these counterparties should have increased profitability in 1995 for two reasons:

1. Higher profit margins are required to compensate Enron for the riskiness of the business.

2. Some firms will not do business with low rated counterparties. Firms like Enron that will do business with such counterparties should achieve higher margins even after the higher provision for credit losses.

5. The level and profitability of ECT's trading activities should increase as it should be able to increase transactions with higher rated counterparties (who may have been unwilling to transact with ECT given Enron's BBB rating) and charge higher rates to below investment grade counterparties (whose credit risk is reduced with Enron's higher debt rating).

6. A. Long-term Debt ($ millions)

	1994	1995
Fair value	$ 2,752	$3,360
Carrying amount	(2,805)	(3,065)
Excess fair value	$ (53)	$ 295

At year-end 1994, the carrying amount of debt exceeded its market value. The estimated fair value was nearly 10% higher than carrying amount at the end of 1995. The company-obligated preferred stock of its subsidiaries presents a similar picture.

B. The 1995 increase in fair value of fixed rate debt is consistent with the decline in interest rates. Higher fixed coupons (relative to declining market rates) are worth more to the holders of such debt.

C. Enron does not state whether fixed rates were swapped for variable rates or vise versa. Average rates received/paid for aggregate dollar notional amounts with corresponding detailed or average maturities would also have been informative. Although rarely provided, disclosure of early termination penalties, credit ratings of counterparties and collateral, if any, would also be useful.

D. The estimated fair value of the swaps has declined during a period of falling interest rates, suggesting the Enron must be a fixed price payer and a variable rate receiver. The reasoning is similar to part B.

7. Under the assumption that the contracts hedged current production, sales of current production would have taken place at higher prices, increasing the profitability of Enron's production activities.

There may, however, be a timing difference. If the production is sold in the quarter ending March 31, 1997 (the next quarter), the higher profitability will be reported in that quarter while the hedging loss is reported in the final quarter of 1996. This suggests a possible motivation for recognizing the loss: Enron may have wished to recognize the loss currently (either because earnings were exceeding expectation or because they were poor anyway) and build in higher profits for the next year.

Case 17-1

Estimated solution time is four to five hours.

Note: Students should have been assigned (or have access to the solution of) Case 10-1 prior to attempting this case. That case provides information as to the market value of the firms' debt.

1. Exhibit 17C1S-1 contains the 1994 current cost balance sheet for ICI. Exhibit 17C1S-2 provides the 1994 current cost balance sheet for Dow. Footnotes explain each adjustment. Major adjustments include:

   A. Replacement of historical cost balance with current cost of fair value (inventories, investments, and debt).
   B. Elimination of assets and liabilities with no predictive value or cash flow consequences (intangible assets and deferred taxes).
   C. Capitalization of off-balance sheet obligations (leases).
   D. Replacement of employee benefit plan accruals with actual plan status.

   U.K. GAAP permits revaluation of tangible fixed assets. ICI reports revalued fixed assets on its balance sheet (see footnote 12, p. 1178). However, revaluations are not permitted under U.S. GAAP making it difficult to adjust Dow's fixed assets to current cost. See pages 420-423 and 939-940 for a discussion of the problems related to the adjustment of operating assets to current cost.

2. Exhibit 17C1S-3 provides reported and current cost capitalization tables for both ICI and Dow as of December 31, 1994.

Exhibit 17C1S-1
ICI Current Cost Balance Sheet 12/31/94 (£ millions)

	Reported	Adjustments	Current Cost
Assets			
Cash and short-term deposits[1]	£1,759	£136	£1,895
Inventories	1,233	---	1,233
Receivables	1,911	---	1,911
Prepaid pension costs (N.33)	69	---	69
Total current assets	£4,972	£136	£5,108
Participating interests[2]	171	15	186
Tangible assets[3,4]	3,861	61	3,922
Take-or-pay contracts[8]	-----	784	784
Total assets	£9,004	£996	£10,000
Liabilities			
Short-term borrowings[1]	142	136	278
Current portion of loans	181	---	181
Accrued pension costs (N. 33)	29	---	29
Other creditors	2,256	---	2,256
Total current liabilities	£2,608	£136	£2,744
Long-term loans[4,5]	1,522	70	1,592
Deferred income & other creditors	125	---	125
Other pension obligations[6]	130	540	670
Provisions for liabilities[7]	545	(90)	455
Off-balance sheet obligations[8]	---	784	784
Total liabilities	£4,930	£1,440	£6,370
Minority interests	338	---	338
Common equity	724	---	724
Additional capital	569	---	569
Reserves	97	---	97
Profit and loss account	2,346	---	2,346
Current value adjustments[9]	-----	(444)	(444)
Total equity	£4,074	£ (444)	£3,630
Total equity and liabilities	£9,004	£996	£10,000

[1]Addback to cash and short-term debt of short-term borrowings reported as a reduction of cash.

[2]Excess of market value over balance sheet amount of listed investments included in Participating interests.

[3]Because U.K. GAAP permits revaluation of fixed assets and Footnote 12 shows the extent of revaluation, no further adjustments were made.

[4] Addition of capitalized operating leases.

[5] Restatement of long-term debt to fair value (see Case 10C-1).

[6]Other pension obligations represent liability for unfunded plans (see Footnote 33). The same footnote states that the market value of plan assets is £5,747m and that amount is 92% of the projected benefit obligation (£6,247m or a shortfall of £500m). ICI has accrued pension costs of £29m and recorded prepaid pension costs of £69m for a net asset of £40m. We have increased the pension liability by £540m to reflect the deficit of £500m net of the reported asset of £40m.

[7]Elimination of deferred tax assets and liabilities.

[8]Addition of the present value of take-or-pay contracts (N.35, p.1190).

[9]Sum of asset, liability, and equity adjustments to current cost.

Exhibit 17C1S-2
Dow Current Cost Balance Sheet 12/31/94

($ millions)	Reported	Adjustments	Current Cost
Assets			
Cash, securities and st deposits	$ 1,134	$ ---	$ 1,134
Inventories[1]	2,712	119	2,831
Receivables	4,458	---	4,458
Deferred income taxes[2]	389	(389)	---
Total current assets	$ 8,693	$ (270)	$ 8,423
Equity method investments	931	---	931
Other investments[3]	1,529	12	1,541
Noncurrent receivables	330	---	330
Plant properties[4]	8,726	1,940	10,666
Goodwill[5]	4,365	(4,365)	---
Deferred taxes receivable[2]	1,132	(1,132)	---
Take-or-pay contracts[8]	---	693	693
Deferred charges	839	---	839
Total assets	$26,545	$(3,122)	$23,423
Liabilities			
Notes payable	741	---	741
LT debt due within one year	534	---	534
Accounts payable and other	5,287		5,287
Deferred taxes[2]	56	(56)	---
Total current liabilities	$ 6,618	$ (56)	$ 6,562
Long-term debt[4,6]	5,303	1,907	7,210
Pensions and OPEB[7]	1,987	(411)	1,576
Other noncurrent obligations	1,253		1,253
Deferred income taxes	644	(644)	---
Off-balance sheet obligations[8]	---	693	693
Total liabilities	$15,805	$ 1,489	$17,294
Minority interests	2,506	---	2,506
Temporary equity	22	---	22
Common equity	818	---	818
Additional capital	326	---	326
Unrealized loss on investments	(21)		(21)
Translation adjustment	(330)	---	(330)
Profit and loss account	8,857	---	8,857
Treasury stock	(1,438)		(1,438)
Current value adjustments[9]	---	(4,611)	(4,611)
Total equity	$10,740	$(4,611)	$ 6,129
Total equity and liabilities	$26,545	$(3,122)	$ 23,423

[1] Addition of LIFO Reserve.
[2] Elimination of deferred tax assets and liabilities.
[3] Footnote J, p.1159 reports FV of investments.
[4] Addition of capitalized operating leases.
[5] Elimination of goodwill
[6] Restatement of long-term debt to fair value. See Footnote J, p.1159.
[7] Footnote O, p. 1162. Dow accrued pension costs of $249 ($377-$128) and the PBO exceeded plan assets by $377 ($411-$34); we add $128 ($377-$249) to pension obligations. The unfunded APBO is $1,124. Dow accrued $1,663; we reduce pensions and other postretirement obligations by $539 ($1,663-$1,124). Net effect is a decrease of $411 ($539-$128).
[8] Addition of the present value of take-or-pay contracts.
[9] Sum of asset, liability, and equity adjustments to current cost.

ICI
Capitalization of Operating Leases
£ in millions

Estimation of interest rate:
Interest expense £ 186 (Footnote 8, p. 1176)
Average debt £ 1,964
Interest rate 9.47%

Source: Footnote 31, p. 1188 (£ millions)

Year	Payments			Present Value
	Land & Buildings	Other Assets	Total	
1995	£ 7.00	£ 9.00	£16.00	£14.62
1996	3.50	6.75	10.25	8.55
1997	3.50	6.75	10.25	7.81
1998	3.50	6.75	10.25	7.14
1999	3.50	6.75	10.25	6.52
2000	3.50	6.75	10.25	5.96
2001	3.50	6.75	10.25	5.44
2002	3.50	3.50	7.00	3.39
2003	2.50	----	2.50	1.11
Total	£34.00	£53.00	£87.00	£60.54

Note: U.K. GAAP lease disclosures differ from those required by U.S. GAAP. ICI reports aggregated operating lease payments for years 2 to 5. U.S. firms would have to provide disclosure of payments made in each of years 2 to 5. We have assumed that equal payments will be made in each of the years 2 to 5. We also use the same payment to determine the annual payment for the remaining years. For land and buildings, we allocated the total amount disclosed, £14, equally (£3.5/year) to years 2 to 5. The remaining amount of £13 was assumed to be paid at the same rate for three more years and the final payment was estimated at £2.5 for aggregate payments of £34.00 over the life of the leases.

DOW
Capitalization of Operating Leases
$ millions

Estimation of interest rate:
Interest expense $ 603
Average debt $ 6,761
Interest rate 8.92%

Source: Footnote H, p. 1157 ($ millions)

Year	Payments	Present Value
1995	$ 297	$ 272.7
1996	272	229.3
1997	250	193.5
1998	402	285.6
1999	360	234.8
2000	360	215.6
2001	360	197.9
2002	360	181.7
2003	278	128.8
Total	$2,939	$1,939.9

Capitalization of take-or-pay contracts
Source: Footnote Q, p. 1164 ($ millions)

Year	Payments	Present Value
1995	$ 200	$ 183.6
1996	168	141.6
1997	155	109.9
1998	142	100.9
1999	73	47.6
2000	73	43.7
2001	73	40.1
2002	51	25.7
Total	$ 935	$ 693.1

Capitalization Table as of December 31, 1994 for ICI
(£millions) and duPont and Dow ($ millions)

	DuPont[1]	ICI	DOW
Short-term debt	$ 1,292	£ 459	$ 1,275
Long-term debt	6,376	1,522	5,303
Total reported debt	$ 7,668	£ 1,981	$ 6,578
Adjustments[2]			
Capitalization of operating leases	980	61	1,940
Payables to banks	321		
Take-or-pay contract obligations		784	693
50% of affiliate debt	1,619		
Restatement of debt to mkt value	232	9	(33)
Adjusted total debt	$ 10,820	£ 2,835	$ 9,178
Preferred stock	237		
Minority interests (MI)	197	338	2,506
Common equity	12,585	3,736	8,234
Total stockholders' equity	$ 13,019	£ 4,074	$10,740
Adjustments[2]			
Preferred stock	(102)		
Current cost adjustment to equity	5,779	(444)	$(4,611)
Adjusted stockholders' equity	$ 18,696	£ 3,630	$ 6,129
Total reported capital	$ 20,687	£ 6,055	$ 17,318
Total adjusted capital	$ 29,516	£ 6,465	$ 15,307
Reported Book value per share[3]	$18.48	£5.16	$36.26
Adjusted Book value per share	$26.97	£4.55	$15.95
Reported price-to-book value	3.03x	1.45x	1.85x
Adjusted price-to-book value	2.08x	1.65x	4.22x
Reported debt-to-equity ratio	0.59	0.49	0.61
Adjusted debt-to-equity ratio	0.37	0.78	1.50
Reported debt-to-capital ratio	0.37	0.33	0.38
Adjusted debt-to-capital ratio	0.37	0.44	0.60

[1]DuPont data from Exhibit 17-2, p. 947.
[2]See Exhibits 17C1S-1 and 17C1S-2 and text for adjustments.
[3]Book value is common equity divided by shares outstanding at year-end.
For Dow outstanding shares are (327.1 million less 50 million treasury
stock) 227.1 million; for ICI shares outstanding are 724 million (see
note 22, p. 1184).

3.   (a)   Exhibit 17C1S-3 also shows the book value per share, debt-to-equity, and debt-to-total capital ratios, based on both reported and current cost data for duPont, ICI, and Dow. The duPont data were obtained from Exhibits 17-1 and 17-2.

     (b)   (i)   The current cost adjustments lower the book value per share for both ICI (by 12%) and Dow (by 56%). The major adjustment for ICI is the recognition of pension obligations. The write-offs of goodwill and deferred taxes are responsible for lower book value in the case of Dow.

           (ii) Dow's price-to-book value ratio shows the largest change from a reported 1.85x to an adjusted 4.22x. It appears to be the most expensive stock of the three studied. DuPont's price-to-book ratio declines reflecting the higher adjusted book value per share. ICI is selling at the lowest multiple to adjusted book value. Note that neither Dow nor duPont report current cost fixed assets and both firms reported intangible assets. However, ICI's reported book value includes revalued fixed assets and excludes goodwill, which has been written off to reserves. These differences partially account for both a lower reported book value and a lower adjustment to current cost.

           (iii) Dow's adjusted leverage (debt-to-equity) ratio is significantly higher after adjustment (1.50 versus 0.61) because of its greater use of operating leases and other off-balance sheet financing techniques. ICI also uses off-balance sheet financing techniques but its reported and adjusted leverage as well as the change in leverage is lower than that reported by Dow.

     (c)   DuPont and Dow reported similar leverage (0.59 and 0.61, respectively) ratios and ICI has the lowest reported leverage. The current cost adjustments show that Dow is the most highly levered of the three firms followed by ICI and duPont. Both Dow and ICI use proportionately more off balance sheet financing techniques compared to duPont. Unlike duPont, Dow and ICI do not benefit from current cost adjustments for equity method investments. Finally, Dow's adjusted equity is lower due to elimination of significant amount of goodwill.

(d) Major differences are:

(1) Use of LIFO (by duPont and Dow) versus FIFO by ICI. This difference is virtually eliminated by adding the LIFO reserve to the adjusted book value of duPont and Dow.

(2) Comprehensive deferred tax allocation by duPont and Dow compared to partial allocation by ICI. This difference does not survive in the current cost statements because we eliminate all deferred taxes for all three firms.

(3) ICI revalues its fixed assets but duPont and Dow do not. This difference remains in the current cost statements because we do not have sufficient data to adjust duPont and Dow.

(4) Goodwill is written off to reserves by ICI; duPont and Dow must amortize goodwill over a maximum of 40 years. We eliminate goodwill in the current cost statements of duPont and Dow.

4. (a) Exhibit 17C1S-4 shows a normalized net income for Dow and ICI for the two years ended December 31, 1994. The total unusual items have been allocated equally over two years.

Exhibit 17C1S-4
Normalization of Reported Net Income of ICI and Dow
1993 and 1994 (£ millions for ICI and $ millions for Dow)

	DUPONT[1]		ICI		DOW	
	1993	*1994*	*1993*	*1994*	*1993*	*1994*
Reported net income	$ 555	$2,727	£ 129	£188	$ 644	$ 938
Items reported aftertax						
Early debt retirement	11	------				
Tax adjustments	(274)	(105)				
LIFO liquidation	(50)	------				
Items reported pretax						
LIFO liquidation[2]					18	(16)
Restructuring provisions[3]	1,835	(142)	153	106	180	
Implant litigation[4]					192	70
Fungicide recall	200	175				
Loss(gain) on asset sales[5]	(198)	(92)	(4)	74	(652)	40
Capitalized interest[6]	(231)	(144)	----	----	(66)	(66)
Subtotal	$1,606	$ (203)	149	180	$(328)	$ 28
Tax offset	(546)	69	(49)	(59)	115	(10)
Net effect	$1,060	$ (134)	100	121	$(213)	$ 18
Normalized net income before nonrecurring items	$1,302	$2,488	£229	£309	$ 431	$ 956
Percentage difference	134.6%	-8.8%	77.5%	64.4%	-33.0%	1.9%
Adjustment	(228)	(228)	(111)	(111)	98	98
Earnings power	$1,074	$2,260	£118	£198	$ 529	$ 1054
Percentage difference	93.5%	-17.1%	-8.5%	5.3%	-17.9%	12.4%

[1]See Chapter 17 for the development of a normalized income statement for duPont.

[2]Dow's 1993 pretax income was decreased by $18 and increased by $16 due to LIFO liquidations.

[3]See Footnote 3, p.1172 for restructuring charges and discontinued operations reported by ICI. The adjustment includes £4 and £(4) for 1993 and 1994, respectively related to amounts written off investments.
See Footnote B, p. 1154 for a discussion of restructuring charges reported by Dow.

[4]Footnote Q, p. 1163 describes the implant litigation and the charges taken by Dow.

[5]Footnote 3 on p.1172 shows profits on disposal of fixed assets by ICI. Footnotes C (p. 1155) and R (p. 1165) contain the following data regarding (gains) and losses on asset and investment sales:

	1993	1994
Shares in Magma	$(62)	$(90)
Dow Schlumberger	(450)	--
Dow Brands	---	132
Crestar Energy	(101)	--
Sale of assets	(73)	(57)
Sale of securities	34	55
Total	$(652)	$ 40

[6]Deduction for interest capitalized by Dow.

(b) The following table shows the price-earnings ratios
     (and calculations) for duPont, Dow, and ICI at December
     31, 1994 using:

     • Reported net income
     • Net income before nonrecurring items
     • Earnings power

(Earnings and number of shares in millions)

	DuPont	ICI	Dow
Earnings (Ex. 17C1S-4)			
Reported	$ 2,727	£ 188	$ 938
Adjusted	2,488	309	956
Normalized	2,260	198	1,054
Average shares	680	723	276.1
EPS			
Reported	$ 4.00	26 p	$ 3.40
Adjusted	$ 3.65	43 p	$ 3.46
Normalized	$ 3.32	27 p	$ 3.82
Price/share	$ 56.125	£ 7.49	$ 67.25
Price-earnings ratio			
Reported	14.03	28.80	19.80
Adjusted	15.38	17.53	19.42
Normalized	16.89	27.35	17.62

(c)   The normalization process applied in Exhibit 17C1S-4
      does not completely account for the following
      differences:

      i.   DuPont, ICI, and Dow operate in many foreign
           countries. Changes in exchange rates and exposures
           affect reported results. Inadequate disclosures
           prevent adjustment for these differences.

      ii. The three firms use different accounting methods,
           assumptions, and estimates for inventory costs,
           depreciation expense, amortization or the write-
           off of goodwill, capitalization of interest
           expense, benefit plans, income taxes, investments
           in affiliates, off-balance-sheet financing
           methods, and contingencies.

      iii. The timing, measurement, and recognition of
           impairments of assets and provisions for
           restructuring activities may differ across the
           companies.

(d)   (i)   Effect of Zeneca's demerger on:

            Trend of ICI's sales and net income

		1993	1994	Change
Sales				
Including Zeneca in 1993	£	10,632	£9,189	− 13.6%
Excluding Zeneca in 1993 & 1994	£	8,430	£9,189	9.0%
Net Income before exceptional items		1993	1994	Change
Including Zeneca in 1993	£	129	£ 188	46%
Excluding Zeneca in 1993 & 1994	£	25	£ 188	652%
Net Income		1993	1994	Change
Including Zeneca in 1993	£	245	£ 270	10.2%
Excluding Zeneca in 1993 & 1994	£	141	£ 270	91.5%

            The subtraction of Zeneca sales and net income (before
            and after exceptional items) from continuing operations
            provides the increase in sales and net income. Note
            that the actual or reported changes (a decrease of
            13.6% in Sales, increase of 46% in net income before
            exceptional items, and an increase of 10.2% in net
            income) would be reported in computerized databases.
            However, since the 1994 data do not include Zeneca,
            this comparison is incorrect.

(ii) Earnings power of the firm.

Exhibit 17C1S-4 shows an increase in earnings power of 67%, from £118 million in 1993 to £198 in 1994.

Exhibit 17C1S-4A

	ICI	
	1993	**1994**
Reported net income	£ 25	£ 188
Items reported pretax		
Restructuring provisions[3]	94	106
Loss(gain) on asset sales[5]	(4)	74
Subtotal	115	180
Tax offset	(38)	(59)
Net effect	77	121
Normalized net income		
before nonrecurring items	£ 102	£ 309
Percentage difference	308%	64.4%
Adjustment	(99)	(99)
Earnings power	£ 3	£ 210
Percentage difference	-88%	11.7%

Exhibit 17C1S-4A depicts the computation of earnings power in 1993 excluding Zeneca. Earnings power rises from £ 3 to £ 210, an increase of 7000%! We do not have any information about growth contributed by Zeneca. However, sales, net income, and earnings power of continuing operations show substantial increases.

5. (a) Exhibit 17C1S-5 contains the 1993 and 1994 free cash
        flow for ICI and Dow. No adjustments were made for
        restructuring charges, severance payments, and other
        business rationalization activities reported by both
        firms as those were neither unusual nor infrequent. For
        Dow, the costs of breast implant litigation (see
        Footnote Q, p.1163) should be regarded as nonrecurring
        and an adjustment is required. However, the firm does
        not separately report the liability and it is not clear
        whether the post-tax charges of $192 million in 1993
        and $70 million in 1994 are net of expected insurance
        recoveries. No adjustment has been made for the
        potential cash consequences of this litigation.

    (b) Both ICI and Dow reported declines in free cash flow
        (CFO plus CFI) and free cash flow after dividends from
        1993 to 1994. Reported CFI is distorted by significant
        asset sales by both companies. In addition, CFI
        reported by ICI is significantly distorted by payments
        from the demerged unit, Zeneca. Adjusted CFO declines
        by 13.7%, a greater decline than reported CFO because
        after tax interest fell from 1993 to 1994. The adjusted
        free cash flow after dividend payments is lower for
        ICI. However, the trend is in the opposite direction;
        it increased 72% from £ 134 in 1993 to £ 231 in 1994
        due to a significant drop (23%) in capital
        expenditures. ICI has generated substantial free cash
        flow augmented by proceeds from asset sales that is
        available for expansion.

        Dow reports a substantial increase in CFO (25%) and
        slightly lower (21%) increase in adjusted CFO. The
        difference in interest payments is minor. The firm
        reports a much higher difference in adjusted free cash
        flow (312% from $213 in 1993 to $878 in 1994) also due
        to a significant drop (16%) in capital expenditures.
        Whether these increases in free cash flow can be
        sustained by Dow and ICI depends on expected CFO and
        required capital expenditures.

Exhibit 17C1S-5
1993 and 1994 Free Cash Flow.
ICI (£ millions) and Dow ($ millions)

	ICI		DOW	
As Reported	*1993*	*1994*	*1993*	*1994*
Cash & equivalents, Jan 1	£ (56)	£ 514	$ 375	$ 407
Cash & equivalents, Dec 31	514	1,040	407	569
Δ in cash & equivalents	£ 570	£ 526	$ 32	$ 162
Cash from operations (CFO)	£ 787	£ 713	$ 2,093	$ 2,635
Cash from investments (CFI)	447	293	(622)	(1,195)
Cash from financing (CFF)	(662)	(444)	(1,437)	(1,277)
Effect of exchange rate changes	(2)	(36)	(2)	(1)
Δ in cash & equivalents	£ 570	£ 526	$ 32	$ 162
Free cash flow[1]	£ 1,234	£1,006	$ 1,471	$ 1,440
Dividends paid[2]	(338)	(231)	(917)	(1,004)
Free cash flow after dividends	£ 896	£ 775	$ 554	$ 436
Adjustments				
Interest paid[3]	£ 254	£ 182	$ 677	$ 642
Less: income tax offset[4]	(84)	(60)	(237)	(212)
After-tax interest paid	£ 170	£ 122	$ 440	$ 430
Capital expenditures[5]	£ (485)	£ (373)	$(1,414)	$(1,183)
After Adjustment				
CFO[6]	£ 957	£ 835	$ 2,533	$ 3,065
CFI	447	293	(622)	(1,195)
CFF[7]	(832)	(566)	(1,877)	(1,707)
Effect of exchange rate changes	(2)	(36)	(2)	(1)
Δ in cash & equivalents	£ 570	£ 526	$ 32	$ 162
Free cash flow[8]	£ 472	£ 462	$ 1,190	$ 1,882
Dividends paid[2]	(338)	(231)	(917)	(1,004)
Free cash flow after dividends	£ 134	£ 231	$ 213	$ 878

[1] CFO plus CFI
[2] Includes distributions to minority interests.
[3] Interest paid for ICI; Interest paid plus capitalized for Dow.
[4] 33% of interest paid for ICI; 35% of interest paid for Dow.
[5] From statement of cash flows
[6] Reported CFO plus after-tax interest
[7] Reported CFF minus after-tax interest
[8] Adjusted CFO plus capital expenditures

6. (a) Exhibit 17C1S-6 shows the required ratios based on both the 1994 reported and adjusted (balance sheet) data.

   (b) (i) *ICI*: Because the firm uses FIFO for inventories, there is no change in the inventory turnover ratio. The total asset turnover declines due to various adjustments to assets. The current ratio declines because of the adjustment for short term debt previously reported as a component of cash equivalents.

      Leverage ratios are higher and return on assets and return on capital ratios are lower than reported because of the adjustments that increased debt and total assets. Return on equity improves as the current cost adjustments decrease the equity.

      Dow: The inventory turnover declines because of the addition of the LIFO reserve. The total assets turnover ratio improves and the liquidity ratio declines due to the decreases in current and long-term assets.

      Adjusted solvency ratios suggest significantly higher leverage after the addition of operating leases and other off-balance sheet financing activities. All return ratios improve because of significant declines in the denominators. However, this change is misleading; its primary cause is the writeoff of goodwill which lowers the asset and capital base. This conflict reflects a basic dilemma discussed elsewhere in the text: goodwill should be eliminated in computing current cost but it reflects excess payments made in acquisitions and its elimination overstates post-acquisition returns.

      In general, the adjusted ratios better reflect risk-return relationships because they are based on more comprehensive and current measures of resources and obligations.

Exhibit 17C1S-6
Adjusted Financial Ratios, Year ended December 31, 1994
(ICI data in £ millions; Dow data in $ millions)

	ICI		DOW	
	Reported	*Adjusted*	*Reported*	*Adjusted*
Activity				
Inventory turnover	5.37	5.37	5.05	4.67
Number of days	68	68	72	78
Total asset turnover	1.00	0.92	0.77	0.85
Liquidity				
Current ratio	1.91	1.86	1.31	1.28
Solvency				
Debt-to-equity	0.49	0.78	0.61	1.50
Debt-to-total-capital	0.33	0.44	0.38	0.63
Profitability				
Return on assets	4.53	4.08	7.88	8.76
Return on total capital	6.74	6.31	11.85	14.05
Return on equity	4.61	5.18	8.73	15.30

7. Value added can be defined as the difference between the value of a company's outputs and that of its inputs. ICI reports the sources and disposal of value added in footnote 36 (page 1191 of the text).

That statement reports that ICI created value added as follows:

	1993		1994	
	£ Millions	% total	£ Millions	% total
Sales	8,430	100.0%	9,189	100.0%
Less: inputs	(6,111)	-72.5%	(6,556)	-71.3%
Gross value added	2,319	27.5%	2,633	28.7%
Less: employee costs	(1,742)	-20.7%	(1,791)	-19.5%
Operating value added	577	6.8%	842	9.2%

We define gross value added as sales less materials and services, and operating value added as gross value added less employee costs. Note that the 1993 data exclude discontinued operations, making the two years comparable.

These data reveal that:

- While ICI's 1994 sales increased 9%, gross value added rose nearly 14% and operating value added 46%. The value added performance trailed that of reported income For example, EBIT rose 63% from £370 to £602 million.

- Value added "margins" rose in 1994; the portion of ICI sales representing value added increased. Both inputs and employee costs declined as a percentage of sales. Again, this performance mirrored that of profit margins.

While the value added data provide little additional information in this case, they do offer another perspective on ICI's performance. Over longer time periods, they should enable financial analysts to obtain a better understanding of changes in profitability. In addition, value added data may yield insights into performance relative to other firms whose value added margins differ.

Case 17-2 Solution

Estimated solution time is four to five hours.

1. Exhibit 17CS-1 (p.17C2-2) shows the 1995 current cost
   balance sheet for ALCOA. The footnotes (p.17C2-3)
   explain each adjustment. These adjustments are of
   several types:

   i. Replacement of historical cost with current cost
      or fair value (inventories and debt).

   ii. Elimination of assets and liabilities that have no
       predictive value (intangible assets and deferred
       income tax).
       The deferred tax adjustment of $35.8 million is
       computed as follows:

Net deferred tax asset (Note R)	$394.0 million
Current deferred tax asset	$ 244.8 million
Long-term deferred tax asset	493.6
Long-term deferred tax liability	(308.6)
Net identifiable adjustments	$ 429.8 million

       The difference between these two amounts ($394.0 –
       $429.8 = $35.8 is assumed to be included in
       "income and other tax" in current liabilities.

   iii. Capitalization of off-balance-sheet obligations
        (leases). We assume an interest rate of 8.5%. The
        data needed to accurately compute the effective
        interest rate on Alcoa debt is not provided.

   iv. Replacement of employee benefit plan accruals with
       actual plan status. There are two adjustments:

       Pension Plan:

Accrued pension cost	$ 400.2 million
Excess of PBO over plan assets	273.3
Liability overstated by	$ 126.9 million
The adjustment has two components:	
Minimum liability (in equity)	$ 9.3 million
Adjust "postretirement benefits"	117.6
Total adjustment	$ 126.9 million

Alcoa Current Cost Balance Sheet

NOTES		Reported	Adjustments	Current Cost
	ASSETS	12/31/1995 ($millions)		
(1)	Inventories	$ 1,418.4	$ 802.1	$ 2,220.5
(2)	Deferred income tax	244.8	(244.8)	-
	Other current assets	3,078.5	-	3,078.5
	Total current assets	$ 4,741.7	$ 557.3	$ 5,299.0
(3)	Property (net)	$ 6,929.7	$ 155.0	$ 7,084.7
(4)	Intangibles	600.0	(600.0)	-
(2)	Deferred income tax	493.6	(493.6)	-
	Other assets	878.4	-	878.4
	TOTAL ASSETS	$ 13,643.4	$ (381.3)	$ 13,262.1
	LIABILITIES			
	Short-term debt	$ 693.2		$ 693.2
(2)	Income and other tax	304.7	(35.8)	268.9
	Other current liabilities	1,654.3	-	1,654.3
	Total current liabilities	$ 2,652.2	$ (35.8)	$ 2,616.4
(3)(5)	Long-term debt	1,215.5	155.0	1,370.5
(6)(7)	Postretirement benefits	1,827.3	(601.5)	1,225.8
	Deferred hedging gains	466.3		466.3
	Other liabilities	1,119.4		1,119.4
(2)	Deferred income tax	308.6	(308.6)	-
	TOTAL LIABILITIES	$ 7,589.3	$ (790.9)	$ 6,798.4
				-
	Minority interest	1,609.4		1,609.4
	Preferred stock	55.8		55.8
	Common stock	178.9		178.9
	Additional capital	637.1		637.1
	Translation adjustment	(79.0)		(79.0)
	Retained earnings	3,800.1		3,800.1
(6)	Minimum pension liability	(9.3)	9.3	-
(8)	Current value adjustments		400.3	400.3
	Treasury stock	(138.9)	-	(138.9)
	TOTAL EQUITY	$ 6,054.1	$ 409.6	$ 6,463.7
				-
	TOTAL EQUITIES	$ 13,643.4	$ (381.3)	$ 13,262.1

(1) Add LIFO reserve
(2) Eliminate deferred tax assets and liabilities
(3) Add capitalized operating leases (see below)
(4) Eliminate intangible assets
(5) Restate long-term debt to fair value
(6) Reduce of accrued pension liability (including
    minimum liability) to excess of PBO over assets.
(7) Reduce accrued cost to excess of APBO over assets.
(8) Sum of asset and liability adjustments to fair value.

Capitalization of Operating Leases
$ millions

Year	Payment	Present Value
1996	$ 46.7	$ 43.0
1997	40.5	34.4
1998	27.7	21.7
1999	22.4	16.1
2000	24.9	16.5
2001	19.8	12.1
2002	19.8	11.2
Total	$ 201.8	$ 155.0

Postretirement Benefits:

Accrued postretirement benefits	$1,920.7 million
Excess of APBO over plan assets	1,436.8
Liability overstated by	$ 483.9 million

The total adjustment to the "postretirement benefit liability" is, therefore $601.5 million ($117.6 + $483.9).

Each of these adjustments moves the balance sheet closer to current cost. The major adjustment *not made* is for property. The text discusses the difficulty of adjusting operating assets to current value on pages 420-423 and 939-940. Minority interest is also unadjusted given the lack of data about the current cost of affiliate assets and liabilities.

2.   (a)   (i)   **Reported BVPS = $24.89** (Exhibit 17C-3)

From this amount, we compute the approximate number of shares at year end:

(Total equity - preferred)/BVPS
($4,444.7 - $55.8) / $24.89
$4,388.9/$24.89 = 176.33 million shares

Adjusted BVPS = Adjusted equity/# shares
= Equity - preferred - minority interest / # shares

= $6,463.7 - $55.8 - $1,609.4)/176.33
= $4,798.5/176.33 = **$27.21**

Note that year-end shares, not average shares, should be used to compute BVPS. While these numbers are similar for Alcoa, they may be quite different when firms issue or retire a significant number of shares during the year.

Exhibit 17CS2-2

Alcoa Normalized Income Statement
1991-1995 ($millions)

	1991	1992	1993	1994	1995	Total
Adjustments:						
Special items	$(330.9)	$(251.6)	$(150.8)	$(79.7)	$(16.2)	$(829.2)
Capital gain				400.2		400.2
Subtotal	(330.9)	(251.6)	(150.8)	320.5	(16.2)	(429.0)
Less income tax	115.8	88.1	52.8	(112.2)	5.7	150.2
Aftertax adjustment	$(215.1)	$(163.5)	$(98.0)	$208.3	$(10.5)	$(278.9)
Income before extraordinary	62.7	22.4	4.8	443.1	790.5	1,323.5
Aftertax adjustment	215.1	163.5	98.0	(208.3)	10.5	278.9
Amortized adjustment	(55.8)	(55.8)	(55.8)	(55.8)	(55.8)	(278.9)
Normalized income	$222.0	$130.2	$47.1	$179.0	$745.3	$1,323.5
Normalized EPS	$1.31	$0.76	$0.27	$1.01	$4.19	$7.53
Reported EPS	$0.36	$(6.70)	$0.02	$2.10	$4.43	$0.21
Before extraordinary	0.36	0.13	0.02	2.49	4.43	7.43

17C2-5

(ii) **Reported debt/equity** = ($693.2 + $1.213.5) / $6,054.1 = $1,906.7/$6,054.1 = **0.31**

Note that neither preferred equity nor minority interest is subtracted from equity.

Adjusted debt/equity = ($693.2 + $1.370.5/ $6,463.7 = $2,063.7/$6,463.7 = **0.32**

(b) **Price to reported BVPS** = $52.875/$24.89 = **2.12**
Price to adjusted BVPS = $52.875/$27.21 = **1.94**

3.   (a)   Exhibit 17CS2-2 (p.17C2-5) shows a normalized income statement for Alcoa for 1991 to 1995. The adjustments are the special items shown in Exhibit 17C-3 as well as the capital gain identified at the beginning of Exhibit 17C-2.

The pretax items for each year are adjusted by the estimated income tax expense (using a 35% tax rate) to estimate aftertax unusual items.

For each year, income before extraordinary items is adjusted to remove special items originating in that year. In addition, the total unusual items over the five year period ($278.9 million aftertax) is amortized equally to each year. The net result of these two adjustments is normalized EPS.

(b)   December 31, 1995 price-earnings ratio (PER) equals $52.875 [part 2(b)] divided by the appropriate EPS amount:

Reported: $52.875/$4.43 =   **11.9**
Normalized: $52.875/$4.19 =   **12.6**
Averaged: $52.875/($7.53/5) =   **35.1**

(c)   The reported PER is least useful as reported EPS contains special items. However, many market participants use that ratio so that it cannot be completely ignored.

The Normalized PER is based on a better measure of 1995 earnings as it excludes special items but includes a "normal" amount of such items. This ratio should provide the best measure of the valuation of Alcoa shares. This ratio, however, is only as good as the adjustment process. If significant special items are undisclosed or if the recent period items are unusually large or small, this ratio is misstated.

Using average EPS has the advantage of capturing cyclical variations in income as well as the erratic nature of special items. The disadvantage is that market participants are usually focused on future EPS rather than prior year amounts.

(d)   Return on total capital = EBIT/debt plus equity, where EBIT = net income + income tax expense + interest expense + minority interest.

Reported ROTC = $1,590/$7,962.8 =   **20.0%**
Adjusted ROTC = $1,590/$8,727.4 =   **18.2%**

Averaged ROTC cannot be computed as short-term debt and other prior year adjustment data are not provided. However the "return on average invested capital" data in Exhibit 17C-3 make it clear that 1995 returns were much higher than those for the five year period.

Return on equity = Net income + minority interest/equity

Reported ROE = $790.5+$233.8/$6,054.1 =   **16.9%**
Adjusted ROE = $745.3+$233.8/$6,463.7 =   **15.1%**
Averaged ROE = $264.7+$178.1/$4,113.9 =   **10.8**

Note that the average ROE uses five year averages for all three data inputs.

(e)   Adjusted returns, based on normalized income, is the best comparative measure. It replaces the effect of special items on the current year with a "normal" amount. The averaged return data might be useful, however, for comparing firms within the same industry, facing the same economic cycle.

4. The price data are useful for the analysis of Alcoa in several respects:

    1. Changes in market prices generally have a significant effect on profitability. While some input prices (e.g. aluminum bearing ores) may be related to output prices, most are not. Thus higher prices tend to increase profitability. It is not coincidental that Alcoa's 1995 earnings were the highest of the years shown; prices were also highest. Thus, earnings estimates for Alcoa for future years must be based on estimates of aluminum prices.

    2. However, not all firms are equally sensitive to price changes. Alcoa's realized price was below the market average in 1994 and 1995, but above that average in prior years. This low sensitivity may indicate that Alcoa sells some output under fixed price contracts, or that some product lines (e.g. consumer products) are not price-sensitive. The reasons for this low sensitivity and their future impact are important inputs for earnings estimates.

    3. Alcoa's sensitivity to aluminum prices can be measured by the ratio of physical output to shares outstanding, using either shipments or capacity. As shipments (output) may vary with prices, some judgment is required.

Case 17-3 Solution

Estimated solution time is five to six hours.

Overview: This case shows how adjustments facilitate financial analysis of a cyclical firm. The analysis covers balance sheet adjustments, normalization of income, and cash flow analysis.

1. Exhibits 17CS-3 A and B (p. 17C3-2 and 4, respectively) show the 1995 and 1994 current cost balance sheets for Castle. The footnotes on page 17CS-3 explain each adjustment, including:

    i. Replacement of historical cost with current cost of inventories (add LIFO reserve).

    ii. Elimination of assets and liabilities that have no predictive value.Goodwill is eliminated for both years. The deferred tax liability for inventories (due to differences between the form of LIFO used for tax and financial reporting) has been retained as its volatility suggests that the likelihood of reversal is high.

    Note (3) reports Castle's 1996 net deferred tax liability of $12,165; $2,799 relates to inventories. The net amount of $9,366 is the adjustment (1994: $10,471 - $3,991 = $6,480).

    iii. Capitalization of off-balance-sheet obligations (leases). 1995 calculations are shown in on page 17CS3-3. For 1994, we estimate a present value of $15,000, noting that 1995 sale and leasebacks total more than $4,000 [note 5(d)].

    iv. Replacement of employee benefit plan accruals with actual plan status. The 1995 accrued pension cost is eliminated and a liability equal to the plan status is created. The 1994 accrued pension cost is reduced to the plan status.

    For both years, the accrued postretirement benefit cost is increased to reflect unrecognized amounts.

    Each adjustment moves the balance sheet closer to current cost. The major adjustment *not made* is for property. The text discusses the difficulty of adjusting operating assets to current value on pages 420-423 and 939-940.

A.M. CASTLE
Adjusted Balance Sheet and Capitalization Table
December 31, 1995 ($ thousands)

	Reported	Adjustment	Adjusted
ASSETS			
Inventories[1]	$ 97,766	$ 66,300	$ 164,066
Other current assets	64,075	-	64,075
Total current assets	$ 161,841	$ 66,300	$ 228,141
Property (net)[2]	44,463	19,860	64,323
Other assets[3,4]	16,245	(10,627)	5,618
TOTAL ASSETS	$ 222,549	$ 75,533	$ 298,082
LIABILITIES			
Current debt	$ 2,756	$ -	$ 2,756
Current income tax	958	-	958
Other current liabilities	73,745	-	73,745
Total current liabilities	$ 77,459	$ -	$ 77,459
Long-term debt[2]	28,015	19,860	47,875
Deferred income tax[5]	10,893	(9,366)	1,527
Postretirement benefits[6,7]	2,819	2,887	5,706
TOTAL LIABILITIES	$ 119,186	$ 13,381	$ 132,567
Stockholders' equity[8]	103,363	62,152	165,515
TOTAL LIABILITIES AND EQUITY	$ 222,549	$ 75,533	$ 298,082
# Shares outstanding	11,156	11,156	11,156
Book value per share	9.27	5.57	14.84
Total debt	$ 30,771	$ 19,860	$ 50,631
Total capital	134,134	82,012	216,146
Total debt-to-equity	29.8%		30.6%
Total debt to total capital	22.9%		23.4%

A.M. CASTLE
Footnotes to Adjusted Balance Sheet

[1] Add LIFO reserve (Exhibit 17C-4).
[2] Add capitalized operating leases (see below).
[3] Eliminate unamortized goodwill ($790 both years).
[4] Eliminate 1995 pension asset; 1994 asset reduced.
[5] Eliminate deferred tax except for inventories (see text).
[6] Establish liability for excess of 1995 PBO over pension assets.
[7] Increase postretirement liability by unrecognized amounts.
[8] Asset revaluations less liability revaluations.

Present Value of Leases

	1995	
	Payments	PV
1996	$ 5,888	$5,434
1997	5,437	4,631
1998	4,239	3,333
1999	3,483	2,527
2000	2,568	1,720
2001	1,864	1,152
2002	1,863	1,063
Total	$ 25,342	$19,860

Interest expense	$ 3,053
Average debt	36,557
Average interest rate	8.35%

A.M.CASTLE
Adjusted Balance Sheet
12/31/1994 ($ thousands)

	Reported	Adjustment	Adjusted
ASSETS			
Inventories[1]	$ 98,215	$ 51,700	$ 149,915
Other current assets	59,868	-	59,868
Total current assets	$ 158,083	$ 51,700	$ 209,783
Property (net)[2]	41,190	15,000	56,190
Other assets[3,4]	13,854	(4,882)	8,972
TOTAL ASSETS	$ 213,127	$ 61,818	$ 274,945
LIABILITIES			
Current debt	$ 3,831	$ -	$ 3,831
Current income tax	2,321	-	2,321
Other current liabilities	75,986	-	75,986
Total current liabilities	$ 82,138	$ -	$ 82,138
Long-term debt[2]	38,531	15,000	53,531
Deferred income tax[5]	7,772	(6,480)	1,292
Postretirement benefits[6,7]	2,525	86	2,611
TOTAL LIABILITIES	$ 130,966	$ 8,606	$ 139,572
Stockholders' equity[8]	82,161	53,212	135,373
TOTAL LIABILITIES AND EQUITY	$ 213,127	$ 61,818	$ 274,945
# Shares outstanding	11,080	11,080	11,080
Book value per share	$ 7.42	$ 4.80	$ 12.22
Total debt	$ 42,362	$ 15,000	$ 57,362
Total capital	124,523	68,212	192,735
Total debt-to-equity	51.6%		42.4%
Total debt to total capital	34.0%		29.8%

2.   Capitalization tables are shown within Exhibits 17CS-3 A and B.

3.   (a) Calculations are shown within Exhibits 17CS-3 A and B.

Note that year-end shares, not average shares, should be used to compute BVPS. While the 1995 numbers are identical for Castle, they may be quite different when firms issue or retire a significant number of shares during the year.

(b) (i) Current cost adjustments increase book value per share by 60%, from $9.27 to $14.84. The adjustment of inventory to current cost is the major factor; all other adjustments largely offset.

(ii) Reported BVPS grew 25% in 1995, reflecting the increase in retained earnings. Adjusted BVPS rose by only 21% from the higher adjusted level. While the 1995 current cost adjustment exceeded the 1994 adjustment, the increase was only 16%.

(iii) **Price to BVPS:**
1995 reported = $28.125/$ 9.27 = **3.03**
1995 adjusted = $28.125/$14.84 = **1.90**

1994 reported = $13.875/$ 7.42 = **1.87**
1995 adjusted = $13.875/$12.22 = **1.14**

Ratios are lower in both years after adjustment. Investors seeking companies whose shares sell at low P/BVPS ratios would have found Castle attractive in 1994 only if adjusted data were used. 1995 ratio significantly higher both before and after adjustment.

(iv) The 1995 debt-to-equity ratio (Exhibit 17CS-3A) is higher after adjustment; debt increases by a greater percentage than equity. The 1994 ratio, however, declines after adjustment.

4. (a) Exhibit 17CS-4 (p.17CS3-7) shows a normalized income statement for Castle for 1991 to 1995. There are no identified special items. (A very small cumulative effect of accounting change in 1992 was ignored for simplicity.)

    However, Castle's earnings are highly cyclical, and rose each year as the U.S. economy expanded. To compute earnings power, we must make some adjustment for that cyclicality.

    The adjustment made in the exhibit uses the ratio of pretax income to sales over the entire five year period:

    $87,706/$$2,498,856 = 3.5%

    The adjusted pretax amounts equal the sales for that year multiplied by 3.5%. The average 40% tax rate for the five year period ($34,978/$87,706) is used to compute net income.

    (b) December 31, 1995 price-earnings ratios:

    (i)   **Reported:** $28.125/$2.40 =   **11.7**
    (ii) **Same as (i)**
    (iii) **Normalized:** $28.125/$1.18 =   **23.8**

    (c) Cyclical normalization, while necessary for meaningful valuation, is difficult. Only in retrospect can the analyst identify the beginning and end of a complete cycle. One the cycle is identified, different normalization methods can be used. In addition to the one demonstrated here, normalization can be based on EBIT/sales, return on total capital, or profit per used of output.

        An additional difficulty with the use of cyclically normalized data is that market participants are usually focused on near term EPS. Such data is most useful when a cyclical turn can be forecast (such turns usually surprise the market).

A.M. CASTLE
Normalization of income statement
1991-1995 ($thousands)

	1991	1992	1993	1994	1995
Net sales	$436,441	$423,913	$474,108	$536,568	$627,826
Cost of material sold	(331,093)	(313,683)	(351,823)	(391,386)	(454,428)
Gross profit	$105,348	$110,230	$122,285	$145,182	$173,398
Operating expenses	(92,848)	(94,944)	(102,089)	(112,070)	(121,652)
Depreciation	(5,273)	(4,865)	(4,784)	(4,603)	(4,459)
Operating income	$ 7,227	$ 10,421	$ 15,412	$ 28,509	$ 47,287
Interest expense	(6,848)	(4,333)	(3,801)	(3,215)	(2,953)
Pretax income	$ 379	$ 6,088	$ 11,611	$ 25,294	$ 44,334
Income tax expense	(178)	(2,696)	(4,712)	(9,884)	(17,508)
Net income	$ 201	$ 3,392	$ 6,899	$ 15,410	$ 26,826
Shares outstanding	10,914	10,914	10,917	11,080	11,156
Earnings per share	$ 0.02	$ 0.31	$ 0.63	$ 1.39	$ 2.40
Tons sold (000)	234	249	308	338	343
Pretax income/Sales	0.09%	1.44%	2.45%	4.71%	7.06%
Adjusted pretax income	$ 15,275	$ 14,837	$ 16,594	$ 18,780	$ 21,974
Adjusted income tax	(6,110)	(5,935)	(6,638)	(7,512)	(8,790)
Adjusted net income	$ 9,165	$ 8,902	$ 9,956	$ 11,268	$ 13,184
Adjusted EPS	$ 0.84	$ 0.82	$ 0.91	$ 1.02	$ 1.18

5. (a) Box 3-2, on pages 113-4 of the text, contains cash flow data for the 1987 to 1991 period and analysis of that data. Despite one overlapping year (1991), the totals are quite different:

	1987-91	1991-95
Cash from operations	$ 30,746	$ 93,331
Capital expenditures	(37,497)	(29,428)
Property sales	8,111	16,610
Acquisitions	(2,529)	0
Cash from investment	$(31,915)	$(12,818)
Less: reclassification	(5,317)	(8,740)
Adjusted CFI	**$(37,232)**	**$(21,558)**
Net change in debt	18,319	(61,961)
Net issue of equity	332	1,208
Dividends paid	(19,980)	(19,395)
Cash from financing	$ (1,329)	$(80,148)
Plus: reclassification	5,317	8,740
Adjusted CFF	**$ 3,988**	**$(71,408)**
Net change in cash	**$ (2,498)**	**$ 365**

Note the reclassification of equipment sold and leased back in 1993 to 1995 (Exhibit 17C-5, note 5(d)). While this adjustment is incomplete (there were sales in 1991 and 1992 as well) it captures most of the cash effect of those transactions.

The 1991 to 1995 data are quite different from those for the five years ended 1991. Cash from operations is nearly four times that of the earlier period. Cash for investment, however, declined sharply. As a result, Castle repaid much of its debt. However dividends paid showed little change.

1991 to 1995 were years of substantial prosperity for Castle. Net income rose to nearly $27 million in 1995 from break-even in 1991; the previous cyclical earnings peak was $13.7 million in 1988.

Despite rising earnings, CFO was positive every year, in contrast to negative CFO in the previous peak earnings year of 1988. Clearly Castle improved its working capital management. Even in 1993 and 1995, when operating working capital increased, CFO remained positive.

CFI, however, fell from the 1987 to 1991 period, despite ample availability of funds. Apparently Castle lacked attractive investment opportunities. Free cash flow (CFO less CFI) exceeded $80 million in 1991 to 1995; FCF was $(7.5) million for the five years ended 1991.

What use did Castle make of this liquidity? While dividends increased in 1995, they had declined in 1992 and 1993 when net income was low; over the five year period there was no increase from the five years ended 1991. The excess liquidity was used to reduce debt by $62 million.

(b)   In retrospect, Castle was creating financial slack during the five years ended 1995. In 1996, when the company started to diversify, Castle started using this built up slack.

Exhibit 17CS-5
A.M.CASTLE
1995 Financial Ratios

		Reported	Adjusted
ACTIVITY			
(i)	Inventory turnover	4.64	2.89
(ii)	Fixed asset turnover	14.66	10.42
(iii)	Total asset turnover	2.88	2.19
LIQUIDITY			
(iv)	Current ratio	2.09	2.95
PROFITABILITY			
(v)	Return-on-assets	21.7%	8.7%
(vi)	Return-on-total-capital	36.6%	12.2%
(vii)	Return-on-equity	14.5%	4.4%

6. (a) Exhibit 17CS-5 (p.17CS3-9) contains 1995 ratios based on both reported and adjusted data. The following points are worthy of mention:

(i) Adjusted inventory turnover uses reported COGS but adjusted inventory (current cost method).

(v) and (vi) return ratios contain EBIT in the numerator. Adjusted EBIT of $24,927 was computed as follows:

Pretax income	$ 21,974	Exhibit 17CS-4
Interest expense	2,953	Exhibit 17CS-4
Adjusted EBIT	$ 24,927	

For simplicity, no adjustment was made for the interest factor in lease payments, or for cyclical variation in debt. (b) The adjusted ratios are quite different, mostly lower. Turnover ratios are reduced by including the current cost of assets in the denominator; the numerators are unchanged.

The current ratio, however, improves as inventory is increased to its current cost.

Profitability ratios decline sharply as numerators decline and denominators increase. Using "cyclically normalized" rather than 1995 income and equity at current cost reduces the high 1995 returns to mediocre levels.

(c) Turnover and liquidity ratios are more informative when current costs are substituted for historic ones. Adjusted ratios also facilitate comparisons of firms using different accounting methods (e.g. LIFO/FIFO).

Profitability analysis of cyclical firms requires consideration of operations over the entire business cycle. Such companies typically earn very high returns at cyclical peaks but very low returns (or negative ones) at troughs. To evaluate the earning power of such firms requires normalization. Analysts should compare earnings power with the current cost of net assets that generate those earnings.

Case 17-4 - Solution

Estimated length of time to solve this case is 2 to 2½ hrs.

Introduction:
Beginning in Chapter 3 and throughout the book we have shown that the SoCF can be affected by the manner in which cash flows are classified into the various categories - operating, investment and financing. Using Deere as an example, this case demonstrates the effects of such classifications on CFO, CFI, CFF and Free Cash Flows.

Before starting the case it may be worthwhile to review a simple example of a sale generating a credit receivable and how Deere would account for it.

Example: Deere sells a customer equipment for $20,000. No cash is paid at the time of the sale; rather Deere provides the customer a five-year installment (interest bearing) loan. Deere then securitizes $5,000 of the loan by selling it to a financing institution with recourse (equivalent to at least the rate of bad debt experience) and Deere continue to process the loan.
If we analyze the events to this point:
- no cash was received from the customer
- the securitization of the receivable is in effect a loan (as argued in Chapter 11).
- the only cash flow is a $5,000 financing inflow.

Assume now that the customer pays $1,000 of the securitized credit receivable.
- That $1,000 is the first $1,000 received from a customer and as such is cash from operations.
- When Deere "passes" it through to the financing institution, it is effectively repaying a portion of the loan.
- ***The net effect of the two transactions is still a cash increase of $5000 which should be treated as CFO = $1,000 and CFF = $4,000***

Deere reports the %5,000 increase in cash as resulting from:
Cash from operations   **$20,000**
Cash from investment:
    Cost of acquiring credit receivable   ($20,000)
    Proceeds from sale of credit receivable <u>$5,000</u>   **(15,000)**
          Change in Cash $5,000

They treat the sale as if they received the cash from the customer immediately[1] (CFO) and then granted the customer a $20,000 loan (CFI). The pass-through of $1,000 is not wxplicitly recognized.

To adjust Deere's reported amounts to the "reality" of having received a $5,000 loan and repaying $1,000 of it from $1,000 generated by CFO, the following adjustments must be made to the reported data.

	CFO	CFI	CFF
Cash flows as reported	$ 20,000	$(15,000)	-
Adjustments:			
Cost of acquiring credit receivables	(20,000)	20,000	
Proceeds from sale of receivables	5,000	(5,000)	
Change in balance of securitized receivables	(4,000)	-	4,000
Adjusted cash flows	$ 1,000	-	$ 4,000

With this background, the analysis done in the case is better understood.

1. (a)

Free Cash Flows 1992-1994

	1992	1993	1994	Total
Cash from operations	$ 358.3	$ 834.1	$ 718.8	$ 1,911.2
Cash from investing	(133.7)	215.0	(1,205.3)	(1,124.0)
Free Cash Flows	$ 224.6	$1,049.1	$ (486.5)	$ 787.2

(b) Overall, FCF indicates strong financial health as the firm is generating positive cash flows after allowing for investment in capital expenditures and other investments. Over the three years on a cumulative basis, free cash flow is positive. Additionally CFO has been positive in each year. The only red flag would seem to be the sharp decline in 1994. However as the decline comes from an increase in investment rather than a decrease in CFO, it perhaps is not as worrisome.

---

[1] Under the indirect method, as the credit receivable is *long-term* the change in that receivable will not be an adjustment to net income.

2.(a) Credit receivables reflect long-term financing which Deere provides its customers. Classifying such transactions as investments distorts the relationship between CFO and CFI. No cash actually changes hands; yet Deere effectively treats such sales as a inflow to CFO and as an outflow of CFI as it "invests" in a long-term loan to its customers. A more appropriate treatment would be to classify credit receivables as any other receivable and changes in such receivables as adjustments to CFO. Changes in credit receivables reflected in CFI are equal to the cost of credit receivables acquired (i.e. new loans) less proceeds from and sales of these receivables.

Change in Credit Receivables reflected in Cash Flow Statement

	1992	1993	1994	Total
Cost of acquiring	$3,460.6	$3,635.1	$4,308.8	$11,404.5
less: Proceeds	(696.7)	(1,148.3)	(561.9)	(2,406.9)
Collections	(3,008.9)	(2,995.5)	(3,012.5)	(9,016.9)
Change	$ (245.0)	$ (508.7)	$ 734.4	$ (19.3)

The impact on CFO however, is not complete until we consider the change in the securitirized receivables. As discussed in Chapter 11, sales of receivables are really borrowings and therefore the true operating cash flow occurs when the sold receivables are collected. Decreases (increases) in these balances reflect increases (decreases) to CFO (outflows) and must be adjusted accordingly. As these sales are really borrowings they should be reflected as an adjustment to CFF.

Changes in Balance of Securitized Receivables

	1991	1992	1993	1994	Total
Balance	$ 242.0	$ 688.0	$ 1,384.0	$ 1,195.0	
Change		446.0	696.0	(189.0)	953.0

Before we consider the impact of the above on CFO, we need also look at operating leases. Similar arguments can be made when the firm "sells" equipment through leases. Changes in these balances need also be CFO. These changes are smaller than the ones computed above.

Changes in Operating Leases

	1992	1993	1994	Total
Cost of acquiring	$ 63.2	$ 106.3	$ 102.5	$ 272.0
less Collections	43.9	46.5	49.2	139.6
Change	$ 19.3	$ 59.8	$ 53.3	$ 132.4

(i) Adjusting CFO

	1992	1993	1994	Total
CFO as reported	$358.3	$834.1	$718.8	$ 1,911.2
Adjustments:				
Δ in credit receivables	245.0	508.7	(734.4)	19.3
Δ in securitized receivables	(446.0)	(696.0)	189.0	(953.0)
CFO adjusted for receivables	$157.3	$646.8	$173.4	$ 977.5
Δ in operating leases	(19.3)	(59.8)	(53.3)	(132.4)
CFO adjusted	$138.0	$587.0	$120.1	$ 845.1

(ii) Adjusting CFI

	1992	1993	1994	Total
CFI as reported	$(133.7)	$215.0	$(1,205.3)	$(1,124.0)
Adjustments: Add				
Δ in credit receivables	(245.0)	(508.7)	734.4	(19.3)
Δ in operating leases	19.3	59.8	53.3	132.4
CFI adjusted	$(359.4)	$(233.9)	$ (417.6)	$(1,010.9)

(iii) Adjusting CFF

	1992	1993	1994	Total
CFF as reported	$(285.6)	$(926.1)	$ 390.9	$ (820.8)
Adjustments: Add				
Δ in securitized receivables	446.0	696.0	(189.0)	953.0
CFF adjusted	$ 160.4	$(230.1)	$ 201.9	$ 132.2

Note that CFF outflows of $821 million have been reversed and turned into inflows. The company did not reduce its external financing; rather it needed additional external financing. (see 2(d) and 3 below).

(b) (i) The reported data treat a (long-term) credit sale as if cash was received from operations immediately. The adjusted numbers reflect the actual cash flows generated by Deere and as such are a better indicator of Deere's cash generating ability. In Deere's case, although adjusted CFO remained positive each year, over the three year period, Deere generated $1.1 billion less cash then the amount reported in the SoCF.

(ii) The reported numbers show acquisition of credit receivables as an outflow of CFI. No such transaction took place; rather the "outflow" is an offset to the artificial "inflow" being credited to CFO discussed in

17C4-4

(i). The adjusted data are more reflective of Deere's actual investments. Note that CFI is less volatile and reflects a reasonably steady investment pattern. The reported CFI is volatile as it is distorted by credit sales and the collection of those sales.

(c) For comparison purposes, we repeat the (pre-adjustment) Free cash flows calculated in 1(a)

	1992	1993	1994	Total
FCF pre-adjustments	$ 224.6	$ 1,049.1	$(486.5)	$ 787.2

The adjusted FCF is calculated below.

	1992	1993	1994	Total
CFO adjusted	$138.0	$ 587.0	$ 120.1	$(1,561.8)
CFI adjusted	(359.4)	(233.9)	(417.6)	1,396.0
FCF adjusted	$(221.4)	$ 353.1	$ (297.5)	$ (165.8)

(d) A different picture emerges. Over the three year period, FCF was not a positive of $787 million; but a negative $166 million, a difference of close to $1 billion. The firm required additional financing to "cover" the negative FCF's.

On a trend basis, there was not a sharp decline in 1994 from previous 1992-1993 levels. The 1994 level was in line with 1992; the 1993 FCF was "out-of-line". It should be pointed out that for businesses such as Deere which provide long term financing for customers, FCF numbers such as these are not unusual. The company requires additional financing to maintain growth. However, the analyst needs to know the actual levels of FCF being generated.

3. (a)-(c) The analysis over the full three years as well as the year by year analysis is provided below:

Cash Flow Analysis - Total 1992 - 1994

Adjusted CFO	$ 845.1	Change in debt	$ 17.0
Capital Expenditures	(720.3)	Common stock issued	625.3
FCF	$ 124.8	Change in mkt sec	(241.5)
Dividends	(477.2)	Other	38.3
Acquisitions	(119.8)	Decrease in cash	33.1
Cash requirements	$(472.2)	Cash provided	$ 472.2

Cash Flow Analysis - 1992

Adjusted CFO	$138.0	Change in debt	$324.3
Capital Expenditures	(285.7)	Common stock issued	2.4
FCF	$(147.7)	Change in mkt sec	(94.0)
Dividends	(152.5)	Other [20.3-12.8-.7]	5.8
Acquisitions	-	Decrease in cash	61.7
Cash requirements	$(300.2)	Cash provided	$300.2

Cash Flow Analysis - 1993

Adjusted CFO	$ 587.0	Change in debt	$(650.3)
Capital Expenditures	(206.5)	Common stock issued	586.0
FCF	380.5	Change in mkt sec	(25.6)
Dividends	(152.9)	Other [-1.8-12.9-1.6]	(16.3)
Acquisitions	-	Increase in cash	(121.4)
Cash excess	$ 227.6	Cash used	$(227.6)

Cash Flow Analysis - 1994

Adjusted CFO	$ 120.1	Change in debt	$343.0
Capital Expenditures	(228.1)	Common stock issued	36.9
FCF	$(108.0)	Change in mkt sec	(121.9)
Dividends	(171.8)	Other [52.2-6.2+2.8]	48.8
Acquisitions	(119.8)	Decrease in cash	92.8
Cash requirements	$(399.6)	Cash provided	$399.6

Explanation of calculations:
Adjusted CFO :   as calculated in 1(a)(i)

Most of the items such as: *Capital Expenditures (purchases of property & equipment), Dividends, Acquisitions, Common stock issued* and *change in cash* are directly obtained from the SoCF. (Exhibit 17C-8)

Change in marketable securities is the difference between proceeds of sales and purchases of marketable securities reported in the SoCF

Change in debt is the sum of
- changes in short-term borrowings
- proceeds from long-term borrowings
- principal payments of long-term borrowings
- changes in balance of securitized receivables

The first three are obtainable from the SoCF; the fourth item is included since we treat sales of securitized receivables as financing. The calculations follow:

       1992 =(533.9)+772.0+(359.8)+ 446 = 324.3
       1993 =(1487.1)+687.1-546.3+ 696 = (650.3)
       1994 = 934.2 + 188.5+(590.7)+(189) = 343.0

The definition of FCF used in the earlier part of the case (which deducts all CFI) can be improved upon by removing investment in marketable securities and acquisitions. Deere is not in the securities business. Therefore investment in marketable securities should not be part of its FCF calculation. *Such investments really reflect how excess cash is being held.* Similarly acquisition of new businesses are not part of "normal operating activities" and as such are better removed from the FCF calculation as well.

The analysis in this format is useful as on one side it provides information on the extent to which operations provide cash from the company's normal activities and how this cash (if available) is used for dividends and expansion by acquisition.

When there is a shortfall, the right side explains how Deere financed the shortfall - from borrowings, stock issuance or from drawing down the company's resources i.e. cash and marketable securities. Conversely, when there is an excess (see 1993) it shows how the excess is used.

For Deere, over the three years, we find (as opposed to what was noted earlier in 2(c)) that FCF was positive. However, that excess was not sufficient to fund dividends paid and acquisitions of other businesses. The company needed approximately $472 million. This $472 million was obtained by stock issuances of $625 million. The excess cash raised by the new stock issue went toward increasing the company's resources ; i.e. cash and marketable securities (net change of $241 - $33 = $188).

It is ironic that the cash requirements resulted from dividends paid of $477.2 million. *Without those dividends, FCF were enough to finance the acquisitions. Cash for dividends paid was obtained by stock issuance. Deere raised money from shareholders to pay shareholders !!* -- a practice not immediately justifiable by finance theory.

Chapter 18 - Solutions

Overview:

Problem Length	*Problem #'s*
{S}	*3*
{M}	*1,2,4,6,7,8,9*

Problems 1-3 deal with the takeover of Kraft by Philip Morris. If assigned together, they would require approximately 1½ hrs of work.

Problem 5 is based on (the solution) to Case 17-2. Students should have been assigned that case previously and/or have access to the solutions to that case before attempting this problem.

1. {M} A.

	Before Kraft	**Consolidated**
Pretax interest coverage[1]	10.64X	3.76X
Long-term debt/total capital[2]	28.11%	61.99%
Cash flow/total debt[3]	71.14%	23.14%

[1]   ($4820+$500)/$500   ($4420+$1600)/$1600

[2] $3883/($3883+$9931) $15,778/($15,778+$9675)

[3] $\dfrac{(\$2820+\$750+\$100-\$125)}{(\$3883 + \$1100)}$ $\dfrac{(\$2564+\$1235+\$390-\$125)}{(\$15,778 + \$ 1783)}$

B. Pretax interest coverage moves from the AA range to the BBB range. Long-term debt/total capital shifts from A to less than B. Cash flow/total debt declines from between A and AA to BB.

C. Prior to the merger, Philip Morris debt would have a strong A rating based on these criteria. After the Kraft merger, BB would be appropriate based on these same criteria.

2. {M}*NOTE: The answers given below concern the effect of the merger on the probability of bankruptcy as predicted by Altman's models. It is not clear that ratio changes caused by external events (such as an acquisition) have the same predictive ability as those resulting from normal operations.*

The variables used in Altman's two models (see Exhibit 18-1) are listed below by category:

	(1977 model)	(1968 model)
Activity		Sales to total assets
Liquidity	Current ratio	Working capital to total assets
Leverage and Solvency	Equity (market) to debt	Equity (market) to capital
	Times interest earned	
Profitability	Return on assets	Return on assets
	Retained earnings to total assets	Retained earnings to total assets
Earnings Variability	Standard error of ROA	
Size	Total assets	

Activity

(1968 model) Sales to total assets

Sales increased by $11,610 (approximately 33%) from $33,080 to $44,690 as a result of the merger. Although Exhibit 18P-1 does not provide the data directly, we can infer from the data available that the increase in assets would be greater.

Debt plus equity increased[1] by $12,322. When we consider that current operating liabilities and other (nondebt) liabilities also increased as a result of the merger, we can infer that total assets grew by *at least* $12,322.

If, prior to the merger, the asset turnover ratio was greater than 1, then adding a given amount ($11,610) to the numerator and a larger amount to the denominator would reduce the ratio, increasing the likelihood of bankruptcy.

If, on the other hand, prior to the merger, the asset turnover ratio was less than 1, then more information about actual asset levels is needed to determine the effect on this ratio.

Liquidity

(1977 model) Current ratio
(1968 model) Working capital to total assets

The information in Exhibit 18P-1 is insufficient to assess the impact of the merger on working capital and the current ratio.

Leverage and Solvency

(1977 model) Market value of equity to debt
(1968 model) Market value of equity to capital

Before the merger, Philip Morris' total debt was $4,983 million ($1,100+$3,883). As a result of the merger, total debt increased more than threefold to $17,561 million ($1,783+$15,778). Unless the market value of equity increased by the same proportion [Philip Morris' market value actually *decreased* following the merger announcement] the equity to debt (capital) ratio would be reduced considerably, increasing the likelihood of bankruptcy.

---

[1] Total debt + equity (pre merger) = $1100 + $3883 + $9931 = $14,914
                        (post merger) = $1783 + $15778 + $9675 = <u>27,236</u>
                                Increase   = $12,322

(1977 model) Times interest earned

From problem 1, we have

	Before Kraft	**Consolidated**
Pretax interest coverage	10.64X	3.76X

Based on the (1977) model, the reduction in the coverage ratio would increase the likelihood of bankruptcy.

Profitability

(Both Models) Return on assets

Philip Morris' EBIT rose from $5320 million ($4820+$500) to $6020 million ($4420+$1600). As a percent of sales, EBIT decreased from 16% ($5320/$33080) to 13.5% ($6020/$44690). The impact on ROA depends on the asset turnover (discussed earlier). However, unless asset turnover increased by (at least) 18.5%, the net effect would be a reduction in ROA.

(Both Models) Retained earnings to total assets

Since the merger is accounted for under the purchase method, Kraft's retained earnings are eliminated. As total assets increase, this ratio would be greatly reduced. The reduced ratio results in prediction by the model of a greater likelihood of bankruptcy.

Earnings Variability

(1977 model) Standard deviation of ROA

Similar to portfolio diversification, the variance of return measures such as ROA should decline following the merger, reducing the likelihood of bankruptcy.

Size

(1977 model) Total assets

As total assets increase as a result of the merger, the model predicts a smaller likelihood of bankruptcy.

3. {S} The theoretical as well as empirical models (Exhibit 18-3), indicate that beta risk is a function of both the operating (unleveraged beta) and financial (leveraged) risk of the company. As Philip Morris' debt increased by approximately $12 billion as a result of the merger without a commensurate increase in equity the firm's financial leverage increased. *Ceteris paribus*, this should result in an increase in financial risk and beta.

The effect on operating risk depends on how Kraft's cost structure compares with that of Philip Morris, that is, on the mix between fixed and variable costs. The impact on beta would depend on the answer to this question.

4. A. {M}

	Coca-Cola Company (KO)	Coca-Cola Enterprises (CCE)
(i) Short-term liquidity		
Current ratio	0.74	1.14
Quick ratio	0.41	0.60
Inventory turnover	6.21	18.96
Receivables turnover	10.63	13.28
(ii) Capital structure & long-term solvency		
Debt to equity	0.75	2.99
Times interest earned	16.92	1.45
(iii) Asset utilization		
Inventory turnover	6.21	18.96
Receivables turnover	10.63	13.28
PP&E turnover	4.16	3.14
Total asset turnover	1.19	0.75
(iv) Operating profitability		
Gross profit	61%	37%
Return on sales	17%	1%
ROA	20%	1%
ROE	55%	6%

(i)   CCE has better short-term liquidity as its current and acid test ratios are higher. Consistent with the above its accounts receivable and inventory turnovers are higher.

(ii) KO's ratio of long-term debt to equity is far lower than CCE's. KO has substantial short-term debt; however, the total debt to equity ratio, is still disparately lower. Additionally, CCE's debt burden and low profitability result in an interest coverage ratio that is far below that of KO.

(iii) As noted CCE's short-term turnover ratios are superior to KO's. However, property and total asset turnover ratios are superior to those of CCE as the latter is more capital intensive.

(iv) KO is more profitable than CCE by all measures. Higher gross margins are carried down to net income. Given its lower capital requirement, KO's return ratios are also higher.

B. & C.   1. Adjustment of KO investments from carrying amount to market value. Effect is to reduce leverage but also turnover ratios and return ratios.

2. KO and CCE's debt should be increased by the OBS debt. For Ko, the amount is $202 million. In CCE's case the amount is considerably larger as it should be the present value of the future payments. Recognition will increase the leverage of CCE by a greater amount than KO, thus enhancing the differences noted above.

3. Additionally, as an offset to the debt, the companies' assets should be increased. The effect will be to decrease return and turnover ratios.

4. Increase CCE debt to its market-value. The effect will be to raise its leverage even more. For comparison purposes, the fair value of KO's debt should also be obtained.

5.{M}A. The ratios and bond rating categories based on both reported and adjusted data follow. Comparing the ratios with those in Exhibit 18-8, we find that all but one are in the AA/AAA range. OCF/sales is much lower, implying a rating of B. Putting these all together suggests an overall rating of AA for Alcoa's debt.

ALCOA
Financial Ratios Used for Bond Ratings
1995

Ratio	Reported		Adjusted	
	Ratio	Rating	Ratio	Rating
Pretax interest coverage[1]	13.27	AA+	12.08	AA+
EBITDA interest coverage[2]	19.22	AAA/AA	17.44	AA+
Free OCF/total debt[3]	0.43	AAA-	0.42	AAA-
Operating income/sales[4]	0.09	B	0.09	B
Long-term debt/capital[5]	0.17	AA	0.17	AA
Total debt/capital[5]	0.24	AAA	0.24	AAA
Overall rating		AA		AA

Calculations based on data from case and solution to Case 17-2:

[1] Reported: EBIT = ($1,024.3 + $445.9 + $119.8) = $1,590.0
    Interest Expense = $119.8
  Adjusted EBIT = $1,590.0 + $16.2 (special charges) = $1,606.2
    Interest Expense adjusted for capitalized leases
        = $119.8 + (8.55% x $155=)$13.2 = 133

[2] EBITDA = EBIT + Depreciation and depletion of 712.9

[3] Reported OCF is given at $1,712.5. To arrive at Free OCF we deduct capital expenditures of $887 yielding $825.5,
  Adjusted free OCF is $825.5 plus adjustment for capitalization of operating leases. Payment of $47 less interest portion of $13.2 is cash from financing. Adjusted OCF=$825.5+($47-$13.2) = $859.3.
  Reported debt = $1,215.5 + 693.2 = $1,908.7
  Adjusted debt includes capitalized leases of $155 ; = $2,063.7

[4] Reported Operating inc. = $1,024.3 + $119.8x(1-tax rate)=$1.104.3
  Adjusted operating inc. = $1,104.3 + $16.2x(1-tax rate)= $1,115.0
  Sales given as $12,499.7

[5,6] LTD: Reported = $1,215.1
              Adjusted = $1,215.1+$155 (lease capitalized) = $1,360.1
  Equity: Reported = $6,054.1 ; Adjusted = $6,463.7

B.   (i)   See table above for adjusted ratios.
     (ii) See table above for ratings based on adjusted data. With
           the ratios only slightly lower, Alcoa still appears to
           be a AA rated credit.

     (iii) There are two reasons. First, the Exhibit 18-8 data are
           for 1992-94 while the Alcoa data is for 1995, a better
           economic year. The companies in S&P's sample may have
           had higher ratios in 1995 than those shown. Second,
           adjustments to the data in Exhibit 18-8 might well have
           reduced the sample ratios as well. It is inappropriate
           the compare adjusted data for one company with
           unadjusted data for another.

     (iv) The adjustments are not large enough to significantly
           change Alcoa's default risk. The only weak ratio is
           operating income to sales, which apparently is
           characteristic of Alcoa's business, even in profitable
           years. In any case, it is unclear whether adjusted data
           can be compared with bond ratings ratios based on
           unadjusted data for other firms.

     (v)   Using data from Case 17-2, the ratios in Altman's Z''-
           score model can be computed:

ALCOA Z''-SCORE

1995 Data ($ in millions)

	As Reported		
RATIO	Numerator	Denominator	Ratio
Working capital/total assets	$2,089.5	$13,643.4	0.153
Retained earnings/total assets	3,800.1	13,643.4	0.279
EBIT/total assets	1,590.0	13,643.4	0.117
BV equity/total liabilities	6,054.1	7,589.3	0.798
Z'' Score			**3.533**

	Adjusted		
	Numerator	Denominator	Ratio
Working capital/total assets	$2,682.6	$13,262.1	0.202
Retained earnings/total assets	3,800.1	13,262.1	0.287
EBIT/total assets	1,606.2	13,262.1	0.121
BV equity/total liabilities	6,463.7	6,598.4	0.951
Z'' Score			**4.103**

Both the reported and adjusted ratios are comfortably over the 2.60 Nonbankruptcy cut-off point (Box 18-2).

Using the Z″ score to assess bond ratings we add (see Exhibit 18-9) 3.25 to the above scores yielding 6.783 for the reported data and 7.353 for the adjusted data. The adjusted score suggests that Alcoa debt should be rated at least AA, as compared to a rating of less than A+ implied by the unadjusted score.

6. {M} A. The following ratios can be computed from the data in Exhibit 18P-3:

	1991	1992
Debt/total capital	0.42	0.58
Operating income/sales	0.05	(0.01)
Interest coverage	1.96	(0.25)
CFO/total debt	0.21	(0.05)
Pretax ROE	0.05	(0.09)

The 1992 data in Exhibit 18P-3 show marked deterioration. Using 1991 data, CFO/total debt suggested an A rating and debt/capital justified a BBB rating. Interest coverage was below BB while the other ratios were poor. In 1992, only the debt/capital ratio justified a BB rating; the others were below CCC. Given these ratios, the S&P decision seems unsurprising.

B. Abbreviated data are not sufficient to evaluate a firm's credit rating. Full financial statements and footnotes are required. Attention should be paid to whether off-balance sheet or other "window dressing" transactions were engaged in during 1992. Detailed cash flow analysis would also be helpful.

C. The difficulty with this comparison is that 1992 was a year of serious recession in the paper industry; 1992-1994, includes 1993 and 1994, improved economic years. In any case, the sample of firms used to compile Exhibit 18-8 may not be comparable to James River.

7. {M}   A.   The following ratios can be computed from the data
              provided:

	1991	1992
Debt/total capital	0.37	0.38
Operating income/sales	0.14	0.13
Interest coverage	3.26	3.02
CFO/total debt	0.34	0.33
Pretax ROE	0.13	0.12

Despite some deterioration in 1992, most of
Westvaco's ratios would justify a BBB rating.

B.   Based on the long-term debt/capital ratio, Westvaco
     should be between BBB and A rated while James River and
     Union Camp are closer to BB. The 1991 interest coverage
     ratios fall into the BB range.

     Thus all three firms would appear to be candidates for
     the downgrading of their debt.

C. and D. The data in Exhibit 18P-5 show the effect of the
         recession on three paper companies. The comparison
         shows that all three firms should be downgraded
         based on 1991 data alone. Given a longer term
         perspective, however, rating agencies should be
         willing to tolerate poor performance during
         recessions as long as operating results (and
         ratios) are at acceptable levels over the entire
         business cycle. Thus, it is not as clear that a
         downgrading is required, especially for Westvaco,
         whose 1992 ratios held up relatively well.

8. {M} The solution to this problem is based on the ratios calculated below. The suggested ratings are based on the data provided in Exhibit 18-8.

	1992	1993	1994	Ratings Based on 1992-94 data	1995	Ratings Based on 1995 data
Interest Coverage	2.5	3.5	3.6	BBB to A	5.6	A
CFO/Total Debt	22.0%	23.0%	21.6%	A	33.8%	AA to AAA
Pretax return on capital	7.1%	8.7%	7.8%	B to BB	19.3%	AA
Operating income/Sales	12.3%	12.2%	10.6%	BBB	16.0%	A to AA
Debt/Capital	45.9%	40.7%	40.9%	BBB to A	50.5%	BB to BBB

A. The BBB+ rating would seem to be an appropriate rating. For two of the ratios, the suggested rating lies between BBB and A (BBB+). For the others, one has a rating of BBB, another a rating of A. The only "anomaly" is the pretax return on capital which suggests a lower rating but its impact is presumably overwhelmed by the others.

B. SCA was probably placed on the Creditwatch list because at the beginning of 1995, the only effect known *at that time* (January 1995) was the effect on the debt/capital ratio. Because of the new debt taken on by SCA for the acquisition, the ratio increased considerably suggesting a possible lower rating.

C.& D. After 1995, all the ratios save one suggest a rating of about AA. These "improved" ratios are ones affected by the company's profitability. However, the leverage ratio remained weak (below BBB), thus limiting the extent to which the rating of SCA was raised.

9. {M}A. *EBIT/Interest expense*, the times interest earned ratio is an indicator of the degree of protection available to creditors with respect to receiving interest payments. The ratio measures the firm's ability to meet interest payments out of current earnings. The higher the ratio, the less risky the firm.

   Long-term debt/total capitalization measures the proportion of a firm's financing provided by debt. The higher that proportion, the higher the firm's financial leverage as the higher debt requires higher fixed interest payments. The firm is riskier as the probability of insolvency increases as the firm may find it difficult to meet interest and principal payments.

Debt, ultimately, is repaid by internally generated cash flows. Funds from operations act as a surrogate for CFO and *Funds from operations/total debt* measures the extent to which internally generated funds or cash flows are available for debt service. The ratio indicates the proportion of debt a firm can pay off from annually generated internal cash flows.

A firm's long-term solvency depends on its ability to generate profits. *Operating income/sales* provides a measure of a firm's profitability.

B. Overall, the ratings indicate that Alpine falls in between the A and BBB ratings:

EBIT/Interest expense ranged from 4.70 to 5.65 in the last four years. Exhibit 18-8 shows that debt given an A rating had a median ratio of 5.67. Thus, based on this ratio, Alpine would fall into the A rating category.

Exhibit 18-8 shows a 28.8% *long-term debt/capital* ratio for the A rating and 40.7% for the BBB rating. Alpine's ratio of 34% in 1990-1992 and 44% in 1993 would be indicative of a BBB rating.

Funds from operations/total debt has declined considerably from 1989. However, the current levels of greater than 50% are just above the 49.1% median ratio indicated by the A rating and would qualify it for that rating.

Operating income/sales in the 12-14% range is consistent with the other ratios. Alpine falls between the BBB and A ratings which show ratios of 12.3% and 14.6% respectively.

C. Alpine is paying 100 basis points more than US Treasury Notes, equivalent to what a BBB-rated firm is paying. As Alpine's ratings are better than BBB; falling between BBB and A, the Alpine bond should trade at a smaller spread. O'Flaherty should recommend the Alpine Chemical bond for purchase.

Case 18-1

Estimated solution time is three hours.

Note: The adjusted data are based on Case 17-1. Students should have been assigned that case first or have access to its solution. (Alternatively, the case can be assigned by omitting the questions requiring adjusted data).

---

1. Z-Scores for duPont, ICI, and Dow are provided below. Data required for calculations (based on reported data on December 31, 1994) are provided in Exhibit 18CS-1

Z-Score Variables	DUPONT	DOW	ICI
1.2(Working Capital/Total Assets)	0.1152	0.0938	0.3151
+ 1.4(Retained Earnings/Total Assets)	0.2810	0.4671	0.3648
+ 3.3(EBIT / Total Assets)	0.4420	0.3219	0.2177
+ 0.6(MV of Equity / BV of Debt)	2.9907	1.6991	1.6424
+ 1.0(Sales / Total Assets)	1.0662	0.7540	1.0205
= Z-Score	**4.8951**	**3.3359**	**3.5604**

2. Adjusted Z-Scores for duPont, ICI, and Dow are provided below. Data required for calculations (based on current cost data) are provided in Exhibit 18CS-1

Z-Score Variables	DUPONT	DOW	ICI
1.2(Working Capital/Total Assets)	0.1126	0.0953	0.2837
+ 1.4(Retained Earnings/Total Assets)	0.2355	0.5294	0.3284
+ 3.3(EBIT / Total Assets)	0.3704	0.3648	0.1960
+ 0.6(MV of Equity / BV of Debt)	2.1195	1.2178	1.1477
+ 1.0(Sales / Total Assets)	0.8935	0.8545	0.9189
= Z-Score	**3.7315**	**3.0618**	**2.8747**

3. The adjusted Z-scores show significant declines for all three firms:

DUPONT	DOW	ICI
23.8%	8.3%	19.23%

The primary causes are significantly higher adjusted total assets and debt. DuPont reports the biggest decline because it has the greatest increase in total assets and debt. The relative ranking does not change but ICI is the worst off after the adjustment. Pre-adjustment Z-scores for all three firms are above the critical value of 2.999. On the current cost basis, ICI is in the zone of ignorance, whereas Dow's Z-score is just marginally over the 2.999 required to be classified as non-bankrupt. [However, the zone of ignorance was defined using reported rather than adjusted data.

We assume that the zone would change if based on current cost data.] Only duPont remains comfortably in the non-bankrupt zone. Nevertheless, its Z-score declined the most on a percentage basis after adjustment.

Exhibit 18CS-1

Data used to calculate Z and Z" scores for questions 1 and 6.
(For duPont and Dow in $ millions, for ICI in £ millions)

	REPORTED			*ADJUSTED*		
	DuPont	**Dow**	**ICI**	**DuPont**	**Dow**	**ICI**
Total Assets	36,892	26,545	9,004	44,019	23,423	10,000
Working Capital	3,543	2,075	2,364	4,130	1,861	2,364
Retained Earnings	7,406	8,857	2,346	7,406	8,857	2,346
EBIT	4,941	2,589	594	4,941	2,589	594
BV of Debt	7,668	6,578	1,981	10,820	9,178	2,835
MV of Equity	38,221	18,628	5,423	38,221	18,628	5,423
BV of Equity	13,019	10,740	4,074	18,696	6,129	3,630
Sales	39,333	20,015	9,189	39,333	20,015	9,189

The data used can be traced to the following sources:

- The reported data were taken directly from the financial statements and/or the calculations in Chapter 4 for duPont and Case 4-1 for Dow and ICI. Additionally, the data for MV of equity is based on closing market price/share (see Case 17-1, P. 967) of $56.125, $67.25 and £7.49 and shares of 681, 327 and 324 million for duPont, Dow and ICI respectively.

- The adjusted data are based on the solution to Case 17-1.

4. (a) and (b) Key Financial Ratios based on Reported Data (see Exhibit 18CS-2 for data used)

Ratios	DUPONT		DOW		ICI	
	Ratio	Rating	Ratio	Rating	Ratio	Rating
Pretax interest coverage (x)	8.84	AA-	4.82	A-	3.19	BBB+
Pretax interest coverage including rents (x)	5.79	AA	3.06	A-	2.39	BBB
EBITDA interest coverage (x)	14.16	AA	7.66	A-	5.40	BBB
Funds from operations/total debt(%)	73.87	AA	40.06	BBB+	32.24	BBB+
Free operating cash flow/total debt(%)	34.09	AA+	23.76	A+	20.44	A+
Pretax return on permanent capital(%)	21.18	AA+	11.85	BBB	6.74	B
Operating income/sales(%)	10.21	BB-	11.72	BB	6.40	B-
Long-term debt/capital (%)	30.82	A	30.62	A-	25.14	A+
Total debt/capitalization including short-term debt (%)	37.07	A	37.98	A	32.72	A+
Total debt/capitalization including short-term debt (including 8 times rents) (%)	44.66	A	48.83	A	41.12	AA-
Overall Rating	**AA/AA-**		**A-/BBB+**		**A-/BBB+**	

5. (a) and (b) Key Financial Ratios based on Adjusted Data (see Exhibit 18CS-2 for data used)

Ratios	DUPONT		DOW		ICI	
	Ratio	Rating	Ratio	Rating	Ratio	Rating
Pretax interest coverage (x)	7.03	A+	4.29	A-	3.19	BBB+
Pretax interest coverage including rents (x)	5.01	AA	2.87	BBB+	2.39	BBB
EBITDA interest coverage (x)	11.26	A+	6.82	A-	5.40	BBB
Funds from operations/total debt(%)	56.80	A	33.40	BBB	29.45	BBB+
Free operating cash flow/total debt(%)	28.61	AA	20.51	A	16.30	A
Pretax return on permanent capital(%)	14.36	A-	13.59	BBB+	6.32	B
Operating income/sales(%)	10.21	BB-	11.72	BB	6.40	B-
Long-term debt/capital (%)	32.28	A-	51.63	BB	36.75	BBB+
Total debt/capitalization including short-term debt (%)	36.66	A	59.96	BB	43.85	BBB
Total debt/capitalization including short-term debt (including 8 times rents) (%)	42.22	AA-	67.71	BB	50.47	A-
Overall Rating	**A+**		**BBB**		**BBB**	

(c) The ratings implicit in the ratios calculated in Exhibit 18-8 are based on unadjusted data. Using them for adjusted data may not be appropriate as the companies which formed the basis of Exhibit 18-8 would also have to be adjusted to make the comparison "fair".

18C-3

Exhibit 18CS-2

Data used to calculate ratios for questions 4 & 5.
(For duPont and Dow in $ millions, for ICI in £ millions)

| | REPORTED | | | ADJUSTED | | |
	DuPont	Dow	ICI	DuPont	Dow	ICI
Sales	39,333	20,015	9,189	39,333	20,015	9,189
Operating Income	4,015	2,345	588	4,015	2,345	588
EBIT	4,941	2,589	594	4,941	2,589	594
Interest	559	537	186	703	603	186
EBT	4,382	2,052	408	4,238	1,986	408
Rent	355	459	108	355	459	108
EBIT + Rent	5,296	3,048	702	5,296	3,048	702
Depreciation	2,976	1,525	411	2,976	1,525	411
EBITDA	7,917	4,114	1,005	7,917	4,114	1,005
Interest + Rent	914	996	294	1,058	1,062	294
Funds (CFO) From Operations	5,664	2,635	612	6,146	3,065	835
Free Cash Flow	2,614	1,563	405	3,096	1,882	462
Long Term Debt	6,376	5,303	1,522	9,528	7,903	2,376
Total Debt	7,668	6,578	1,981	10,820	9,178	2,835
Equity	13,019	10,740	4,074	18,696	6,129	3,630
Total Capitalization	20,687	17,318	6,055	29,516	15,307	6,465

The data used can be traced to the following sources:

- The reported data were taken directly from the financial statements and/or the calculations in Chapter 4 for duPont and Case 4-1 for Dow and ICI. Additionally, the data for rents were obtained from Note 20 for duPont; Note H for Dow and Note 31 for ICI from the companies' respective financial statements.

- The adjusted data are based on the solution to Case 17-1. Interest expense is adjusted by including the capitalized portion of interest.

6. The Z"-Scores for duPont, ICI, and Dow and the implied ratings for those scores, based on reported data on December 31, 1994, are reported below. Data used in calculations are provided in Exhibit 18CS-1

Z-Score Variables	DUPONT	DOW	ICI
6.56(Working Capital / Total Assets)	0.6300	0.5128	1.7223
+3.26(Retained Earnings / Total Assets)	0.6544	1.0877	0.8494
+6.72(EBIT / Total Assets)	0.9000	0.6554	0.4433
+1.05(BV of Equity / Total Liabilities)	1.7827	1.6327	1.7144
+3.25	3.2500	3.2500	3.2500
= Z"-Score	7.2171	7.2203	8.4244
Implied rating (see Exhibit 18-9)	AA	AA	AAA

The Z"-Scores for duPont, ICI, and Dow and the implied ratings for those scores, based on current cost data on December 31, 1994 are reported below. Data used in calculations are provided in Exhibit 18CS-1

Z-Score Variables	DUPONT	DOW	ICI
6.56(Working Capital / Total Assets)	0.6155	0.5212	1.5508
+3.26(Retained Earnings / Total Assets)	0.5485	1.2327	0.7648
+6.72(EBIT / Total Assets)	0.7543	0.7428	0.3992
+1.05(BV of Equity / Total Liabilities)	1.8143	0.7012	1.3444
+3.25	3.2500	3.2500	3.2500
= Z"-Score	6.9825	6.4479	7.3092
Implied rating (see Exhibit 18-9)	AA-	A-	AA

The table below summarizes the ratings derived in questions 4-6.

Question	Data Source	DUPONT	DOW	ICI
4	Reported	AA/AA-	A-/BBB+	A
5	Adjusted	A+	BBB	BBB
6(a)	Reported	AA	AA	A-/BBB+
6(b)	Adjusted	AA-	A-	BBB+

The relative rankings among the firms is maintained in all cases with duPont being "best" followed by Dow and then ICI. In each case, "ratings" based on adjusted data are lower than those based on unadjusted data. The ratings are relatively consistent for each firm with duPont's between A and AA; and Dow and ICI between BBB and A.[1]

---

[1] The only exception would seem to be the Z"-score for Dow based on reported data which assigns a rating of AA.

7. Overall, the adjustments resulted in a downgrading of the firms' ratings. This was primarily a result of two factors. First, off-balance sheet debt was added to the firms' liabilities, increasing their leverage and risk. Second, by increasing assets to current costs, the denominator in ratios (such as those used in the Z"-score analysis) was increased and the ratios themselves were reduced. Additionally, capitalized interest was expensed, thus reducing times interest earned and profitability ratios.

Chapter 19 - Solutions

Overview:

Problem Length	*Problem #'s*
{S}	1,2,15,16,17
{M}	3,4,5,7,10,11,12,14
{L}	6,8,9,13

1.{S}The models should give identical results. Using 19X3 expected dividends of $4.50, a discount rate r of 20%, and growth rate g of 15%, we find that:

$$P = \frac{D}{r-g} = \frac{\$4.50}{.20-.15} = \$90$$

The dividend payout ratio for both 19X2 ($4.05/$10.03 = 40.4%) and 19X3 ($4.50/$11.40 = 39.5%) is approximately 40%. The long term growth rates for earnings and dividends differ. This is possible only if the payout rate will change over time. Thus, in an earnings based model using the earnings growth rate of 14%, we must use another (higher than 40%) estimate for the payout ratio. A payout ratio of 47.5% would result in the same valuation:

$$P = \frac{kE}{r-g} = \frac{(.475)(\$11.40)}{.20-.14} = \$90$$

Based on these models, Emfil shares are not attractive at a price of $115, and should not be added to the portfolio.

2.{S}A.

$$P = \frac{E}{r}$$

$$\frac{P}{E} = \frac{1}{r}$$

$$r = \frac{1}{P/E}$$

For a firm with a P/E ratio of 12

r = 8.25%

B. (i) The increase of $3 is transitory. The market is saying that the price/earnings ratio should reflect only the "normal" earnings of $10 per share.

(ii) The increase of $3 is permanent and earnings in the future are expected to remain at $13. The market value is based on $13 per share of normal earnings.

(iii) The increase of $3 implies not only permanence but growth as future earnings are expected to increase above the present level of $13.

3.{M}A. The P/E ratio with a dividend payout of k, discount rate of r and growth rate equal to g can be derived as:

$$P = \frac{kE(1+g)}{r-g} \quad and \quad \frac{P}{E} = \frac{k(1+g)}{r-g}$$

For the Lo Company:

$$\frac{P}{E} = \frac{.2(\$1+.04)}{.10-.04} = 3.467$$

B. Hi's P/E ratio must be identical to that of Lo (3.467) as both firms have the same market value and earnings.

C. **Lo Company**

	1988	1989	1990	1991	1992
1) Earnings/ share	$1.00	$1.04	$1.08	$1.12	$1.17
2) Number of shares	1,000	1,000	1,000	1,000	1,000
3) Net income	$1,000	$1,040	$1,082	$1,125	$1,170
4) Dividends paid	200	208	216	225	234
5) New investment	800	832	865	900	936
6) Firm value at period end	3,467	3,605	3,750	3,900	4,056
7) Price per share	3.47	3.61	3.75	3.90	4.06
8) P/E ratio	3.467	3.467	3.467	3.467	3.467

Calculations:
1) Given
2) Since no new financing and no stock dividends or splits; shares must remain constant over time.
3) Earnings per share x number of shares
4) Dividends per share (given) x number of shares
5) Net income - dividends paid
6) (.2 x next year's income)/(.10-.04); 1992 value assumes that net income continues to grow at 4% rate.
7) Firm value/number of shares
8) Firm value/current year net income

Hi Company

	1988	1989	1990	1991	1992
1) Earnings/share	$1.00	$0.80	$0.64	$0.51	$0.41
2) Number of shares	1,000	1,300	1,690	2,197	2,856
3) Net income	$1,000	$1,040	$1,082	$1,125	$1,170
4) Dividends paid	1,000	1,040	1,082	1,125	1,170
5) New investment	800	832	865	900	936
6) New financing	800	832	865	900	936
7) Firm value at period end	3,467	3,605	3,750	3,900	4,056
8) Price/share before new issue	3.47	2.77	2.22	1.77	1.42
9) P/E ratio	3.467	3.467	3.467	3.467	3.467
10) Shares issued	300	390	507	659	857
11) Price/share at new issue	$2.67	$2.13	$1.71	$1.37	$1.09

Calculations based on issuance of shares at end of year:
1) Given
2) 1988 given; From 1989 on, previous year shares plus new shares issued
3) Earnings per share x number of shares
4) Dividends per share (given) x number of shares
5) Identical in amount to that computed for Lo Company
6) Equal to (5)
7) Identical to Lo Company [(.2 x next year's income)/(.10-.04)]; 1992 value assumes that net income continues to grow at 4% rate.
8) Firm value/number of shares
9) Firm value/current year net income

10) and 11) Since (number of shares + shares issued) x price per share at new issue = firm value; and
Shares issued x price per share at new issue = new financing, therefore:
10) shares issued = new financing/price per share at new issue
11) price per share at new issue = (firm value - new financing)/ number of shares (item 2)

D. The growth rate is 4% for net income, dividends, and firm value. For the Lo Company, EPS also grows at 4% since the number of shares is constant. The Hi Company, on the other hand, keeps issuing new shares. Therefore, although net income is growing, earnings per share declines. This problem demonstrates the effect of dividend policy on reported growth rates.

E. The company's return on new investments is 5%.

Using the formula for growth,
$$g = (1-k) \times ROE,$$

with k = 20% and g =4%, ROE = 5%.

Alternatively, using 1989 as an example, on the additional investment of $800 the company's income increases by $40 or 5%.

This return is lower than the required rate of return of 10%. Hence, the low P/E ratio. Both companies would be better off paying out all earnings as dividends and not making any new investments.

Firm value would then equal $1,000/.10 = $10,000

4.{M} A.   The EBO model defines value =

current book value + present value of abnormal earnings

To compare the situation of all dividends being paid out versus one of only some dividends paid out we need only compare the present value of abnormal earnings since opening book value is identical.

If all income is paid out as dividends, then book value will remain constant at $10,000 and income will stay at $1000/year. With a dividend payout of 20% as in problem 3, income will grow at 4%.

	Dividends = 100%; no growth			**Dividend payout=20%; Growth = 4%**			
	Open			Open			
	Book	Income	**Abnormal**	Book	Income	Dividends	**Abnormal**
YEAR	Value		**Earnings**	Value			**Earnings**
19X0	$10,000	$1,000	0	$10,000	1,000	$200	0
19X1	10,000	1,000	0	10,800	1,040	208	**(40)**
19X2	10,000	1,000	0	11,632	1,082	216	**(82)**
19X3	10,000	1,000	0	12,497	1,125	225	**(125)**
19X4	10,000	1,000	0	13,397	1,170	234	**(170)**
19X5	10,000	1,000	0	14,333	1,217	243	**(217)**

Reinvesting some income results in negative abnormal earnings whereas 100% dividend payout results in abnormal earnings = 0. Thus, it is clearly preferable to pay out all earnings as dividends.

When all income is paid out as dividends, the value of the firm will equal the opening book value of $10,000 (the same as in problem 3) since the present value of the abnormal earnings is zero.

B. The pattern of income and dividends will be identical as these are independent of book value. Abnormal earnings, however, will differ.

(i) Open Book Value = $9,000

Dividends = 100%; no growth

YEAR	Open Book Value	Income	Abnormal Earnings
19X0	$9,000	$1,000	**$100**
19X1	9,000	1,000	**100**
19X2	9,000	1,000	**100**
19X3	9,000	1,000	**100**
19X4	9,000	1,000	**100**
19X5	9,000	1,000	**100**

Dividend payout=20%; Growth = 4%

Open Book Value	Income	Dividends	Abnormal Earnings
$9,000	$1,000	$200	**$100**
9,800	1,040	208	**60**
10,632	1,082	216	**18**
11,497	1,125	225	**(25)**
12,397	1,170	234	**(70)**
13,333	1,217	243	**(117)**

Here again, abnormal earnings for the 100% payout is greater (or equal) to abnormal earnings for the 20% payout. Hence, all income should be paid out as dividends. Note that for 100% payout, abnormal earnings are a perpetuity of $100. Therefore their present value is $100/.1 = $1,000 and

value = current book value + present value of abnormal earnings
      = $9,000 + $1,000 = $10,000 as before

(ii) Open Book Value = $11,000

Dividends = 100%; no Growth

YEAR	Open Book Value	Income	Abnormal Earnings
19X0	$11,000	$1,000	**$(100)**
19X1	11,000	1,000	**(100)**
19X2	11,000	1,000	**(100)**
19X3	11,000	1,000	**(100)**
19X4	11,000	1,000	**(100)**
19X5	11,000	1,000	**(100)**

Dividend payout=20%; Growth = 4%

Open Book Value	Income	Dividends	Abnormal Earnings
$11,000	$1,000	$200	**$(100)**
11,800	1,040	208	**(140)**
12,632	1,082	216	**(182)**
13,497	1,125	225	**(225)**
14,397	1,170	234	**(270)**
15,333	1,217	243	**(317)**

Once again, abnormal earnings for the 100% payout is greater (or equal) to abnormal earnings for the 20% payout. Hence, all income should be paid out as dividends. Note that for 100% payout, abnormal earnings are a perpetuity of ($100). Therefore their present value is ($100)/.1 = ($1000) and

value = current book value + present value of abnormal earnings
      = $11,000 - $1,000 = $10,000 as before

5.{M}A. Cash flow before interest payments (i.e., free cash flow to the firm) is the same regardless of which bond is issued:

(in $ millions)	Conventional		Zero Coupon	
	19X6	19X7	19X6	19X7
EBIT	$ 20	$ 20	$ 20	$ 20
Taxes	6	6	6	6
Free cash flow	$ 14	$ 14	$ 14	$ 14

However cash flows reported in accordance with SFAS 95 differ:

(in $ million)	Conventional		Zero Coupon	
	19X6	19X7	19X6	19X7
Cash flow pre interest	$ 14.0	$ 14.0	$ 14.0	$ 14.00
Interest paid	(1.0)	(1.0)	---	----
Tax benefit	0.3	0.3	0.3	0.33
	$ 13.3	$ 13.3	$ 14.3	$ 14.33

The venture receives a tax benefit of 30% of interest expense in both cases because of the deductibility of interest expense.

B. For the conventional bond, bondholders will receive $1 million annually. The zero coupon bondholders will receive no cash interest. The after-tax interest paid by the firm is $0.7 million for the conventional bond, but a $0.3 million *inflow* for the zero coupon bond.

C. and D. The answers to parts A and B imply that the amount available for dividends is based on reported cash flows that depend on the form of the bond. This implication is incorrect. The "fallacy" is that, on January 1, 19X8 the conventional bond will require a debt repayment of $10 million. The zero coupon bond, however, will require payment of $12.1 million. The extra $2.1 million[*] precludes

19-8

the use of the "extra" cash flow for dividends.
Focusing on the free cash flows, however,
indicates that firm values are identical as long
as their WACCs are equivalent.**

*$1 million for two years   = $ 2.0 million
10% interest on first year's $1 million =   __.1__
Total accrued interest at 1-1-X8 $ 2.1 million

**The relative WACCs are also a consideration as, after
19X6, the zero coupon bond will result in higher debt. In
most cases, the debt/equity ratio will rise.

6.{L}A.   g   = (1 - dividend payout) x ROE

12% = (1-k) x 20%

1-k = .6

 k = .4

Dividend payout ratio is 40%

B.   With a dividend payout ratio of 40 %, new investment
(from equity) must be .6 x $30,000 = $18,000

Current interest expense of $5000 at an interest rate
of 10% implies debt of $50,000. At a growth rate of
12%; new investment from debt will equal .12 x $50,000
= $6000. [Alternate calculation: interest expense used
to calculate debt level; $5600/.10 = $56,000.]

Total investment:
Replacement (depreciation)=$ 8,000
New investment   = 24,000 ($18,000 + $6,000)
 Total $32,000

C. **Cash Flow Statement**

	Current	Forecast
Net income	$30,000	$33,600
Depreciation	8,000	8,960
Cash from operations	$38,000	$42,560
Cash for investment	(32,000)	(35,840)
Cash for financing:		
New debt	6,000	6,720
Dividends paid	(12,000)	(13,440)
	$(6,000)	$ (6,720)
Change in Cash	0	0

NOTE: *this cash flow statement assumes no change in working capital accounts.*

D. **Free Cash Flow Calculation**

	Current	Forecast
Operating income	$ 35,000	$ 39,200
Depreciation	8,000	8,960
	$ 43,000	$ 48,160
Investment	(32,000)	(35,840)
Free cash flow	**$ 11,000**	**$ 12,320**
Financing cash flows:		
New debt	6,000	6,720
Interest paid	(5,000)	(5,600)
	$ 1,000	$ 1,120
Dividends paid	(12,000)	(13,440)
Financing cash flow*	**$(11,000)**	**$(12,320)**

*Remember that interest paid must be reclassified from operating to financing cash flow for purposes of valuation.

E. The value of the debt is:

$$($50,000 + $6,000) = \$ 56,000$$

The value of the equity is:

$$\frac{\$12,000 \times (1.12)}{.15 - .12} = \frac{\$13,440}{.03} = \underline{448,000}$$

Value of the firm is: $\underline{\$504,000}$

Check: WACC=($56,000/$504,000)(.10) + ($448,000/$504,000)(.15) = .14444

[FCF(1+g)]/(WACC-g)=[$11,000(1.12)]/(.14444-.12)=$12,320/.02444=$504,000

7. {M} (i) When the open book value is $168,000, then forecasted net
income of $33,600 yields an ROE of 20%. This amount is
equal to the return assumed for new investment
opportunities and the ROE in any year (see table below)
is consistent with that long term rate of return.

Year	Open Book Value	Net Income grows by 12%	.15 x Open Book Value	Abnormal Earnings	ROE = Net Income Open Book Value
1	$168,000	$33,600	$25,200	$ 8,400	20%
2	188,160	37,632	28,224	9,408	20%
3	210,739	42,148	31,611	10,537	20%
4	236,028	47,206	35,404	11,801	20%
5	264,351	52,870	39,653	13,218	20%

In this case all factors, net income, book value and
abnormal earnings grow by 12%. Therefore in an EBO framework
the valuation is straightforward and equal to

$$EBO \text{ Valuation } = B_0 + \frac{(ROE - r)}{r - g} B_0 = \$168,000 + \frac{.20 - .15}{.15 - .12} \$168,000 = \$448,000$$

identical to the amount obtained in problem 7.

(ii) When the opening book value is $212,000 then the
(accounting) ROE will not immediately equal 20% but will
converge towards that amount over time as the table below
indicates. Were we to extend this table and apply the EBO
valuation we would obtain the $448,000 as above.

Year	Open Book Value	Net Income grows by 12%	.15 x Open Book Value	Abnormal Earnings	ROE = Net Income Open Book Value
1	$212,000	$33,600	$31,800	$ 1,800	15.8%
2	232,160	37,632	34,824	2,808	16.2%
3	254,739	42,148	38,211	3,937	16.5%
4	280,028	47,206	42,004	5,201	16.9%
5	308,351	52,870	46,253	6,618	17.1%
6	340,073	59,215	51,011	8,204	17.4%
7	375,602	66,320	56,340	9,980	17.7%
8	415,394	74,279	62,309	11,970	17.9%
9	459,962	83,192	68,994	14,198	18.1%
10	509,877	93,175	76,482	16,694	18.3%

As extending the table indefinitely is not feasible (or desirable)[1], we make use of the following formula (presented in Appendix 19-B; text P. 1102) to estimate value.

$$P_0 = B_0 + \sum_{j=1}^{T} \frac{\left(ROE_j - r\right)B_{j-1}}{\left(1+r\right)^j} + \left\{ \frac{B_{T-1}}{\left(1+r\right)^T}\left[\frac{\left(ROE_T - \overline{ROE}\right)c}{1+r-c(1+g)} + \frac{\left(\overline{ROE}-r\right)}{r-g} \right] \right\}$$

The formula makes explicit forecasts of abnormal earnings for a number of years (in our case we use 5 years) and then estimates (discounted aggregate) abnormal earnings after that based on the rate of convergence of ROE_t to the long-run rate of return. The rate of convergence c, is based on the following relationship (see text 1103)

$$ROE_t = \overline{ROE} + c(ROE_{t-1} - \overline{ROE})$$

where $\overline{ROE}$ is the long-run ROE that in our case, equals 20%.

After 5 periods ROE_T=17.1% and ROE_{T-1}=16.9%; B_{T-1}= \$308,351

Therefore ROE_6 = 20% + c(ROE_5 - 20%)

17.1% = 20% + c(16.9% - 20%)

Thus, c is approximately equal to .9. Substituting in the valuation formula yields.

$$P_0 = 212000 + \frac{1800}{1.15} + \frac{2808}{1.15^2} + \frac{3937}{1.15^3} + \frac{5201}{1.15^4} + \frac{6618}{1.15^5} + \left\{ \frac{308351}{\left(1.15\right)^5}\left[\frac{.(174-.20).9}{1.15-.9(1+.12)} + \frac{\left(.20-.15\right)}{.15-.12} \right] \right\}$$

P_0 = \$451,021

This amount differs from the \$448,000 by approximately one-half percent.

---

[1] This does not mean that the EBO model does not work as well as the DCF models. First, we picked a "poor" starting point for book value. In part (i) the EBO model was as efficient as the DCF models. More important, in this example we assume that abnormal earnings opportunities are available indefinitely (to infinity). The advantages of the EBO model are in those (more realistic) situations where equilibrium conditions result in abnormal earnings dissipating and convergence to steady-state is quicker.

8.{L}A. From problem 6 we have $6,000 of new investment
        financed by debt. The present value factor for 5 years
        at 10% is 3.79 yielding lease payments of:

$$\frac{\$6,000}{3.79} = \$1,583 \text{ per year}$$

   B.   The difference between the two forecast statements is
        in the selling and interest expense categories. We
        begin by disaggregating these items from the current
        and forecast income statements of problem 5:

Selling Expense:

	Current	12% Increase	Forecast
Depreciation	$ 8,000	$ 960	$ 8,960
Other	17,000	2,040	19,040
Total	$25,000	$ 3,000	$28,000

Interest Expense	$ 5,000	$ 600	$ 5,600

The new investment of $24,000 increases depreciation by
$960. With $6,000 of the new investment as a lease, the
additional depreciation (on the remaining $18,000) is
only $720.

Reconciliation for operating lease:

Selling Expense:

	Current	Increase	Forecast
Depreciation	$ 8,000	$ 720	$ 8,720
Other	17,000	2,040	19,040
Rent expense			1,583
Total			$29,343

The difference of $1,343 ($29,343 - $28,000) between
selling expense for the operating lease method and that
for Problem 6 is due to $1,583 rent expense replacing
$240 of depreciation.

Interest Expense: The $600 difference between the two
methods represents the interest expense on the leased
asset. Under the operating expense all payments are
included in selling expense.

19-13

Reconciliation for capital lease:

Selling Expense:

	Current	Increase	Forecast
Depreciation	$ 8,000	$ 720	$ 8,720
Other	17,000	2,040	19,040
Amortization of leased asset			1,200
Total			$28,960

The $1200 amortization of leased assets replaces $240 of depreciation, increasing selling expense by $960 ($28,960 - $28,000) as compared with the problem 6 forecast. Note that amortization is not equal to depreciation because the leased assets must be amortized over the (5 year) lease term unless there is a bargain purchase option.

Interest Expense: is the same as interest on the capital lease equals interest on the debt that it replaces.

C. Before presenting the cash flow statements, we discuss note the cash flow consequences of the lease.

Increased cash outflow to lessors: The lease requires annual outlays of $1583, all charged to cash from operations for the operating lease. [$600 is interest and the remaining $983 is principal repayment for the capital lease]. In the problem 5 scenario, only $600 in interest is paid.

Decrease in replacement cost: Our example assumes that depreciation equals replacement cost for acquired assets. When some assets are leased, this equality no longer holds as depreciation is reduced by $240. However, leased assets "used up" must still be replaced. We assume that such replacement is effected through additional leases.

To maintain similar levels of debt and equity the company must obtain additional cash of $743 ($983-$240) each year by borrowing.

Cash Flow Statement, Operating Lease:

	Current	Forecast
Net income	$30,000	$32,857
Depreciation	8,000	8,720
Cash from operations	$38,000	$41,577
Cash for investment	(26,000)	(28,880)
Cash for financing:		
Dividends paid	(12,000)	(13,440)
New debt	---	743
Total	(12,000)	(12,697)
Change in cash	0	0

Lease payments are included in cash from operations. The "acquisition" of the leased asset, however, is ignored in the statement of cash flows.

D. **Cash Flow Statement, Capital Lease:**

	Current	Forecast
Net income	$ 30,000	$ 32,640
Depreciation/amortization	8,000	9,920
Cash from operations	$ 38,000	$ 42,560
Cash for investment	(26,000)	(28,880)
Cash for financing:		
Dividends paid	(12,000)	(13,440)
Debt repayment (lease)		(983)
New debt	---	743
Total	$(12,000)	$(13,680)
Change in cash	0	0

Principal payments for the leased assets are included in cash for financing but the interest payment is part of cash from operations. The actual acquisition of the leased assets is not shown directly in the cash flow statement. Rather, it is disclosed as a "significant noncash investment and financing activity."

E. **Free Cash Flow Calculation**

Based on reported cash flows alone, free cash flow (after removing interest) appears to be:

		Forecast Year	
	Current	Operating	Capital
Operating income	$35,000	$37,857	$38,240
Depreciation	8,000	8,720	9,920
Cash from operations	$43,000	$46,577	$48,160
Cash for investment	(26,000)	(28,880)	(28,880)
Reported free cash flow	$17,000	$17,697	$19,280

However, economically, these cases are identical to the problem 6 case, where free cash flow is $12,320 (6-D). The only difference from that case is that the LZ company has leased assets rather than purchasing them, and two different accounting methods are used to account for the lease.

To obtain this result we must adjust reported free cash flow by treating leases as investment and financing activities:

		Forecast Year	
	Current	Operating	Capital
Reported free cash flow	$17,000	$17,697	$19,280
Rent expense	---	1,583	---
Acquisition of leased assets	(6,000)	(6,960)	(6,960)
Free cash flow	$11,000	$12,320	$12,320

For the forecast year, leased assets acquired = $6720 + $240. The first component is 12% above the current year amount, reflecting the assumed 12% growth rate. The second component is required to replace "used up" assets (see Part C).

Free cash flows are identical to those of problem 6.

F. The solutions will be identical to problem 5E as the leases are another form of investment and debt and should be so treated in any valuation model.

G. Leases should not affect a valuation model as long as appropriate analytic adjustments are made. Leases are a form of investment and debt and their substitution should not affect valuation.

19-16

9.(L) *NOTE: The FAB example illustrates the difficulty of applying theoretical valuation models to an actual company and the sensitivity of the results to the assumptions made.*

The data provided were available as of September 1, 1989, well into that year. Thus, in the valuation analysis, although 1989 data is forecast, in many cases we treat 1989 as the "current" year.

A. FAB's 1988 book value is $26.62 per share; the 1989 forecast is $28.95. The market value of $36 per share is well above these amounts. This suggests that FAB has some economic goodwill.

Alternative explanations may be that the historical value of its inventories and/or fixed costs are below market values. The LIFO valuation basis gives some credence to this viewpoint. Also see Exhibit 14-1 (page 1020) for other possible adjustments to book value.

B. (i) **Implicit Growth Rate**

	1985	1986	1987	1988	1989
All per share:					
Earnings	$2.39	$2.95	$2.94	$2.62	$3.20
Dividends	0.50	0.60	0.60	0.70	0.80
Book value	19.52	21.86	24.70	26.62	28.95
Payout ratio	20.9%	20.3%	20.4%	26.7%	25.0%
ROE = EPS / Ave. BPS*	12.9%	14.3%	12.6%	10.2%	11.5%
Estimated growth**	10.2%	11.4%	10.1%	7.5%	8.6%

*1984 BPS approximated as 1985 BPS - 1985 EPS + 1985 DPS
**Implicit growth rate = (1 - payout ratio) x ROE

Historical Growth Rate (from prior year)

	1986	1987	1988	1989
Earnings per share: Arithmetic Average: 8.5% Geometric Average: 7.6%	23%	0%	(11%)	22%
Dividends per share: Arithmetic Average: 10.0% Geometric average: 12.5%	20%	0%	16%	14%

Value Line Forecast Growth Rates
Earnings per share: 10%
Dividends per share: 9.5%

The implicit growth rate has been erratic and declined over the period to about 8.00%. This is in line with the historical growth rate for earnings but considerably less than the historical growth rate for dividends. Value Line's forecast growth rates seem to be "compromise" estimates. They have estimated a higher growth rate for EPS, implicitly assuming a recovery in ROE but lowered the rate for DPS, assuming that the payout ratio will return to the lower level of earlier years.

The implicit growth rate estimates have the advantage of being derived from the actual operating results of FAB and, therefore, showing the declining trends of ROE and the implicit growth rate. Using this estimate for forecast purposes requires assumptions about whether these trends will continue.

The historical growth rates are very erratic, limiting their usefulness for forecasting. Using averages solves the variability problem but gives little insight into trends.

The Value Line estimates have the advantage of reflecting some informed judgment about the company and may also reflect "guidance" from management. On the other hand, these estimates are only as good as the analyst making the forecast. Comparisons of companies followed by different analysts may suffer from differing forecast methods and biases.

(ii) Historical growth rates of per share data may be distorted as FAB has repurchased shares, distorting the data in two ways:
   (1) since the number of shares has changed the per share growth pattern may differ from the pattern in total dollars.
   (2) in the context of valuation models, share repurchases should be treated as dividends.

We can estimate the amount of repurchases by converting the per share data into total dollars (multiplying by the number of shares). The resulting data can be used to calculate adjusted historical growth rates:

(data in millions)	1985	1986	1987	1988	1989
Number of shares*	3.63	3.63	3.53	3.43	3.28

*This is the number of shares at year end. EPS and DPS should be multiplied by the *average* number of shares outstanding. Using the year end shares understates dollar earnings and dividends when shares outstanding are declining.

($ millions)	1985	1986	1987	1988	1989
Earnings	$ 8.68	$10.71	$10.38	$ 8.99	$10.50
Dividends	1.82	2.18	2.12	2.40	2.62
Book value	70.90	79.40	87.20	91.30	95.00
Implied book value[1]		79.40	87.66	93.79	99.18
Repurchases		$ 0	$ .46	$ 2.49	$ 4.18
Total dividends[2]		2.18	2.58	4.89	6.80

[1]Implied book value can be calculated by adding earnings and subtracting dividends from the prior year's book value.
[2]Actual dividends plus share repurchases

	1986	1987	1988	1989
Implicit Growth Rate				
Adjusted payout ratio	20.3%	24.9%	54.4%	64.8%
Adjusted ROE	14.3%	12.5%	10.1%	11.3%
Adjusted implicit growth	11.4%	9.4%	4.3%	4.0%
Historical Growth Rate				
Earnings	23.0%	(3.1%)	(13.4%)	16.8%
Arithmetic average: 5.8%				
Geometric average: 4.9%				
Dividends (ignoring repurchases)	19.8%	(2.8%)	13.2%	9.2%
Arithmetic average: 9.8%				
Geometric average: 9.5%				
Dividends (including repurchases)	19.8%	18.3%	89.5%	39.1%
Arithmetic average: 41.7%				
Geometric average: 43.1%				

C. Using the CAPM allows us to estimate FAB's cost of equity as:

$$r = R_f + B(R_m - R_f) = .08 + .8(.06) = \quad 12.8\%$$

As we shall see, valuation is sensitive to the estimates used for the relevant parameters.

Dividend discount model

For this model, as well as the other models, we must forecast the future level of dividends. Is the starting point $2.62 million (ignoring repurchases) or $6.80 (including repurchases)? That is, which level is more indicative of future payments to shareholders? Will management continue to make share repurchases?

With current dividends of $2.62 million (ignoring repurchases) as the appropriate starting point, we use a 9.5% growth rate. This rate is the Value Line

19-20

forecast and is consistent with historical growth rates. Thus:

$$P = \frac{D(1+g)}{r-g} = \frac{(\$2.62)(1.095)}{.128-.095} = \$86.94 \, million$$

The value of $86.94 million translates to $26.51/share ($86.94/3.28), approximately 25% less than the market price of $36/share. The sensitivity of the model to the assumed growth rate can be illustrated by increasing the growth rate by 0.5% to 10%. The model now yields a value of $31.40 per share, an increase of close to 20%.

With dividends of $6.80 million (including share repurchases) as the appropriate starting point, the choice of growth rate is more difficult. The historical growth rate of 40% for dividends (including repurchases) seems untenable in the long run. At the other extreme is the 4% implicit rate. The following table shows the per share value of Fab with varying growth rates:

Growth rate	Per share value
5%	$27.91
8%	$46.65
10%	$81.45

Given the 1989 payout ratio of 64.8% and the declining ROE, 5% seems like a maximum expectation. Yet a growth rate of approximately 6.3% is required to predict the market price of $36 per share.

Earnings Based Model

Earnings growth rates are considerably more volatile and, on average, below those of dividends. The historical growth rate as well as the implicit rate [g = (1-k)ROE], imply a growth rate of 4 to 5% when the dividend payout includes the repurchase of stock. When the dividend payout excludes repurchases, the growth rate is 7.5 to 8.5%.

Value Line's growth rate forecast of 10% seems high as it is based on per share data that, as we have shown, may be distorted by the repurchases. We use a growth rate of 8% and assume a dividend payout of 40%, allowing for continued stock repurchases.

$$P = \frac{kE(1+g)}{r-g} = \frac{(.40)(\$10.50)(1.08)}{.128-.08} = \$94.50 \text{ million}$$

or $28.81 per share ($94.50/3.28), approximately 20% below the market price of $36/share.

Similar to the dividend model, the following table shows the sensitivity of the valuations to assumed growth rates and payout ratios:

FAB price per share
Effect of payout ratios and growth assumptions

Growth Rates	Payout Ratios				
	20%	25%	40%	50%	60%
5%	8.6	10.8	17.2	21.6	25.9
8%	14.4	18.0	28.8	36.0	43.2
10%	25.2	31.4	50.3	63.0	75.5

At a payout ratio of 50% (consistent with the repurchase program) and a growth rate of 8%, the predicted price is identical to the market price.

Free Cash Flows
Based on the data available, free cash flows can only be approximated. On a per share basis, they are:

	1985	1986	1987	1988	1989
"Cash flow"	$3.18	$3.07	$4.13	$4.02	$4.70
Capital spending	1.04	1.71	2.47	0.95	1.15

Converting to millions of dollars by multiplying by the number of shares:

	1985	1986	1987	1988	1989
"Cash flow"	$11.54	$14.05	$14.58	$13.79	$15.42
Capital spending	3.78	6.21	8.72	3.26	3.77
"Free cash flow"	$ 7.76	$ 7.84	$ 5.86	$10.53	$11.65

19-22

These amounts are not actual free cash flows as they do not include changes in operating working capital. However, in the absence of better data, we use them to estimate the growth rate:

	1986	1987	1988	1989
Change from prior year	1%	(25.3%)	79.6%	10.6%

Arithmetic average: 16.5%
Geometric average: 10.0%

The changes are very erratic and we use Value Line's forecast of 9.5%

For the changes in operating accounts we have one year's data (Part C of Exhibit 19P-1). These data show increased receivables of $3 million, increased inventory of $0.1, and decreased accounts payable of $1.1. [The increase in cash of $0.9 is assumed not to be required for operations (see part D).] These amounts reduce cash flows by $4.2 million ($3.0 + $0.1 + $1.1), bringing our 1989 estimate of free cash flows to $11.65 - $4.2 = $7.45 million. Ignoring any effect that the changes in operating accounts may have on growth rates, the free cash flow forecast becomes:

$$P = \frac{FCF(1+g)}{r-g} = \frac{(\$7.45)(1.095)}{.128-.095} = \$247.20 \text{ million}$$

The value is $75 per share ($247.20/3.28), more than twice the market price of $36/share. This should not surprise us. As dividends are paid in the long run from free cash flow, a dividend growth rate of perhaps 5% and a free cash flow growth rate of 9.5% are not consistent. Growth rates should be examined for consistency; they cannot be used mechanically.

If we accept the market price as the benchmark, then the models do not do very well. However, even if the actual price is ignored, the results are troublesome. The dividend and earnings models yield valuations that are far below those of the free cash flow model. As suggested in the previous paragraph, more attention to the growth rates used is required. It is also possible that earnings and/or free cash flow (and the growth rates derived from their historical amounts) require adjustment because of accounting methods or other transactions that distort reported amounts.

D. Dividend and earnings based DCF models assume that cash generated is used either for dividends or for new investment. When cash is "hoarded", the results of the models are distorted as both dividend payments and new investments become subject to management discretion. [This problem also exists for the free cash flow model to the extent any change in cash is treated as a working capital "requirement."]

Thus, the discrepancy between the dividend/earnings models and the free cash flow model may result from the fact that the free cash flow model "correctly" accounts for this "excess" cash. Hence its higher value for FAB.

One method of adjusting the earnings/dividend models is to consider FAB's cash position of more than $10/share. If these funds are not needed for operations then $10/share should be added to the valuations generated by the DCF models. This adjustment would have the effect of raising the dividend and earnings model valuations above the current market price. This adjustment still leaves values below that computed by the free cash flow model. The adjustment has valued only the excess cash arising from past operations and excludes the effect of excess cash to be generated in future periods.

On this basis, all models now indicate (to varying degrees) that FAB common stock was underpriced. *It is interesting to note that over the next eighteen months FAB's stock price increased by approximately 100% to over $70/share.*

E. We use Value Line's forecasts (after adjusting to dollars) for 1990 and 1992-1994 as follows:

1990	Given
1991	Average of 1990 and 1992-1994
1992-1994	Base level for future

We assume a growth rate of 9.5%.

	1990	1991	1992 & later
Dividends	$2.93	$3.17	$3.41

$$Value = \frac{\$2.93}{1.128} + \frac{\$3.17}{(1.128)^2} + [\frac{1}{(1.128)^2} \times \frac{\$3.41}{(.128-.095)}] = \$86.30 \ million$$

or $26.31 per share ($86.30/3.28)

Earnings

Using the payout ratios forecast by Value Line, the earnings based model will be identical to the dividend model.

Free Cash Flows ($ millions)

	1990	**1991**	**1992**
"Cash flow"	$16.58	$19.07	$21.55
Capital spending	4.55	5.77	6.98
"Free cash flow"	$12.03	$13.30	$14.57

For the free cash flow model we need the changes in working capital. We will make the assumption that operating working capital (accounts receivable + inventory - accounts payable) increases by 10%/year. Since in 1989 these components totaled $43.9 million ($28.5 + $23.8 -$8.4), the requirement for 1990 and succeeding years will be:

Working capital change	4.39	4.83	5.31
Free cash flows	$7.64	$ 8.47	$9.26

where the last line is free cash flow as generally used in the chapter. Therefore:

$$Value = \frac{\$7.64}{1.128} + \frac{\$8.47}{(1.128)^2} + [\frac{1}{(1.128)^2} \times \frac{\$9.26}{(.128-.095)}] = \$233.96 \ million$$

or $71.33 per share ($233.96/3.28)

The results are very similar to those calculated in part C.

F.   In Part B, an estimate of r^*, ROE, was calculated at approximately 11-12%. Based on these values, r is approximately = r^* and reinvestment should not make a difference.

Using the 1990 level of earnings (in $ millions) of $11.375 ($3.50 x 3.25), a no reinvestment, no growth policy would yield:

Value = $11.375/.128 = $88.87 million or $27.09 per share ($88.87/3.28)

which is comparable to the estimates derived using reinvestment and growth.

10. {M} FAB's "normal" P/E ratio should be

$$(1+r)/r \text{ or } 1.128/.128 = 8.8$$

The current[2] P/E ratio of 11.3 is considerably higher.

The current P/B ratio of $36/$28.95 = 1.24 is also higher than the "normal" level of 1.

The high P/E and P/B ratios place FAB in quadrant I of (text) Figure 19.1 implying that FAB is a company with strong growth potential. Future abnormal earnings will be high and will be larger than current levels of abnormal earnings. The data in the table below,[3] based on Exhibit 19P-1, bear these results out. Current year (1989) abnormal earnings are negative. From 1990 on, future abnormal earnings (ROE - r) improve and grow considerably.

	Opening Book Value	Earnings	Dividends	ROE = Earnings Open B.V.	ROE-r =ROE-12.8%	Book Value Growth
1989	$91.307	$10.496	$2.62	11.50%	(1.18%)	
1990	94.956	11.375	2.93	11.98%	(0.82%)	N/A
1991	103.406	13.388	3.17	12.95%	0.15%	8.9%
1992	113.619	15.500	3.41	13.64%	0.84%	9.8%

For EBO valuation based on the above data, we will express the valuation in terms of the price/book value ratio, making explicit forecasts through 1992 and terminal assumptions based on the 1992 data. (See p. 1066 in text).

The efficacy of the forecasts depends on the terminal assumptions made. We assume first that steady-state abnormal earnings levels are reached after two periods (from 1992 on). Abnormal earnings do not grow after that point, although book value does. The growth rate is assumed to be (see table above) 9.8%; consistent with Value Line's growth (forcasted) rate of 9.5% for 5 years. Based on these parameters, the P/B ratio is

---

[2] The P/E ratio "cum dividend" would be even higher!

[3] The table was prepared by multiplying the per share data by the number of shares. As in problem 9, we assume that the level of the 1991 forecasted variables is the average of the 1990 and the 1992-1994 levels.

$$\frac{P_0}{B_0} = 1 + \frac{(ROE_1 - r)}{(1+r)} + \frac{(ROE_2 - r)(1+g_1)}{(1+r)^2} + \frac{(ROE_3 - r)(1+g_1)(1+g_2)}{r(1+r)^2}$$

$$= 1 + \frac{-0.82\%}{1.128} + \frac{.15\%(1.089)}{(1.128)^2} + \frac{.84\%(1.089)(1.098)}{.128(1.128)^2}$$

$$= 1 - .0073 + .0013 + .0617$$

$$= 1.0557$$

A price/book ratio of 1.0557 implies a price of
1.0557 x $28.95 = **$30.56/share**

This forecast is closer to the actual price of $36 than (any of) the DCF forecasts made in problem 9. When we assume that abnormal earnings also grow at the same rate as book value[4] our forecast improves:

$$\frac{P_0}{B_0} = 1 + \frac{(ROE_1 - r)}{(1+r)} + \frac{(ROE_2 - r)(1+g_1)}{(1+r)^2} + \frac{(ROE_3 - r)(1+g_1)(1+g_2)}{(r-g_2)(1+r)^2}$$

$$= 1 + \frac{-0.82\%}{1.128} + \frac{.15\%(1.089)}{(1.128)^2} + \frac{.84\%(1.089)(1.098)}{(.03)(1.128)^2}$$

$$= 1 - .0073 + .0013 + .2633$$

$$= 1.2573$$

A price/book ratio of 1.2573 implies a price of
1.2573 x $28.95 = **$36.40/share**

approximately the current price of $36/share

---

[4] Note, that Value Line forecasts earnings growth at 10% for the next five years and book value growth of 9.5%. These forecasts are consistent with a growth rate of 9.8% for abnormal earnings.

11. {M}   The first step is to convert per share amounts to
            dollars by multiplying by the number of shares
            outstanding (as in problem 9, we use *average* shares):

$ millions	1990	1991	1992
Earnings	$10.11	$15.57	$16.32
Dividends	2.50	3.09	3.08
"Cash flow"	15.35	20.39	22.48
Capital spending	6.80	3.03	7.39
"Free cash flow"	$ 8.55	$17.36	$15.09

Assuming a growth rate of 9.5% after 1992 yields, for the
dividend model:

$$Value = \frac{\$2.50}{1.128} + \frac{\$3.09}{(1.128)^2} + [\frac{1}{(1.128)^2} \times \frac{\$3.08}{(.128-.095)}] = \$77.99 \text{ million}$$

or $23.71 per share ($77.99/3.28)

For the earnings model, unless we alter the growth
assumption, the results are identical to those of problem 9.

It should, however, be noted that these calculations ignore
share repurchases--a form of dividends. For 1990, if we
treat repurchases as dividends, they would be ($ millions):

Book value at 1989 year end	$ 95.81	(3.29 x $29.12)
1990 earnings	10.11	
Cash dividends	(2.50)	
"Implicit" net worth	$103.42	
Actual net worth	97.72	(3.12 x $31.32)
Implied repurchases	$ 5.70	

This result can be approximated as follows:

Reduction in shares	.17 million (3.29 - 3.12)
Current price (1990)	$36
Approximate repurchase	$6.1 million (.17 million x $36)

     It appears that FAB bought shares at an average price
below $36 ($5.70/.17=$33.53).

Including stock repurchases triples the 1990 dividend. In later years the repurchase amounts were lower, although it appears that the firm continued to generate "excess" cash. (The firm may not have continued repurchases because of the higher stock price in later years.) By using the free cash flow model, the effects of dividend and repurchase policy can be mitigated if we assume that the company has enough cash for its operations.

As in question 9, we assume that operating working capital needs increase by 10% annually. Thus free cash flows are ($millions):

	1990	1991	1992
"Cash flow"	$15.35	$20.39	$22.48
Capital spending	6.80	3.03	7.39
"Free cash flow"	$ 8.55	$17.36	$15.09
Working capital change	4.39	4.83	5.31
Free cash flow	$ 4.16	$12.53	$ 9.78

Therefore:

$$Value = \frac{\$4.16}{1.128} + \frac{\$12.53}{(1.128)^2} + [\frac{1}{(1.128)^2} x \frac{\$9.78}{(.128-.095)}] = \$246.43 \, million$$

or $75.13 per share ($246.43/3.28)

For the EBO valuation, we calculate the relevant inputs using the actual data shown below.

	Opening Book Value	Earnings	Dividends	ROE = Earnings Open B.V.	ROE-r =ROE-12.8%	Book Value Growth
1989	$91.307	$10.496	$2.62	11.50%	(1.18%)	
1990	94.956	10.11	2.50	10.55%	(2.25%)	N/A
1991	103.406	15.57	3.09	15.93%	3.13%	2.0%
1992	113.619	16.32	3.08	14.92%	2.12%	12.0%

Again, we find low (negative) current abnormal earnings followed by higher (and positive) abnormal earnings in the future. The actual data differ from the expected data in that abnormal earnings (growth) is more dramatic; near-term results were worse than expected; whereas future results were better. Additionally, once positive abnormal earnings are reached they level off but with a higher growth rate for book value.

When these data are used in EBO valuation models, the results again are dependent on expectations as to the pattern of abnormal earning after 1992. If it is assumed that they level off, and ROE remains at 14.92%, the EBO valuation results in a price of $33-$34 a share; approximately equal to the current (1989) level of $36. With an assumption of future growth in abnormal earnings, value increases to $43. Overall, however, if we assume that the current market price is the appropriate benchmark, the EBO model values FAB more correctly than the DCF models.

12. {M}*NOTE: FAB's cost of equity of 12.8% (computed in 9-C) is based on its current beta of 0.8. As noted in Chapter 18, the beta of a leveraged firm differs from that of an unlevered firm. Consequently, the appropriate return on equity would also differ. For this example we have ignored the adjustment as it would change ROE by an immaterial amount (0.2%).*

A. The problem can be simplified readily if we assume that FAB maintains a constant debt to equity ratio. In that case, we can estimate 1990 free cash flow as follows:

FCF (1989) = $7.45 million (computed in 9-C)
FCF (1990) = $8.16 million, assuming a 9.5% growth rate

Interest (net of taxes) on current debt of $50 million: (1-.34) x 11% x $50 million = $3.63 million.

To maintain the constant debt/equity ratio, debt must grow at the same 9.5% rate. New debt = $50 x 9.5% = $4.75 million.

Thus free cash flow available for equity holders equals unlevered FCF less interest expense + new debt:

$$\$8.158 - \$3.63 + \$4.75 = \$9.278 \text{ million}$$

and the value of equity $= \dfrac{\$ 9.278}{(.128-.095)} = \$281.15 \text{ million}$

B.   Adding the value of equity to the value of debt:

Value of equity	$281.15 million
Value of debt	50.00
Value of firm	$331.15 million

Alternatively, the WACC can be computed as follows:

$$\{\frac{\$281.15}{\$331.15}x.128\} \ + \ \{\frac{\$50}{\$331.15}x[.11x(1-.34)]\} = .1196$$

Using 1990 unlevered FCF yields the value of the firm:

$$Value \ = \ \frac{FCF(1+g)}{r-g} \ = \ \frac{(\$7.45)(1.095)}{.1196-.095} \ = \ \$331.15 \ million$$

13. (L)A. **Statement of Cash Flows**

Net income	$19,200
Depreciation	8,500
	$27,700
Changes in operating accounts:	
Account receivable	(500)
Accounts payable	500
Cash from operations	$27,700
Cash for investment:	
Fixed assets	(9,000)
Cash for financing:	
Dividends paid	(16,700)
Change in cash	$ 2,000

To estimate free cash flow we assume that the increase in cash of $2000 is needed for operations, not held as "excess" cash by the firm. After reclassifying interest expense (after tax) from cash from operations to cash for financing:

Operating income (net of tax)	$ 21,000
Depreciation	8,500
Funds from operations	$ 29,500
Changes in operating accounts:	
Cash	$ (2000)
Accounts receivable	(500)
Accounts payable	500
	(2,000)
Adjusted cash from operations	$ 27,500
Cash for investment:	(9,000)
Free cash flow	**$ 18,500**
Cash for financing:	
Interest (net of tax)	(1,800)
Dividends paid	(16,700)
Total	$(18,500)

B. Begin by estimating the fixed and variable cost components of the income statement. We use the method shown in Appendix 4-A and the equation:

Fixed costs = total costs - (variable cost % x sales)

COGS: Increase in cost of $3,000 for sales increase of $10,000 implies variable cost percentage of 30% and fixed costs of $20,000.

Selling and General: Increase of $2,000 for sales increase of $10,000 implies variable cost percentage of 20% and fixed selling and general costs of 0.

If fixed selling costs are 0, $8,500 of depreciation must be included in cost of goods sold. To complete the forecast of operating income we must forecast depreciation expense.

Estimating Fixed Asset Investments and Depreciation:

Average fixed asset turnover ratio for 19X1 and 19X2 is
    Using gross assets   1.06
    Using net assets   1.70

Our forecast should maintain these ratios and also be consistent with depreciation expense of 8%-9% of gross fixed assets (implying an average life of about 12 years). That forecast is:

	19X3	19X4	19X5
Sales	$150,000	$180,000	$200,000
Fixed assets (gross)	140,000	170,000	190,000
Accumulated depreciation	(52,500)	(66,500)	(81,500)
Fixed assets (net)	$ 87,500	$103,500	$108,500

As 19X2 accumulated depreciation was $(41,000), we can derive depreciation expense from the annual change in accumulated depreciation (assuming no retirement of fixed assets):

	19X3	19X4	19X5
Depreciation expense	$ 11,500	$ 14,000	$ 15,000

19-34

These estimates yield the following turnover ratios (consistent with the historical pattern):

	19X3	19X4	19X5
Fixed assets (gross)	1.07	1.06	1.05
Fixed assets (net)	1.71	1.74	1.84
and depreciation rates of	8.2%	8.2%	7.9%

These estimates allow us to forecast (pre and posttax) operating income:

	19X3	19X4	19X5
Sales	$150,000	$180,000	$200,000
Cost of goods sold	(68,000)	(79,500)	(86,500)
Selling and general	(30,000)	(36,000)	(40,000)
Operating income	$ 52,000	$ 64,500	$ 73,500
Operating income (after 40% tax)	$ 31,200	$ 38,700	$ 44,100

To complete the income statement we need to estimate the firm's interest expense.

Forecast of borrowing needs and interest expense:

Turnover ratios for current operating accounts are:

Cash	10
Accounts receivable	12
Inventory	8.5
Accounts payable	6

These turnover ratios imply the following working capital accounts, based on the sales and cost of goods sold figures determined earlier:

	19X3	19X4	19X5
Cash	$ 15,000	$18,000	$ 20,000
Accounts receivable	12,500	14,500	16,500
Inventory	7,500	9,000	10,000
Accounts payable	(11,500)	(13,500)	(14,500)
Operating working capital	$ 23,500	$28,000	$32,000

19-35

To estimate the company's borrowing needs, we need the following additional assumptions:

(1) The present level of dividends ($16,700) will be maintained as funds are needed to finance expansion.

(2) Any cash needed will be borrowed. Excess cash will be used to repay debt.

(3) Although borrowing would most likely be done throughout the year, for simplification we assume that borrowings occur at year end.(This will also be relevant for valuation purposes.)

	19X3	19X4	19X5
Opening balance of debt	$ 30,000	$ 49,300	$50,758
Interest expense (10%)	3,000	4,930	5,076
Net of tax (60%)	1,800	2,958	3,046
Operating income after tax	31,200	38,700	44,100
Depreciation expense	11,500	14,000	15,000
Change in operating w.c.	(6,500)	(4,500)	(4,000)
Cash from operations [before interest exp.]	$ 36,200	$ 48,200	$55,100
*Cash for investment and financing:			
Increased fixed assets (gross)	(37,000)	(30,000)	(20,000)
Dividends paid	(16,700)	(16,700)	(16,700)
Interest (net of tax)	(1,800)	(2,958)	(3,046)
Subtotal	$(55,500)	$(49,658)	$(39,746)
Borrowing (repayment) [Cash from operations less cash for investment and financing]	19,300	1,458	(15,354)
Closing balance of debt [Opening balance plus borrowing (less repayment)]	$ 49,300	$ 50,758	$35,404

Income statements and balance sheets follow:

	19X3	19X4	19X5
Income Statement:			
Sales	$150,000	$180,000	$200,000
Cost of goods sold	(68,000)	(79,500)	(86,500)
Selling and general	(30,000)	(36,000)	(40,000)
Operating income	$ 52,000	$ 64,500	$ 73,500
Interest expense	(3,000)	(4,930)	(5,076)
Pretax income	$ 49,000	$ 59,570	$ 68,424
Tax expense	(19,600)	(23,828)	(27,370)
Net income	$ 29,400	$ 35,742	$ 41,054
Balance Sheet:			
Cash	$ 15,000	$ 18,000	$ 20,000
Accounts receivable	12,500	14,500	16,500
Inventory	7,500	9,000	10,000
Current assets	$ 35,000	$ 41,500	$ 46,500
Fixed assets (gross)	$140,000	$170,000	$190,000
Accumulated depreciation	(52,500)	(66,500)	(81,500)
Fixed assets (net)	$ 87,500	$103,500	$108,500
Total assets	$122,500	$145,000	$155,000
Accounts payable	$ 11,500	$ 13,500	$ 14,500
Debt	49,300	50,758	35,404
Stockholders' equity	61,700	80,742	105,096
Total liabilities & equity	$122,500	$145,000	$155,000

C. Estimate of free cash flow:

	19X3	19X4	19X5
Operating income after tax	$ 31,200	$ 38,700	$ 44,100
Depreciation	11,500	14,000	15,000
Change in operating w.c.	(6,500)	(4,500)	(4,000)
	$ 36,200	$ 48,200	$ 55,100
Increased fixed assets	(37,000)	(30,000)	(20,000)
Free cash flow	$ (800)	$ 18,200	$ 35,100
Cash for financing:			
Interest (net of tax)	(1,800)	(2,958)	(3,046)
Borrowing (repayment)	19,300	1,458	(15,354)
Dividends paid	(16,700)	(16,700)	(16,700)
Total	$ 800	$(18,200)	$(35,100)

D. After 19X5, the company will reach "steady state" and maintain operations equal to that year. At that point, it will not need new investments in fixed assets or working capital. Cash for investments will be required only for replacement. If we assume that depreciation approximates replacement of assets we have the following forecast:

	19X6 and later
Operating income after tax	$44,100
Depreciation	15,000
Change in operating working capital	0
Cash from operations	$59,100
Increase in fixed assets	(15,000)
Free cash flow	$44,100

If we assume that all free cash flows are used to pay interest and dividends:

Cash for financing:	
Interest (net of tax)	$ (2,025)
Dividends paid	(42,075)
Total	$(44,100)

Dividends to equity shareholders are ($ thousands):

	19X3	**19X4**	**19X5**	**19X6 and later**
Dividends	16.7	16.7	16.7	42.1

Value of equity at end of 19X5 $= \dfrac{\$42.1}{.15} = \$280.7$

Value at end of 19X2 $= \dfrac{\$16.7}{(1.15)} + \dfrac{\$16.7}{(1.15)^2} + \dfrac{\$16.7 + \$280.7}{(1.15)^3}$

$$= \$222.7$$

As value of equity $= \$222.7$
and value of debt $= \underline{\quad 30.0}$
Value of firm $\quad \$252.7$

Alternatively, the value of the firm can be determined using free cash flows:

($ thousands)	**19X3**	**19X4**	**19X5**	**19X6 and later**
Free cash flows	(.8)	18.2	35.1	44.1

We must first estimate WACC.
As the after tax cost of debt = .06:

$$WACC = \frac{\$222}{\$252} \, x \, .15 + \frac{\$30}{\$252} \, x \, .06 = .139$$

Value of firm at end of 19X5 $= \dfrac{\$44.1}{.139} = \$316.6$

Value at end of 19X2 $= \dfrac{\$(.8)}{(1.139)} + \dfrac{\$18.2}{(1.139)^2} + \dfrac{\$35.1 + \$316.6}{(1.139)^3}$

$$= \$251.3$$

The slight discrepancy between the two answers ($252.2 and $251.3) is due mainly to rounding. In addition, since the amount of debt (relative to the value of equity) changes from period to period, the WACC changes also. We have ignored this refinement and used a constant WACC as the changes from period to period are slight.

14. (M)

$300 Charge Taken in 19X0

	Open Book Value	Income Before Restruct.	Restruct. Charge	Net Income	.10xOpen Book Value	Abnormal Earnings
19x1	$5,700	$1,050	0	$1,050	$570	$480
19x2	6,750	1,100	0	1,100	675	425
19x3	7,850	1,150	0	1,150	785	365

Book Value at end of 19x3: $7,850 + $1,150 = $9,000

EBO Valuation =

B_{19x0}	+ PV of Abnormal Earnings in Year 19x1, 19x2 and 19x3
$5,700	+ $480/(1.1) + \$425/(1.1)^2 + \$365/(1.1)^3$
$5,700	+ $1,062 = **$6,762**

Restructuring Charge Recognized Over Three Years

	Open Book Value	Income Before Restruct.	Restruct. Charge	Net Income	.10xOpen Book Value	Abnormal Earnings
19x1	$6,000	$1,050	150	$ 900	$600	$300
19x2	6,900	1,100	100	1,000	690	310
19x3	7,900	1,150	50	1,100	790	310

Book Value at end of 19X3: $7,900 + $1,100 = $9,000

EBO Valuation =

B_{19x0}	+ PV of Abnormal Earnings in Year 19x1, 19x2 and 19x3
$6,000	+ $300/(1.1) + \$310/(1.1)^2 + \$310/(1.1)^3$
$6,000	+ $762 = **$6,762**

This exercise shows that the EBO valuation is indifferent to accounting methods. Both yield a valuation of $6,762 at the end of 19X0. The differences in open book value is offset by the differences in abnormal earnings.

B. (i) and (ii) When the valuation is done as at the beginning of 19X0, the result is similar[5]. The EBO valuations are identical at $6,147.1. Abnormal earnings in years 19X1-19X3 are identical to those calculated in A; abnormal earnings for 19X0, however, must be included in the calculations.

$300 Charge Taken in 19X0

	Open Book Value	Income Before Restructuring	Restructuring Charge	Net Income	.10xOpen Book Value	Abnormal Earnings
19X0	$5,000	$1,000	$300	$ 700	$500	$200
19X1	5,700	1,050	0	1,050	570	480
19X2	6,750	1,100	0	1,100	675	425
19X3	7,850	1,150	0	1,150	785	365

EBO Valuation =
Open Book Value + PV of Abnormal Earnings in Year 19x0 to 19x3

$$= \text{Open Book Value} + \frac{\$200}{1.1} + \frac{\$480}{1.1^2} + \frac{\$425}{1.1^3} + \frac{\$365}{1.1^4}$$

$$= \ \mathbf{\$5,000} \quad + \$181.8 + \$396.7 + \$319.3 + \$249.3 = \mathbf{\$6,147.1}$$

---

[5] Note that the valuation calculated at the end of 19X0 is 10% (the required rate of return) higher than the valuation calculated at the beginning of 19X0; i.e. 6761.8 = 1.1 x 6147.1. An alternative way of viewing the problem is presented below:

  Choice 1 - **Immediate Writeoff**

```
        PV of abnormal earnings (19x1 - 19x3) = 1,062
        Discounted to beginning of year 19x0 = 1062/1.1  = $  965
        19x0 abnormal earnings  = 700 - 500 = 200
        Discounted to beginning of year 19x0 = 200/1.1   =    182
        PV of abnormal earnings (19x0 - 19x3)            $1,147
        Opening Book Value                               5,000
                                                         $6,147
```

  Choice 2 - **Charge over 3 years**

```
        PV of abnormal earnings (19x1 - 19x3) = 762
        Discounted to beginning of year 19x0 = 762/1.1 =     693
        19x0 abnormal earnings  = 1000 - 500 = 500
        Discounted to beginning of year 19x0 = 500/1.1   =   454
        PV of abnormal earnings (19x0 - 19x3)            $1,147
        Opening Book Value                               5,000
                                                         $6,147
```

Restructuring Charge Recognized Over Three Years

	Open Book Value	Income Before Restructur.	Restructur. Charge	Net Income	.10xOpen Book Value	Abnormal Earnings
19X0	$5,000	$1,000	0	$1,000	$500	$500
19X1	6,000	1,050	150	900	600	300
19X2	6,900	1,100	100	1,000	690	310
19X3	7,900	1,150	50	1,100	790	310

EBO Valuation =

Open Book Value + PV of Abnormal Earnings in Year 19x0 to 19x3

$$= \text{Open Book Value} + \frac{\$500}{1.1} + \frac{\$300}{1.1^2} + \frac{\$310}{1.1^3} + \frac{\$310}{1.1^4}$$

= \quad $5,000 \quad + $454.5 + $247.9 + $232.9 + $211.7 = **$6,147.1**

15. (S) A. Assuming that the market value of Kraft prior to the merger was "appropriate" the amount by which Philip Morris "overpaid" can be calculated (in $ millions) as:

Market value of Kraft prior to merger $ 7,800
    ($65 x 120)

Amount paid for acquisition of Kraft   (10,800)
    ($90 x 12)

        "Overpayment" $(3,000)

On a per share basis, the overpayment should have decreased the market price of Philip Morris shares by:

$$\frac{\$3,000}{234} = \$12.80 \text{ per share}$$

The actual market price decrease of $4.50 was considerably less than the amount determined by the asset based approach.

B. The smaller decline in the price of Philip Morris shares suggests that the market expected synergistic effects from the merger that partly offset the "overpayment". Investors in Philip Morris may have believed that Kraft was "undermanaged" and that its profitability would be improved by Philip Morris management.

C.   The problem in using any of the DCF models is predicting the effect of the acquisition on the parameters of the model.

1.   For example, the acquisition of Kraft would be expected to have no immediate effect on dividends paid to Philip Morris shareholders. The need to service the debt incurred to buy Kraft, however, might reduce the future growth rate of dividend payments, reducing their present value. The higher leverage of Philip Morris following the merger would also increase the required discount rate, further decreasing the stock price.

2.   For an earnings-based model, the effect on current earnings (dilution) as well as the effect on the growth rate and discount rate, must be considered.

3.   The Kraft acquisition reduces the free cash flow of Philip Morris initially. After tax interest expense of $770 million [11% x $10,800 x (1-.35) exceeds the free cash flow of Kraft (estimated as CFO + interest - capital expenditures = $607 + $81 - $260). As in the other cases, the effect on the growth rate and discount rate must also be considered.

The advantage of the dividend model is that there is no effect on the current level of dividends; thus only the growth rate and discount rate effects must be estimated.

16.(S)   From a theoretical perspective there are a number of
          problems with the price to cash flow ratio suggested
          by the article.

    1.   The measure used, net income + depreciation +
          amortization, is equal to funds from operations (FFO),
          an incomplete measure of cash flow. It does not reflect
          changes in operating working capital accounts or other
          adjustments required to calculate CFO as defined by
          SFAS 95. FFO has been shown to have little or no
          explanatory power beyond that provided by net income.

    2.   The theoretical basis for a price to cash flow ratio is
          based on a free cash flow model. As noted in the
          chapter, free cash flow is considerably different from
          CFO, and is even more distant from FFO.

          Notwithstanding the above, the price to cash flow ratio
    may be a useful "filter," similar to the price to earnings
    ratio (PER). As noted in the chapter, the PER itself is
    predicated on the assumption that earnings is a useful
    surrogate for or predictor of cash flows to investors. Thus,
    the efficacy of both ratios depends to some extent on how
    well they can predict relevant variables of interest.

          In this respect CFO may be more useful than earnings as
    it is less subject to manipulation by the selection of
    accounting principles. On the other hand, CFO suffers from a
    conceptual limitation relevant to valuation in that it does
    not reflect the cost of asset replacement (whereas the
    depreciation component of earnings may approximate this
    cost). This limitation may be overcome if replacement cost
    is a constant proportion of cash flow. In this case, it will
    be imbedded in the price to cash flow ratio.

          Ultimately, however, the usefulness of the ratio should
    be tested empirically.

17.{S}A. IIMR headline earnings attempts to take on some of the characteristics of each of the four definitions of income. However, ultimately it is not identical to any of them.

Although, headline earnings excludes capital items (e.g. sale of assets) it differs from operating income as it includes interest income/expense. By including items that are abnormal in nature and size, as well as discontinued operations, headline earnings differs from both permanent and sustainable income. Finally, it is not equivalent to economic income as it excludes capital items and valuation adjustments that are part of economic earnings.

B. The purpose of IIMR earnings appears to be the desire to have a reported income amount that is relatively free from capital gains and losses and other nonoperating adjustments. This measure should be less affected by the timing of asset sales and such extraneous items as prior period adjustments.

Towards that end, IIMR headline earnings exclude gains or losses from the sale of net assets, the disposal of operating segments, and acquisitions. Prior period adjustments are also excluded. Finally, income tax expense is adjusted for any components of net income excluded from IIMR headline earnings.

The result is a normalized earnings amount. However the operating results of discontinued operations as well as many nonrecurring items, remain within the IIMR earnings report. The proposal appears to leave further adjustment for these items to the individual analyst rather than permitting management to make those judgments.

C. To Whom It May Concern:

My major concern is related to the three reasons given for the delineation of earnings. They suffer from two faults: (1) the reason itself is not compelling; and (2) the reason contradicts one of the other reasons.

The first reason given is that "in evaluating a company the stock market must order published information in some useful way. If this so, ... information should ... be ordered in that way...." Since we do not know the manner in which the markets order the information, or even whether or not markets do so, how can we attempt to order the information in this "unknown" manner?

The second reason relates to those who do not have any expertise in "distilling" information contained in the accounts. While one may be sympathetic to their plight, it is not clear that these investors actually influence the market (see discussion in Chapter 5). Even if they do, why should we assume that headline earnings is the appropriate input for their use? In addition, this reason contradicts the previous one, that is geared to providing a number that will satisfy the manner in which the markets "order published information in some useful way". That implies a sophisticated level of information processing.

Finally, there is the argument that there is a need for an unambiguous reference point. That may be true. It does not however point to headline earnings. Any agreed upon number will do.

Case 19-1

Estimated solution time is three hours

The case illustrates the sensitivity of valuation results to both the valuation model used and parameter assumptions.

A beta of 1 with a risk-free rate of 6.5% and a risk premium of 6.0% implies equity cost of capital of 12.5%.

1.(a) (i) *Dividend discount model*

Value Line Forecast of 1995 dividends is $1.88/share. Value Line also forecasts a growth rate of 7% for dividends over the next five years. Given a historical growth rate of 7.5% over the last 10 years and 9% in the past 5 years, the 7% forecast seems conservative.[1] Using that forecast, however, yields a valuation of

Value = Dividends/(r-g) = $1.88/(.125-.07) = $34.18/share.

This value is considerably below duPont's actual price of $56.125/share

(ii) *Earnings-based model*

Value Line Forecast of 1995 earnings is $4.70/share with an earnings growth rate of 18% over the next five years. Given the historical growth rate of 6% over the last 10 years, this rate would seem to be high and not sustainable for an extended period of time. Thus, we assume that, after 5 years, duPont's earnings growth rate reverts to 8%. This rate is consistent [(1-k)ROE=g] with the payout ratio, k, of 40% used by Value Line in estimating duPont's dividends and an ROE of approximately 13% (the average ROE over the last five years - see Exhibit 19-3).

---

[1] It should be noted that for 1997-1999, Value Line forecasts dividends at $2.70/share. This number is inconsistent with their own forecast of 7% growth in the next five years. Using Value Line's explicit forecasts for 1995-1999 we obtain the following forecast.

$$Value = \frac{\$1.88}{1.125} + \frac{\$2.00}{1.125^2} + \frac{\$2.23}{1.125^3} + \frac{\$2.46}{1.125^4} + \frac{\$2.70}{1.125^5} + \frac{\$2.70(1.07)}{1.125^5(.125-.07)} = \$37.00$$

The above is based on assuming that growth between 1997 and 1999 is linear and that after 1999 the growth rate is 7%. A higher price is arrived at by this method but it is still considerably lower than duPont's actual price.

$$Value = \frac{(.4)4.70}{1.125} + \frac{(.4)(4.70)(1.18)}{1.125^2} + \frac{(.4)(4.70)(1.18)^2}{1.125^3} + \frac{(.4)(4.70)(1.18)^3}{1.125^4} + \frac{(.4)(4.70)(1.18)^4}{1.125^5}$$

$$+ \frac{(.4)(4.70)(1.18)^4(1.08)}{1.125^5(.125-.08)} = \$57.75$$

The earnings-based forecasting model yields a value almost identical to the market price of $56.125.

Normalized Earnings

In Exhibit 17-1 we find that duPont's normalized net earnings for 1994 were $2,488 million. As duPont had 680 million shares outstanding, on a per share basis, this translates to $3.66/share. Assuming an 18% growth rate,[2] value becomes

$$Value = \frac{(.4)(3.66)(1.18)}{1.125} + \frac{(.4)(3.66)(1.18)^2}{1.125^2} + \frac{(.4)(3.66)(1.18)^3}{1.125^3} + \frac{(.4)(3.66)(1.18)^4}{1.125^4}$$

$$+ \frac{(.4)(3.66)(1.18)^5}{1.125^5} + \frac{(.4)(3.66)(1.18)^5(1.08)}{1.125^5(.125-.08)} = \$53.10$$

The above forecasted value is also consistent with the market price of $56.125.

(iii) *Free Cash Flows*

Estimating WACC: DuPont's market value of equity is 56.125 x 680 million or approximately $38,100 million. Note 17 and Note 19 of duPont's financial statements provide an estimate of the fair value of duPont's short term and long term debt. They are estimated to be $1,300 million and $6,600 respectively or $7,900 million in total. From Exhibit 10P-1, the interest rate on AA rated debt is 8.5%. Thus, the WACC is approximately equal[3] to 11.8%.

Exhibit 17-4 derives free cash flows of $3,096 for duPont in 1994. Using Value Line's "cash flow" growth rate of 11.5% for the next five years and consistent with income

---

[2] Note that an 18% growth rate implies a starting point of $4.32 as 1995 "normalized" earnings. Using reported earnings of $2,727/680 = $4.01 and an 18% growth rate implies 1995 forecasted earnings of $4.72 consistent with Value Line's forecast of $4.70

[3] $WACC = \left[\frac{38,100}{38,100+7,900} x.125\right] + \left[\frac{7,900}{38,100+7,900} x.085\right] = 11.8\%$

11.5% for the next five years and consistent with income and dividends a growth rate of 7.5% after that yields (in $ millions)

$$Value = \frac{3{,}096(1.115)}{1.118} + \frac{3{,}096(1.18)^2}{1.118^2} + \frac{3{,}096(1.18)^3}{1.118^3} + \frac{3{,}096 1.18)^4}{1.118^4} + \frac{3{,}096(1.18)^5}{1.118^5}$$

$$+ \frac{3{,}096(1.18)^5(1.075)}{1.118^5(.118-.075)} = \$91{,}723$$

That $91,723 million is the value of debt and equity. Subtracting the $7,900 million debt leaves the value of equity at $83,823 or, on a per share basis, ($83,823/680=) $123.27/share, twice the actual market value!

(b) Valuation models are extremely sensitive to parameter assumptions. For the (constant-growth) dividend model, the key parameters are the growth rate (g) in income and discount rate (r). Dividends in 1994 were $1.82/share. The table below presents the value of the firm's equity under combinations of r and g. For g=7% and r=12.5%, the assumptions used in part (a), a value of $35.21/share is arrived at.[4] We have indicated by bold numbers the combination of assumptions which would be consistent with the market valuation of $56.125. Thus, for example, for an r of 10%, the growth rate would have to be between 6% and 7% to arrive at the market valuation.

Sensitivity analysis of dividend discount model.

g r	6%	7%	8%	9%	10%
9.0%	$ 64.31	$ 97.37	$196.56	n/a	n/a
10.0%	48.23	64.91	98.28	198.38	n/a
11.0%	38.58	48.69	65.52	99.19	200.20
12.0%	32.15	38.95	49.14	66.13	100.10
12.5%	29.68	35.41	43.68	56.68	80.08
13.0%	27.56	32.46	39.31	49.60	66.73

Earnings-based models require, in addition to r and g, an estimate of the dividend payout, k. In part (a) we found that assuming

[4] This value is slightly different than the $34.18 found in part (a) because we use different starting points. In part (a) we used Value Line's 1995 forecast of $1.88/share. In part (b) we used 1994 actual dividends of $1.82 multiplied by a growth rate of 7%, implying dividends in 1995 of $1.95/share

- dividend payout (k) of .4
- a growth rate assumption of 18% for the next five years and 8% thereafter; and
- r = .125

the model yielded a valuation consistent with that of the market.

In that valuation we made two differing growth assumptions, one for the first five years and another assumption thereafter. Below, we present a sensitivity analysis using a constant growth assumption and varying k from .3 to .5.

Sensitivity analysis of earnings based model for k=.3

g / r	7%	8%	9%	10%	12%
9.0%	$ 64.20	$ 129.60	n/a	n/a	n/a
10.0%	42.80	64.80	130.80	n/a	n/a
11.0%	32.10	43.20	65.40	132.00	n/a
12.0%	25.68	32.40	43.60	66.00	n/a
12.5%	23.35	28.80	37.37	52.80	268.80
13.0%	21.40	25.92	32.70	44.00	134.40

Sensitivity analysis of earnings based model for k=.4

g / r	7%	8%	9%	10%	12%
9.0%	$ 85.60	$ 172.80	n/a	n/a	n/a
10.0%	57.07	86.40	174.40	n/a	n/a
11.0%	42.80	57.60	87.20	176.00	n/a
12.0%	34.24	43.20	58.13	88.00	n/a
12.5%	31.13	38.40	49.83	70.40	358.40
13.0%	28.53	34.56	43.60	58.67	179.20

Sensitivity analysis of earnings based model for k=.5

g / r	7%	8%	9%	10%	12%
9.0%	$ 107.00	$ 216.00	n/a	n/a	n/a
10.0%	71.33	108.00	218.00	n/a	n/a
11.0%	53.50	72.00	109.00	220.00	n/a
12.0%	42.80	54.00	72.67	110.00	n/a
12.5%	38.91	48.00	62.29	88.00	448.00
13.0%	35.67	43.20	54.50	73.33	224.00

The free cash flow model arrived at a valuation almost twice that of the market. Consistent with that, we find that only for low levels of growth in the range of 5%-6% can a valuation level similar to that of the market be arrived at. Note that the discount rate used below is WACC, not r. That is why we denote the valuation of $57.33 at WACC=13% and r=6% in quotation marks. Given the lower interest rate on debt WACC<r. Since our initial estimate of r is 12.5%, it is unlikely that WACC would be 13%.

Sensitivity analysis of free cash flow model

g	5%	6%	7%	8%	10%
WACC					
9.0%	$ 107.90	$ 149.25	$231.96	$480.10	n/a
10.0%	83.99	109.04	150.77	234.24	n/a
11.0%	68.06	84.90	110.17	152.29	489.21
12.0%	**56.68**	68.82	85.82	111.31	238.79
12.5%	52.12	62.63	76.96	97.65	188.71
13.0%	48.14	"57.33"	69.58	86.73	155.32

2.   (a) - (c)
P/B ratio
DuPont's Price to Book ratio is ($56.125/$18.48) 3.04, considerably higher than the "normal" level of 1 suggesting positive future abnormal earnings.

P/E ratio
The *normal* P/E *cum dividend* ratio for a firm with r of .125 is

$$(1+r)/r = 1.125/.125 = 9$$

DuPont's P/E *cum dividend* ratio is considerably higher;
$$(P+D)/E = (\$56.125 + \$1.82)/\$4.00 = 14.48$$

This suggests that duPont's future abnormal earnings are expected to be higher than current abnormal earnings.

Taken together, duPont's price suggest abnormal earnings which are positive and above current levels. This places duPont in sector 1 of Figure 19-1; i.e. firms with strong growth potential.

3.(a) Per the EBO model, it should not make a difference which accounting regime is followed as long as
- the clean surplus relationship is maintained,
- the accounting policies are internally consistent; i.e. the balance sheet and income statement use similar basis of accounting.

The difference between any set of accounting principles would be the "speed" with which the model converges to a solution, For our purposes, however since forecasts available through Value Line are based on reported numbers we shall limit ourselves to those in our valuation model.

(b) Opening book value is 18.48. As forecasted earnings for 1995 is 4.70, this implies an ROE of approximately 25%, considerably higher than the r of .125. Assuming that this "abnormal" level can be maintained for 5 years with the forecasted growth rate of 18%, the EBO valuation model becomes (expressed in P/B form)

$$\frac{P}{B} = 1 + \frac{(.25-.125)}{1.125} + \frac{(.25-.125)(1.18)}{1.125^2} + \frac{(.25-.125)(1.18)^2}{1.125^3} + \frac{(.25-.125)(1.18)^3}{1.125^4} + \frac{(.25-.125)(1.18)^4}{1.125^5}$$

$$+ \frac{(.25-.125)(1.18)^4}{1.125^5(.125)} = 2.69$$

The P/B ratio of 2.64 implies a price of (2.64 x 18.48) $49.71/share, approximately 11% below the current market price. The above, however, assumes
1. no new projects with abnormal earnings opportunities (ROE=r=12.5%)
2. the current level of abnormal returns (ROE - r = 25% -12.5%)on current projects will be maintained in the future

If the first assumption were to be relaxed then the P/B would be higher. If the second assumption is unrealistic (e.g. competitive pressures drive abnormal earnings on current projects towards zero) the P/B would be lower.